Modern CMake for (

Second Edition

Effortlessly build cutting-edge C++ code and deliver high-quality
solutions

Rafał Świdziński

Modern CMake for C++

Second Edition

Copyright © 2024 Packt Publishing

Senior Publishing Product Manager: Denim Pinto

Acquisition Editor – Peer Reviews: Gaurav Gavas

Project Editor: Amisha Vathare

Content Development Editor: Tanya D'cruz

Copy Editor: Safis Editing

Technical Editor: Anjitha Murali

Proofreader: Safis Editing

Indexer: Rekha Nair

Presentation Designer: Ganesh Bhadwalkar

Developer Relations Marketing Executive: Vipanshu Parashar

First published: February 2022

Second edition: May 2024

Production reference: 1230524

Published by Packt Publishing Ltd.

Grosvenor House

11 St Paul's Square

Birmingham

B3 1RB, UK.

ISBN 978-1-80512-180-0

www.packt.com

Foreword

In the ever-evolving landscape of C++, mastering CMake is indispensable for any developer striving to write efficient, maintainable, and scalable code. *Modern CMake for C++* by Rafał Świdziński serves as a beacon, guiding both novices and seasoned programmers through the intricacies of CMake.

This book is not just a manual; it is a journey. It starts with the basics, ensuring that even those new to CMake can grasp its concepts. As the chapters progress, readers are equipped with advanced techniques, empowering them to harness the full potential of CMake.

What sets this book apart is its pragmatic approach. Real-world examples and best practices are interwoven throughout the text, ensuring that readers not only understand the concepts but also know how to apply them effectively in their projects.

By the end of this book, readers will not only have a deep understanding of CMake but also a newfound confidence in their ability to navigate the complexities of C++ development. They will be armed with the knowledge and skills needed to write cleaner, more efficient code, setting them on a path to becoming proficient CMake developers.

Modern CMake for C++ is not just a book; it is a tool that will empower its readers to elevate their C++ development skills to new heights. Whether you're a beginner or an expert, this book will help you unlock the full potential of CMake, making your code more robust, maintainable, and scalable.

Alexander Kushnir

Principal Software Engineer, Biosense Webster

Contributors

About the author

Rafał Świdziński, a seasoned staff engineer at Google, boasts over 12 years of full-stack development expertise. With a track record of spearheading projects for industry giants like Cisco Meraki, Amazon, and Ericsson, he embodies a commitment to innovation. As a Londoner by choice, he remains at the forefront of technological progress, engaging in a myriad of personal ventures. His recent pivot toward AI in healthcare reflects his dedication to impactful advancements. Rafał values top-notch code quality and craftsmanship, sharing insights through his YouTube channel and published books.

To Zoe – I couldn't have written this book without you.

About the reviewers

Eric Noulard has an engineering degree from ENSEEIHT and a PhD in computer science from UVSQ in France. Eric boasts a rich 25-year history in writing and compiling source code across various languages. A user of CMake since 2006, he has also actively contributed to its evolution. Eric has served both private companies and government agencies. He currently works at Antidot, a software vendor specialized in semantic search, AI, and content accessibility. Eric is in the research team, which brings new technology like generative AI and advanced NLP processing to Antidot's flagship product, Fluid Topics.

Giovanni Romano has 28 years of experience in IT ranging from software development to design of apps/components. Currently employed at Leica Geosystem AG as a Senior Software Engineer, he specializes in designing SDKs, microservices, and low-latency backends. As a Nokia/Blackberry Qt Ambassador, he believes in open-source software and contributing to the framework. His interests are cloud-native apps, Kubernetes, Docker, and GitOps. He loves working with the C language and playing tennis.

Join our community on Discord

Join our community's Discord space for discussions with the author and other readers:

https://discord.com/invite/vXN53A7ZcA

Table of Contents

Chapter 3: Using CMake in Popular IDEs   **77**

Chapter 4: Setting Up Your First CMake Project   **97**

Chapter 7: Compiling C++ Sources with CMake   169

Preface

Creating top-notch software is no easy task. Developers researching this subject online often struggle to determine which advice is current and which methods have been superseded by newer, better practices. Moreover, most resources explain the process chaotically, lacking proper background, context, and structure.

Modern CMake for C++ provides an end-to-end guide that offers a simpler experience by treating the building of C++ solutions comprehensively. It not only teaches you how to use CMake in your projects but also highlights what makes them maintainable, elegant, and clean. The guide walks you through automating complex tasks common in many projects, including building, testing, and packaging.

The book instructs you on organizing source directories, building targets, and creating packages. As you progress, you will learn to compile and link executables and libraries, understand these processes in detail, and optimize each step for the best results. Additionally, you will discover how to incorporate external dependencies into your project, such as third-party libraries, testing frameworks, program analysis tools, and documentation generators. Finally, you'll learn how to export, install, and package your solution for both internal and external use.

After completing this book, you'll be able to use CMake confidently on a professional level.

Who this book is for

After you've learned C++, you'll quickly discover that proficiency with the language alone isn't enough to prepare you for delivering projects at the highest standards. This book fills that gap: it is addressed to anyone aspiring to become a better software developer or even a professional build engineer!

Read it if you want to learn modern CMake from scratch or elevate and refresh your current CMake skills. It will help you understand how to make top-notch C++ projects and transition from other build environments.

What this book covers

Chapter 1, First Steps with CMake, covers the installation of CMake, the use of its command line interface, and introduces the fundamental building blocks necessary for a CMake project.

Chapter 2, The CMake Language, cover the essential concepts of the CMake language, including command invocations, arguments, variables, control structures, and comments.

Chapter 3, Using CMake in Popular IDEs, emphasizes the importance of **Integrated Development Environments (IDEs)**, guides you through selecting an IDE, and provides setup instructions for Clion, Visual Studio Code, and Visual Studio IDE.

Chapter 4, Setting up Your First CMake Project, will teach you how to configure a basic CMake project in its top-level file, structure the file tree, and prepare the toolchain necessary for development.

Chapter 5, Working with Targets, explores the concept of logical build targets, understand their properties and different types, and learn how to define custom commands for CMake projects.

Chapter 6, Using Generator Expressions, explains the purpose and syntax of generator expressions, including how to use them for conditional expansion, queries, and transformations.

Chapter 7, Compiling C++ Sources with CMake, delves into the compilation process, configure the preprocessor and optimizer, and discover techniques to reduce build time and improve debugging.

Chapter 8, Linking Executables and Libraries, understands the linking mechanism, different types of libraries, the One Definition Rule, the order of linking, and how to prepare your project for testing.

Chapter 9, Managing Dependencies in CMake, will teach you to manage third-party libraries, add CMake support for those that lack it, and fetch external dependencies from the internet.

Chapter 10, Using the C++20 Modules, introduces C++20 modules, shows how to enable their support in CMake, and configure the toolchain accordingly.

Chapter 11, Testing Frameworks, will help you understand the importance of automated testing, leverage built-in testing support in CMake, and get started with unit testing using popular frameworks.

Chapter 12, Program Analysis Tools, will show you how to automatically format source code and detect software errors during both build time and runtime.

Chapter 13, Generating Documentation, presents how to use Doxygen for automating documentation creation from source code and add styling to enhance your documentation's appearance.

Chapter 14, *Installing and Packaging*, prepares your project for release with and without installation, create reusable packages, and designate individual components for packaging.

Chapter 15, *Creating Your Professional Project*, applies all the knowledge acquired throughout the book to develop a comprehensive, professional-grade project.

Chapter 16, *Writing CMake Presets*, encapsulates high-level project configurations into workflows using CMake preset files, making project setup and management more efficient.

Appendix - Miscellaneous Commands, serves as a reference for various CMake commands related to strings, lists, files, and mathematical operations.

To get the most out of this book

Basic familiarity with C++ and Unix-like systems is assumed throughout the book. Although Unix knowledge isn't a strict requirement, it will prove helpful in fully understanding the examples given in this book.

This book targets CMake 3.26, but most of the techniques described should work from CMake 3.15 (features that were added after are usually highlighted). Some chapters have been updated to CMake 3.28 to cover the latest features.

Preparation of the environment to run examples is covered in *Chapters 1-3*, but we specifically recommend using the Docker image provided with this book if you're familiar with this tool.

Download the example code files

The code bundle for the book is hosted on GitHub at `https://github.com/PacktPublishing/Modern-CMake-for-Cpp-2E`. We also have other code bundles from our rich catalog of books and videos available at `https://github.com/PacktPublishing/`. Check them out!

Download the color images

We also provide a PDF file that has color images of the screenshots/diagrams used in this book. You can download it here: `https://packt.link/gbp/9781805121800`.

Conventions used

There are a number of text conventions used throughout this book.

`CodeInText`: Indicates code words in text, database table names, folder names, filenames, file extensions, pathnames, dummy URLs, user input, and Twitter handles. For example: "Mount the downloaded `WebStorm-10*.dmg` disk image file as another disk in your system."

A block of code is set as follows:

```
cmake_minimum_required(VERSION 3.26)
project(Hello)
add_executable(Hello hello.cpp)
```

When we wish to draw your attention to a particular part of a code block, the relevant lines or items are set in bold:

```
cmake_minimum_required(VERSION 3.26)
project(Hello)
add_executable(Hello hello.cpp)
add_subdirectory(api)
```

Any command-line input or output is written as follows:

```
cmake --build <dir> --parallel [<number-of-jobs>]
cmake --build <dir> -j [<number-of-jobs>]
```

Bold: Indicates a new term, an important word, or words that you see on the screen. For example: "Select **System info** from the **Administration** panel."

 Warnings or important notes appear like this.

 Tips and tricks appear like this.

Get in touch

Feedback from our readers is always welcome.

General feedback: Email `feedback@packtpub.com`, and mention the book's title in the subject of your message. If you have questions about any aspect of this book, please email us at `questions@packtpub.com`.

Errata: Although we have taken every care to ensure the accuracy of our content, mistakes do happen. If you have found a mistake in this book we would be grateful if you would report this to us. Please visit, `http://www.packtpub.com/submit-errata`, selecting your book, clicking on the Errata Submission Form link, and entering the details.

Piracy: If you come across any illegal copies of our works in any form on the Internet, we would be grateful if you would provide us with the location address or website name. Please contact us at `copyright@packtpub.com` with a link to the material.

If you are interested in becoming an author: If there is a topic that you have expertise in and you are interested in either writing or contributing to a book, please visit `http://authors.packtpub.com`.

Share your thoughts

Once you've read *Modern CMake for C++, Secon Edition*, we'd love to hear your thoughts! Scan the QR code below to go straight to the Amazon review page for this book and share your feedback.

https://packt.link/r/1805121804

Your review is important to us and the tech community and will help us make sure we're delivering excellent quality content.

Download a free PDF copy of this book

Thanks for purchasing this book!

Do you like to read on the go but are unable to carry your print books everywhere?

Is your eBook purchase not compatible with the device of your choice?

Don't worry, now with every Packt book you get a DRM-free PDF version of that book at no cost.

Read anywhere, any place, on any device. Search, copy, and paste code from your favorite technical books directly into your application.

The perks don't stop there, you can get exclusive access to discounts, newsletters, and great free content in your inbox daily.

Follow these simple steps to get the benefits:

1. Scan the QR code or visit the link below:

https://packt.link/free-ebook/9781805121800

2. Submit your proof of purchase.
3. That's it! We'll send your free PDF and other benefits to your email directly.

1

First Steps with CMake

There is something magical about software creation. We're not only creating a working mechanism that gets brought to life but we're also often authoring the very idea behind the functionality of the solution.

To cast our ideas into existence, we work in the following loop: design, code, and test. We invent changes, we phrase them in a language that the compiler understands, and we check whether they work as intended. To create proper, high-quality software from our source code, we need to meticulously execute repetitive, error-prone tasks: invoking the correct commands, checking the syntax, linking binary files, running tests, reporting issues, and more.

It takes great effort to remember each step every single time. Instead, we want to stay focused on the actual coding and delegate everything else to automated tooling. Ideally, this process would start with a single button, right after we have changed our code. It would be smart, fast, extensible, and work in the same way across different OSs and environments. It would be supported by multiple **Integrated Development Environments (IDEs)**. Going even further, we could streamline this process into **Continuous Integration** (**CI**) pipelines that build and test our software every time a change is submitted to a shared repository.

CMake is the answer to many such needs; however, it requires a bit of work to configure and use correctly. CMake isn't the source of the complexity; that stems from the subject that we're dealing with here. Don't worry, we will go through this whole learning process very methodically. Before you know it, you will become a software-building guru.

I know you're eager to rush off to start writing your own CMake projects, and this is exactly what we will be doing for most of this book. But since you'll be creating your projects primarily for users (yourself included), it's important for you to understand their perspective first.

So, let's start with just that: becoming a *CMake power user*. We'll go through a few basics: what this tool is, how it works in principle, and how to install it. Then, we'll do a deep dive into the command line and modes of operation. Finally, we'll wrap up with the purposes of different files in a project, and we'll explain how to use CMake without creating projects at all.

In this chapter, we're going to cover the following main topics:

- Understanding the basics
- Installing CMake on different platforms
- Mastering the command line
- Navigating project files
- Discovering scripts and modules

Technical requirements

You can find the code files that are present in this chapter on GitHub at `https://github.com/PacktPublishing/Modern-CMake-for-Cpp-2E/tree/main/examples/ch01`.

To build the examples provided in this book, always execute all the recommended commands:

```
cmake -B <build tree> -S <source tree>
cmake --build <build tree>
```

Be sure to replace the placeholders `<build tree>` and `<source tree>` with the appropriate paths. As you will learn in this chapter, **build tree** is the path of your output directory, and **source tree** is the path at which your source code is located.

To build C++ programs, you also need a compiler appropriate for your platform. If you're familiar with Docker, you can use a fully tooled image introduced in the *Installing CMake on different platforms* section. If you'd rather set up CMake manually, we'll explain the installation in the same section.

Understanding the basics

The compilation of C++ source code appears to be a fairly straightforward process. Let's start with the classic Hello World example.

The following code is found in `ch01/01-hello/hello.cpp`, *Hello world in the C++ language*:

```cpp
#include <iostream>
int main() {
```

```
    std::cout << "Hello World!" << std::endl;
    return 0;
}
```

To produce an executable, we of course need a C++ compiler. CMake doesn't come with one, so you'll need to pick and install one on your own. Popular choices include:

- Microsoft Visual C++ compiler
- The GNU compiler collection
- Clang/LLVM

Most readers are familiar with *a compiler*, as it is indispensable when learning C++, so we won't go into picking one and installation. Examples in this book will use GNU GCC as it is a well-established, open-source software compiler available for free across many platforms.

Assuming that we have our compiler already installed, running it is similar for most vendors and systems. We should call it with the filename as an argument:

```
$ g++ hello.cpp -o hello
```

Our code is correct, so the compiler will silently produce an executable binary file that our machine can understand. We can run it by calling its name:

```
$ ./hello
Hello World!
```

Running one command to build your program is simple enough; however, as our projects grow, you will quickly understand that keeping everything in a single file is simply not possible. Clean code practices recommend that source code files should be kept small and in well-organized structures. The manual compilation of every file can be a tiresome and fragile process. There must be a better way.

What is CMake?

Let's say we automate building by writing a script that goes through our project tree and compiles everything. To avoid any unnecessary compilations, our script will detect whether the source has been modified since the last time we ran the script. Now, we'd like a convenient way to manage arguments that are passed to the compiler for each file – preferably, we'd like to do that based on configurable criteria. Additionally, our script should know how to link all of the compiled files into a single binary file or, even better, build whole solutions that can be reused and incorporated as modules into bigger projects.

Building software is a very versatile process and can span multiple different aspects:

- Compiling executables and libraries
- Managing dependencies
- Testing
- Installing
- Packaging
- Producing documentation
- Testing some more

It would take a very long time to come up with a truly modular and powerful C++ building utility that is fit for every purpose. And it did. Bill Hoffman at Kitware implemented the first versions of CMake over 20 years ago. As you might have already guessed, it was very successful. Today, it has a lot of features and extensive support from the community. CMake is being actively developed and has become the industry standard for C and C++ programmers.

The problem of building code in an automated way is much older than CMake, so naturally, there are plenty of options out there: GNU Make, Autotools, SCons, Ninja, Premake, and more. But why does CMake have the upper hand?

There are a couple of things about CMake that I find (granted, subjectively) important:

- It stays focused on supporting modern compilers and toolchains.
- CMake is truly cross-platform – it supports building for Windows, Linux, macOS, and Cygwin.
- It generates project files for popular IDEs: Microsoft Visual Studio, Xcode, and Eclipse CDT. Additionally, it is a project model for others, like CLion.
- CMake operates on just the right level of abstraction – it allows you to group files in reusable targets and projects.
- There are tons of projects that are built with CMake and offer an easy way to plug them into your project.
- CMake views testing, packaging, and installing as an inherent part of the build process.
- Old, unused features get deprecated to keep CMake lean.

CMake provides a unified, streamlined experience across the board. It doesn't matter whether you're building your software in an IDE or directly from the command line; what's really important is that it takes care of post-build stages as well.

Your CI/CD pipeline can easily use the same CMake configuration and build projects using a single standard even if all of the preceding environments differ.

How does it work?

You might be under the impression that CMake is a tool that reads source code on one end and produces binaries on the other – while that's true in principle, it's not the full picture.

CMake can't build anything on its own – it relies on other tools in the system to perform the actual compilation, linking, and other tasks. You can think of it as the orchestrator of your building process: it knows what steps need to be done, what the end goal is, and how to find the right workers and materials for the job.

This process has three stages:

- Configuration
- Generation
- Building

Let's explore them in some detail.

The configuration stage

This stage is about reading project details stored in a directory, called the **source tree**, and preparing an output directory or **build tree** for the generation stage.

CMake starts by checking whether the project was configured before and reads cached configuration variables from a CMakeCache.txt file. On a first run, this is not the case, so it creates an empty build tree and collects all of the details about the environment it is working in: for example, what the architecture is, what compilers are available, and what linkers and archivers are installed. Additionally, it checks whether a simple test program can be compiled correctly.

Next, the CMakeLists.txt project configuration file is parsed and executed (yes, CMake projects are configured with CMake's coding language). This file is the bare minimum of a CMake project (source files can be added later). It tells CMake about the project structure, its targets, and its dependencies (libraries and other CMake packages).

During this process, CMake stores collected information in the build tree, such as system details, project configurations, logs, and temp files, which are used for the next step. Specifically, a CMakeCache.txt file is created to store more stable information (such as paths to compilers and other tools), which saves time when the whole build sequence is executed again.

The generation stage

After reading the project configuration, CMake will generate a **buildsystem** for the exact environment it is working in. Buildsystems are simply cut-to-size configuration files for other build tools (for example, Makefiles for GNU Make or Ninja and IDE project files for Visual Studio). During this stage, CMake can still apply some final touches to the build configuration by evaluating **generator expressions**.

 The generation stage is executed automatically after the configuration stage. For this reason, this book and other resources sometimes refer to both of these stages interchangeably when mentioning the "configuration" or "generation" of a buildsystem. To explicitly run just the configuration stage, you can use the cmake-gui utility.

The building stage

To produce the final artifacts specified in our project (like executables and libraries), CMake has to run the appropriate **build tool**. This can be invoked directly, through an IDE, or using the appropriate CMake command. In turn, these build tools will execute steps to produce **target artifacts** with compilers, linkers, static and dynamic analysis tools, test frameworks, reporting tools, and anything else you can think of.

The beauty of this solution lies in the ability to produce buildsystems on demand for every platform with a single configuration (that is, the same project files):

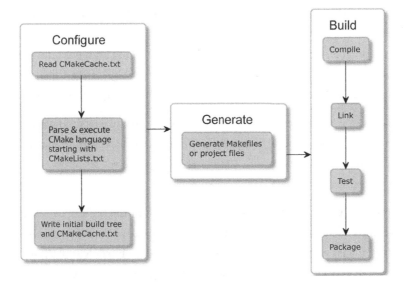

Figure 1.1: The stages of CMake

Do you remember our hello.cpp application from the *Understanding the basics* section? It is really easy to build it with CMake. All we need is the following CMakeLists.txt file in the same directory as our source.

ch01/01-hello/CMakeLists.txt

```
cmake_minimum_required(VERSION 3.26)
project(Hello)
add_executable(Hello hello.cpp)
```

After creating this file, execute the following commands in the same directory:

```
cmake -B <build tree>
cmake --build <build tree>
```

Note that <build tree> is a placeholder that should be replaced with a path to a temporary directory that will hold generated files.

Here is the output from an Ubuntu system running in Docker (Docker is a virtual machine that can run within other systems; we'll discuss it in the *Installing CMake on different platforms* section). The first command generates a **buildsystem**:

```
~/examples/ch01/01-hello# cmake -B ~/build_tree
-- The C compiler identification is GNU 11.3.0
-- The CXX compiler identification is GNU 11.3.0
-- Detecting C compiler ABI info
-- Detecting C compiler ABI info - done
-- Check for working C compiler: /usr/bin/cc - skipped
-- Detecting C compile features
-- Detecting C compile features - done
-- Detecting CXX compiler ABI info
-- Detecting CXX compiler ABI info - done
-- Check for working CXX compiler: /usr/bin/c++ - skipped
-- Detecting CXX compile features
-- Detecting CXX compile features - done
-- Configuring done (1.0s)
-- Generating done (0.1s)
-- Build files have been written to: /root/build_tree
```

The second command actually **builds** the project:

```
~/examples/ch01/01-hello# cmake --build ~/build_tree
Scanning dependencies of target Hello
[ 50%] Building CXX object CMakeFiles/Hello.dir/hello.cpp.o
[100%] Linking CXX executable Hello
[100%] Built target Hello
```

All that's left is to run the compiled program:

```
~/examples/ch01/01-hello# ~/build_tree/Hello
Hello World!
```

Here, we have generated a buildsystem that is stored in the **build tree** directory. Following this, we executed the build stage and produced a final binary that we were able to run.

Now you know what the result looks like, I'm sure you will be full of questions: what are the prerequisites to this process? What do these commands mean? Why do we need two of them? How do I write my own project files? Don't worry – these questions will be answered in the following sections.

 This book will provide you with the most important information that is relevant to the current version of CMake (at the time of writing, this is 3.26). To provide you with the best advice, I have explicitly avoided any deprecated and no longer recommended features and I highly recommend using, at the very least, CMake version 3.15, which is considered *the modern CMake*. If you require more information, you can find the latest, complete documentation online at https://cmake.org/cmake/help/.

Installing CMake on different platforms

CMake is a cross-platform, open-source software written in C++. That means you can, of course, compile it yourself; however, the most likely scenario is that you won't have to. This is because precompiled binaries are available for you to download from the official web page at https://cmake.org/download/.

Unix-based systems provide ready-to-install packages directly from the command line.

Remember that CMake doesn't come with compilers. If your system doesn't have them installed yet, you'll need to provide them before using CMake. Make sure to add the paths to their executables to the PATH environment variable so that CMake can find them.

To avoid facing tooling and dependency problems while learning from this book, I recommend practicing by following the first installation method: Docker. In a real-world scenario, you will of course want to use a native version, unless you're working in a virtualized environment to begin with.

Let's go through some different environments in which CMake can be used.

Docker

Docker (https://www.docker.com/) is a cross-platform tool that provides OS-level virtualization, allowing applications to be shipped in well-defined packages called containers. These are self-sufficient bundles that contain a piece of software with all of the libraries, dependencies, and tools required to run it. Docker executes its containers in lightweight environments that are isolated one from another.

This concept makes it extremely convenient to share whole toolchains that are necessary for a given process, configured and ready to go. I can't stress enough how easy things become when you don't need to worry about minuscule environmental differences.

The Docker platform has a public repository of container images, https://registry.hub.docker.com/, that provides millions of ready-to-use images.

For your convenience, I have published two Docker repositories:

- `swidzinski/cmake2:base`: An Ubuntu-based image that contains the curated tools and dependencies that are necessary to build with CMake
- `swidzinski/cmake2:examples`: An image based on the preceding toolchain with all of the projects and examples from this book

The first option is for readers who simply want a clean-slate image ready to build their own projects, and the second option is for hands-on practice with examples as we go through the chapters.

You can install Docker by following the instructions from its official documentation (please refer to docs.docker.com/get-docker). Then, execute the following commands in your terminal to download the image and start the container:

```
$ docker pull swidzinski/cmake2:examples
$ docker run -it swidzinski/cmake2:examples
root@b55e271a85b2:root@b55e271a85b2:#
```

Note that examples are available in the directories matching this format:

```
devuser/examples/examples/ch<N>/<M>-<title>
```

Here, <N> and <M> are zero-padded chapter and example numbers, respectively (like 01, 08, and 12).

Windows

Installing in Windows is straightforward – simply download the version for 32 or 64 bits from the official website. You can also pick a portable ZIP or MSI package for Windows Installer, which will add the CMake bin directory to the PATH environment variable (*Figure 1.2*) so that you can use it in any directory without any such errors:

cmake is not recognized as an internal or external command, operable program, or batch file.

If you select the ZIP package, you will have to do it manually. The MSI installer comes with a convenient GUI:

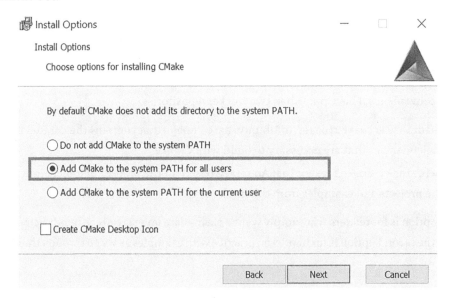

Figure 1.2: The installation wizard can set up the PATH environment variable for you

As I mentioned earlier, this is open-source software, so it is possible to build CMake yourself. However, on Windows, you will have to get a binary copy of CMake on your system first. This scenario is used by CMake contributors to generate newer versions.

The Windows platform is no different from others, and it also requires a build tool that can finalize the build process started by CMake. A popular choice here is the Visual Studio IDE, which comes bundled with a C++ compiler. The Community edition is available for free from Microsoft's website: `https://visualstudio.microsoft.com/downloads/`.

Linux

Installing CMake on Linux follows the same process as with any other popular package: call your package manager from the command line. Package repositories are usually kept up to date with fairly recent versions of CMake, but usually not the latest. If you're fine with this and using a distribution like Debian or Ubuntu, it is simplest to just install the appropriate package:

```
$ sudo apt-get install cmake
```

For a Red Hat distribution, use the following command:

```
$ yum install cmake
```

 Note that when installing a package, your package manager will fetch the latest available version in the repository configured for your OS. In many cases, package repositories don't provide the latest version but, rather, a stable one that has been proven over time to work reliably. Pick according to your needs, but be aware that older versions won't have all the features described in this book.

To get the latest version, reference the download section of the official CMake website. If you know the current version number, you can use one of the following commands.

The command for Linux x86_64 is:

```
$ VER=3.26.0 && wget https://github.com/Kitware/CMake/releases/download/
v$VER/cmake-$VER-linux-x86_64.sh && chmod +x cmake-$VER-linux-x86_64.sh &&
./cmake-$VER-linux-x86_64.sh
```

The command for Linux AArch64 is:

```
$ VER=3.26.0 && wget https://github.com/Kitware/CMake/releases/download/
v$VER/cmake-$VER-Linux-aarch64.sh && chmod +x cmake-$VER-Linux-aarch64.sh
&& ./cmake-$VER-Linux-aarch64.sh
```

Alternatively, check out the *Building from the source* section to learn how to compile CMake on your platform yourself.

macOS

This platform is also strongly supported by CMake developers. The most popular choice of installation is through MacPorts with the following command:

```
$ sudo port install cmake
```

Do note that at the time of writing, the latest version available in MacPorts was 3.24.4. To get the latest version, install the `cmake-devel` package:

```
$ sudo port install cmake-devel
```

Alternatively, you can use the Homebrew package manager:

```
$ brew install cmake
```

macOS package managers will cover all necessary steps, but be mindful that you might not get the latest version unless you're building from the source.

Building from the source

If you're using another platform, or just want to experience the latest builds that haven't been promoted to a release (or adopted by your favorite package repository), download the source from the official website and compile it yourself:

```
$ wget https://github.com/Kitware/CMake/releases/
download/v3.26.0/cmake-3.26.0.tar.gz
$ tar xzf cmake-3.26.0.tar.gz
$ cd cmake-3.26.0
$ ./bootstrap
$ make
$ make install
```

Building from the source is relatively slow and requires more steps. However, there is no other way to have the freedom of picking any version of CMake. This is especially useful when packages that are available in repositories of your operating system are stale: the older the version of the system, the fewer updates it gets.

Now that we have installed CMake, let's learn how to use it!

Mastering the command line

The majority of this book will teach you how to prepare CMake projects for your users. To cater to their needs, we need to thoroughly understand how users interact with CMake in different scenarios. This will allow you to test your project files and ensure they're working correctly.

CMake is a family of tools and consists of five executables:

- cmake: The main executable that configures, generates, and builds projects
- ctest: The test driver program used to run and report test results
- cpack: The packaging program used to generate installers and source packages
- cmake-gui: The graphical wrapper around cmake
- ccmake: The console-based GUI wrapper around cmake

Additionally, Kitware, the company behind CMake, offers a separate tool called CDash to provide advanced oversight over the health of our projects' builds.

CMake command line

The cmake is the main binary of the CMake suite, and provides a few modes of operation (also sometimes called actions):

- Generating a project buildsystem
- Building a project
- Installing a project
- Running a script
- Running a command-line tool
- Running a workflow preset
- Getting help

Let's see how they work.

Generating a project buildsystem

The first step required to build our project is to generate a buildsystem. Here are three forms of command to execute the CMake *generating a project buildsystem* action:

```
cmake [<options>] -S <source tree> -B <build tree>
cmake [<options>] <source tree>
cmake [<options>] <build tree>
```

We'll discuss available <options> in the upcoming sections. Right now, let's focus on choosing the right form of the command. One important feature of CMake is the support for *out-of-source builds* or the support for storing *build artifacts* in a directory different from the source tree. This is a preferred approach to keep the source directory clean from any build-related files and avoid polluting the **Version Control Systems** (**VCSs**) with accidental files or ignore directives.

This is why the first form of command is the most practical. It allows us to specify the paths to the source tree and the produced buildsystem specified with -S and -B, respectively:

```
cmake -S ./project -B ./build
```

CMake will read the project files from the ./project directory and generate a buildsystem in the ./build directory (creating it beforehand if needed).

We can skip one of the arguments and cmake will "guess" that we intended to use the current directory for it. Note that skipping both will produce an *in-source build* and store the *build artifacts* along with source files, which we don't want.

BE EXPLICIT WHEN RUNNING CMAKE

Do not use the second or third form of the cmake <directory> command, because they can produce a messy *in-source build*. In *Chapter 4, Setting Up Your First CMake Project*, we'll learn how to prevent users from doing that.

As hinted in the syntax snippet, the same command behaves differently if a previous build already exists in <directory>: it will use the cached path to the sources and rebuild from there. Since we often invoke the same commands from the Terminal command history, we might get into trouble here; before using this form, always check whether your shell is currently working in the right directory.

Examples

Generate the build tree in the current directory using the source from one directory up:

```
cmake -S ..
```

Generate the build tree in the ./build directory using the source from the current directory:

```
cmake -B build
```

Choosing a generator

As discussed earlier, you can specify a few options during the generation stage. Selecting and configuring a generator decides which build tool from our system will be used for building in the subsequent *Building a project* section, what build files will look like, and what the structure of the build tree will be.

So, should you care? Luckily, the answer is often "no." CMake does support multiple native buildsystems on many platforms; however, unless you have installed a few generators at the same time, CMake will correctly select one for you. This can be overridden by the CMAKE_GENERATOR environment variable or by specifying the generator directly on the command line, like so:

```
cmake -G <generator name> -S <source tree> -B <build tree>
```

Some generators (such as Visual Studio) support a more in-depth specification of a toolset (compiler) and platform (compiler or SDK). Additionally, CMake will scan environment variables that override the defaults: CMAKE_GENERATOR_TOOLSET and CMAKE_GENERATOR_PLATFORM. Alternatively, the values can be specified directly in the command line:

```
cmake -G <generator name>
      -T <toolset spec>
      -A <platform name>
      -S <source tree> -B <build tree>
```

Windows users usually want to generate a buildsystem for their preferred IDE. On Linux and macOS, it's very common to use the **Unix Makefiles** or **Ninja** generators.

To check which generators are available on your system, use the following command:

```
cmake --help
```

At the end of the help printout, you will get a full list of generators, like this one produced on Windows 10 (some output was truncated for readability):

The following generators are available on this platform:

```
Visual Studio 17 2022
Visual Studio 16 2019
Visual Studio 15 2017 [arch]
Visual Studio 14 2015 [arch]
Visual Studio 12 2013 [arch]
```

```
Visual Studio 11 2012 [arch]
Visual Studio 9 2008 [arch]
Borland Makefiles
NMake Makefiles
NMake Makefiles JOM
MSYS Makefiles
MinGW Makefiles
Green Hills MULTI
Unix Makefiles
Ninja
Ninja Multi-Config
Watcom WMake
CodeBlocks - MinGW Makefiles
CodeBlocks - NMake Makefiles
CodeBlocks - NMake Makefiles JOM
CodeBlocks - Ninja
CodeBlocks - Unix Makefiles
CodeLite - MinGW Makefiles
CodeLite - NMake Makefiles
CodeLite - Ninja
CodeLite - Unix Makefiles
Eclipse CDT4 - NMake Makefiles
Eclipse CDT4 - MinGW Makefiles
Eclipse CDT4 - Ninja
Eclipse CDT4 - Unix Makefiles
Kate - MinGW Makefiles
Kate - NMake Makefiles
Kate - Ninja
Kate - Unix Makefiles
Sublime Text 2 - MinGW Makefiles
Sublime Text 2 - NMake Makefiles
Sublime Text 2 - Ninja
Sublime Text 2 - Unix Makefiles
```

As you can see, CMake supports a lot of different generator flavors and IDEs.

Managing the project cache

CMake queries the system for all kinds of information during the configuration stage. Because these operations can take a bit of time, the collected information is cached in the CMakeCache.txt file in the build tree directory. There are a few command-line options that allow you to manage the behavior of the cache more conveniently.

The first option at our disposal is the ability to *prepopulate cached information*:

```
cmake -C <initial cache script> -S <source tree> -B <build tree>
```

We can provide a path to the CMake listfile, which (only) contains a list of set() commands to specify variables that will be used to initialize an empty build tree. We'll discuss writing the listfiles in the next chapter.

The *initialization and modification* of existing cache variables can be done in another way (for instance, when creating a file is a bit much to only set a few variables). You can set them directly in a command line, as follows:

```
cmake -D <var>[:<type>]=<value> -S <source tree> -B <build tree>
```

The :<type> section is optional (it is used by GUIs) and it accepts the following types: BOOL, FILEPATH, PATH, STRING or INTERNAL. If you omit the type, CMake will check if the variable exists in the CMakeCache.txt file and use its type; otherwise, it will be set to UNINITIALIZED.

One particularly important variable that we'll often set through the command line specifies the **build type** (CMAKE_BUILD_TYPE). Most CMake projects will use it on numerous occasions to decide things such as the verbosity of diagnostic messages, the presence of debugging information, and the level of optimization for created artifacts.

For single-configuration generators (such as GNU Make and Ninja), you should specify the **build type** during the configuration phase and generate a separate build tree for each type of config. Values used here are Debug, Release, MinSizeRel, or RelWithDebInfo. Missing this information may have undefined effects on projects that rely on it for configuration.

Here's an example:

```
cmake -S . -B ../build -D CMAKE_BUILD_TYPE=Release
```

Note that multi-configuration generators are configured during the build stage.

For diagnostic purposes, we can also list cache variables with the -L option:

```
cmake -L -S <source tree> -B <build tree>
```

Sometimes, project authors may provide insightful help messages with variables – to print them, add the H modifier:

```
cmake -LH -S <source tree> -B <build tree>
cmake -LAH -S <source tree> -B <build tree>
```

Surprisingly, custom variables that are added manually with the -D option won't be visible in this printout unless you specify one of the supported types.

The *removal* of one or more variables can be done with the following option:

```
cmake -U <globbing_expr> -S <source tree> -B <build tree>
```

Here, the *globbing expression* supports the * (wildcard) and ? (any character) symbols. Be careful when using these, as it is easy to erase more variables than intended.

Both the -U and -D options can be repeated multiple times.

Debugging and tracing

The cmake command can be run with a multitude of options that allow you to peek under the hood. To get general information about variables, commands, macros, and other settings, run the following:

```
cmake --system-information [file]
```

The optional file argument allows you to store the output in a file. Running it in the **build tree** directory will print additional information about the cache variables and build messages from the log files.

In our projects, we'll be using message() commands to report details of the build process. CMake filters the log output of these based on the current log level (by default, this is STATUS). The following line specifies the log level that we're interested in:

```
cmake --log-level=<level>
```

Here, level can be any of the following: ERROR, WARNING, NOTICE, STATUS, VERBOSE, DEBUG, or TRACE. You can specify this setting permanently in the CMAKE_MESSAGE_LOG_LEVEL cache variable.

Another interesting option allows you to *display log context* with each message() call. To debug very complex projects, the CMAKE_MESSAGE_CONTEXT variable can be used like a stack. Whenever your code enters an interesting context, you can name it descriptively. By doing this, our messages will be decorated with the current CMAKE_MESSAGE_CONTEXT variable, like so:

```
[some.context.example] Debug message.
```

The option to enable this kind of log output is as follows:

```
cmake --log-context <source tree>
```

We'll discuss naming contexts and logging commands in more detail in *Chapter 2, The CMake Language*.

If all else fails and we need to use the big guns, there is always *trace mode*, which will print every executed command with its filename, the line number it is called from, and a list of passed arguments. You can enable it as follows:

```
cmake --trace
```

As you can imagine, it's not recommended for everyday use, as the output is very long.

Configuring presets

There are many, many options that users can specify to generate a **build tree** from your project. When dealing with the build tree path, generator, cache, and environmental variable, it's easy to get confused or miss something. Developers can simplify how users interact with their projects and provide a CMakePresets.json file that specifies some defaults.

To list all of the available presets, execute the following:

```
cmake --list-presets
```

You can use one of the available presets as follows:

```
cmake --preset=<preset> -S <source> -B <build tree>
```

To learn more, please refer to the *Navigating the project files* section of this chapter and *Chapter 16, Writing CMake Presets*.

Cleaning the build tree

Every now and then, we might need to erase generated files. This may be due to some changes in the environment that were made between builds, or just to ensure that we are working on a clean slate. We can go ahead and delete the build tree directory manually, or just add the --fresh parameter to the command line:

```
cmake --fresh -S <source tree> -B <build tree>
```

CMake will then erase CMakeCache.txt and CMakeFiles/ in a system-agnostic way and generate the buildsystem from scratch.

Building a project

After generating our build tree, we're ready for the *building a project* action. Not only does CMake know how to generate input files for many different builders but it can also run them for us providing appropriate arguments, as required by our project.

AVOID CALLING MAKE DIRECTLY

Many online sources recommend running GNU Make directly after the generation stage by calling the make command directly. Because GNU Make is a default generator for Linux and macOS, this recommendation can work. However, use the method described in this section instead, as it is generator-independent and is officially supported across all platforms. As a result, you won't need to worry about the exact environment of every user of your application.

The syntax of build mode is:

```
cmake --build <build tree> [<options>] [-- <build-tool-options>]
```

In the majority of cases, it is enough to simply provide the bare minimum to get a successful build:

```
cmake --build <build tree>
```

The only required argument is the path to the generated *build tree*. This is the same path that was passed with the -B argument in the generation stage.

CMake allows you to specify key build parameters that work for every builder. If you need to provide special arguments to your chosen native builder, pass them at the end of the command after the -- token:

```
cmake --build <build tree> -- <build tool options>
```

Let's see what other options are available.

Running parallel builds

By default, many build tools will use multiple concurrent processes to leverage modern processors and compile your sources in parallel. Builders know the structure of project dependencies, so they can simultaneously process steps that have their dependencies met to save users' time.

You might want to override that setting if you'd like to build faster on a multi-core machine (or to force a single-threaded build for debugging).

Simply specify the number of jobs with either of the following options:

```
cmake --build <build tree> --parallel [<number of jobs>]
cmake --build <build tree> -j [<number of jobs>]
```

The alternative is to set it with the CMAKE_BUILD_PARALLEL_LEVEL environment variable. The command-line option will override this variable.

Selecting targets to build and clean

Every project is made up of one or more parts, called **targets** (we'll discuss these in the second part of the book). Usually, we'll want to build all available targets; however, on occasion, we might be interested in skipping some or explicitly building a target that was deliberately excluded from normal builds. We can do this as follows:

```
cmake --build <build tree> --target <target1> --target <target2> …
```

We can specify multiple targets to build by repeating the –target argument. Also, there's a short-hand version, -t <target>, that can be used instead.

Cleaning the build tree

One special target that isn't normally built is called clean. Building it has the special effect of removing all artifacts from the build directory, so everything can be created from scratch later. You can start this process like this:

```
cmake --build <build tree> -t clean
```

Additionally, CMake offers a convenient alias if you'd like to clean first and then implement a normal build:

```
cmake --build <build tree> --clean-first
```

This action is different from cleaning mentioned in the *Cleaning the build tree* section, as it only affects target artifacts and nothing else (like the cache).

Configuring the build type for multi-configuration generators

So, we already know a bit about generators: they come in different shapes and sizes. Some of them offer the ability to build both Debug and Release build types in a single build tree. Generators that support this feature include Ninja Multi-Config, Xcode, and Visual Studio. Every other generator is a single-configuration generator, and they require a separate build tree for every config type we want to build.

Select Debug, Release, MinSizeRel, or RelWithDebInfo and specify it as follows:

```
cmake --build <build tree> --config <cfg>
```

Otherwise, CMake will use Debug as the default.

Debugging the build process

When things go bad, the first thing we should do is check the output messages. However, veteran developers know that printing all the details all the time is confusing, so they often hide them by default. When we need to peek under the hood, we can ask for far more detailed logs by telling CMake to be verbose:

```
cmake --build <build tree> --verbose
cmake --build <build tree> -v
```

The same effect can be achieved by setting the CMAKE_VERBOSE_MAKEFILE cached variable.

Installing a project

When artifacts are built, users can install them on the system. Usually, this means copying files into the correct directories, installing libraries, or running some custom installation logic from a CMake script.

The syntax of installation mode is:

```
cmake --install <build tree> [<options>]
```

As with other modes of operation, CMake requires a path to a generated build tree:

```
cmake --install <build tree>
```

The install action also has plenty of additional options. Let's see what they can do.

Choosing the installation directory

We can prepend the installation path with a prefix of our choice (for example, when we have limited write access to some directories). The /usr/local path that is prefixed with /home/user becomes /home/user/usr/local.

The signature for this option is as follows:

```
cmake --install <build tree> --install-prefix <prefix>
```

If you use CMake 3.21 or older, you'll have to use a less explicit option:

```
cmake --install <build tree> --prefix <prefix>
```

Note that this won't work on Windows, as paths on this platform usually start with the drive letter.

Installation for multi-configuration generators

Just like in the build stage, we can specify which build type we want to use for our installation (for more details, please refer to the *Building a project* section). The available types include Debug, Release, MinSizeRel, and RelWithDebInfo. The signature is as follows:

```
cmake --install <build tree> --config <cfg>
```

Selecting components to install

As a developer, you might choose to split your project into components that can be installed independently. We'll discuss the concept of components in further detail in *Chapter 14, Installing and Packaging*. For now, let's just assume they represent sets of artifacts that don't need to be used in every case. This might be something like application, docs, and extra-tools.

To install a single component, use the following option:

```
cmake --install <build tree> --component <component>
```

Setting file permissions

If the installation is performed on a Unix-like platform, you can specify default permissions for the installed directories with the following option, using the format of u=rwx,g=rx,o=rx:

```
cmake --install <build tree>
      --default-directory-permissions <permissions>
```

Debugging the installation process

Similarly to the build stage, we can also choose to view a detailed output of the installation stage. To do this, use any of the following:

```
cmake --install <build tree> --verbose
cmake --install <build tree> -v
```

The same effect can be achieved if the VERBOSE environment variable is set.

Running a script

CMake projects are configured using CMake's custom language. It's cross-platform and quite powerful. Since it's already there, why not make it available for other tasks? Sure enough, CMake can run standalone scripts (more on that in the *Discovering scripts and modules* section), like so:

```
cmake [{-D <var>=<value>}...] -P <cmake script file>
      [-- <unparsed options>...]
```

Running such a script won't run any *configuration* or *generate* stages, and it won't affect the cache.

There are two ways you can pass values to this script:

- Through variables defined with the -D option
- Through arguments that can be passed after a -- token

CMake will create CMAKE_ARGV<n> variables for all arguments passed to the script with the latter (including the -- token).

Running a command-line tool

On rare occasions, we might need to run a single command in a platform-independent way – perhaps copy a file or compute a checksum. Not all platforms were created equal, so not all commands are available in every system (or they have been named differently).

CMake offers a mode in which most common commands can be executed in the same way across platforms. Its syntax is:

```
cmake -E <command> [<options>]
```

As the use of this particular mode is fairly limited, we won't cover it in depth. However, if you're interested in the details, I recommend calling cmake -E to list all the available commands. To simply get a glimpse of what's on offer, CMake 3.26 supports the following commands: capabilities, cat, chdir, compare_files, copy, copy_directory, copy_directory_if_different, copy_if_different, echo, echo_append, env, environment, make_directory, md5sum, sha1sum, sha224sum, sha256sum, sha384sum, sha512sum, remove, remove_directory, rename, rm, sleep, tar, time, touch, touch_nocreate, create_symlink, create_hardlink, true, and false.

If a command you'd like to use is missing or you need a more complex behavior, consider wrapping it in a script and running it in -P mode.

Running a workflow preset

We mentioned in the *How does it work?* section that building with CMake has three stages: configure, generate, and build. Additionally, we can also run automated tests and even create redistributable packages with CMake. Usually, users need to manually execute every such step separately by calling the appropriate cmake action through the command line. However, advanced projects can specify **workflow presets** that bundle multiple steps into a single action that can be executed with just one command. For now, we'll only mention that users can get the list of available presets by running:

```
cmake --workflow --list-presets
```

They can execute a workflow preset with:

```
cmake --workflow --preset <name>
```

This will be explained in depth in *Chapter 16*, *Writing CMake Presets*.

Getting help

It isn't a surprise that CMake offers extensive help that is accessible through its command line. The syntax of help mode is:

```
cmake --help
```

This will print the list of the possible topics to dive deeper into and explain which parameters need to be added to the command to get more help.

CTest command line

Automated testing is very important in order to produce and maintain high-quality code. The CMake suite comes with a dedicated command-line tool for this purpose called CTest. It is provided to standardize the way tests are run and reported. As a CMake user, you don't need to know the details of testing this particular project: what framework is used or how to run it. CTest provides a convenient interface to list, filter, shuffle, retry, and timebox test runs.

To run tests for a built project, we just need to call ctest in the generated build tree:

```
$ ctest
Test project /tmp/build
Guessing configuration Debug
    Start 1: SystemInformationNew
1/1 Test #1: SystemInformationNew ........   Passed 3.19 sec
```

```
100% tests passed, 0 tests failed out of 1
Total Test time (real) =    3.24 sec
```

We devoted an entire chapter to this subject: *Chapter 11, Testing Frameworks*.

CPack command line

After we have built and tested our amazing software, we are ready to share it with the world. The rare few power users are completely fine with the source code. However, the vast majority of the world uses precompiled binaries for convenience and time-saving reasons.

CMake doesn't leave you stranded here; it comes with batteries included. CPack is a tool that will create redistributable packages for various platforms: compressed archives, executable installers, wizards, NuGet packages, macOS bundles, DMG packages, RPMs, and more.

CPack works in a very similar way to CMake: it is configured with the CMake language and has many *package generators* to pick from (not to be confused with CMake buildsystem generators). We'll go through all the details in *Chapter 14, Installing and Packaging*, as this tool is meant to be used by mature CMake projects.

CMake GUI

CMake for Windows comes with a GUI version to configure the building process of previously prepared projects. For Unix-like platforms, there is a version built with Qt libraries. Ubuntu provides it in the cmake-qt-gui package.

To access the CMake GUI, run the `cmake-gui` executable:

Figure 1.3: The CMake GUI – the configuring stage for a buildsystem using a generator for Visual Studio 2019

The GUI application is a convenience for users of your application: it can be useful for those who aren't familiar with the command line and would prefer a graphical interface.

USE COMMAND-LINE TOOLS INSTEAD

I would definitely recommend the GUI to end users, but for programmers like you, I suggest avoiding any manual blocking steps that require clicking on forms every time you build your programs. This is especially advantageous in mature projects, where entire builds can be fully executed without any user interaction.

CCMake command line

The ccmake executable is an interactive text user interface for CMake on Unix-like platforms (it's unavailable for Windows unless explicitly built). I'm mentioning it here so you know what it is when you see it (*Figure 1.4*, but as with the GUI, developers will benefit more from editing the CMakeCache.txt file directly.

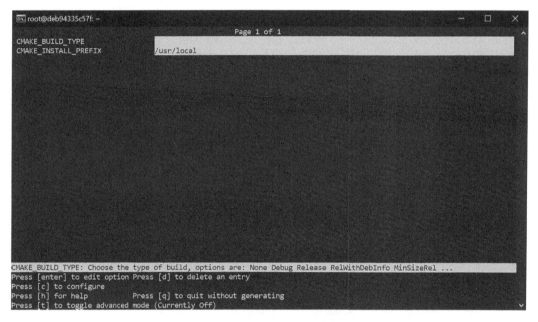

Figure 1.4: The configuring stage in ccmake

Having this out of the way, we have concluded the basic introduction to the command line of the CMake suite. It's time to discover the structure of a typical CMake project.

Navigating project directories and files

Quite a lot of files and directories make up CMake projects. Let's get a general idea of what each one does so we can start tinkering with them. There are several general categories:

- Of course, we'll have project files that we, as developers, prepare and change as our project grows.

- There will be files that CMake generates for itself, and even though they will contain CMake language commands, they aren't meant for developers to edit. Any manual changes made there will be overwritten by CMake.

- Some files are meant for advanced users (as in: not project developers) to customize how CMake builds the project to their individual needs.

- Finally, there are some temporary files that provide valuable information in specific contexts.

This section will also suggest which files you can put in the *ignore* file of your **Version Control System (VCS)**.

The source tree

This is the directory where your project will live (it is also called the **project root**). It contains all of the C++ sources and CMake project files.

Here are the most important takeaways from this directory:

- It requires a CMakeLists.txt configuration file.
- The path to this directory is given by the user with a -S argument of the cmake command when *generating a buildsystem*.
- Avoid hardcoding any absolute paths to the *source tree* in your CMake code – users of your software will store the project in another path.

It's a good idea to initialize a repository in this directory, perhaps using a VCS like Git.

The build tree

CMake creates this directory in a path specified by the user. It will store the buildsystem and everything that gets created during the build: the artifacts of the project, the transient configuration, the cache, the build logs, and the output of your native build tool (like GNU Make). Alternative names for this directory include **build root** and **binary tree**.

Key things to remember:

- Your build configuration (buildsystem) and build artifacts will be created here (such as binary files, executables, and libraries, along with *object files* and archives used for final linking).
- CMake recommends that this directory be placed outside the source tree directory (a practice known as **out-of-source builds**). This way, we can prevent the pollution of our project (**in-source builds**).
- It is specified with -B to the cmake command when *generating a buildsystem*.

- This directory isn't meant as a final destination for generated files. Rather, it's recommended that your projects include an installation stage that copies the final artifacts where they should be in the system and removes all temporary files used for building.

Don't add this directory to your VCS – every user picks one for themselves. If you have a good reason to do an in-source build, make sure to add this directory to the VCS ignore file (like `.gitignore`).

Listfiles

Files that contain the CMake language are called listfiles and can be included one in another by calling `include()` and `find_package()`, or indirectly with `add_subdirectory()`. CMake doesn't enforce any naming rules for these files but, by convention, they have a `.cmake` extension.

Project file

CMake projects are configured with a `CMakeLists.txt` listfile (notice that due to historical reasons, this file has an unconventional extension). This file is required at the top of the source tree of every project and is the first to be executed in the configuration stage.

A top-level `CMakeLists.txt` should contain at least two commands:

- `cmake_minimum_required(VERSION <x.xx>)`: Sets an expected version of CMake and tells CMake how to handle legacy behaviors with policies
- `project(<name> <OPTIONS>)`: Names the project (the provided name will be stored in the `PROJECT_NAME` variable) and specifies the options to configure it (more on this in *Chapter 2, The CMake Language*)

As your software grows, you might want to partition it into smaller units that can be configured and reasoned about separately. CMake supports this through the notion of subdirectories with their own `CMakeLists.txt` files. Your project structure might look similar to the following example:

```
myProject/CMakeLists.txt
myProject/api/CMakeLists.txt
myProject/api/api.h
myProject/api/api.cpp
```

A very simple top-level `CMakeLists.txt` file can then be used to bring it all together:

```
cmake_minimum_required(VERSION 3.26)
project(app)
message("Top level CMakeLists.txt")
add_subdirectory(api)
```

The main aspects of the project are covered in the top-level file: managing the dependencies, stating the requirements, and detecting the environment. We also have an add_subdirectory(api) command to include another `CMakeListst.txt` file from the api subdirectory to perform steps that are specific to the API part of our application.

Cache file

Cache variables will be generated from the listfiles and stored in `CMakeCache.txt` when the configure stage is run for the first time. This file resides in the root of the build tree and has a fairly simple format (some lines removed for brevity):

```
# This is the CMakeCache file.
# For build in directory: /root/build tree
# It was generated by CMake: /usr/local/bin/cmake
# The syntax for the file is as follows:
# KEY:TYPE=VALUE
# KEY is the name of a variable in the cache.
# TYPE is a hint to GUIs for the type of VALUE, DO NOT EDIT
  #TYPE!.
# VALUE is the current value for the KEY.
########################
# EXTERNAL cache entries
########################

# Flags used by the CXX compiler during DEBUG builds.
CMAKE_CXX_FLAGS_DEBUG:STRING=/MDd /Zi /Ob0 /Od /RTC1
# ... more variables here ...

########################
# INTERNAL cache entries
########################

# Minor version of cmake used to create the current loaded
  cache
CMAKE_CACHE_MINOR_VERSION:INTERNAL=19
# ... more variables here ...
```

As you can see from the header comments, this format is pretty self-explanatory. Cache entries in the EXTERNAL section are meant for users to modify, while the INTERNAL section is managed by CMake.

Here are a couple of key takeaways to bear in mind:

- You can manage this file manually, by calling cmake (see *Options for caching* in the *Mastering the command line* section of this chapter), or through ccmake or cmake-gui.
- You can reset the project to its default configuration by deleting this file; it will be regenerated from the listfiles.

Cache variables can be read and written from the listfiles. Sometimes, variable reference evaluation is a bit complicated; we will cover that in more detail in *Chapter 2, The CMake Language*.

Package definition file

A big part of the CMake ecosystem is the external packages that projects can depend on. They provide libraries and tools in a seamless, cross-platform way. Package authors that want to provide CMake support will ship it with a CMake package configuration file.

We'll learn how to write those files in *Chapter 14, Installing and Packaging*. Meanwhile, here's a few interesting details to bear in mind:

- **Config-files** (original spelling) contain information regarding how to use the library binaries, headers, and helper tools. Sometimes, they expose CMake macros and functions that can be used in your project.
- **Config-files** are named <PackageName>-config.cmake or <PackageName>Config.cmake.
- Use the find_package() command to include packages.

If a specific version of the package is required, CMake will check this against the associated <PackageName>-config-version.cmake or <PackageName>ConfigVersion.cmake.

If a vendor doesn't provide a config file for the package, sometimes, the configuration is bundled with the CMake itself or can be provided in the project with **Find-module** (original spelling).

Generated files

Many files are generated in the build tree by the cmake executable in the generation stage. As such, they shouldn't be edited manually. CMake uses them as a configuration for the cmake install action, CTest, and CPack.

Files that you may encounter are:

- `cmake_install.cmake`
- `CTestTestfile.cmake`
- `CPackConfig.cmake`

If you're implementing an in-source build, it's probably a good idea to add them to the VCS ignore file.

JSON and YAML files

Other formats used by CMake are **JavaScript Object Notation (JSON)** and **Yet Another Markup Language (YAML)**. These files are introduced as an interface to communicate with external tools (like IDEs) or to provide configuration that can be easily generated and parsed.

Preset files

The advanced configuration of the projects can become a relatively busy task when we need to be specific about things such as cache variables, chosen generators, the path of the build tree, and more – especially when we have more than one way of building our project. This is where the presets come in – instead of manually configuring these values through the command line, we can just provide a file that stores all the details and ship it with the project. Since CMake 3.25, presets also allow us to configure **workflows**, which tie stages (configure, build, test, and package) into a named list of steps to execute.

As mentioned in the *Mastering the command line* section of this chapter, users can choose presets through the GUI or use the command `--list-presets` and select a preset for the buildsystem with the `--preset=<preset>` option.

Presets are stored in two files:

- `CMakePresets.json`: This is meant for project authors to provide official presets.
- `CMakeUserPresets.json`: This is dedicated to users who want to customize the project configuration to their liking (you can add it to your VCS ignore file).

Presets are not required in projects and only become useful in advanced scenarios. See *Chapter 16, Writing CMake Presets*, for details.

File-based API

CMake 3.14 introduced an API that allows external tools to query the buildsystem information: paths to generated files, cache entries, toolchains, and such. We only mention this very advanced topic to avoid confusion if you come across a *file-based API* phrase in the documentation. The name suggests how it works: a JSON file with a query has to be placed in a special path inside the build tree. CMake will read this file during the buildsystem generation and write a response to another file, so it can be parsed by external applications.

The file-based API was introduced to replace a deprecated mechanism called *server mode* (or cmake-server), which was finally removed in CMake 3.26.

Configure log

Since version 3.26, CMake will provide a structured log file for really advanced debugging of the *configure stage* at:

```
<build tree>/CMakeFiles/CMakeConfigureLog.yaml
```

It's one of these features that you don't normally need to pay attention to – until you do.

Ignoring files in Git

There are many VCSs; one of the most popular out there is Git. Whenever we start a new project, it is good to make sure that we only *add* the necessary files to the repository. Project hygiene is easier to maintain if we specify unwanted files in the .gitignore file. For example, we might exclude files that are generated, user-specific, or temporary.

Git will automatically skip them when forming new commits. Here's the file that I use in my projects:

ch01/01-hello/.gitignore

```
CMakeUserPresets.json
# If in-source builds are used, exclude their output like so:
build_debug/
build_release/

# Generated and user files
**/CMakeCache.txt
**/CMakeUserPresets.json
**/CTestTestfile.cmake
```

```
**/CPackConfig.cmake
**/cmake_install.cmake
**/install_manifest.txt
**/compile_commands.json
```

Now you hold a map to the sea of project files. Some files are very important and you will use them all the time – others, not so much. While it might seem like a waste to learn about them, it can be invaluable to know where *not to look* for answers. In any case, one last question for this chapter remains: what other self-contained units can you create with CMake?

Discovering scripts and modules

CMake is primarily focused on projects built to produce artifacts that get consumed by other systems (such as CI/CD pipelines and test platforms, or deployed to machines or stored in artifact repositories). However, there are two other concepts in CMake that use its language: scripts and modules. Let's explain what they are and how they differ.

Scripts

CMake offers a platform-agnostic programming language, which comes with many useful commands. Scripts written in it can be bundled with a bigger project or be completely independent.

Think of it as a consistent way to do cross-platform work. Normally, to perform a task, you would have to create a separate Bash script for Linux and separate batch files or PowerShell scripts for Windows, and so on. CMake abstracts this away so you can have one file that works fine on all platforms. Sure, you could use external tools such as Python, Perl, or Ruby scripts, but that's an added dependency and will increase the complexity of your C/C++ projects. So why introduce another language, when most of the time, you can get the job done with something far simpler? Use CMake!

We have already learned from the *Mastering the command line* section that we can execute scripts using the -P option: `cmake -P script.cmake`.

But what are the actual requirements for the script file that we want to use? Not that big: the script can be as complex as you like, or just an empty file. It is still recommended to call the `cmake_minimum_required()` command at the beginning of every script though. This command tells CMake which policies should be applied to subsequent commands in this project (more in *Chapter 4, Setting Up Your First CMake Project*).

Here's an example of a simple script:

ch01/02-script/script.cmake

```cmake
# An example of a script
cmake_minimum_required(VERSION 3.26.0)
message("Hello world")
file(WRITE Hello.txt "I am writing to a file")
```

When running scripts, CMake won't execute any of the usual stages (such as configuration or generation), and it won't use the cache, since there is no concept of **source tree** or **build tree** in scripts. This means that project-specific CMake commands are not available/usable in scripting mode. That's all. Happy scripting!

Utility modules

CMake projects can use external modules to enhance their functionality. Modules are written in the CMake language and contain macro definitions, variables, and commands that perform all kinds of functions. They range from quite complex scripts (like those provided by CPack and CTest) to fairly simple ones, such as AddFileDependencies or TestBigEndian.

The CMake distribution comes packed with over 80 different utility modules. If that's not enough, you can download more from the internet by browsing curated lists, such as the one found at https://github.com/onqtam/awesome-cmake, or write your own module from scratch.

To use a utility module, we need to call an include(<MODULE>) command. Here's a simple project showing this in action:

ch01/03-module/CMakeLists.txt

```cmake
cmake_minimum_required(VERSION 3.26.0)
project(ModuleExample)
include (TestBigEndian)
test_big_endian(IS_BIG_ENDIAN)
if(IS_BIG_ENDIAN)
message("BIG_ENDIAN")
else()
message("LITTLE_ENDIAN")
endif()
```

We'll learn what modules are available as they become relevant to the subject at hand. If you're curious, a full list of bundled modules can be found at https://cmake.org/cmake/help/latest/manual/cmake-modules.7.html.

Find-modules

In the *Package definition File* section, I mentioned that CMake has a mechanism to find files belonging to external dependencies that don't support CMake and don't provide a CMake package config-file. That's what find-modules are for. CMake provides over 150 find-modules that are able to locate those packages if they are installed in the system. As was the case with utility modules, there are plenty more find-modules available online. As a last resort, you can always write your own.

You can use them by calling the `find_package()` command and providing the name of the package in question. Such a find-module will then play a little game of hide and seek and check all known locations of the software it is looking for. If the files are found, variables with their path will be defined (as specified in that module's manual). Now, CMake can build against that dependency.

For example, the `FindCURL` module searches for a popular *Client URL* library and defines the following variables: `CURL_FOUND`, `CURL_INCLUDE_DIRS`, `CURL_LIBRARIES`, and `CURL_VERSION_STRING`.

We will cover find-modules in more depth in *Chapter 9, Managing Dependencies in CMake*.

Summary

Now you understand what CMake is and how it works; you learned about the key components of the CMake tool family and how it is installed on a variety of systems. Like a true power user, you know all the ways in which to run CMake through the command line: buildsystem generation, building a project, installing, running scripts, command-line tools, and printing help. You are aware of the CTest, CPack, and GUI applications. This will help you to create projects with the right perspective for users and other developers. Additionally, you learned what makes up a project: directories, listfiles, configs, presets, and helper files, along with what to ignore in your VCS. Finally, you took a sneak peek at other non-project files: standalone scripts and two kinds of modules – utility modules and find-modules.

In the next chapter, we will learn how to use the CMake programming language. This will allow you to write your own listfiles and will open the door to your first script, project, and module.

Further reading

For more information, you can refer to the following resources:

- The official CMake web page and documentation:
  `https://cmake.org/`

- Single-configuration generators:
  `https://cgold.readthedocs.io/en/latest/glossary/single-config.html`
- The separation of stages in the CMake GUI:
  `https://stackoverflow.com/questions/39401003/`

Leave a review!

Enjoying this book? Help readers like you by leaving an Amazon review. Scan the QR code below to get a free eBook of your choice.

2

The CMake Language

Writing in the **CMake language** is trickier than one might expect. When you read a CMake listfile for the first time, you may be under the impression that the language in it is so simple that it can be just practiced without any theory. You may then attempt to introduce changes and experiment with the code without a thorough understanding of how it actually works. I wouldn't blame you. We programmers are usually very busy, and build-related issues aren't usually something that sounds exciting to invest lots of time in. In an effort to go fast, we tend to make gut-based changes hoping they just might do the trick. This approach to solving technical problems is called *voodoo programming*.

The CMake language appears trivial: after introducing our small extension, fix, hack, or one-liner, we suddenly realize that something isn't working. Usually, the duration spent on debugging exceeds the time required for comprehending the topic itself. Luckily, this won't be our fate because this chapter covers most of the critical knowledge needed to use the CMake language in practice.

In this chapter, we'll not only learn about the building blocks of the CMake language – **comments**, **commands**, **variables**, and **control structures** – but we'll also understand the necessary background and try out examples following the latest practices.

CMake puts you in a bit of a unique position. On one hand, you perform the role of a build engineer and must have a comprehensive grasp of compilers, platforms, and all related aspects. On the other hand, you're a developer who writes the code that generates a buildsystem. Crafting high-quality code is a challenging task that demands a multifaceted approach. Not only must the code be functional and legible but it should also be easy to analyze, extend, and maintain.

To conclude, we will present a selection of the most practical and frequently utilized commands in CMake. Commands that are also commonly used, but not to the same extent, will be placed in *Appendix, Miscellaneous Commands* (reference guides for the string, list, file, and math commands).

In this chapter, we're going to cover the following main topics:

- The basics of the CMake language syntax
- Working with variables
- Using lists
- Understanding control structures in CMake
- Exploring the frequently used commands

Technical requirements

You can find the code files that are present in this chapter on GitHub at https://github.com/ PacktPublishing/Modern-CMake-for-Cpp-2E/tree/main/examples/ch02.

To build the examples provided in this book, always use the recommended commands:

```
cmake -B <build tree> -S <source tree>
cmake --build <build tree>
```

Be sure to replace the placeholders <build tree> and <source tree> with appropriate paths. As a reminder: **build tree** is the path to the target/output directory and **source tree** is the path at which your source code is located.

The basics of the CMake language syntax

Composing CMake code is very much like writing in any other imperative language: lines are executed from top to bottom and from left to right, occasionally stepping into an included file or a called function. The starting point of execution is determined by the mode (see the *Mastering the command line* section in *Chapter 1, First Steps with CMake*), either from the root file of the source tree (CMakeLists.txt) or a .cmake script file provided as an argument to cmake.

Since CMake scripts offer extensive support for the CMake language, except for project-related features, we will utilize them to practice CMake syntax in this chapter. Once we become proficient in composing simple listfiles, we can advance to creating actual project files, which we will cover in *Chapter 4, Setting Up Your First CMake Project*.

As a reminder, scripts can be run with the following command: cmake -P script.cmake.

CMake supports **7-bit ASCII** text files for portability across all platforms. You can use both \n or \r\n line endings. CMake versions above 3.2 support **UTF-8** and **UTF-16** with optional **byte-order markers (BOMs)**.

Everything in a CMake listfile is either a *comment* or a *command invocation*.

Comments

Just like in **C++**, there are two kinds of comments: *single-line* comments and *bracket* (multiline) comments. But unlike in C++, bracket comments can be nested. Single-line comments start with a hash sign, #:

```
# they can be placed on an empty line
message("Hi"); # or after a command like here.
```

Multiline bracket comments get their name from their symbol – they start with # followed by opening square bracket [, any number of equal signs = (which can also include 0), and another square bracket [. To close a bracket comment, use the same number of equal signs and reverse the brackets]:

```
#[=[
bracket comment
  #[[
    nested bracket comment
  #]]
#]=]
```

You can deactivate a multiline comment swiftly by adding another # to the initial line of the bracket comment, as demonstrated in the following:

```
##[=[ this is a single-line comment now
no longer commented
  #[[
    still, a nested comment
  #]]
#]=] this is a single-line comment now
```

Knowing how to use comments is definitely useful, but it raises another question: when should we do it? Since writing listfiles is essentially programming, it is a good idea to bring our best coding practices to them as well.

Code that follows such practices is often called *clean code* – a term used over the years by software development gurus like Robert C. Martin, Martin Fowler, and many other authors.

There is often a lot of controversy surrounding which practices are considered beneficial or detrimental, and as you might expect, comments have not been exempt from these debates. Everything should be judged on a case-by-case basis, but generally agreed-upon guidelines say that good comments provide at least one of the following:

- **Information**: They can untangle complexities such as regex patterns or formatting strings.
- **Intent**: They can explain the intent of the code when it is not obvious from the implementation or interface.
- **Clarification**: They can explain concepts that can't be easily refactored or changed.
- **Warnings of consequences**: They can provide warnings, especially around code that can break other things.
- **Amplification**: They can underline the importance of an idea that is hard to express in code.
- **Legal clauses**: They can add this necessary evil, which is usually not the domain of a programmer.

It's best to avoid comments by applying better naming, refactoring or correcting your code. Omit comments that are:

- **Mandated**: These are added for completeness but they are not really important.
- **Redundant**: These repeat what is already clearly written in the code.
- **Misleading**: These could be outdated or incorrect if they don't follow code changes.
- **Journal**: These note what has been changed and when (use **Version Control Systems (VCS)** for this instead).
- **Dividers**: These mark sections.

If you can, avoid adding comments, adopt better naming practices, and refactor or correct your code. Crafting elegant code is a challenging task but it enhances the reader's experience. Since we spend more time reading code than composing it, we should always strive to write code that is easy to read, instead of just trying to finish it quickly. I recommend checking out the *Further reading* section at the end of this chapter for some good references on *clean code*. If you're interested in comments, you'll find a link to my YouTube video *Which comments in your code ARE GOOD?* touching on this subject in depth.

Command invocations

Time for some action! Invoking commands is the bread and butter of CMake listfiles. In order to run a command, you must specify its name followed by parentheses, in which you can enclose a list of **command arguments** separated by whitespace.

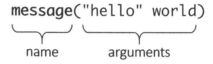

Figure 2.1: An example of a command

Command names aren't case-sensitive, but there is a convention in the CMake community to use snake_case (that is, lowercase words joined with underscores). You can also define your own commands, which we'll cover in the *Understanding control structures in CMake* section of this chapter.

One significant difference between CMake and C++ is that command invocations in CMake are not expressions. This means that you cannot pass another command as an argument to a called command because *everything* inside the parentheses is treated as an argument for that specific command.

CMake commands are also not followed with semicolons. This is because each line of source code can only contain one command.

A command can be optionally followed by a comment:

```
command(argument1 "argument2" argument3) # comment
command2() #[[ multiline comment
```

But not the other way around:

```
#[[ bracket
]] command()
```

As we said earlier, everything in a CMake listfile is either a *comment* or a *command invocation*. CMake syntax really is that simple, and for the most part, it's a good thing. While there are some constraints (for instance, you can't increment a counter variable using an expression), for the most part, these limitations are mostly acceptable because CMake is not intended to be a general-purpose language.

CMake provides commands to manipulate variables, direct the flow of execution, modify files, and much more. To make things easier, we will be introducing the relevant commands as we progress through different examples. These commands can be categorized into two groups:

- **Scripting commands**: These are always available and they change the state of the command processor and access variables, and affect other commands and the environment.
- **Project commands**: These are available in projects and they manipulate the project state and build targets.

Virtually every command relies on other elements of the language in order to function: variables, conditional statements, and, most importantly, command-line arguments. Now, let's explore how we can utilize them.

Command arguments

A number of commands in CMake necessitate whitespace-separated arguments to configure their behavior. As demonstrated in *Figure 2.1*, the quotation marks used around the arguments can be quite peculiar. While certain arguments require quotes, others do not. What's the reasoning behind this distinction?

Under the hood, the only data type recognized by CMake is a string. This is why every command expects zero or more strings for its arguments. CMake will **evaluate** every argument to a static string and then pass them into the command. *Evaluating* means **string interpolation**, or substituting parts of a string with another value. This can mean replacing the **escape sequences,** expanding the **variable references** (also called *variable interpolation*), and unpacking **lists**.

Depending on the context, we might want to enable such evaluation as needed. For that reason, CMake offers three types of arguments:

- Bracket arguments
- Quoted arguments
- Unquoted arguments

Every argument type in CMake has its own peculiarities and provides a distinct level of evaluation.

Bracket arguments

Bracket arguments aren't evaluated because they are used to pass multiline strings, verbatim, as a single argument to commands. This means that such an argument will include whitespace in the form of tabs and newlines.

Bracket arguments are formatted identically to comments. They are initiated with [=[and concluded with]=], and the number of equal signs in both the opening and closing tokens must match (omitting equal signs is permissible as long as they match). The only difference from the comments is that bracket arguments cannot be nested.

Here's an example of the use of such an argument with the message() command, which prints all passed arguments to the screen:

ch02/01-arguments/bracket.cmake

```
message([[multiline
  bracket
  argument
]])
message([==[
  because we used two equal-signs "=="
  this command receives only a single argument
  even if it includes two square brackets in a row
  { "petsArray" = [["mouse","cat"],["dog"]] }
]==])
```

In the preceding example, we can see different forms of bracket arguments. Note how putting closing tags on a separate line in the first call introduces an empty line in the output:

```
$ cmake -P ch02/01-arguments/bracket.cmake
multiline
bracket
argument
  because we used two equal-signs "=="
  following is still a single argument:
  { "petsArray" = [["mouse","cat"],["dog"]] }
```

The second form is useful when we're passing text that contains double brackets (]]) (highlighted in the code snippet), as they won't be interpreted as marking the end of the argument.

These kinds of bracket arguments have limited use – typically, they contain lengthier blocks of text with messages that are displayed to the user. In most cases, we'll need something more dynamic, such as quoted arguments.

Quoted arguments

Quoted arguments resemble a regular C++ string – these arguments group together multiple characters, including whitespace, and they will expand *escape sequences*. Like C++ strings, they are opened and closed with a double quote character, ", so to include a quote character within the output string, you have to escape it with a backslash, \". Other well-known escape sequences are supported as well: \\ denotes a literal backslash, \t is a tab character, \n is a newline, and \r is a carriage return.

This is where the similarities with C++ strings end. Quoted arguments can span multiple lines, and they will interpolate variable references. Think of them as having a built-in sprintf function from **C** or a std::format function from **C++20**. To insert a variable reference to your argument, wrap the name of the variable in a token like so: ${name}. We'll talk more about variable references in the *Working with variables* section of this chapter.

Can you guess how many lines will be in the output of the following script?

ch02/01-arguments/quoted.cmake

```
message("1. escape sequence: \" \n in a quoted argument")
message("2. multi...
  line")
message("3. and a variable reference: ${CMAKE_VERSION}")
```

Let's see it in action:

```
$ cmake -P ch02/01-arguments/quoted.cmake
1. escape sequence: "
in a quoted argument
2. multi...
line
3. and a variable reference: 3.26.0
```

That's right – we have one escaped quote character, one newline escape sequence, and a literal newline. We also accessed a built-in CMAKE_VERSION variable, which we can see interpolated on the last line. Let's take a look at how CMake treats arguments without quotes.

Unquoted arguments

In the programming world, we have gotten used to the fact that strings must be delimited in one form or another, for example, by using single quotes, double quotes, or a backslash. CMake deviates from this convention and introduces *unquoted arguments*. We might argue that dropping delimiters makes the code easier to read. Is that true? I'll let you form your own opinion.

Unquoted arguments evaluate both *escape sequences* and *variable references*. However, be careful with semicolons (;) as, in CMake, semicolons are treated as *list* delimiters. If an argument contains a semicolon, CMake will split it into multiple arguments. If you need to use them, escape every semicolon with a backslash, \ ; . We'll talk more about semicolons in the *Using lists* section of this chapter.

You may find that these arguments are the most perplexing to work with, so here's an illustration to help clarify how these arguments are partitioned:

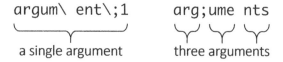

Figure 2.2: Escape sequences cause separate tokens to be interpreted as a single argument

It's always worth being careful with unquoted arguments. Some CMake commands require a specific number of arguments and ignore any overhead. If your arguments become accidentally separated, you'll get hard-to-debug errors.

Unquoted arguments cannot contain unescaped *quotes ("), hashes (#), and backslashes (\). And if that's not enough to remember, parentheses, ( ), are allowed only if they form correct, matching pairs. That is, you'll start with an opening parenthesis and close it before closing the command argument list.

Here are some examples that demonstrate the rules we have discussed:

ch02/01-arguments/unquoted.cmake

```
message(a\ single\ argument)
message(two arguments)
message(three;separated;arguments)
message(${CMAKE_VERSION})   # a variable reference
message(()()())             # matching parentheses
```

What will be the output of the preceding? Let's have a look:

```
$ cmake -P ch02/01-arguments/unquoted.cmake
a single argument
twoarguments
threeseparatedarguments
3.16.3
()()()
```

Even a simple command such as message() is very particular about separated unquoted arguments. The space in a single argument was correctly printed when it was explicitly escaped. However, twoarguments and threeseparatearguments were *glued* together, since message() doesn't add any spaces on its own.

Given all these complexities, when is it beneficial to use unquoted arguments? Some CMake commands allow optional arguments that are preceded by a keyword to signify that an optional argument will be provided. In such instances, using an unquoted argument for the keyword can make the code more legible. For example:

```
project(myProject VERSION 1.2.3)
```

In this command, the VERSION keyword and the following argument 1.2.3 are optional. As you can see, both are left unquoted for readability. Note that keywords are case-sensitive.

Now that we understand how to deal with the complexities and quirks of CMake arguments, we are ready to tackle the next interesting subject – working with all kinds of variables in CMake.

Working with variables

Variables in CMake are a surprisingly complex subject. Not only are there three categories of variables – **normal**, **cache**, and **environment** – but they also reside in different **variable scopes**, with specific rules on how one *scope* affects the other. Very often, a poor understanding of these rules becomes a source of bugs and headaches. I recommend you study this section with care and make sure you understand all of the concepts before moving on.

Let's start with some key facts about variables in CMake:

- Variable names are case-sensitive and can include almost any character.
- All variables are stored internally as strings, even if some commands can interpret them as values of other data types (even *lists*!).

The basic variable manipulation commands are set() and unset(), but there are other commands that can alter variable values, such as string() and list().

To declare a **normal variable**, we simply call set(), providing its name and the value:

ch02/02-variables/set.cmake

```
set(MyString1 "Text1")
set([[My String2]] "Text2")
```

```
set("My String 3" "Text3")
message(${MyString1})
message(${My\ String2})
message(${My\ String\ 3})
```

As you can see, the use of brackets and quoted arguments allows for spaces to be included in the variable name. However, when referencing it later, we have to escape the whitespace with a backslash, \. For that reason, it is recommended to use only alphanumeric characters, dashes (-), and underscores (_) in variable names.

Also avoid reserved names (in uppercase, lowercase, or mixed case) that begin with any of the following: CMAKE_, _CMAKE_, or an underscore, _, followed by the name of any CMake command.

To unset a variable, we can use unset() in the following way: unset(MyString1).

 The set() command accepts a plain text variable name as its first argument, but the message() command uses a variable reference wrapped in the ${} syntax.

What would happen if we were to provide a variable wrapped in the ${} syntax to the set() command?

To answer that, we'll need to understand *variable references* better.

Variable references

I already mentioned references briefly in the *Command arguments* section, as they're evaluated for quoted and unquoted arguments. We learned that to create a reference to a defined variable, we need to use the ${} syntax, like so: message(${MyString1}).

On evaluation, CMake will traverse the *variable scopes* from the innermost scope to the outermost scope and replace ${MyString1} with a value, or an empty string if no variable is found (CMake won't produce any error messages). This process is also called *variable evaluation, expansion*, or *interpolation*.

Interpolation is performed in an inside-out manner, beginning from the innermost curly brace pair and moving outward. For example, if the ${MyOuter${MyInner}} reference is encountered:

1. CMake will try to evaluate MyInner first, rather than searching for a variable named MyOuter${MyInner}.

2. If the MyInner variable is successfully expanded, CMake will repeat the expansion process using the newly formed reference until no further expansion is possible.

To avoid receiving unexpected outcomes, it is recommended to refrain from storing variable expansion tokens in variable values.

CMake will perform variable expansion to the full extent, and only after completion will it pass the resulting values as arguments to the command. This is why when we call `set(${MyInner}` `"Hi")`; we won't actually be changing the `MyInner` variable, but instead, we'll change the variable named after the value stored in `MyInner`. Very often, this is not what we want.

Variable references are a bit peculiar in how they work when it comes to variable categories, but in general, the following applies:

- The `${}` syntax is used to reference *normal* or *cache* variables.
- The `$ENV{}` syntax is used to reference *environment* variables.
- The `$CACHE{}` syntax is used to reference *cache* variables.

That's right, with `${}`, you might get a value from one category or the other: the *normal* variable will be used if it was set in the current scope, but if it wasn't set, or was unset, CMake will use the *cache* variable with the same name. If there's no such variable, the reference evaluates to an empty string.

CMake predefines a lot of built-in normal variables that serve different purposes. For example, you can pass command-line arguments to scripts after the `--` token and they will be stored in the `CMAKE_ARGV<n>` variables (the `CMAKE_ARGC` variable will contain the count).

Let's introduce other categories of variables so that we understand clearly what they are.

Using environment variables

This is the least complicated kind of variable. CMake makes a copy of the variables that were in the environment used to start the `cmake` process and makes them available in a single, global scope. To reference these variables, use the `$ENV{<name>}` syntax.

CMake changes these variables, but changes will only be made to a local copy in the running `cmake` process and not the actual system environment; moreover, these changes won't be visible to subsequent runs of builds or tests, so it is not recommended.

Be aware that there are a few environment variables that affect different aspects of CMake behavior. For example, the `CXX` variable specifies what executable will be used for compiling C++ files. We'll cover environment variables, as they will become relevant to this book. A full list is available in the documentation: `https://cmake.org/cmake/help/latest/manual/cmake-env-variables.7.html`.

It's important to realize that if you use ENV variables as arguments to your commands, the values will be interpolated during the generation of the buildsystem. This means that they will get permanently baked into the build tree, and changing the environment for the build stage won't have any effect.

For example, take the following project file:

ch02/03-environment/CMakeLists.txt

```
cmake_minimum_required(VERSION 3.20.0)
project(Environment)
message("generated with " $ENV{myenv})
add_custom_target(EchoEnv ALL COMMAND echo "myenv in build
  is" $ENV{myenv})
```

The preceding example has two steps: it will print the myenv environment variable during the configuration, and it will add a build stage through add_custom_target(), which echoes the same variable as part of the build process. We can test what happens with a bash script that uses one value for the configuration stage and another for the build stage:

ch02/03-environment/build.sh

```
#!/bin/bash
export myenv=first
echo myenv is now $myenv
cmake -B build .
cd build
export myenv=second
echo myenv is now $myenv
cmake --build .
```

Running the preceding code clearly shows that the value set during the configuration is persisted to the generated buildsystem:

```
$ ./build.sh | grep -v "\-\-"
myenv is now first
generated with first
myenv is now second
Scanning dependencies of target EchoEnv
myenv in build is first
Built target EchoEnv
```

This concludes our discussion on environmental variables for the time being. Let us now move on to the final category of variables: cache variables.

Using cache variables

We first mentioned cache variables when discussing command-line options for cmake in *Chapter 1, First Steps with CMake*. Essentially, they're persistent variables stored in a CMakeCache.txt file in your build tree. They contain information gathered during the *configuration stage* of your project. They originate from the system (path to compilers, linkers, tools, and others) and from the user, provided through the GUI or from the command line with the -D option. Again, cache variables are not available in *scripts*; they only exist in *projects*.

Cache variables will be used if the ${<name>} reference can't find a normal variable defined in the current scope but a cache variable with the same name exists. However, they can also be explicitly referenced with the $CACHE{<name>} syntax and defined with a special form of the set() command:

```
set(<variable> <value> CACHE <type> <docstring> [FORCE])
```

In contrast to the set() command for *normal variables*, extra arguments are necessary for cache variables: <type> and <docstring>. This is because these variables can be configured by the user, and the GUI requires this information to display them appropriately.

The following *types* are accepted:

- BOOL: A Boolean on/off value. The GUI will show a checkbox.
- FILEPATH: A path to a file on a disk. The GUI will open a file dialog.
- PATH: A path to a directory on a disk. The GUI will open a directory dialog.
- STRING: A line of text. The GUI offers a text field to be filled. It can be replaced by a drop-down control by calling set_property(CACHE <variable> STRINGS <values>).
- INTERNAL: A line of text. The GUI skips internal entries. The internal entries may be used to store variables persistently across runs. Use of this type implicitly adds the FORCE keyword.

The <doctring> value is simply a label that will be displayed by the GUI next to the field to provide more detail about this setting to the user. It is required even for an INTERNAL type.

Setting cache variables in the code follows the same rules as environmental variables to some extent – values are overwritten only for the current execution of CMake. However, if the variable doesn't exist in the cache file or an optional FORCE argument is specified, the value will be persisted:

```
set(FOO "BAR" CACHE STRING "interesting value" FORCE)
```

Similar to C++, CMake supports *variable scopes*, albeit implemented in a rather specific way.

How to correctly use variable scopes in CMake

Variable scope is probably the strangest concept in the CMake language. This is maybe because we're so accustomed to how it is implemented in general-purpose languages. We're explaining this early because incorrect understanding of scopes is often a source of bugs that are difficult to find and fix.

Just to clarify, variable scope as a general concept is meant to separate different layers of abstraction expressed with code. Scopes are nested inside one another in a tree-like fashion. The outermost scope (root) is called the **global scope**. Any scope can be called the **local scope**, to indicate the currently executed or discussed scope. Scopes create boundaries between variables, so that the *nested scope* can access variables defined in the *outer scope*, but not the other way around.

CMake has two kinds of variable scopes:

- **File**: Used when blocks and custom functions are executed within a file
- **Directory**: Used when the add_subdirectory() command is called to execute another CMakeLists.txt listfile in a nested directory

 Conditional blocks, loop blocks, and macros don't create separate scopes.

So, what's so different about how a variable scope is implemented in CMake? When a *nested scope* is created, CMake simply fills it with copies of all the variables from the *outer scope*. Subsequent commands will affect these copies. But as soon as the execution of the *nested scope* is completed, all copies are deleted and the original variables from the *outer scope* are restored.

How the concept of scope works in CMake has interesting implications that aren't that common in other languages. When executing in a nested scope, if you unset (unset()) a variable created in the *outer scope*, it will disappear, but only in the current *nested scope*, because the variable is a local copy. If you now reference this variable, CMake will determine that no such variable is defined, it will ignore the *outer scopes*, and continue searching through the cache variables (which are considered separate). That's a possible gotcha.

File variable scopes are opened using the block() and function() commands (but not macro()) and closed with the endblock() and endfunction() commands, respectively. We'll cover functions in the *Command definitions* section of this chapter. For now, let's see how variable scope works in practice with the simpler block() command (introduced in CMake 3.25).

Consider the following example:

ch02/04-scope/scope.cmake

```
cmake_minimum_required(VERSION 3.26)

set(V 1)
message("> Global: ${V}")
block() # outer block
  message(" > Outer: ${V}")
  set(V 2)
  block() # inner block
    message("  > Inner: ${V}")
    set(V 3)
    message("  < Inner: ${V}")
  endblock()
  message(" < Outer: ${V}")
endblock()
message("< Global: ${V}")
```

We initially set the variable V to 1 in the *global scope*. After entering the outer and inner blocks, we immediately change them to 2 and 3, respectively. We also print the variable upon entering and exiting each scope:

```
> Global: 1
 > Outer: 1
  > Inner: 2
  < Inner: 3
 < Outer: 2
< Global: 1
```

As explained previously, as we enter each *nested scope,* the variable values are temporarily copied from the *outer scope* but their original values are restored upon exiting. This is reflected in the last two lines of the output.

The block() command can also propagate values to outer scopes (like C++ would do by default), but it has to be explicitly enabled with the PROPAGATE keyword. If we were to enable propagation for the inner block with block(PROPAGATE V), the output would be as follows:

```
> Global: 1
> Outer: 1
  > Inner: 2
  < Inner: 3
< Outer: 3
< Global: 1
```

Again, we affected the scope of the outer block but not the global scope.

Another method for modifying a variable in the outer scope is to set the PARENT_SCOPE flag for the set() and unset() commands:

```
set(MyVariable "New Value" PARENT_SCOPE)
unset(MyVariable PARENT_SCOPE)
```

That workaround is a bit limited, as it doesn't allow accessing variables more than one level up. Another thing worth noting is the fact that using PARENT_SCOPE doesn't change variables in the current scope.

Now that we know how to handle basic variables, let's take a look at one special case: since all variables are stored as strings, CMake has to take a more creative approach to more complex data structures such as *lists*.

Using lists

To store a **list**, CMake concatenates all elements into a string, using a semicolon, ;, as a delimiter: a;list;of;5;elements. You can escape a semicolon in an element with a backslash, like so: a\;single\;element.

To create a list, we can use the set() command:

```
set(myList a list of five elements)
```

Because of how lists are stored, the following commands will have exactly the same effect:

```
set(myList "a;list;of;five;elements")
set(myList a list "of;five;elements")
```

CMake automatically unpacks lists in unquoted arguments. By passing an unquoted `myList` reference, we effectively send more arguments to the command:

```
message("the list is:" ${myList})
```

The `message()` command will receive six arguments: "the list is:", "a", "list", "of", "five", and "elements". This may have unintended consequences, as the output will be printed without any additional spaces between the arguments:

```
the list is:alistoffiveelements
```

As you can see, this is a very simple mechanism, and it should be used carefully.

CMake offers a `list()` command that provides a multitude of subcommands to read, search, modify, and order lists. Here's a short summary:

```
list(LENGTH <list> <out-var>)
list(GET <list> <element index> [<index> ...] <out-var>)
list(JOIN <list> <glue> <out-var>)
list(SUBLIST <list> <begin> <length> <out-var>)
list(FIND <list> <value> <out-var>)
list(APPEND <list> [<element>...])
list(FILTER <list> {INCLUDE | EXCLUDE} REGEX <regex>)
list(INSERT <list> <index> [<element>...])
list(POP_BACK <list> [<out-var>...])
list(POP_FRONT <list> [<out-var>...])
list(PREPEND <list> [<element>...])
list(REMOVE_ITEM <list> <value>...)
list(REMOVE_AT <list> <index>...)
list(REMOVE_DUPLICATES <list>)
list(TRANSFORM <list> <ACTION> [...])
list(REVERSE <list>)
list(SORT <list> [...])
```

Most of the time, we don't really need to use lists in our projects. However, if you find yourself in that rare case where this concept would be convenient, you'll find a more in-depth reference of the `list()` command in *Appendix, Miscellaneous Commands*.

Now that we know how to work with lists and variables of all kinds, let's shift our focus to controlling the execution flow and learn about control structures available in CMake.

Understanding control structures in CMake

The CMake language wouldn't be complete without **control structures**! Like everything else, they are provided in the form of a command, and they come in three categories: **conditional blocks**, **loops**, and **command definitions**. Control structures are executed in scripts and during buildsystem generation for projects.

Conditional blocks

The only conditional block supported in CMake is the humble if() command. All conditional blocks have to be closed with an endif() command, and they may have any number of elseif() commands and one optional else() command in this order:

```
if(<condition>)
  <commands>
elseif(<condition>) # optional block, can be repeated
  <commands>
else()              # optional block
  <commands>
endif()
```

As in many other imperative languages, the if()-endif() block controls which sets of commands will be executed:

- If the <condition> expression specified in the if() command is met, the first section will be executed.
- Otherwise, CMake will execute commands in the section belonging to the first elseif() command in this block that has met its condition.
- If there are no such commands, CMake will check whether the else() command is provided and execute any commands in that section of the code.
- If none of the preceding conditions are met, the execution continues after the endif() command.

Note that no local *variable scope* is created in any of the conditional blocks.

The provided <condition> expression is evaluated according to a very simple syntax – let's learn more about it.

The syntax for conditional commands

The same syntax is valid for if(), elseif(), and while() commands.

Logical operators

The if() conditions support the NOT, AND, and OR logical operators:

- NOT <condition>
- <condition> AND <condition>
- <condition> OR <condition>

Also, the nesting of conditions is possible with matching pairs of parentheses (()). As in all decent languages, the CMake language respects the order of evaluation and starts from the innermost parenthesis:

```
(<condition>) AND (<condition> OR (<condition>))
```

The evaluation of a string and a variable

For legacy reasons (because the variable reference (${}) syntax wasn't always around), CMake will try to evaluate *unquoted arguments* as if they are *variable references*. In other words, using a plain variable name (for example, QUX) inside a condition is equal to writing ${QUX}. Here's an example for you to consider, and a gotcha:

```
set(BAZ FALSE)
set(QUX "BAZ")
if(${QUX})
```

The if() condition works in a bit of a convoluted way here – first, it will evaluate ${QUX} to BAZ, which is a recognized variable, and this in turn is evaluated to a string containing five characters spelling FALSE. Strings are considered *Boolean true* only if they equal any of the following constants (these comparisons are case-insensitive): ON, Y, YES, TRUE, or a *non-zero number*.

This brings us to the conclusion that the condition in the preceding example will evaluate to *Boolean false*.

However, here's another catch – what would be the evaluation of a condition with an unquoted argument with the name of a variable containing a value such as BAR? Consider the following code example:

```
set(FOO BAR)
if(FOO)
```

According to what we have said so far, it would be `false`, as the BAR string doesn't meet the criteria to evaluate to a *Boolean true* value. That's unfortunately not the case, because CMake makes an exception when it comes to unquoted variable references. Unlike quoted arguments, FOO won't be evaluated to BAR to produce an `if("BAR")` statement (which would be `false`). Instead, CMake will only evaluate `if(FOO)` to `false` if it is any of the following constants (these comparisons are case-insensitive):

- `OFF`, `NO`, `FALSE`, `N`, `IGNORE`, or `NOTFOUND`
- A string ending with `-NOTFOUND`
- An empty string
- Zero

So, simply asking for an undefined variable will be evaluated to `false`:

```
if (CORGE)
```

When a variable is defined beforehand, the scenario changes and the condition evaluates to `true`:

```
set(CORGE "A VALUE")
if (CORGE)
```

> If you think that the recursive evaluation of unquoted `if()` arguments is confusing, wrap variable references in quoted arguments: `if("${CORGE}")`. This will result in argument evaluation before the provided argument is passed into the `if()` command, and the behavior will be consistent with the evaluation of strings.

In other words, CMake assumes that the user passing a variable name to the `if()` command is asking whether the variable is defined with a value that does not evaluate to *Boolean false*. To explicitly check whether the variable is defined or not (and ignore its value), we can use the following:

```
if(DEFINED <name>)
if(DEFINED CACHE{<name>})
if(DEFINED ENV{<name>})
```

Comparing values

Comparison operations are supported with the following operators:

`EQUAL`, `LESS`, `LESS_EQUAL`, `GREATER`, and `GREATER_EQUAL`

The usual comparison operators found in other languages do not work in CMake: ==, >, <, !=, and so on.

They can be used to compare numeric values, like so:

```
if (1 LESS 2)
```

You can compare software versions following the `major[.minor[.patch[.tweak]]]` format by adding a `VERSION_` prefix to any of the operators:

```
if (1.3.4 VERSION_LESS_EQUAL 1.4)
```

Omitted components are treated as zeros, and non-integer version components truncate the compared string at that point.

For *lexicographic* string comparisons, we need to prepend an operator with the `STR` prefix (note the lack of an underscore):

```
if ("A" STREQUAL "${B}")
```

We often need more advanced mechanisms than simple equality comparisons. Fortunately, CMake also supports **POSIX regex** matching (the CMake documentation hints at an **Extended Regular Expression** (ERE) flavor, but no support for specific regex character classes is mentioned). We can use the `MATCHES` operator as follows:

```
<VARIABLE|STRING> MATCHES <regex>
```

Any matched groups are captured in `CMAKE_MATCH_<n>` variables.

Simple checks

We already mentioned one simple check, `DEFINED`, but there are others that simply return `true` if a condition is met.

We can check the following:

- Whether a value is in a list: `<VARIABLE|STRING> IN_LIST <VARIABLE>`
- Whether a command is available for invocation in this version of CMake: `COMMAND <command-name>`
- Whether a CMake policy exists: `POLICY <policy-id>` (this is covered in *Chapter 4, Setting Up Your First CMake Project*)
- Whether a CTest test was added with `add_test()`: `TEST <test-name>`
- Whether a build target is defined: `TARGET <target-name>`

We'll explore build targets in *Chapter 5, Working with Targets*, but for now, let's just say that targets are logical units of a build process in a project created with add_executable(), add_library(), or add_custom_target() commands.

Examining the filesystem

CMake provides many ways of working with files. We rarely need to manipulate them directly, and normally, we'd rather use a high-level approach. For reference, this book will provide a short list of the file-related commands in the *Appendix*. But most often, only the following operators will be needed (behavior is well-defined only for absolute paths):

- EXISTS <path-to-file-or-directory>: Checks if a file or directory exists.

- This resolves symbolic links (it returns true if the target of the symbolic link exists).

- <file1> IS_NEWER_THAN <file2>: Checks which file is newer.

  This returns true if file1 is newer than (or equal to) file2 or if one of the two files doesn't exist.

- IS_DIRECTORY path-to-directory: Checks if a path is a directory.

- IS_SYMLINK file-name: Checks if a path is a symbolic link.

- IS_ABSOLUTE path: Checks if a path is absolute.

Additionally, since 3.24 CMake supports a simple path comparison check, that will collapse multiple path separators but won't do any other normalization:

```
if ("/a////b/c" PATH_EQUAL "/a/b/c") # returns true
```

For more advanced path manipulation, refer to the documentation on the cmake_path() command.

This completes the syntax for conditional commands; the next control structure we'll discuss is a loop.

Loops

Loops in CMake are fairly straightforward – we can use either a while() loop or a foreach() loop to repeatedly execute the same set of commands. Both of these commands support loop control mechanisms:

- The break() loop stops the execution of the remaining block and breaks from the enclosing loop.

- The continue() loop stops the execution of the current iteration and starts at the top of the next one.

Note that no local *variable scope* is created in any of the loop blocks.

while()

The loop block is opened with a `while()` command and closed with an `endwhile()` command. Any enclosed commands will be executed as long as the `<condition>` expression provided in `while()` is `true`. The syntax for phrasing the condition is the same as for the `if()` command:

```
while(<condition>)
  <commands>
endwhile()
```

You probably guessed that – with some additional variables – the `while` loop can replace a `for` loop. Actually, it's way easier to use a `foreach()` loop for that – let's take a look.

foreach() loops

There are several variations of the `foreach()` block, which execute the enclosed commands for each value in the given list. Like other blocks, it has opening and closing commands: `foreach()` and `endforeach()`.

The simplest form of `foreach()` is meant to provide a C++-style for loop:

```
foreach(<loop_var> RANGE <max>)
  <commands>
endforeach()
```

CMake will iterate from 0 to `<max>` (inclusive). If we need more control, we can use the second variant, providing `<min>`, `<max>`, and, optionally, `<step>`. All arguments must be non-negative integers, and `<min>` has to be smaller than `<max>`:

```
foreach(<loop_var> RANGE <min> <max> [<step>])
```

However, `foreach()` shows its true colors when it is working with lists:

```
foreach(<loop_variable> IN [LISTS <lists>] [ITEMS <items>])
```

CMake will retrieve elements from one or more specified `<lists>` list variables, as well as a list of `<items>` values defined in-line, and put them in `<loop variable>`. Then, it will execute all commands for each item in the list. You can choose to provide only lists, only values, or both:

ch02/06-loops/foreach.cmake

```
set(MyList 1 2 3)
foreach(VAR IN LISTS MyList ITEMS e f)
```

```
    message(${VAR})
endforeach()
```

The preceding code will print the following:

```
1
2
3
e
f
```

Or, we can use a short version (skipping the IN keyword) for the same result:

```
foreach(VAR 1 2 3 e f)
```

Since version 3.17, foreach() has learned how to zip lists (ZIP_LISTS):

```
foreach(<loop_var>... IN ZIP_LISTS <lists>)
```

The process of zipping lists involves iterating through multiple lists and operating on corresponding items that have the same index. Let's look at an example:

ch02/06-loops/foreach.cmake

```
set(L1 "one;two;three;four")
set(L2 "1;2;3;4;5")
foreach(num IN ZIP_LISTS L1 L2)
    message("word=${num_0}, num=${num_1}")
endforeach()
```

CMake will create a num_<N> variable for each list provided, which it will fill with items from each list.

You can pass multiple variable names (one for every list) and each list will use a separate variable to store its items:

```
foreach(word num IN ZIP_LISTS L1 L2)
    message("word=${word}, num=${num}")
```

Both examples on ZIP_LISTS will produce the same output:

```
word=one, num=1
word=two, num=2
word=three, num=3
word=four, num=4
```

In the event that the item counts between lists vary, variables for the shorter lists will be empty.

It is worth noting that, as of version 3.21, the loop variables in foreach() are restricted to the local scope of the loop. This concludes our discussion on loops.

Command definitions

There are two ways to define your own command: you can use the macro() command or the function() command. The easiest way to explain the differences between these commands is by comparing them to *C-style preprocessor macros* and actual C++ functions:

A macro() command works more like a find-and-replace instruction than an actual subroutine call such as function(). Contrary to functions, macros don't create a separate entry on a call stack. This means that calling return() in a macro will return to the calling statement one level higher than it would for a function (possibly terminating the execution if we're already in the top scope).

The function() command creates a *local scope* for its variables, unlike the macro() command, which works in the *variable scope* of the caller. This may lead to confusing results. Let's talk about these details in the next section.

Both methods of defining commands allow the defining of named arguments that can be referred to in the local scope of the defined command. Moreover, CMake offers the following variables for accessing call-related values:

- ${ARGC}: The count of arguments
- ${ARGV}: All arguments as list
- ${ARGV<index>}: The value of an argument at a specific index (starting from 0), regardless of whether this argument was expected or not
- ${ARGN}: A list of anonymous arguments that were passed by a caller after the last expected argument

Accessing a numeric argument with an index outside of the ARGC bounds is an undefined behavior. To handle advanced scenarios (usually with an unknown number of arguments), you may be interested to read about cmake_parse_arguments() in the official documentation. If you decide to define a command with named arguments, every call has to pass all of them or it will be invalid.

Macros

Defining a macro is similar to any other block:

```
macro(<name> [<argument>…])
```

```
  <commands>
endmacro()
```

After this declaration, we may execute our macro by calling its name (function calls are case-insensitive).

As we know, macros don't create a separate entry on a call stack or a *variable scope*. The following example highlights some of the problems relating to this behavior in macros:

ch02/08-definitions/macro.cmake

```
macro(MyMacro myVar)
  set(myVar "new value")
  message("argument: ${myVar}")
endmacro()
set(myVar "first value")
message("myVar is now: ${myVar}")
MyMacro("called value")
message("myVar is now: ${myVar}")
```

Here's the output from this script:

```
$ cmake -P ch02/08-definitions/macro.cmake
myVar is now: first value
argument: called value
myVar is now: new value
```

What happened? Despite explicitly setting myVar to new value, it didn't affect the output for message("argument: ${myVar}")! This is because arguments passed to macros aren't treated as real variables but rather, as constant find-and-replace instructions.

On the other hand, the myVar variable in the global scope was changed from first value to new value. This behavior is a *side effect* and is considered a bad practice, as it's impossible to tell which global variables will be changed by a macro without reading it. It is advisable to utilize functions whenever possible, as they are likely to prevent many issues.

Functions

To declare a command as a function, follow this syntax:

```
function(<name> [<argument>...])
  <commands>
endfunction()
```

A function requires a name and optionally accepts a list of names of expected arguments. As mentioned before, functions create their own *variable scopes*. You can call set(), providing one of the named arguments of the function, and any change will be local to the function (unless PARENT_SCOPE is specified, as we discussed in the *How to correctly use variable scopes in CMake* section).

Functions follow the rules of the call stack, enabling returning to the calling scope with the return() command. Starting from CMake 3.25, the return() command allows an optional PROPAGATE keyword followed by a list of variable names. Its purpose is similar to the one in the block() command – it transfers the values of the specified variables from the *local scope* to the scope of the call.

CMake sets the following variables for each function (these have been available since version 3.17):

- CMAKE_CURRENT_FUNCTION
- CMAKE_CURRENT_FUNCTION_LIST_DIR
- CMAKE_CURRENT_FUNCTION_LIST_FILE
- CMAKE_CURRENT_FUNCTION_LIST_LINE

Let's take a look at these function variables in practice:

ch02/08-definitions/function.cmake

```
function(MyFunction FirstArg)
  message("Function: ${CMAKE_CURRENT_FUNCTION}")
  message("File: ${CMAKE_CURRENT_FUNCTION_LIST_FILE}")
  message("FirstArg: ${FirstArg}")
  set(FirstArg "new value")
  message("FirstArg again: ${FirstArg}")
  message("ARGV0: ${ARGV0} ARGV1: ${ARGV1} ARGC: ${ARGC}")
endfunction()
set(FirstArg "first value")
MyFunction("Value1" "Value2")
message("FirstArg in global scope: ${FirstArg}")
```

Running this script with cmake -P function.cmake prints the following output:

```
Function: MyFunction
File: /root/examples/ch02/08-definitions/function.cmake
FirstArg: Value1
FirstArg again: new value
```

```
ARGV0: Value1 ARGV1: Value2 ARGC: 2
FirstArg in global scope: first value
```

As you can see, the general syntax and concept of the functions are very similar to macros but less susceptible to implicit errors.

The procedural paradigm in CMake

Let us suppose that we want to write CMake code similar to how we write a program in C++. We'll make a CMakeLists.txt listfile that will call three defined commands that may call defined commands of their own. *Figure 2.3* illustrates that:

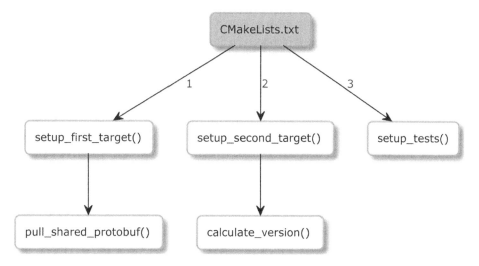

Figure 2.3: A procedural call graph

In CMake, writing in a procedural style can be problematic since you must provide command definitions before calling them. The CMake parser will not have it any other way. Your code could look something like this:

```
cmake_minimum_required(...)
project(Procedural)

# Definitions
function(pull_shared_protobuf)
function(setup_first_target)
function(calculate_version)
function(setup_second_target)
function(setup_tests)
```

```
# Calls
setup_first_target()
setup_second_target()
setup_tests()
```

What a nightmare! Everything is reversed! It will be very difficult to understand because the code with the lowest level of abstraction is at the beginning of the file. A correctly structured piece of code lists the most general steps in the first subroutine, after which it provides the slightly more detailed subroutines, and keeps the most detailed steps at the very end of the file.

There are solutions to this problem, such as moving command definitions to other files and partitioning scopes across directories (scoped directories will be explained in detail in *Chapter 4, Setting Up Your First CMake Project*). But there is also a simple and elegant approach – declaring an entry-point macro at the top of the file and calling it at the very end of the file:

```
macro(main)
    first_step()
    second_step()
    third_step()
endmacro()

function(first_step)
function(second_step)
function(third_step)

main()
```

With this approach, our code is written with a gradually narrowing scope, and because we're not actually calling the main() macro until the very end, CMake won't complain about the execution of undefined commands.

Why use a macro over a function in this case? It's good to have unrestricted access to global variables, and since we're not passing any arguments to main(), we don't need to worry about the usual caveats.

You'll find a simple example of this concept in the ch02/09-procedural/CMakeLists.txt listfile in the GitHub repository for this book.

A word on naming conventions

Naming is famously hard in software development, but nevertheless, it's very important to maintain a solution that is easy to read and understand. When it comes to CMake scripts and projects, we should follow the rules of the *clean code* approach, as we would with any software development solution:

- Follow a consistent naming style (snake_case is an accepted standard in the CMake community).
- Use short but meaningful names (for example, avoid func(), f(), and similar).
- Avoid puns and cleverness in your naming.
- Use pronounceable, searchable names that don't require mental mapping.

Now that we know how to properly invoke the commands with the correct syntax, let's explore which commands will be the most beneficial to us to begin with.

Exploring the frequently used commands

CMake offers many scripting commands that allow you to work with variables and the environment. Some of them have been extensively covered in the *Appendix*: for example, list(), string(), and file(). Others, such as find_file(), find_package(), and find_path(), fit better in chapters that talk about their respective subjects. In this section, we will provide a brief overview of the common commands that are useful in most situations:

- message()
- include()
- include_guard()
- file()
- execute_process()

Let's get to it.

The message() command

We already know and love our trusty message() command, which prints text to standard output. However, there's a lot more to it than meets the eye. By providing a MODE argument, you can customize the behavior of the command like so: message(<MODE> "text to print").

The recognized modes are as follows:

- `FATAL_ERROR`: This stops processing and generation.

- `SEND_ERROR`: This continues processing but skips generation.

- `WARNING`: This continues processing.

- `AUTHOR_WARNING`: A CMake warning. This continues processing.

- `DEPRECATION`: This works accordingly if either of the `CMAKE_ERROR_DEPRECATED` or `CMAKE_WARN_DEPRECATED` variables are enabled.

- `NOTICE` or omitted mode (default): This prints a message to `stderr` to attract the user's attention.

- `STATUS`: This continues processing and is recommended for main messages to users.

- `VERBOSE`: This continues processing and should be used for more detailed information that usually isn't very necessary.

- `DEBUG`: This continues processing and should contain any fine details that might be helpful when there's an issue with a project.

- `TRACE`: This continues processing and is recommended to print messages during project development. Usually, these sorts of messages would be removed before publishing the project.

Picking the right mode is extra work, but it can save debugging time by coloring the output text based on the severity (since 3.21) or even stop the execution after declaring an irrecoverable error:

ch02/10-useful/message_error.cmake

```
message(FATAL_ERROR "Stop processing")
message("This won't be printed.")
```

Messages will be printed depending on the current log level (which is `STATUS` by default). We discussed how to change this in the previous chapter in the *Options for debugging and tracing* section.

In *Chapter 1*, *First Steps with CMake*, I mentioned debugging with `CMAKE_MESSAGE_CONTEXT`, and now it's time to delve into it. In the meantime, we have gained insights into three crucial pieces of this subject: lists, scopes, and functions.

In complex debugging scenarios, it can be extremely useful to indicate in which context the message is occurring. Consider the following output, where messages printed in the foo function have the appropriate prefix:

```
$ cmake -P message_context.cmake --log-context
[top] Before `foo`
[top.foo] foo message
[top] After `foo`
```

Here's how this works:

ch02/10-useful/message_context.cmake

```
function(foo)
  list(APPEND CMAKE_MESSAGE_CONTEXT "foo")
  message("foo message")
endfunction()

list(APPEND CMAKE_MESSAGE_CONTEXT "top")
message("Before `foo`")
foo()
message("After `foo`")
```

Let's break this down:

1. First, we append the top to the context-tracking variable CMAKE_MESSAGE_CONTEXT, then we print the initial Before `foo` message, and the matching prefix [top] will be added to the output.

2. Next, upon entering the foo() function, we append a new context to the list named foo after the function it belongs to and output another message, which appears with the extended [top.foo] prefix in the output.

3. Finally, after function execution has completed, we print the After `foo` message. The message is printed with the original [foo] scope. Why? Because of the *variable scope* rules: the changed CMAKE_MESSAGE_CONTEXT variable only lives until the end of the function scope, and is then restored to the original unchanged version.

Another cool trick with message() is to add indentation to the CMAKE_MESSAGE_INDENT list (in exactly the same way as with CMAKE_MESSAGE_CONTEXT):

```
list(APPEND CMAKE_MESSAGE_INDENT "  ")
message("Before `foo`")
foo()
message("After `foo`")
```

The output from our scripts can then look a bit simpler:

```
Before `foo`
    foo message
After `foo`
```

Since CMake doesn't offer any real debugger with breakpoints or other tools, the ability to produce clean log messages comes in very handy when things don't go exactly as planned.

The include() command

Partitioning code into different files to keep things ordered and, well, *separate*, is quite useful. Then, we can reference them from our parent listfile by calling include(), like so:

```
include(<file|module> [OPTIONAL] [RESULT_VARIABLE <var>])
```

If we provide a filename (a path with a .cmake extension), CMake will try to open and execute it.

Note that no nested, separate *variable scope* will be created, so any changes to variables made in that file will affect the calling scope.

CMake will raise an error if a file doesn't exist unless we specify that it is optional with the OPTIONAL keyword. When we need to know whether include() was successful, we can provide a RESULT_ VARIABLE keyword with the name of the variable. It will be filled with a full path to the included file on success or not found (NOTFOUND) on failure.

When running in script mode, any relative paths will be resolved from the current working directory. To force searching in relation to the script itself, provide an absolute path:

```
include("${CMAKE_CURRENT_LIST_DIR}/<filename>.cmake")
```

If we don't provide a path but do provide the name of a module (without .cmake or otherwise), CMake will try to find a module and include it. CMake will search for a file with the name of <module>.cmake in CMAKE_MODULE_PATH and then in the CMake module directory.

As CMake walks the source tree and includes different listfiles, the following variables are set: CMAKE_CURRENT_LIST_DIR, CMAKE_CURRENT_LIST_FILE, CMAKE_PARENT_LIST_FILE, and CMAKE_ CURRENT_LIST_LINE.

The include_guard() command

When we include files that have side effects, we might want to restrict them so that they're only included once. This is where include_guard([DIRECTORY|GLOBAL]) comes in.

Put include_guard() at the top of the included file. When CMake encounters it for the first time, it will make a note of this fact in the current scope. If the file gets included again (maybe because we don't control all the files in our project), it won't be processed any further.

If we want to protect against inclusion in unrelated function scopes that won't share variables with each other, we should provide DIRECTORY or GLOBAL arguments. As the names suggest, the DIRECTORY keyword will apply the protection within the current directory and below it, and the GLOBAL keyword applies the protection to the whole build.

The file() command

To give you an idea of what you can do with CMake scripts, let's take a quick look at the most useful variants of the file manipulation command:

```
file(READ <filename> <out-var> [...])
file({WRITE | APPEND} <filename> <content>...)
file(DOWNLOAD <url> [<file>] [...])
```

In short, the file() command will let you read, write, and transfer files and work with the filesystem, file locks, paths, and archives, all in a system-independent manner. Please see the *Appendix* for more details.

The execute_process() command

Every now and then, you'll need to resort to using tools available in the system (after all, CMake is primarily a buildsystem generator). CMake offers a command for this purpose: you can use execute_process() to run other processes and collect their output. This command is a great fit for scripts and it can also be used in projects, but it **only works during the configuration stage**. Here's the general form of the command:

```
execute_process(COMMAND <cmd1> [<arguments>]... [OPTIONS])
```

CMake will use the API of the operating system to create a child process (so, shell operators such as &&, ||, and > won't work). However, you can still chain commands and pass the output of one to another simply by providing the COMMAND <cmd> <arguments> arguments more than once.

Optionally, you may use a TIMEOUT <seconds> argument to terminate the process if it hasn't finished the task within the required limit, and you can set the WORKING_DIRECTORY <directory> as you need.

The exit codes of all tasks can be collected in a list by providing RESULTS_VARIABLE <variable> arguments. If you're only interested in the result of the last executed command, use the singular form: RESULT_VARIABLE <variable>.

To collect the output, CMake provides two arguments: OUTPUT_VARIABLE and ERROR_VARIABLE (which are used in a similar fashion). If you would like to merge both stdout and stderr, use the same variable for both arguments.

Remember that when writing projects for other users, you should make sure that the command you're planning to use is available on the platforms you claim to support.

Summary

This chapter opened the door to actual programming with CMake – you're now able to write great, informative comments and utilize built-in commands, and you understand how to correctly provide all kinds of arguments to them. This knowledge alone will help you understand the unusual syntax of CMake listfiles that you might have seen in projects created by others. We have covered variables in CMake – specifically, how to reference, set, and unset *normal*, *cache*, and *environment variables*. We delved into how file and directory *variable scopes* work, how to create them, and what issues we might encounter and how to solve them. We also covered lists and control structures. We examined the syntax of conditions, their logical operations, the evaluation of unquoted arguments, as well as strings and variables. We learned how to compare values, do simple checks, and examine the state of the files in the system. This allows us to write conditional blocks and while loops; while we were talking about loops, we also grasped the syntax of foreach loops.

Understanding how to define custom commands using macro and function statements will undoubtedly facilitate cleaner, more procedural code. We also discussed strategies for improving code structure and creating more readable names.

Finally, we formally introduced the message() command and its multiple log levels. We also studied how to partition and include listfiles, and we discovered a few other useful commands. With this information, we are well prepared to take on the next chapter, *Chapter 3, Using CMake in Popular IDEs*.

Further reading

For more information on the topics covered in this chapter, you can refer to the following links:

- Clean Code: A Handbook of Agile Software Craftsmanship (Robert C. Martin):
  `https://amzn.to/3cm69DD`

- Refactoring: Improving the Design of Existing Code (Martin Fowler):
  `https://amzn.to/3cmWk8o`

- Which comments in your code ARE GOOD? (Rafał Świdzinski):
  `https://youtu.be/4t9bpo0THb8`

- What's the CMake syntax to set and use variables? (StackOverflow):
  `https://stackoverflow.com/questions/31037882/whats-the-cmake-syntax-to-set-and-use-variables`

Join our community on Discord

Join our community's Discord space for discussions with the author and other readers:

`https://discord.com/invite/vXN53A7ZcA`

3

Using CMake in Popular IDEs

Programming is as much an art as it is a deeply technical process, and as we know all too well, it's very difficult. Therefore, we should be looking to optimize this process as much as possible. There aren't too many instances where we can just flip a switch and get better outcomes, but using **Integrated Development Environments (IDEs)** is definitely one of those rare cases.

If you haven't worked with a proper IDE before (or you believe that a text processor like Emacs or Vim is the best you can hope for), this chapter is for you. If you're a seasoned professional and are already familiar with the subject, you can use this chapter as a quick overview of the current top choices and maybe consider a switch or, even better, get clear confirmation that your current tool is the best.

With an emphasis on accessibility for those new to the field, this chapter provides a gentle introduction to the critical choice of an IDE. We will cover why you'd want one and how to pick one that best suits your needs. Sure, there are many choices out there, but as usual, some are just better than others. Unfortunately, this isn't a universal, one-size-fits-all kind of deal. Many factors contribute toward the productivity levels that you might get if you choose right. We'll discuss a few considerations that might be important if your work is in an organization of a certain size, ensuring that you grasp the nuances without becoming mired in complexity. This will be followed by a quick introduction to toolchains, where we'll discuss available choices.

We will then highlight the distinctive qualities of several popular IDEs, such as the sophisticated CLion, the adaptable nature of Visual Studio Code, and then the powerhouse that is the Visual Studio IDE. Each section is tailored to showcase the strengths and advanced features that these environments offer, providing you with the knowledge of how to take your initial steps with the IDE. Additionally, we highlight one advanced feature that was subjectively picked from many others, just to let you know what you might expect if you decide to use this suite.

In this chapter, we're going to cover the following main topics:

- Getting to know IDEs
- Starting with the CLion IDE
- Starting with Visual Studio Code
- Starting with the Visual Studio IDE

Getting to know IDEs

In this section, we will discuss IDEs and how they can significantly enhance development speed and code quality. Let's begin by explaining what an IDE is for those new to this topic.

Why and how do you choose an IDE? An IDE, or integrated development environment, is a comprehensive tool that combines various specialized tools to simplify the software development process. The journey of creating a professional project involves numerous steps: designing, coding, building, testing, packaging, releasing, and maintaining. Each step comprises many smaller tasks, and the complexity can be overwhelming. IDEs offer a solution by providing a platform with a set of tools that are curated and configured by the IDE creators. This integration allows you to use these tools seamlessly without having to set them up individually for each project.

IDEs are mainly centered around the code editor, compiler, and debugger. They are designed to provide sufficient integration, enabling you to edit code, compile it immediately, and run it with a debugger attached. IDEs can include build toolchains or allow developers to choose their preferred compilers and debuggers. Editors are usually a core part of the software but can often be greatly extended with plugins, like code highlighting, formatting, and more.

More advanced IDEs offer very sophisticated features like Hot Reload debugging (available in Visual Studio 2022; read on to learn more). This feature lets you run your code in a debugger, edit it, and continue execution without restarting the program. You will also find refactoring tools to rename symbols or extract code into a separate function, and static analysis to identify errors before compilation. Additionally, IDEs provide tools to work with Git and other version control systems, which are invaluable for resolving conflicts, among other benefits.

I'm sure you can see now how beneficial it can be to learn how to use an IDE early and standardize this usage in your organization. Let's find out why choosing an IDE that is *right for you* is important.

Choosing an IDE

There are plenty of code editors that are on the verge of being recognized by the community as fully featured IDEs. It's always recommended to research the space a bit before committing to a specific choice, especially because of the pace of current software release cycles and rapid changes in the space.

In my few years of corporate experience, it's quite uncommon for an IDE to offer a feature compelling enough to make someone switch from one IDE to another. Force of habit is really second nature to a developer, and it shouldn't be ignored. Remember that as soon as you feel comfortable in an IDE, it's likely going to be your tool of choice for the considerable future. This is why you still see developers using Vim (a console-based text editor released in 1991), extended with a bunch of plugins to make it as powerful as more modern, GUI-based IDEs. No pressure then.

There are varied reasons why programmers choose one IDE over another; some of them are really important (speed, reliability, comprehensiveness, completeness), while others... not so much. I'd like to share my subjective perspective on this choice, which I hope you'll find useful too.

Choose a comprehensive IDE

If you're just starting out, you might think about using a simple text editor and running a few commands to build your code. This approach is definitely workable, especially when you're trying to understand the basics (I encourage you to use the actual commands to monitor your progress throughout this book). It also helps you grasp what a beginner might experience without an IDE.

On the other hand, IDEs are created for a purpose. They streamline numerous processes that developers handle during a project's lifecycle, which can be extremely valuable. Although it might seem overwhelming initially, choose a comprehensive IDE that includes all the necessary features. Ensure it's as complete as possible, but be mindful of the cost, as IDEs can be expensive for small businesses or individual developers. It's a balance between the time spent on manual management and the cost of the features provided by the IDE.

Regardless of the cost, always select an IDE with strong community support to assist you if you encounter issues. Explore community forums and popular Q&A sites like `StackOverflow.com` to check if users get their questions answered. Additionally, choose an IDE that is actively developed by a reputable company. You don't want to waste your time on something that hasn't been updated in a while and might get deprecated or abandoned in the near future. For example, not so long ago, Atom, an editor created by GitHub, was sunset after 7 years of releases.

Choose an IDE that is widely supported in your organization

Counterintuitively, this might not align with every developer's preference. You may already be comfortable with a different tool from your university, previous job, or a personal project. Such a habit, as mentioned earlier, can tempt you to ignore your company's recommendations and stick with what you know. Resist this. Such a choice becomes increasingly challenging over time. From my experiences at Ericsson, Amazon, and Cisco, only once did the effort to configure and maintain a non-standard IDE prove worthwhile. That was because I managed to get enough organizational support to address issues collectively.

Your primary goal should be writing code, not struggling with an unsupported IDE. Learning the recommended software may require effort, but it's less than what's needed to go against the norm (and yes, Vim lost this battle; it's time to move on).

Don't pick an IDE based on the target OS and platform

You might think that if you're developing software for Linux, you need to use a Linux machine and a Linux-based IDE. However, C++ is a portable language, which means it should compile and run the same way on any platform, provided you've written it correctly. Of course, you might encounter issues with libraries, as not all of them are installed by default, and some may be specific to your platform.

Adhering strictly to the target platform isn't always necessary and can sometimes be counterproductive. For instance, if you're targeting an older or **Long-Term Support** (**LTS**) version of an OS, you might not be able to use the latest toolchain versions. If you wish to develop on a different platform than your target, you can.

In that case, consider **cross-compilation** or **remote development**. Cross-compilation involves using a specialized toolchain that allows a compiler running on one platform (like Windows) to produce artifacts for another platform (like Linux). This approach is widely used in the industry and is supported by CMake. Alternatively, I recommend remote development, where you send your code to the target machine and build it there using the local toolchain. This method is supported by many IDEs and offers several benefits, which we'll explore in the next section.

Pick an IDE with remote development support

While it shouldn't be your primary criterion, considering remote development support in an IDE is beneficial after meeting other requirements. Over time, even seasoned developers encounter projects requiring a different target platform than their usual OS due to changing teams, projects, or even companies.

If your preferred IDE supports remote development, you can continue using it, leveraging the ability to compile and debug code on a different OS and view results in the IDE's GUI. The main advantage of remote development over cross-compilation is its integrated debugger support, offering a cleaner process without needing CMake project-level configuration. Additionally, companies often provide powerful remote machines, allowing developers to use less expensive, lightweight local devices.

Sure, there's an argument to be made that cross-compilation offers greater control over the development environment, allowing temporary changes for testing. It doesn't necessitate bandwidth for code transfers, supporting low-end internet connections, or offline work. However, considering most software development involves internet access for information, this might be a less critical advantage. Using virtualized environments like Docker enables running a local production copy and setting up remote development connections, offering security, customizability, and the ability to build and deploy containers.

The considerations mentioned here are slightly tilted toward working in big corporations, where things move slower, and it's difficult to make highly impactful changes. These suggestions don't negate the possibility of having a perfectly complete experience with CMake if you decide to prioritize other aspects of IDEs, as needed by your use case.

Installing toolchains

As we discussed earlier, an IDE integrates all the necessary tools to streamline software development. A key part of this process is building binaries, sometimes in the background or on the fly, to provide additional information to developers. Toolchains are collections of tools like compilers, linkers, archivers, optimizers, debuggers, and implementations of the standard C++ library. They may also include other handy utilities like `bash`, `make`, `gawk`, `grep`, and so on, which are used to build programs.

Some IDEs come with toolchains or toolchain downloaders, while others do not. It's best to just run an installed IDE and check if you're able to compile a basic test program. CMake typically does this by default during the configuration stage, which most IDEs execute as part of the initialization of new projects. If this process fails, you might be prompted by the IDE or the OS's package manager to install the necessary tools. Just follow along, as this flow is usually well prepared.

If you're not prompted, or if you'd like to use a specific toolchain, here are some options based on your platform:

- **GNU GCC** (`https://gcc.gnu.org/`) for Linux, Windows (via MinGW or Cygwin), macOS, and many others. GCC is one of the most popular and widely used C++ compilers, supporting a wide range of platforms and architectures.

- **Clang/LLVM** (`https://clang.llvm.org/`) for Linux, Windows, macOS, and many others. Clang is a compiler frontend for the C, C++, and Objective-C programming languages, utilizing LLVM as its backend.

- **Microsoft Visual Studio/MSVC** (`https://visualstudio.microsoft.com/`) for Windows primarily, with cross-platform support via Visual Studio Code and CMake. MSVC is the C++ compiler provided by Microsoft, typically used within the Visual Studio IDE.

- **MinGW-w64** (`http://mingw-w64.org/`) for Windows. MinGW-w64 is an advancement of the original MinGW project, aimed at providing better support for 64-bit Windows and new APIs.

- **Apple Clang** (`https://developer.apple.com/xcode/cpp/`) for macOS, iOS, iPadOS, watchOS, and tvOS. Apple's version of Clang, optimized for Apple's hardware and software ecosystem, is integrated with Xcode.

- **Cygwin** (`https://www.cygwin.com/`) for Windows. Cygwin provides a POSIX-compatible environment on Windows, allowing the use of GCC and other GNU tools.

If you're looking to start quickly without delving deeply into the specifics of each toolchain, you can follow my personal preference: if there's no toolchain provided by the IDE, go with MinGW on Windows, Clang/LLVM on Linux, and Apple Clang on macOS. Each of these is well suited to its primary platform and typically offers the best experience.

Using this book's examples with IDEs

This book comes with an extensive collection of examples of CMake projects, available in the official GitHub repository here:

`https://github.com/PacktPublishing/Modern-CMake-for-Cpp-2E`.

Naturally, as we explore the subject of IDEs, a question arises: how do we use this repository with all the IDEs presented here? Well, we need to recognize that the book teaching you how to create professional projects isn't a professional project itself. It's a collection of such projects with varied levels of completion, reasonably simplified where possible. Unfortunately (or, maybe fortunately?), IDEs aren't built to load tens of projects and conveniently manage them. They generally focus their features on loading one actively edited project.

This puts us in a somewhat awkward position: it's really difficult to navigate the example set with IDEs. Upon using an IDE to load the example set, by selecting the example directory to open it, most IDEs will detect multiple `CMakeLists.txt` files and ask you to pick one. After doing so, the usual initialization process will occur, temporary files will be written, and essentially, the CMake configuration and generation stages will be run to get the project into a state where it can be built. As you might guess, this only works for the example whose `CMakeLists.txt` file was selected. Most IDEs do offer ways to switch between different directories (or projects) in the workspace, but it might not be as straightforward as we'd like it to be.

If you're struggling with this, there are two options: either don't use the IDE to build examples (and go with console commands instead) or load an example into a fresh project every time. I would recommend the first option if you're keen on practicing the commands, as they may come in handy in the future and will give you a better understanding of what is going on behind the scenes. This is usually a good choice for build engineers, as this knowledge will be used often. On the other hand, if you're working on a single project, mostly as a developer focusing on the business side of the code, perhaps going with the IDEs early on is the best. In any case, choosing one doesn't prevent you from going with the other from time to time.

With this out of the way, let's focus on reviewing today's top IDEs and seeing which one might be the best for you. All of them will serve you well, regardless of whether you work in a corporation or not.

Starting with the CLion IDE

CLion is a paid, cross-platform IDE available for Windows, macOS, and Linux, developed by JetBrains. That's right – this piece of software is subscription-based; starting from $99.00 (early 2024), you can get a one-year license for individual use. Bigger organizations pay more, and startups pay less. If you're a student or release an open-source project, you can get a free license. On top of that, there's a 30-day trial to test the software. This is the only IDE in this listing that doesn't offer a "community" or stripped-down version available free of charge. Regardless, this is a solid piece of software that is developed by a reputable company, and it very well might be worth the cost.

Figure 3.1 shows how the IDE looks in light mode (dark mode is the default option):

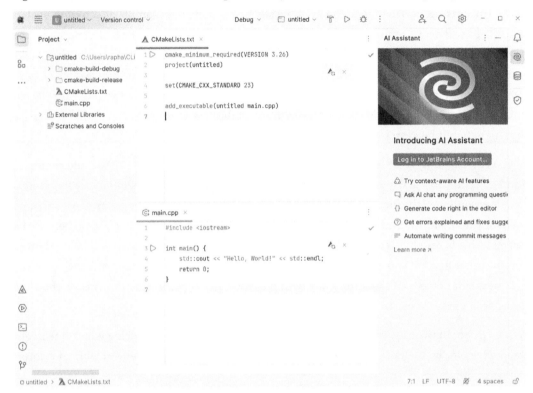

Figure 3.1: The main window of the CLion IDE

As you can see, this is a fully featured IDE, ready for anything and everything you might throw at it. Let's talk about how it stands out.

Why you might like it

Unlike the alternatives, C and C++ are the first and only languages supported by CLion. Many features of this IDE are specifically designed to support this environment and align with the C/C++ mindset. This is very visible when we compare features from other IDEs: code analysis, code navigation, integrated debugger, and refactoring tools can be found in competing software like the Visual Studio IDE. However, they are not as deeply and robustly oriented toward C/C++. This, of course, is a very difficult thing to measure objectively.

Regardless, CMake is fully integrated into CLion out of the box and is the primary choice for the project format in this IDE. However, alternatives like Autotools and Makefile projects are in early support and can be used to eventually migrate toward CMake. It's worth noting that CLion natively supports CMake's CTest with many unit-testing frameworks and has dedicated flows to generate code, run tests, and collect and present results. You can use Google Test, Catch, Boost.Test, and doctest.

A feature I especially like is the ability to work with Docker to develop C++ programs in containers – more on that later. Meanwhile, let's see how to start with CLion.

Take your first steps

After downloading CLion from the official website (`https://www.jetbrains.com/clion`), you can proceed with the usual installation process on the platform you're using. CLion comes with an adequate visual installer on Windows (*Figure 3.2*) and macOS (*Figure 3.3*).

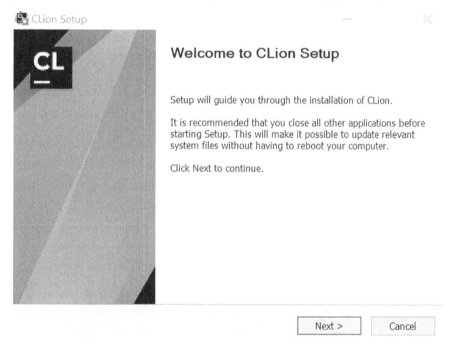

Figure 3.2: CLion Setup for Windows

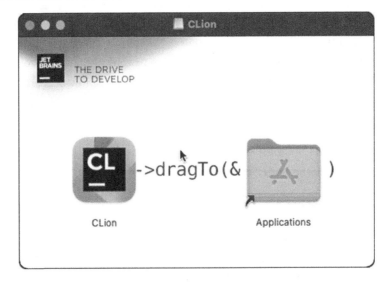

Figure 3.3: CLion Setup for macOS

On Linux, you'll need to unpack the downloaded archive and run the installation script:

```
tar -xzf CLion-<version>.tar.gz
./CLion-<version>/bin/CLion.sh
```

These instructions may be outdated, so make sure to confirm with the CLion website.

On the first run, you'll be asked to provide a license code or to start a 30-day free trial. Selecting the second option will allow you to experiment with the IDE and determine if it's right for you. Next, you'll be able to create a new project and select the targeted C++ version. Immediately after, CLion will detect the available compilers and CMake versions and attempt to build a test project to confirm everything is set up correctly. On some platforms (like macOS), you may get an automatic prompt to install developer tools as needed. On others, you may need to set them up yourself and ensure they're available in the PATH environment variable.

Next, ensure your toolchain is configured according to your needs. Toolchains are configured per project, so go ahead and create a default CMake project. Then, navigate to your **Settings/Preferences** (*Ctrl/Command + Alt + S*) and select **Build, Execution, Deployment > CMake**. On this tab, you can configure the build profile (*Figure 3.3*). It may be useful to add a Release profile to build optimized artifacts without the debugging symbols. To add one, simply press the plus icon above the profile list. CLion will create a default Release profile for you. You can switch between profiles using the dropdown at the top of the main window.

Now, you can simply press *F9* to compile and run the program with the debugger attached. Follow up by reading the official documentation of CLion, as there are plenty of useful features to explore. I'd like to introduce you to one of my favorites: the debugger.

Advanced feature: Debugger on steroids

The debugging capabilities of CLion are truly cutting-edge and especially designed for C++. I was very pleased to discover one of the latest additions, CMake debugging, which includes many standard debugging features: stepping through code, breakpoints, watches, inlined value exploration, and more. The ability to explore variables in different scopes (cache, ENV, and the current scope) is extremely convenient when things don't quite work as expected.

For C++ debugging, you will get many standard features provided by the **GNU Project Debugger (GDB)**, such as assembly view, breakpoints, step through, watchpoints, and so on, but there are also some major enhancements. In CLion, you'll find a parallel stack view, which enables you to see all the threads in a graph-like diagram with all the current stack frames for each thread. There's an advanced memory view feature to see the layout of the running program in RAM and modify the memory on the fly. CLion provides multiple other tools to help you understand what's happening: register view, code disassembly, debugger console, core dump debugging, debugging of arbitrary executables, and many more.

To top it off, CLion has a very well-executed **Evaluate Expression** feature, which works wonders and even allows you to modify objects during program execution. Just right-click on a line of code and select this feature from the menu.

That's all on CLion; it's time to take a look at another IDE.

Starting with Visual Studio Code

Visual Studio Code (VS Code) is a free, cross-platform IDE available for Windows, macOS, and Linux, developed by Microsoft. Don't confuse it with another Microsoft product, the Visual Studio IDE (usually named after the year it was released, for example, Visual Studio 2022).

VS Code is favored for its vast extension ecosystem and support for hundreds of programming languages (an estimated are over 220 different languages!). When GitHub was acquired by Microsoft, VS Code was introduced as something of a replacement for Atom.

The overall design of the IDE is top-notch, as you can see in *Figure 3.4*.

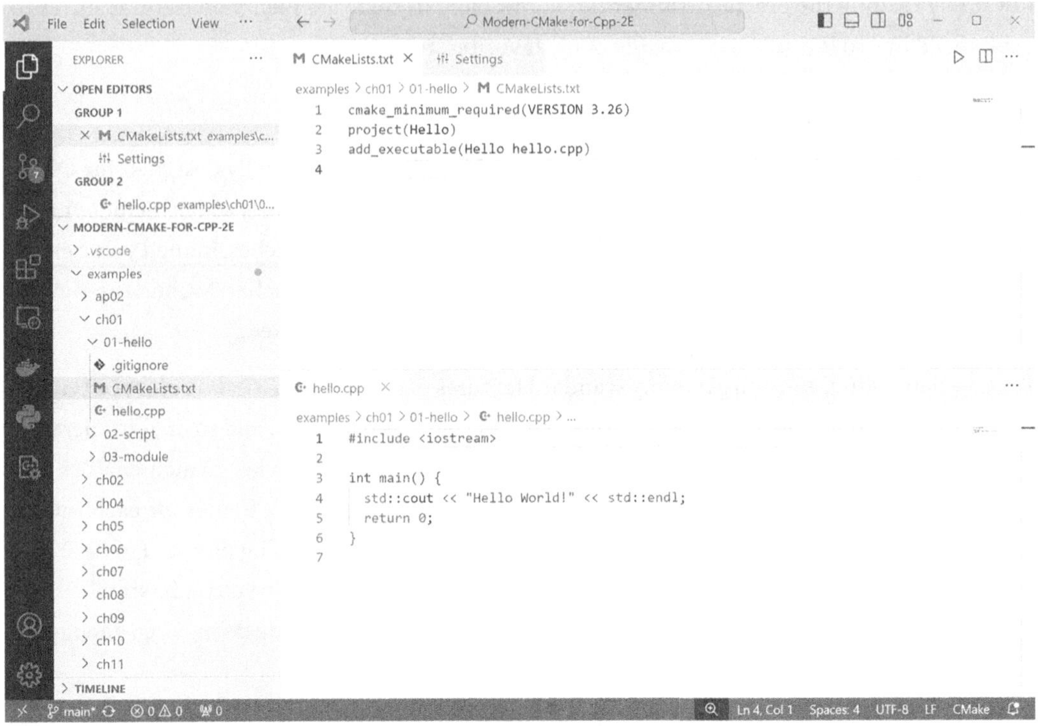

Figure 3.4: The main window of VS Code

Now, let's find out what makes VS Code so special.

Why you might like it

C++ isn't the priority in terms of languages supported by VSC, but it's quite close to the top, thanks to the many sophisticated language extensions available. This trade-off is rewarded with the ability to switch between many languages as needed while working in the same environment.

There's a bit of a learning curve to this tool, as most extensions conform to the basic UI functionalities provided, rather than implementing advanced interfaces on their own. Many of the features will be available through the command palette (accessible by pressing *F1*), which requires you to type the name of the command instead of clicking an icon or a button. This is a reasonable sacrifice to keep VSC clean, fast, and free of charge. In fact, this IDE is so quick to load that I prefer to use it as a general-purpose text editor, even when I'm not working on a project.

That said, VS Code is truly powerful thanks to an enormous library of really good extensions, the vast majority of which are available for free. There are special extensions available for C++ and CMake, so let's see how to configure them in the next section.

Take your first steps

VSC is available from the official website: `https://code.visualstudio.com/`. The website provide quite an extensive list of downloads for Windows and macOS, as well as for many Linux distributions: Debian, Ubuntu, Red Hat, Fedora, and SUSE. Follow the usual process on your platform to install the software. After that, you'll want to install a bunch of extensions by going to the **Extensions Marketplace** (*Ctrl/Command + Shift + X*). The following are recommended to start with:

- C/C++ by Microsoft
- C/C++ Extension Pack by Microsoft
- CMake by twxs
- CMake Tools by Microsoft

They will provide the usual code highlighting and the ability to compile, run, and debug code straight from the IDE, but you might need to install the toolchain yourself. Usually, VS Code will suggest extensions to install in a pop - up window as you start opening relevant files, so you don't necessarily need to go out on a hunt.

I also suggest installing the **Remote – SSH by Microsoft** extension if you're involved with remote projects, as this will make the experience much more coherent and comfortable; this extension not only takes care of file synchronization but will also enable you to remotely debug by attaching to the debugger on the remote machine.

However, there's one more interesting extension that shifts the paradigm of working with projects; let's see how.

Advanced feature: Dev Containers

If you're deploying your application to a production environment, whether you're shipping the compiled artifact or running a build process, it's crucial to ensure that all dependencies are present. Otherwise, you'll get all sorts of problems. Even with all dependencies accounted for, different versions or configurations might cause your solution to behave differently from the development or staging environment. I've experienced such cases on numerous occasions. Before virtualization became prevalent, dealing with environmental issues was just a part of life.

With the introduction of lightweight containers like Docker, things got much simpler. Suddenly, you were able to run a minified operating system with your service isolated to its own space. This isolation allowed all dependencies to be packaged with the container, freeing developers from a major headache.

Until recently, developing inside a container involved manually building, running, and connecting to the container with a remote session from the IDE. This process wasn't overly difficult, but it required manual steps that could be executed differently by various developers.

In recent years, Microsoft released an open standard called Dev Containers (`https://containers.dev/`) to help address this slight inconvenience. The specification mainly consists of a `devcontainer.json` file that you can place in your project repository, instructing IDEs on how to set up their development environment in a container.

To use this feature, simply install the **Dev Containers by Microsoft** extension and point it to a repository of an appropriately prepared project. If you're undeterred by the challenges of switching the main `CMakeLists.txt`, feel free to try it with the book's repository:

`git@github.com:PacktPublishing/Modern-CMake-for-Cpp-2E.git`

I can confirm that other IDEs, like CLion, are adopting this standard, so it seems like a good practice to adopt if you're facing the circumstances described. Time to move on to the next product from the Microsoft family.

Starting with the Visual Studio IDE

The **Visual Studio (VS)** IDE is an IDE available for Windows developed by Microsoft. VS was available for macOS but is being deprecated in August 2024. It's important to distinguish it from VS Code, *the other IDE* by Microsoft.

VS comes in a few flavors: Community, Professional, and Enterprise. The Community version is free, allowing up to five users in a company. More mature companies will need to pay licensing fees, which start from $45 per user monthly. *Figure 3.5* shows what VS Community looks like:

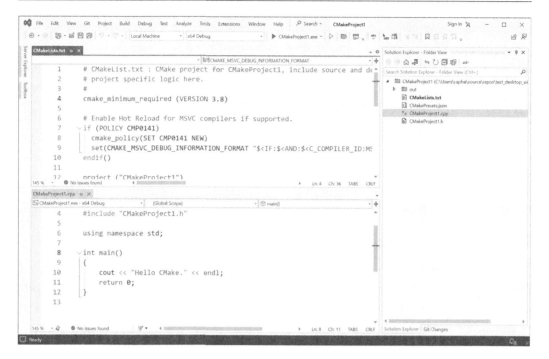

Figure 3.5: The main window of VS 2022

Like the other IDEs discussed in this chapter, you can enable dark mode if you prefer. Let's move on to the noteworthy features of this IDE.

Why you might like it

This IDE shares many features with VS Code, offering an experience of a similar flavor but in a much more refined form. The suite is full of features, many of which utilize GUIs, wizards, and visual elements. Most of these features are available straight out of the box, rather than through extensions (although there is still a large and extensive package marketplace for additional functionality). In other words, it's like VSC but much more advanced.

Depending on the version, your testing tools will cover a wide range of tests: unit testing, performance testing, load testing, manual testing, Test Explorer, test coverage, IntelliTest, and code profiling. The profiler, in particular, is quite a valuable tool, and it's available in the Community edition.

If you're designing Windows desktop applications, VS provides visual editors and a large collection of components. There's extensive support for the **Universal Windows Platform (UWP)**, which is the UI standard for Windows-based applications introduced in Windows 10. This support allows for a sleek, modern design, heavily optimized for adaptive controls that scale well on different screens.

Another thing worth mentioning is that even though VS is a Windows-only IDE, you can develop projects targeted for Linux and mobile platforms (Android and iOS). There's also support for game developers using Windows-native libraries and Unreal Engine.

Ready to see for yourself how it works? Here's how to start.

Take your first steps

This IDE is only available for Windows, and it follows a standard installation process. Start by downloading the installer from `https://visualstudio.microsoft.com/free-developer-offers/`. After running the installer, you'll be asked to pick the version (Community, Professional, or Enterprise) and select the workloads you want:

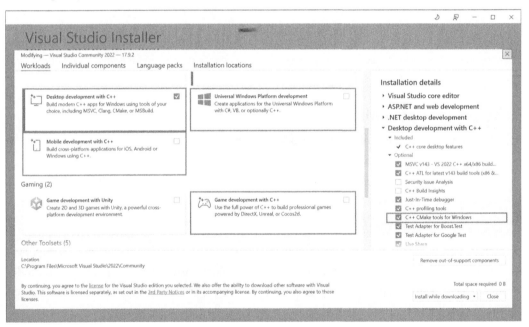

Figure 3.6: Installer window for the VS IDE

Workloads are simply feature sets that allow VS to support the specific language, environment, or format of the program. Some workloads include Python, Node.js, or .NET. We're of course interested in the ones related to C++ (*Figure 3.6*); there's extensive support available for different use cases:

- Desktop development with C++
- Universal Windows Platform development
- Game development with C++
- Mobile development with C++
- Linux development with C++

Pick the ones that fit your desired application and press **Install**. Don't worry about installing all options just in case – you can always modify your selection later by running the installer again. If you decide to configure the workload components more precisely, ensure to keep the **C++ CMake tools for Windows** or **C++ CMake tools for Linux** option enabled to get access to CMake support.

After installation, you can start the IDE and select **Create a new project** on the start window. You'll be presented with multiple templates based on the workloads you installed previously. To work with CMake, choose the **CMake Project** template. Other options don't necessarily use it. Upon creating your project, you can start it by pressing the green play button at the top of the window; the code will compile, and you'll see the basic program executed with the following output:

```
Hello CMake.
```

Now, you're ready to work with CMake in Visual Studio.

Advanced feature: Hot Reload debugging

While running Visual Studio might be more resource-intensive and take more time to start, it offers numerous unmatched features. One significant game-changer is Hot Reload. Here's how it works: open a C++ project, start it with a debugger attached, make a change in a code file, press the **Hot Reload** button (or *Alt + F10*), and your changes will immediately be reflected in the running application while maintaining the state.

To ensure Hot Reload support is enabled, set these two options in the **Project > Properties > C/C++ > General** menu:

- **Debug Information Format** must be set to **Program Database for Edit and Continue /ZI**
- **Enable Incremental Linking** must be set to **Yes /INCREMENTAL**

The behind-the-scenes mechanics of Hot Reload might seem like sorcery, but it's an incredibly useful feature to have. There are some limitations, such as changes to global/static data, object layouts, or "time-traveling" changes (like altering the constructor of an already constructed object).

You can find more about Hot Reload in the official documentation here: `https://learn.microsoft.com/en-us/visualstudio/debugger/hot-reload`.

This concludes our discovery of the three main IDEs. The initial learning curve might look steep, but I promise that the effort put in to learn any of these platforms will pay off very quickly when you move on to more advanced tasks.

Summary

This chapter provides an in-depth look at using IDEs to optimize the programming process, particularly focusing on IDEs that deeply integrate with CMake. It offers a comprehensive guide for both beginners and experienced professionals, detailing the benefits of using an IDE and how to select one that best fits individual or organizational needs.

We started with a discussion on the importance of IDEs in enhancing development speed and code quality, explaining what an IDE is and how it simplifies the various steps involved in software development by integrating tools like code editors, compilers, and debuggers. This was followed by a short reminder about toolchains, where we explained the necessity of their installation if they aren't present in the system, and we presented a short list of the most common choices.

We discussed how to start with CLion and its unique features, and we took an advanced look at its debugging capabilities. VS Code, a free, cross-platform IDE by Microsoft, is recognized for its vast extension ecosystem and support for numerous programming languages. We guided you through the initial setup and its key extension installations, and we introduced an advanced feature called Dev Containers. The VS IDE, exclusive to Windows, provides a refined, feature-rich environment tailored to various user needs. The setup process, key features, and the advanced Hot Reload debugging feature were also covered.

Each IDE section provided insights into why you might choose a particular IDE, the steps to get started, and a look at an advanced feature that sets the IDE apart. We also emphasized the concept of remote development support, highlighting its growing importance in the industry.

In summary, this chapter serves as a foundational guide for programmers seeking to understand and choose an IDE, offering a clear overview of the top options, their unique benefits, and how to effectively use them in conjunction with CMake to enhance coding efficiency and project management. In the next chapter, we'll learn the basics of project setup using CMake.

Further reading

For more information on the topics covered in this chapter, you can refer to the following:

- Qt Creator IDE, another CMake-supporting option to explore:
  `https://www.qt.io/product/development-tools`

- Eclipse IDE for C/C++ developers, which supports CMake as well:
  `https://www.eclipse.org/downloads/packages/release/2023-12/r/eclipse-ide-cc-developers`

- Xcode for macOS can also be used with CMake:
  `https://medium.com/practical-coding/migrating-to-cmake-in-c-and-getting-it-working-with-xcode-50b7bb80ae3d`

- CodeLite is another choice, thanks to the CMake plugin:
  `https://docs.codelite.org/plugins/cmake/`

Join our community on Discord

Join our community's Discord space for discussions with the author and other readers:

`https://discord.com/invite/vXN53A7ZcA`

4

Setting Up Your First CMake Project

We have now gathered enough information to start talking about the core function of CMake: *building projects*. In CMake, a **project** contains all the source files and the configuration necessary to manage the process of bringing our solutions to life. Configuration starts by performing all the checks: verifying if the target platform is supported, ensuring the presence of all essential dependencies and tools, and confirming the compatibility of the provided compiler with the required features.

Once the preliminary checks are completed, CMake proceeds to generate a buildsystem tailored to the selected build tool. Then, the buildsystem is executed, which means compiling the source files and linking them together with their respective dependencies to create the output artifacts.

The resulting artifacts can be distributed to consumers in different ways. They can be shared directly with users as binary packages, allowing them to install them on their systems using package managers. Alternatively, they can be distributed as single-executable installers. Additionally, end-users have the option to create the artifacts themselves by accessing projects shared in an open-source repository. In this scenario, users can utilize CMake to compile the projects on their own machines and subsequently install them.

Leveraging CMake projects to their fullest extent can significantly enhance the development experience and the overall quality of the generated code. By harnessing the power of CMake, numerous mundane tasks can be automated, such as executing tests after the build and running code coverage checkers, formatters, validators, linters, and other tools. This automation not only saves time but also ensures consistency and promotes code quality throughout the development process.

To unlock the power of CMake projects, we'll make a few key decisions first: how to correctly configure the project as a whole and how to partition it and set up the source tree so that all files are neatly organized in the right directories. By establishing a coherent structure and organization from the beginning, the CMake project can be effectively managed and scaled as it evolves.

Next up, we'll take a look at the project's build environment. We'll find out things like the architecture we're working with, the tools at our disposal, the features they support, and the language standard we're using. To make sure everything is in sync, we'll compile a test C++ file and see if our chosen compiler meets the standard requirements we've set for our project. It's all about ensuring a smooth fit between our project, the tools we're using, and the standards we've chosen.

In this chapter, we're going to cover the following main topics:

- Understanding the basic directives and commands
- Partitioning your project
- Thinking about the project structure
- Scoping the environment
- Configuring the toolchain
- Disabling in-source builds

Technical requirements

You can find the code files that are present in this chapter on GitHub at https://github.com/ PacktPublishing/Modern-CMake-for-Cpp-2E/tree/main/examples/ch04.

To build the examples provided in this book, always use the recommended commands:

```
cmake -B <build tree> -S <source tree>
cmake --build <build tree>
```

Be sure to replace the placeholders <build tree> and <source tree> with appropriate paths. As a reminder: **build tree** is the path to the target/output directory and **source tree** is the path at which your source code is located.

Understanding the basic directives and commands

In *Chapter 1*, *First Steps with CMake*, we already looked at a simple project definition. Let's revisit it. It is a directory with a CMakeLists.txt file that contains a few commands configuring the language processor:

chapter01/01-hello/CMakeLists.txt

```
cmake_minimum_required(VERSION 3.26)
project(Hello)
add_executable(Hello hello.cpp)
```

In the same chapter, in the section named *Project files*, we learned about a few basic commands. Let's explain them in depth here.

Specifying the minimum CMake version

It's important to use the `cmake_minimum_required()` command at the very top of your project files and scripts. This command not only verifies if the system has the correct CMake version but also implicitly triggers another command, `cmake_policy(VERSION)`, which specifies the policies to be used for the project. These policies define how commands behave within CMake, and they have been introduced over the course of CMake's development to accommodate changes and improvements in the supported languages and CMake itself.

To keep the language clean and simple, the CMake team introduced policies whenever there was a backward-incompatible change. Each policy enables the new behavior associated with that change. These policies ensure that projects can adapt to the evolving features and functionalities of CMake, while preserving compatibility with older codebases.

By calling `cmake_minimum_required()`, we tell CMake that it needs to apply the default policies configured at the version provided in the argument. When CMake gets upgraded, we don't need to worry about it breaking our project, as the new policies coming with the new version won't be enabled.

Policies can affect every single aspect of CMake, including other important commands like `project()`. For that reason, it is important to start your `CMakeLists.txt` file by setting the version you're working with. Otherwise, you will get warnings and errors.

Each CMake version introduces numerous policies. However, it's not necessary to delve into details unless you encounter challenges when upgrading older projects to the latest CMake version. In such cases, it is recommended to refer to the official documentation on policies for comprehensive information and guidance: `https://cmake.org/cmake/help/latest/manual/cmake-policies.7.html`.

Defining languages and metadata

It's recommended to put the project() command just after cmake_minimum_required(), even though it's technically not. Doing so will ensure that we use the right policies when configuring the project. We can use one of its two forms:

```
project(<PROJECT-NAME> [<language-name>...])
```

Or:

```
project(<PROJECT-NAME>
        [VERSION <major>[.<minor>[.<patch>[.<tweak>]]]]
        [DESCRIPTION <project-description-string>]
        [HOMEPAGE_URL <url-string>]
        [LANGUAGES <language-name>...])
```

We need to specify <PROJECT-NAME>, but the other arguments are optional. Calling this command will implicitly set the following variables:

```
PROJECT_NAME
CMAKE_PROJECT_NAME (only in the top-level CMakeLists.txt)
PROJECT_IS_TOP_LEVEL, <PROJECT-NAME>_IS_TOP_LEVEL
PROJECT_SOURCE_DIR, <PROJECT-NAME>_SOURCE_DIR
PROJECT_BINARY_DIR, <PROJECT-NAME>_BINARY_DIR
```

What languages are supported? Quite a few. And you can use more than one at a time! Here's a list of language keywords you can use to configure your project:

- ASM, ASM_NASM, ASM_MASM, ASMMARMASM, ASM-ATT: Dialects of Assembler
- C: C
- CXX: C++
- CUDA: Compute Unified Device Architecture by Nvidia
- OBJC: Objective-C
- OBJCXX: Objective-C++
- Fortran: Fortran
- HIP: Heterogeneous(-compute) Interface for Portability (for Nvidia and AMD platforms)
- ISPC: Implicit SPMD Program Compiler's language
- CSharp: C#
- Java: Java (requires extra steps, see official documentation)

CMake enables both C and C++ by default, so you may want to explicitly specify only CXX for your C++ projects. Why? The project() command will detect and test the available compilers for your chosen language, so stating the required ones will allow you to save time during the configuration stage, by skipping any checks for unused languages.

Specifying the VERSION keyword will automatically set the variables that can be used to configure packages, or exposed in the header files to be consumed during the compilation (we'll cover this in the *Configuring the headers* section of *Chapter 7, Compiling C++ Sources with CMake*):

```
PROJECT_VERSION, <PROJECT-NAME>_VERSION
CMAKE_PROJECT_VERSION (only in the top-level CMakeLists.txt)
PROJECT_VERSION_MAJOR, <PROJECT-NAME>_VERSION_MAJOR
PROJECT_VERSION_MINOR, <PROJECT-NAME>_VERSION_MINOR
PROJECT_VERSION_PATCH, <PROJECT-NAME>_VERSION_PATCH
PROJECT_VERSION_TWEAK, <PROJECT-NAME>_VERSION_TWEAK
```

We can also set DESCRIPTION and HOMEPAGE_URL, which will set the following variables for similar purposes:

```
PROJECT_DESCRIPTION, <PROJECT-NAME>_DESCRIPTION
PROJECT_HOMEPAGE_URL, <PROJECT-NAME>_HOMEPAGE_URL
```

The cmake_minimum_required() and project() commands will allow us to create a basic listfile and initialize an empty project. While the structure may not have been a significant concern for the small, single-file projects, it becomes crucial as the codebase expands. How do you prepare for that?

Partitioning your project

As our solutions grow in terms of lines of code and the number of files they contain, it becomes apparent that we must address the looming challenge: either we begin partitioning the project, or risk being overwhelmed by its complexity. There are two ways we can tackle this problem: splitting the CMake code and relocating the source files to subdirectories. In both cases, we aim to follow the design principle called **separation of concerns**. Put simply, we break down the code into smaller parts, grouping together closely related functionality while keeping other pieces of code separate to establish clear boundaries.

We talked a bit about partitioning CMake code when discussing listfiles in *Chapter 1, First Steps with CMake*. We spoke about the include() command, which allows CMake to execute the code from an external file.

This method helps with the separation of concerns, but only a little – specialized code is extracted to separate files and can even be shared across unrelated projects, but it can still pollute the global variable scope with its internal logic, if the author is not careful.

You see, calling `include()` doesn't introduce any additional scopes or isolations beyond what is already defined within the file. Let's see why this is a potential problem by considering an example, a piece of software that supports a small car rental company. It will have many source files defining different aspects of the software: managing customers, cars, parking spots, long-term contracts, maintenance records, employee records, and so on. If we were to put all these files in a single directory, finding anything would be a nightmare. Therefore, we create a number of directories in the main directory of our project and move the related files inside it. Our `CMakeLists.txt` file might look similar to this:

ch04/01-partition/CMakeLists.txt

```
cmake_minimum_required(VERSION 3.26.0)
project(Rental CXX)
add_executable(Rental
              main.cpp
              cars/car.cpp
              # more files in other directories
)
```

That's all great, but as you can see, we still have the list of source files from the nested directory in a top-level file! To increase the separation of concerns, we could extract the list of sources to another listfile and store it in a `sources` variable:

ch04/02-include/cars/cars.cmake

```
set(sources
    cars/car.cpp
#    more files in other directories
)
```

Now we can reference this file with the `include()` command to gain access to the sources variable:

ch04/02-include/CMakeLists.txt

```
cmake_minimum_required(VERSION 3.26.0)
project(Rental CXX)
include(cars/cars.cmake)
add_executable(Rental
              main.cpp
```

```
        ${sources} # for cars/
)
```

CMake would effectively set sources in the same scope as add_executable, filling the variable with all the files. This solution works, but it has a few flaws:

- **The variables from the nested directory will pollute the top-level scope (and vice versa):**

  While it's not an issue in a simple example, in more complex, multi-level trees with multiple variables used in the process, it can quickly become a hard-to-debug problem. What if we have multiple included listfiles that define their sources variable?

- **All of the directories will share the same configuration:**

  This issue shows its true colors as projects mature over the years. Without any granularity, we have to treat every source file the same, and we cannot specify different compilation flags, choose a newer language version for some parts of the code, and silence warnings in chosen areas of the code. Everything is global, meaning that we need to introduce changes to all of the translation units at the same time.

- **There are shared compilation triggers:**

  Any changes to the configuration will mean that all the files will have to be recompiled, even if the change is meaningless for some of them.

- **All the paths are relative to the top level:**

  Note that in cars.cmake, we had to provide a full path to the cars/car.cpp file. This results in a lot of repeated text ruining the readability and going against the **Don't Repeat Yourself (DRY)** principle of clean coding (unnecessary repetition leads to mistakes). Renaming a directory would be a struggle.

The alternative is to use the add_subdirectory() command, which introduces a variable scope and more. Let's take a look.

Managing scope with subdirectories

It's a common practice to structure your project following the natural structure of the filesystem, where nested directories represent the discrete elements of the application, the business logic, GUI, API, and reporting, and finally, separate directories with tests, external dependencies, scripts, and documentation. To support this concept, CMake offers the following command:

```
add_subdirectory(source_dir [binary_dir] [EXCLUDE_FROM_ALL])
```

As already established, this adds a source directory to our build. Optionally, we may provide a path that built files will be written to (`binary_dir` or the build tree). The `EXCLUDE_FROM_ALL` keyword will disable the automatic building of targets defined in the subdirectory (we'll cover **targets** in the next chapter). This may be useful for separating parts of the project that aren't needed for the core functionality (like *examples* or *extensions*).

`add_subdirectory()` will evaluate the `source_dir` path (relative to the current directory) and parse the `CMakeLists.txt` file in it. This file is parsed within the directory scope, eliminating the issues mentioned in the previous method:

- Variables are isolated to the nested scope.
- The nested artifacts can be configured independently.
- Modifying the nested `CMakeLists.txt` file doesn't require rebuilding unrelated targets.
- Paths are localized to the directory and can be added to the parent **include path** if desired.

This is what the directory structure looks like for our `add_subdirectory()` example:

```
├── CMakeLists.txt
├── cars
│   ├── CMakeLists.txt
│   ├── car.cpp
│   └── car.h
└── main.cpp
```

Here, we have two `CMakeLists.txt` files. The top-level file will use the nested directory, `cars`:

ch04/03-add_subdirectory/CMakeLists.txt

```
cmake_minimum_required(VERSION 3.26.0)
project(Rental CXX)
add_executable(Rental main.cpp)
add_subdirectory(cars)
target_link_libraries(Rental PRIVATE cars)
```

The last line is used to link the artifacts from the `cars` directory to the `Rental` executable. It is a target-specific command, which we'll discuss in depth in the next chapter: *Chapter 5, Working with Targets*.

Let's see what the nested listfile looks like:

ch04/03-add_subdirectory/cars/CMakeLists.txt

```
add_library(cars OBJECT
    car.cpp
#   more files in other directories
)
target_include_directories(cars PUBLIC .)
```

In this example, I have used add_library() to produce a globally visible **target** cars, and added the cars directory to its public **include directories** with target_include_directories(). This informs CMake where the cars.h resides, so when target_link_libraries() is used, the main. cpp file can consume the header without providing a relative path:

```
#include "car.h"
```

We can see the add_library() command in the nested listfile, so did we start working with libraries in this example? Actually, no. Since we used the OBJECT keyword, we're indicating we're only interested in producing the **object files** (exactly as we did in the previous example). We just grouped them under a single logical target (cars). You may already have a sense of what a **target** is. Hold that thought – we'll explain the details in the next chapter.

When to use nested projects

In the previous section, we briefly mentioned the EXCLUDE_FROM_ALL argument used in the add_ subdirectory() command to indicate extraneous elements of our codebase. The CMake documentation suggests that if we have such parts living inside the source tree, they should have their own project() commands in their CMakeLists.txt files so that they can generate their own buildsystems and can be built independently.

Are there any other scenarios where this would be useful? Sure. For example, one scenario would be when you're working with multiple C++ projects built in one **CI/CD** pipeline (perhaps when building a framework or a set of libraries). Alternatively, maybe you're porting the buildsystem from a legacy solution, such as GNU Make, which uses plain **makefiles**. In such a case, you might want an option to slowly break things down into more independent pieces – possibly to put them in a separate build pipeline, or just to work on a smaller scope, which could be loaded by an IDE such as **CLion**. You can achieve that by adding the project() command to the listfile in the nested directory. Just don't forget to prepend it with cmake_minimum_required().

Since project nesting is supported, could we somehow connect related projects that are built side by side?

Keeping external projects external

While it is technically possible to reference the internals of one project from another in CMake, it is not a regular or recommended practice. CMake does provide some support for this, including the load_cache() command to load values from another project's cache. However, using this approach can result in problems with cyclical dependencies and project coupling. It's best to avoid this command and make a decision: should our related projects be nested, connected through libraries, or merged into a single project?

These are the partitioning tools at our disposal: *including listfiles*, *adding subdirectories*, and *nesting projects*. But how should we use them so our projects stay maintainable and easy to navigate and extend? To do this, we need a well-defined project structure.

Thinking about the project structure

It's no secret that as a project grows, it becomes harder and harder to find things in it – both in listfiles and in the source code. Therefore, it is very important to maintain the project hygiene right from the start.

Imagine a scenario where you need to deliver some important, time-sensitive changes, and they don't fit well in either of the two directories in your project. Now, you need to additionally push a *cleanup commit* to restructure the file hierarchy to fit your changes neatly. Or, worse, you decide to just shove them anywhere and add a TODO to deal with the issue later.

Over the course of the year, these problems accumulate, the technical debt grows, and so does the cost of maintaining the code. This becomes extremely troublesome when there's a crippling bug in a live system that needs a quick fix or when people unfamiliar with the codebase need to introduce occasional changes.

So, we need a good project structure. But what does this mean? There are a few rules that we can borrow from other areas of software development like system design. The project should have the following characteristics:

- Easy to navigate and extend
- Well bounded (project-specific files should be contained to the project directory)
- Individual targets follow the hierarchical tree

There isn't one definitive solution, but out of the various project structure templates available online, I suggest using this one as it is simple and extensible:

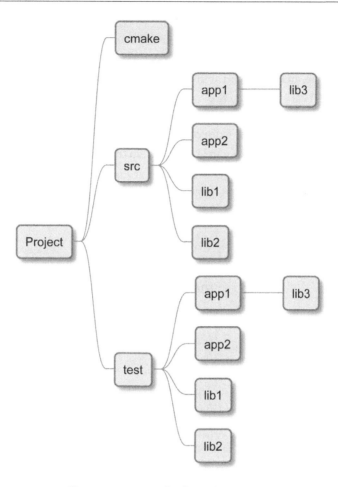

Figure 4.1: An example of a project structure

This project outlines the directories for the following components:

- cmake: Shared macros and functions, find_modules, and one-off scripts
- src: Source and header files for binaries and libraries
- test: Source code for automated tests

In this structure, the CMakeLists.txt file should exist in the following directories: the top-level project directory, test, and src and all its subdirectories. The main listfile shouldn't declare any build steps on its own, but instead, it should configure the general aspects of the project and delegate the responsibility of building to the nested listfiles with the add_subdirectory() command. In turn, these listfiles may delegate this work to even deeper layers if needed.

Some developers suggest separating the executables from the libraries and creating two top-level directories instead of one: src and lib. CMake treats both artifacts the same, and separation at this level doesn't really matter. Feel free to follow that model if it's your preference.

Having multiple directories in the src directory comes in handy for bigger projects. But if you're building just a single executable or library, you may skip them and store your source files directly in src. In any case, remember to add a CMakeLists.txt file there and execute any nested listfiles as well. This is how your file tree might look for a single, simple target:

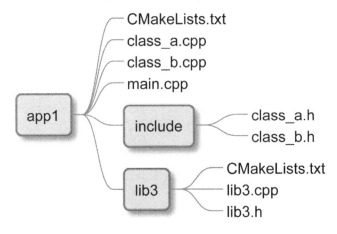

Figure 4.2: The directory structure of an executable

In *Figure 4.1*, we see a CMakeLists.txt file in the root of the src directory – it will configure the key project settings and include all listfiles from nested directories. The app1 directory (visible in *Figure 4.2*) contains another CMakeLists.txt file along with the .cpp implementation files: class_a.cpp and class_b.cpp. There's also the main.cpp file with the executable's entry point. The CMakeLists.txt file should define a target that uses these sources to build an executable – again, we'll learn how to do that in the next chapter.

Our header files are placed in the include directory and can be used to declare symbols for other C++ translation units.

Next, we have a lib3 directory, which contains a library specific to this executable only (libraries used elsewhere in the project or exported externally should live in the src directory). This structure offers great flexibility and allows for easy project extensions. As we continue adding more classes, we can conveniently group them into libraries to improve compilation speed. Let's see what a library looks like:

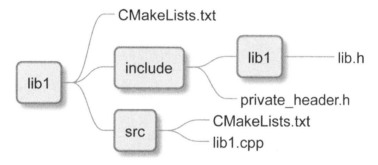

Figure 4.3: The directory structure of a library

Libraries should adhere to the same structure as executables, with a minor distinction: an optional lib1 directory is added to the include directory. This directory is included when the library is intended for external use beyond the project. It contains public header files that other projects will consume during compilation. We'll return to this subject when we start building our own libraries in *Chapter 7, Compiling C++ Sources with CMake.*

So, we have discussed how files are laid out in a directory structure. Now, it's time to take a look at how individual CMakeLists.txt files come together to form a single project and what their role is in a bigger scenario.

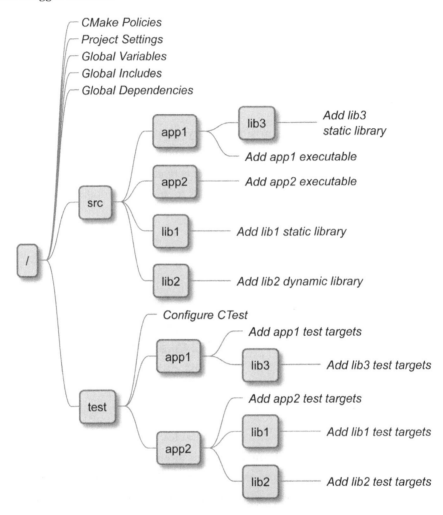

Figure 4.4: How CMake merges listfiles together in a single project

In the preceding figure, each box represents a CMakeLists.txt listfile residing in each directory, while the labels in italics represent the actions executed by each file (from top to bottom). Let's analyze this project once more from CMake's perspective (for all the details, look at the example in the ch04/05-structure directory):

1. The execution starts from the root of the project – that is, from a CMakeLists.txt listfile residing at the top of the source tree. This file will set the minimum required CMake version with the appropriate policies, set the project name, supported languages, and global variables, and include the files from the cmake directory, so that their contents are available globally.

2. The next step is to enter the scope of the src directory by calling the add_subdirectory(src bin) command (we'd like to put compiled artifacts in <binary_tree>/bin rather than <binary_tree>/src).

3. CMake reads the src/CMakeLists.txt file and discovers that its only purpose is to add four nested subdirectories: app1, app2, lib1, and lib2.

4. CMake enters the variable scope of app1 and learns about another nested library, lib3, which has its own CMakeLists.txt file; then the scope of lib3 is entered. As you may have noticed, this is a depth-first traversal of the directory structure.

5. The lib3 library adds a static library target with the same name. CMake returns to the parent scope of app1.

6. The app1 subdirectory adds an executable that depends on lib3. CMake returns to the parent scope of src.

7. CMake will continue entering the remaining nested scopes and executing their listfiles until all add_subdirectory() invocations have been completed.

8. CMake returns to the top-level scope and executes the remaining command add_subdirectory(test). Each time, CMake enters the new scope and executes commands from the appropriate listfile.

9. All the targets are collected and checked for their correctness. CMake now has all the necessary information to generate a buildsystem.

It's important to note that the previous steps occur in the exact order in which we wrote the commands in our listfiles. In some cases, this order is significant, while in others, it may not be as crucial. We will delve deeper into this topic in the next chapter, *Chapter 5, Working with Targets*, to understand its implications.

So, when is the right time to create the directories to contain all of the elements of the project? Should we do it right from the start – create everything needed for the future and keep the directories empty – or wait until we actually have the files that need to go in their own category? This is a choice – we could follow the **Extreme Programming (XP)** rule **YAGNI (you aren't gonna need it)**, or we could try to make our project future-proof and lay good foundations for new developers to come.

Try to aim for a good balance between these approaches – if you suspect that your project might someday need an extern directory, then add it (your version control system may require an empty .keep file to check a directory into the repository).

Another effective approach to guide others in placing their external dependencies is by creating a README file that outlines the recommended structure. This can be particularly beneficial for less experienced programmers who will work on the project in the future. You may have observed this yourself: developers are reluctant to create directories, especially in the root of the project. If we provide a good project structure, others will be inclined to follow it.

Some projects can be built in almost every environment, while others are quite particular about their requirements. The top-level listfile is the perfect place to determine the appropriate course of action. Let's see how to do this.

Scoping the environment

CMake provides multiple ways of querying the environment with CMAKE_ variables, ENV variables, and special commands. For example, collected information can be used to support cross-platform scripts. These mechanisms allow us to avoid using platform-specific shell commands that may not be easily portable or differ in naming across environments.

For performance-critical applications, it will be useful to know all the features of the building platform (for example, instruction sets, CPU core count, and more). This information can then be passed to the compiled binaries so that they can be tuned to perfection (we'll learn how to do the passing in the next chapter). Let's explore the native information provided by CMake.

Detecting the operating system

There are many occasions when it is useful to know what the target operating system is. Even as mundane a thing as a filesystem differs greatly between Windows and Unix in things such as case sensitivity, file path structures, the presence of extensions, privileges, and so on. Most commands present on one system won't be available on another; they could be named differently (for example, ifconfig on Unix and ipconfig on Windows) or produce totally different output altogether.

If you ever need to support multiple target operating systems with a single CMake script, just check the CMAKE_SYSTEM_NAME variable so that you can act accordingly. Here's a simple example:

```
if(CMAKE_SYSTEM_NAME STREQUAL "Linux")
  message(STATUS "Doing things the usual way")
elseif(CMAKE_SYSTEM_NAME STREQUAL "Darwin")
  message(STATUS "Thinking differently")
```

```
elseif(CMAKE_SYSTEM_NAME STREQUAL "Windows")
  message(STATUS "I'm supported here too.")
elseif(CMAKE_SYSTEM_NAME STREQUAL "AIX")
  message(STATUS "I buy mainframes.")
else()
  message(STATUS "This is ${CMAKE_SYSTEM_NAME} speaking.")
endif()
```

If needed, there's a variable containing the operating system version: CMAKE_SYSTEM_VERSION. However, my recommendation is to try and make your solutions as system-agnostic as possible and use the built-in CMake cross-platform functionality. Especially for operations on filesystems, you should use the file() command described in the *Appendix*.

Cross-compilation — what are host and target systems?

Cross-compilation refers to the process of compiling code on one machine to be executed on a different target platform. For example, using the appropriate toolset, it is possible to compile applications for Android by running CMake on a Windows machine. Although cross-compilation is beyond the scope of this book, it's important to understand how it impacts some parts of CMake.

One of the necessary steps to allow cross-compilation is setting the CMAKE_SYSTEM_NAME and CMAKE_SYSTEM_VERSION variables to the values appropriate for the operating system that you're compiling for (the CMake documentation refers to it as the **target system**). The operating system used to perform the build is called a **host system**.

Regardless of the configuration, the information on the host system is always accessible in variables with the HOST keyword in their name: CMAKE_HOST_SYSTEM, CMAKE_HOST_SYSTEM_NAME, CMAKE_HOST_SYSTEM_PROCESSOR, and CMAKE_HOST_SYSTEM_VERSION.

There are a few more variables with a HOST keyword in their name, so just keep in mind that they're explicitly referencing the host system. Otherwise, all variables reference the target system (which is normally the host system anyway, unless we're cross-compiling).

If you're interested in reading more about cross-compilation, I suggest referencing the CMake documentation at https://cmake.org/cmake/help/latest/manual/cmake-toolchains.7.html.

Abbreviated variables

CMake will predefine a few variables that will provide information about the host and target systems. If a specific system is used, an appropriate variable will be set to a non-false value (that is, 1 or true):

- ANDROID, APPLE, CYGWIN, UNIX, IOS, WIN32, WINCE, WINDOWS_PHONE

- CMAKE_HOST_APPLE, CMAKE_HOST_SOLARIS, CMAKE_HOST_UNIX, CMAKE_HOST_WIN32

The WIN32 and CMAKE_HOST_WIN32 variables will be true for 32- and 64-bit versions of Windows and MSYS (this value is kept for legacy reasons). Also, UNIX will be true for Linux, macOS, and Cygwin.

Host system information

CMake could provide more variables, but to save time, it doesn't query the environment for rarely needed information, such as *whether a processor supports MMX* or *what the total physical memory is*. That doesn't mean this information isn't available – you just need to ask for it explicitly with the following command:

```
cmake_host_system_information(RESULT <VARIABLE> QUERY <KEY>...)
```

We need to provide a target variable and a list of keys we're interested in. If we provide just one key, the variable will contain a single value; otherwise, it will be a list of values. We can ask for many details about the environment and the OS:

Key	Description
HOSTNAME	Hostname
FQDN	Fully qualified domain name
TOTAL_VIRTUAL_MEMORY	Total virtual memory in MiB
AVAILABLE_VIRTUAL_MEMORY	Available virtual memory in MiB
TOTAL_PHYSICAL_MEMORY	Total physical memory in MiB
AVAILABLE_PHYSICAL_MEMORY	Available physical memory in MiB
OS_NAME	Output of uname -s if this command is present; either Windows, Linux, or Darwin
OS_RELEASE	The OS sub-type, such as on Windows Professional
OS_VERSION	The OS build ID
OS_PLATFORM	On Windows, $ENV{PROCESSOR_ARCHITECTURE}. On Unix/macOS, uname -m

If needed, we can even query processor-specific information:

Key	Description
NUMBER_OF_LOGICAL_CORES	Number of logical cores
NUMBER_OF_PHYSICAL_CORES	Number of physical cores
HAS_SERIAL_NUMBER	1 if the processor has a serial number
PROCESSOR_SERIAL_NUMBER	Processor serial number
PROCESSOR_NAME	Human-readable processor name
PROCESSOR_DESCRIPTION	Human-readable full processor description
IS_64BIT	1 if processor is 64-bit
HAS_FPU	1 if processor has floating-point units
HAS_MMX	1 if processor supports MMX instructions
HAS_MMX_PLUS	1 if processor supports Ext. MMX instructions
HAS_SSE	1 if processor supports SSE instructions
HAS_SSE2	1 if processor supports SSE2 instructions
HAS_SSE_FP	1 if processor supports SSE FP instructions
HAS_SSE_MMX	1 if processor supports SSE MMX instructions
HAS_AMD_3DNOW	1 if processor supports 3DNow instructions
HAS_AMD_3DNOW_PLUS	1 if processor supports 3DNow+ instructions
HAS_IA64	1 if IA64 processor is emulating x86

Does the platform have 32-bit or 64-bit architecture?

In 64-bit architecture, memory addresses, processor registers, processor instructions, address buses, and data buses are 64 bits wide. While this is a simplified definition, it gives a rough idea of how 64-bit platforms are different from 32-bit platforms.

In C++, different architectures mean different bit widths for some fundamental data types (int and long) and pointers. CMake utilizes the pointer size to gather information about the target machine. This information is available through the CMAKE_SIZEOF_VOID_P variable, and it will contain a value of 8 for 64 bits (because a pointer is 8 bytes wide) and 4 for 32 bits (4 bytes):

```
if(CMAKE_SIZEOF_VOID_P EQUAL 8)
  message(STATUS "Target is 64 bits")
endif()
```

What is the endianness of the system?

Architectures can be categorized as either **big-endian** or **little-endian** based on the byte order within a word or the natural unit of data for a processor. In a **big-endian** system, the most significant byte is stored at the lowest memory address, while the least significant byte is stored at the highest memory address. On the other hand, in a **little-endian** system, the byte order is reversed, with the least significant byte stored at the lowest memory address and the most significant byte at the highest memory address.

In most cases, **endianness** doesn't matter, but when you're writing bit-wise code that needs to be portable, CMake will provide you with a `BIG_ENDIAN` or `LITTLE_ENDIAN` value stored in the `CMAKE_<LANG>_BYTE_ORDER` variable, where `<LANG>` is C, CXX, OBJC, or CUDA.

Now that we know how to query the environment, let's shift our focus to the key settings of the project.

Configuring the toolchain

For CMake projects, a toolchain consists of all the tools used in building and running the application – for example, the working environment, the generator, the CMake executable itself, and the compilers.

Imagine what a less-experienced user feels when your build stops with some mysterious compilation and syntax errors. They must dig into the source code and try to understand what happened. After an hour of debugging, they discover that the correct solution is to update their compiler. Could we provide a better experience for users and check if all the required functions are present in the compiler before starting the build?

Sure! There are ways to specify these requirements. If the toolchain doesn't support all of the required features, CMake will stop early and show a clear message of what happened, asking the user to step in.

Setting the C++ standard

One of the initial steps we may consider is specifying the required C++ standard that the compiler should support for building our project. For new projects, it is recommended to set a minimum of C++14, but preferably C++17 or C++20. Starting from CMake 3.20, it is possible to set the required standard to C++23 if the compiler supports it. Additionally, since CMake 3.25, there is an option to set the standard to C++26, although this is currently a placeholder.

It has been over 10 years since the official release of **C++11**, and it is no longer considered to be *the modern C++ standard*. It's not recommended to start projects with this version unless your target environment is very old.

Another reason to stick to old standards is if you are building legacy targets that are too hard to upgrade. However, the C++ committee works very hard to keep C++ backward compatible, and in most cases, you won't have any problems bumping the standard to a higher version.

CMake supports setting the standard on a target-by-target basis (this is useful if parts of your codebase are really old), but it's better to converge to a single standard across the project. This can be done by setting the CMAKE_CXX_STANDARD variable to one of the following values: 98, 11, 14, 17, 20, 23, or 26, like so:

```
set(CMAKE_CXX_STANDARD 23)
```

This will be a default value for all subsequently defined targets (so it's best to set it close to the top of the root listfile). You can override it on a per-target basis if needed, like so:

```
set_property(TARGET <target> PROPERTY CXX_STANDARD <version>)
```

Or:

```
set_target_properties(<targets> PROPERTIES CXX_STANDARD <version>)
```

The second version allows us to specify multiple targets if that's needed.

Insisting on standard support

The CXX_STANDARD property mentioned in the previous section won't stop CMake from continuing with the build, even if the compiler isn't supporting the desired version – it's treated as a preference. CMake doesn't know if our code actually uses the brand-new features that aren't available in the previous compilers, and it will try to work with what it has available.

If we know for certain that this won't be successful, we can set another variable (which is overridable per target in the same manner as the previous one) to explicitly require the standard we target:

```
set(CMAKE_CXX_STANDARD_REQUIRED ON)
```

In this case, if the compiler present in the system doesn't support the required standard, the user will see the following message and the build will stop:

```
Target "Standard" requires the language dialect "CXX23" (with compiler
extensions), but CMake does not know the compile flags to use to enable
it.
```

Asking for C++23 might be a bit excessive, even for a modern environment. But C++20 should be fine on up-to-date systems, as it has been generally supported in **GCC/Clang/MSVC** since 2021/2022.

Vendor-specific extensions

Depending on the policy you implement in your organization, you might be interested in allowing or disabling vendor-specific extensions. What are these? Well, let's just say that the C++ standard is moving a bit slow for the needs of some compiler producers, so they decided to add their own enhancements to the language – *extensions*, if you like. For example, C++ **Technical Report 1 (TR1)** was a library extension that introduced regular expressions, smart pointers, hash tables, and random number generators before they became commonplace. To support such plugins released by the GNU project, CMake will substitute the compiler flag responsible for standard (-std=c++14) with -std=gnu++14.

On the one hand, this may be desired, as it allows for some convenient functionality. On the other hand, your code will lose portability as it will fail to build if you switch to a different compiler (or if your users do!). This is also a per-target property for which there is a default variable, CMAKE_CXX_EXTENSIONS. CMake is more liberal here, and allows the extensions unless we specifically tell it not to:

```
set(CMAKE_CXX_EXTENSIONS OFF)
```

I recommend doing so, if possible, as this option will insist on having vendor-agnostic code. Such code won't impose any unnecessary requirements on the users. Similarly to previous options, you can use set_property() to change this value on a per-target basis.

Interprocedural optimization

Usually, compilers optimize the code on the level of a single translation unit, which means that your .cpp file will be preprocessed, compiled, and then optimized. The intermediary files generated during these operations are then passed to the linker to create a single binary. However, modern compilers have the capability of performing **interprocedural optimization** at link time, also known as **link-time optimization**. This allows all compilation units to be optimized as a unified module, which in principle will achieve better results (sometimes at the cost of slower builds and more memory consumption).

If your compiler supports interprocedural optimization, it may be a good idea to use it. We'll follow the same method. The variable responsible for this setting is called CMAKE_INTERPROCEDURAL_ OPTIMIZATION. But before we set it, we need to make sure it is supported to avoid errors:

```
include(CheckIPOSupported)
check_ipo_supported(RESULT ipo_supported)
set(CMAKE_INTERPROCEDURAL_OPTIMIZATION ${ipo_supported})
```

As you can see, we had to include a built-in module to get access to the check_ipo_supported() command. This code will fail gracefully, and fall back to default behavior if the optimization is not supported.

Checking for supported compiler features

As we discussed earlier, if our build is to fail, it's best if it fails early, so we can provide a clear feedback message to the user and shorten the wait. Sometimes we're specifically interested in which C++ features are supported (and which aren't). CMake will question the compiler during the configuration stage and store a list of the available features in the CMAKE_CXX_COMPILE_FEATURES variable. We may write a very specific check and ask if a certain feature is available:

ch04/07-features/CMakeLists.txt

```
list(FIND CMAKE_CXX_COMPILE_FEATURES cxx_variable_templates result)
if(result EQUAL -1)
  message(FATAL_ERROR "Variable templates are required for compilation.")
endif()
```

As you may guess, writing one for every feature we use is a daunting task. Even the authors of CMake recommend only checking if certain high-level **meta-features** are present: cxx_std_98, cxx_std_11, cxx_std_14, cxx_std_17, cxx_std_20, cxx_std_23, and cxx_std_26. Each **meta-feature** indicates that the compiler supports a specific C++ standard. If you wish, you can use them exactly as we did in the previous example.

A full list of features known to CMake can be found in the documentation: https://cmake.org/ cmake/help/latest/prop_gbl/CMAKE_CXX_KNOWN_FEATURES.html.

Compiling a test file

One particularly interesting scenario occurred to me when I was compiling an application with GCC 4.7.x. I had manually confirmed in the compiler's reference that all of the C++11 features we were using were supported. However, the solution still didn't work correctly. The code silently ignored the call to the standard <regex> header. As it turned out, this specific compiler had a bug, and the regex library wasn't implemented.

No single check can protect you from such rare bugs (and you shouldn't need to check for them!), but there's a chance you may want to use some cutting-edge experimental feature of the latest standard, and you're not sure which compilers support it. You can test if your project is going to work by creating a test file that uses those specially required features in a small sample that can be quickly compiled and executed.

CMake provides two configure-time commands, try_compile() and try_run(), to verify that everything you need is supported on the target platform.

The try_run() command gives you more freedom, as you can ensure that the code is not only compiling but that it is also executing correctly (you could potentially test if regex is working). Of course, this won't work for cross-compilation scenarios (as the host won't be able to run an executable built for a different target). Just remember that the aim of this check is to provide a quick piece of feedback to the user if the compilation is working, so it's not meant to run any unit tests or anything complex – keep the file as basic as possible. For example, something like this:

ch04/08-test_run/main.cpp

```cpp
#include <iostream>
int main()
{
  std::cout << "Quick check if things work." << std::endl;
}
```

Calling try_run() isn't very complicated at all. We start by setting the required standard, after which we call try_run() and print the collected information to the user:

ch04/08-test_run/CMakeLists.txt

```cmake
set(CMAKE_CXX_STANDARD 20)
set(CMAKE_CXX_STANDARD_REQUIRED ON)
set(CMAKE_CXX_EXTENSIONS OFF)
try_run(run_result compile_result
        ${CMAKE_BINARY_DIR}/test_output
        ${CMAKE_SOURCE_DIR}/main.cpp
        RUN_OUTPUT_VARIABLE output)
message("run_result: ${run_result}")
message("compile_result: ${compile_result}")
message("output:\n" ${output})
```

This command may seem overwhelming at first, but only a few arguments are actually required to compile and run a very basic test file. I additionally used the optional RUN_OUTPUT_VARIABLE keyword to collect the output from stdout.

The next step is to extend our basic test file by using some of the more modern C++ features that we're going to use throughout the actual project – perhaps by adding a variadic template to see if the compiler on the target machine can digest it.

Finally, we can check in the conditional blocks if the collected output is meeting our expectations and message(SEND_ERROR <error>) is printed when something isn't right. Remember that SEND_ERROR keyword will allow CMake to continue through the configuration stage but will prevent the generation of the buildsystem. This is useful to show all the encountered errors before aborting the build. We now know how to ensure the compilation can complete in full. Let's move on to the next subject, disabling in-source builds.

Disabling in-source builds

In *Chapter 1, First Steps with CMake*, we talked about in-source builds, and how it is recommended to always specify the build path to be out of source. This not only allows for a cleaner build tree and a simpler .gitignore file, but it also decreases the chances you'll accidentally overwrite or delete any source files.

To stop the build early you may use the following check:

ch04/09-in-source/CMakeLists.txt

```
cmake_minimum_required(VERSION 3.26.0)
project(NoInSource CXX)
if(PROJECT_SOURCE_DIR STREQUAL PROJECT_BINARY_DIR)
  message(FATAL_ERROR "In-source builds are not allowed")
endif()
message("Build successful!")
```

If you would like more information about the STR prefix and variable references, please revisit *Chapter 2, The CMake Language*.

Notice, however, that no matter what you do in the preceding code, it seems like CMake will still create a CMakeFiles/ directory and a CMakeCache.txt file.

You might find online suggestions to use undocumented variables to make sure that the user can't write in the source directory under any circumstances. Relying on undocumented variables to restrict writing in the source directory is not recommended. They may not work in all versions and can be subject to removal or modification without warning.

If you're worried about users leaving those files in the source directory, add them to the `.gitignore` (or equivalent), and change the message to request a manual cleanup.

Summary

In this chapter, we covered valuable concepts that lay a strong foundation for building robust and future-proof projects. We discussed setting the minimum CMake version and configuring essential project aspects like name, languages, and metadata fields. Establishing these foundations enables our projects to scale effectively.

We explored project partitioning, comparing the use of basic `include()` with `add_subdirectory`, which offers benefits such as scoped variable management, simplified paths, and increased modularity. The ability to create nested projects and build them separately proved useful in gradually breaking down code into more independent units. After understanding the available partitioning mechanisms, we delved into creating transparent, resilient, and extensible project structures. We examined CMake's traversal of listfiles and the correct order of configuration steps. Next, we studied how we can scope the environment of our target and host machines, what the differences are between them, and what kind of information about the platform and system is available through different queries. We also covered configuring the toolchain, including specifying the required C++ version, handling vendor-specific compiler extensions, and enabling important optimizations. We learned how to test the compiler for required features and execute sample files to test compilation support.

Although the technical aspects covered so far are essential for a project, they are not sufficient to make it truly useful. To increase the project's utility, we need to understand the concept of **targets**. We briefly touched on the topic earlier, but now we are ready to approach it in full, as we finally have a solid understanding of related fundamentals. Targets, introduced in the next chapter, will play a crucial role in further enhancing the functionality and effectiveness of our projects.

Further reading

For more information on the topics covered in this chapter, you can refer to the following links:

- Separation of concerns:

  `https://nalexn.github.io/separation-of-concerns/`

- Complete CMake variable reference:

  `https://cmake.org/cmake/help/latest/manual/cmake-variables.7.html`

- `try_compile` and `try_run` references:

  `https://cmake.org/cmake/help/latest/command/try_compile.html`,

  `https://cmake.org/cmake/help/latest/command/try_run.html`

- CheckIPOSupported reference:

  `https://cmake.org/cmake/help/latest/module/CheckIPOSupported.html`

Leave a review!

Enjoying this book? Help readers like you by leaving an Amazon review. Scan the QR code below to get a free eBook of your choice.

5

Working with Targets

The entire application in CMake can be built from a single source code file (such as the classic `helloworld.cpp`). But it's equally possible to create a project where the executable is built from many source files: dozens or even thousands. Many beginners follow this path: they build their binaries with only a few files and let their projects grow organically without strict planning. They keep adding files as required and before they know it, everything is linked directly to a single binary without any structure whatsoever.

As software developers, we deliberately draw boundaries and designate components to group one or more units of translation (`.cpp` files). We do it to increase code readability, manage coupling and connascence, speed up the build process, and finally, discover and extract reusable components into autonomic units.

Every big project will push you to introduce some form of partitioning. This is where CMake targets find their use. A CMake target represents a logical unit that focuses on a specific objective. Targets can have dependencies on other targets, and their construction follows a declarative approach. CMake takes care of determining the proper order for building targets, optimizing with parallel builds where possible, and executing the necessary steps accordingly. As a general principle, when a target is built, it generates an artifact that can be utilized by other targets or serve as the final output of the build process.

Notice the usage of the word *artifact*. I intentionally refrain from using specific terms because CMake offers flexibility beyond just generating executables or libraries. In practice, we can utilize generated buildsystems to produce various types of outputs: additional source files, headers, object files, archives, configuration files, and more. The only requirements are a command-line tool (like a compiler), optional input files, and a designated output path.

Targets are an incredibly powerful concept that greatly streamlines the process of building a project. Understanding how they function and mastering the art of configuring them in an elegant and organized manner is crucial. This knowledge ensures a smooth and efficient development experience.

In this chapter, we're going to cover the following main topics:

- Understanding the concept of a target
- Setting properties of targets
- Writing custom commands

Technical requirements

You can find the code files that are present in this chapter on GitHub at `https://github.com/PacktPublishing/Modern-CMake-for-Cpp-2E/tree/main/examples/ch05`.

To build the examples provided in this book, always use the recommended commands:

```
cmake -B <build tree> -S <source tree>
cmake --build <build tree>
```

Be sure to replace the `<build tree>` and `<source tree>` placeholders with appropriate paths. As a reminder: **build tree** is the path to the target/output directory, while **source tree** is the path at which your source code is located.

Understanding the concept of a target

If you have ever used GNU Make, you have already seen the concept of a target. Essentially, it's a recipe that a buildsystem follows to compile a set of files into another file. It can be a `.cpp` implementation file compiled into a `.o` **object file** or a group of `.o` files packaged into a `.a` static library. There are numerous combinations and possibilities when it comes to targets and their transformations within a buildsystem.

CMake, however, allows you to save time and skip defining the intermediate steps of those recipes; it works on a higher level of abstraction. It understands how most languages build an executable directly from their source files. So, you don't need to write explicit commands to compile your C++ **object files** (as you would using GNU Make). All that's required is an `add_executable()` command with the name of the executable target followed by a list of the source files:

```
add_executable(app1 a.cpp b.cpp c.cpp)
```

We have used this command in the previous chapters, and we already know how executable targets are used in practice – during the generation step, CMake will create a buildsystem and fill it with appropriate recipes to compile each of the source files and link them together into a single binary executable.

In CMake, we can create a target using these three commands:

- `add_executable()`
- `add_library()`
- `add_custom_target()`

Before building executables or libraries, CMake performs a check to determine whether the generated output is older than the source files. This mechanism helps CMake avoid recreating artifacts that are already up to date. By comparing timestamps, CMake efficiently identifies which targets need to be rebuilt, reducing unnecessary recompilation.

All commands defining targets require the name of the target to be provided as a first argument, so it can be later referenced in other commands that do things with targets, like `target_link_libraries()`, `target_sources()`, or `target_include_directories()`. We'll learn about those commands later, but for now, let's take a closer look at what kind of targets we can define.

Defining executable targets

The command to define an executable target, `add_executable()`, is self-explanatory (we leaned on this fact and used it already in previous chapters). The formal structure looks like this:

```
add_executable(<name> [WIN32] [MACOSX_BUNDLE]
               [EXCLUDE_FROM_ALL]
               [source1] [source2 ...])
```

If we're compiling for Windows, by adding the optional argument, the `WIN32` keyword, we'll produce an executable that won't show the default console window (where we usually see the output streamed to `std::cout`). Instead, the application will be expected to generate its own GUI.

The next optional argument, `MACOSX_BUNDLE`, is quite similar in a way; it makes the applications produced for macOS/iOS launchable from the Finder as GUI apps.

The `EXCLUDE_FROM_ALL` keyword, when used, will prevent the executable target from being built in a regular, default build. Such a target will have to be explicitly mentioned in the *build command*:

```
cmake --build -t <target>
```

Finally, we're expected to provide the list of sources that will be compiled into the target. The following extensions are supported:

- For C: c, m

- For C++: C, M, c++, cc, cpp, cxx, m, mm, mpp, CPP, ixx, cppm, ccm, cxxm, c++m

Note that we're not adding any **header files** to the sources list. That can be done either implicitly, by providing a path to the directory where those files are with the target_include_directories() command, or by using a FILE_SET feature of the target_sources() command (added in CMake 3.23). This is an important topic for executables, but since it's complex and orthogonally related to targets, we'll dive into its details in *Chapter 7, Compiling C++ Sources with CMake*.

Defining library targets

Defining the libraries is very similar to defining executables, but, of course, it doesn't require keywords that define how GUI aspects will be handled. Here's the signature of the command:

```
add_library(<name> [STATIC | SHARED | MODULE]
            [EXCLUDE_FROM_ALL]
            [<source>...])
```

Rules regarding the name, *exclusion from all*, and sources match the executable targets exactly. The only difference is in the STATIC, SHARED, and MODULE keywords. If you have any experience with libraries, you'll know that these define what sort of artifact CMake will generate: statically linked libraries, shared (dynamic libraries), or modules. Again, it is quite a vast subject, which will be covered in depth in *Chapter 8, Linking Executables and Libraries*.

Custom targets

Custom targets are a bit different than executables or libraries. They extend the build functionality beyond what CMake provides out of the box by executing explicitly given command lines; for example, they can be used to:

- Calculate the checksums of other binaries.

- Run the code sanitizer and collect the results.

- Send a compilation report to the metrics pipeline.

As you can guess from this list, custom targets are only useful in quite advanced projects, so we'll just cover the basics to move on to more important topics.

To define a custom target, use the following syntax (some options have been removed for brevity):

```
add_custom_target(Name [ALL] [COMMAND command2 [args2...] ...])
```

Custom targets have certain drawbacks to consider. Since they involve shell commands, they can be system specific, potentially limiting portability. Additionally, custom targets may not provide a straightforward means for CMake to determine the specific artifacts or byproducts being generated, if any.

Custom targets also don't apply the staleness check like executables and libraries (they don't verify whether the sources are newer than the binaries), because by default they're not added to the **dependency graph** (so the ALL keyword works in opposite to EXCLUDE_FROM_ALL). Let's find out what that dependency graph is about.

Dependency graph

Mature applications are often built from many components, specifically, internal libraries. Partitioning the project is useful from a structural perspective. When related things are packaged together in a single logical entity, they can be linked with other targets: another library or an executable. This is especially convenient when multiple targets are using the same library. Take a look at *Figure 5.1*, which describes an exemplary dependency graph:

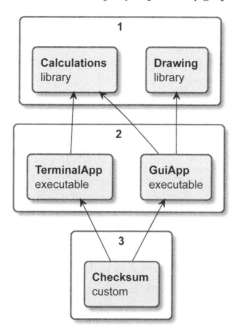

Figure 5.1: Order of building dependencies in the BankApp project

In this project, we have two libraries, two executables, and a custom target. Our use case here is to provide a banking application with a nice GUI for users (**GuiApp**) and a command-line version to be used as part of an automated script (**TerminalApp**). Both executables depend on the same **Calculations** library, but only one of them needs the **Drawing** library. To guarantee that our app's binaries were downloaded from a genuine source, we'll also calculate a checksum, and distribute it through separate secure channels. CMake is pretty flexible when it comes to writing listfiles for such a solution:

ch05/01-targets/CMakeLists.txt

```
cmake_minimum_required(VERSION 3.26)
project(BankApp CXX)

add_executable(terminal_app terminal_app.cpp)
add_executable(gui_app gui_app.cpp)
target_link_libraries(terminal_app calculations)
target_link_libraries(gui_app calculations drawing)

add_library(calculations calculations.cpp)
add_library(drawing drawing.cpp)

add_custom_target(checksum ALL
    COMMAND sh -c "cksum terminal_app>terminal.ck"
    COMMAND sh -c "cksum gui_app>gui.ck"
    BYPRODUCTS terminal.ck gui.ck
    COMMENT "Checking the sums..."
)
```

We link our libraries with executables by using the target_link_libraries() command. Without it, the building of executables would fail because of undefined symbols. Have you noticed that we invoked this command before declaring any of the libraries? When CMake configures the project, it collects information about targets and their properties – their names, dependencies, source files, and other details.

After parsing all the files, CMake will attempt to build a dependency graph. Like with all valid dependency graphs, they're **Directed Acyclic Graph** (**DAGs**). This means that there is a clear direction of which target depends on which, and such dependencies cannot form cycles.

When we execute cmake in build mode, the generated buildsystem will check what top-level targets we have defined and recursively build their dependencies. Let's consider our example from *Figure 5.1*:

1. Start from the top and build both libraries in group 1.

2. When the **Calculations** and **Drawing** libraries are complete, build group 2 – **GuiApp** and **TerminalApp**.

3. Build a checksum target; run specified command lines to generate checksums (cksum is a Unix checksum tool, which means that this example won't build on other platforms).

There's a slight issue, though – the preceding solution doesn't guarantee that a checksum target will be built after the executables. CMake doesn't know that a checksum depends on the executable binaries being present, so it's free to start building it first. To resolve this problem, we can put the add_dependencies() command at the end of the file:

```
add_dependencies(checksum terminal_app gui_app)
```

This will ensure that CMake understands the relationship between the checksum target and the executables.

That's great, but what's the difference between `target_link_libraries()` and `add_dependencies()`? `target_link_libraries()` is intended to be used with actual libraries and allows you to control property propagation. The second is meant to be used only with top-level targets to set their build order.

As projects grow in complexity, the dependency tree gets harder to understand. How can we simplify this process?

Visualizing dependencies

Even small projects can be difficult to reason about and share with other developers. A neat diagram will go a long way here. After all, a picture is worth a thousand words. We can do the work and draw a diagram ourselves, just like I did in *Figure 5.1*. But this is tedious and requires updates whenever the project changes. Luckily, CMake has a great module to generate dependency graphs in the dot/graphviz format, and it supports both internal and external dependencies!

To use it, we can simply execute this command:

```
cmake --graphviz=test.dot .
```

The module will produce a text file that we can import to the Graphviz visualization software, which can render an image or produce a PDF or SVG file that can be stored as part of the software documentation. Everybody loves great documentation, but hardly anyone likes to create it – now, you don't need to!

Custom targets are not visible by default and we need to create a special configuration file, CMakeGraphVizOptions.cmake, that will allow us to customize the graph. Use the set(GRAPHVIZ_CUSTOM_TARGETS TRUE) command to enable custom targets in your graph:

ch05/01-targets/CMakeGraphVizOptions.cmake

```
set(GRAPHVIZ_CUSTOM_TARGETS TRUE)
```

Other options allow the addition of a graph name, a header, and node prefixes and configure which targets should be included or excluded from the output (by name or type). Visit the official CMake documentation for the CMakeGraphVizOptions full description of this module.

If you're in a rush, you can even run Graphviz straight from your browser at this address: https://dreampuf.github.io/GraphvizOnline/.

All you need to do is copy and paste the contents of the test.dot file into the window on the left and your project will be visualized (*Figure 5.2*). Quite convenient, isn't it?

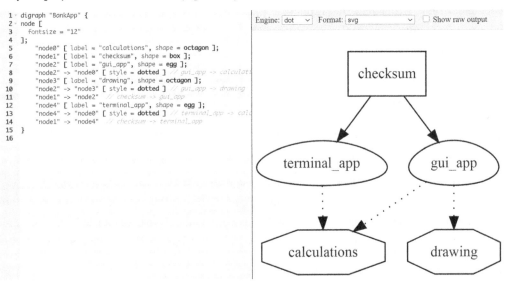

Figure 5.2: A visualization of the BankApp example in Graphviz

Using this method, we can quickly see all the explicitly defined targets.

Now that we understand the concept of a target, we know how to define different types of targets, including executables, libraries, and custom targets, as well as how to create a dependency graph and print it. Let's use this information to do a deeper dive and see how to configure them.

Setting properties of targets

Targets have properties that work in a similar way to fields of C++ objects. Some of these properties are meant to be modified, and some are read only. CMake defines a large list of "known properties" (see the *Further reading* section) that are available depending on the type of the target (executable, library, or custom). You can also add your own properties if you like. Use the following commands to manipulate the properties of a target:

```
get_target_property(<var> <target> <property-name>)
set_target_properties(<target1> <target2> ...
                      PROPERTIES <prop1-name> <value1>
                      <prop2-name> <value2> ...)
```

To print a target property on the screen, we first need to store it in the `<var>` variable and then message it to the user. Reading of the properties has to be done one by one; setting properties on a target allows us to specify multiple properties at the same time, on multiple targets.

> The concept of properties isn't unique to targets; CMake supports setting properties of other scopes as well: `GLOBAL`, `DIRECTORY`, `SOURCE`, `INSTALL`, `TEST`, and `CACHE`. To manipulate all kinds of properties, there are general `get_property()` and `set_property()` commands. In some projects, you'll see these low-level commands used to do exactly what the `set_target_properties()` command does, just with a bit more work:
>
> ```
> set_property(TARGET <target> PROPERTY <name> <value>)
> ```

Generally, it's better to use as many high-level commands as you can. In some cases, CMake offers short-hand commands that come with additional mechanisms. For example, `add_dependencies(<target> <dep>)` is a shorthand for appending dependencies to the `MANUALLY_ADDED_DEPENDENCIES` target property. In this case, we can query it with `get_target_property()` exactly as with any other property. However, we can't use `set_target_properties()` to change it (it's read only), as CMake insists on using the `add_dependencies()` command to restrict operations to appending only.

We'll introduce more property-setting commands when we discuss compiling and linking in upcoming chapters. Meanwhile, let's focus on how the properties of one target can be carried over to another.

What are Transitive Usage Requirements?

Let's just agree that naming is hard, and sometimes one ends up with a label that's difficult to understand. "Transitive Usage Requirements" is, unfortunately, one of those cryptic titles that you will encounter in the online CMake documentation. Let's untangle this strange name and perhaps propose a term that is easier to understand.

Starting from the middle term: **Usage**. As we previously discussed, one target may depend on another. CMake documentation sometimes refers to such dependency as **usage**, as in one target *uses* another.

There will be cases when such a *used target* sets specific *properties* or *dependencies* for itself, which, in turn, constitute **requirements** for *other targets* that use it: link some libraries, include a directory, or require specific compiler features.

The last part of our puzzle, **transitive**, describes the behavior correctly (maybe could be a bit simpler). CMake appends some properties/requirements of *used targets* to properties of *using targets*. You can say that some properties can transition (or simply propagate) across targets implicitly, so it's easier to express dependencies.

Simplifying this whole concept, I see it as **propagated properties** between the **source target** (targets that get used) and **destination targets** (targets that use other targets).

Let's look at a concrete example to understand why it's there and how it works:

```
target_compile_definitions(<source> <INTERFACE|PUBLIC|PRIVATE>
[items1...])
```

This target command will populate the COMPILE_DEFINITIONS property of a <source> target. **Compile definitions** are simply -Dname=definition flags passed to the compiler that configure the C++ preprocessor definitions (we'll get to that in *Chapter 7, Compiling C++ Sources with CMake*). The interesting part here is the second argument. We need to specify one of three values, INTERFACE, PUBLIC, or PRIVATE, to control which targets the property should be passed to. Now, don't confuse these with C++ access specifiers – this is a separate concept in its own right.

Propagation keywords work like this:

- PRIVATE sets the property of the source target.

- INTERFACE sets the property of the destination targets.

- PUBLIC sets the property of the source and destination targets.

When a property is not to be transitioned to any destination targets, set it to PRIVATE. When such a transition is needed, go with PUBLIC. If you're in a situation where the source target doesn't use the property in its implementation (.cpp files) and only in the headers, and these are passed to the consumer targets, INTERFACE is the keyword to use.

How does this work under the hood? To manage those properties, CMake provides a few commands such as the aforementioned target_compile_definitions(). When you specify a PRIVATE or PUBLIC keyword, CMake will store provided values in the property of the target, in this case, COMPILE_DEFINITIONS. Additionally, if a keyword is INTERFACE or PUBLIC, it will store the value in a property with an INTERFACE_ prefix – INTERFACE_COMPILE_DEFINITIONS. During the configuration stage, CMake will read the interface properties of source targets and append their contents to destination targets. There you have it – propagated properties, or Transitive Usage Requirements, as CMake calls them.

Properties managed with the set_target_properties() command can be found at https://cmake.org/cmake/help/latest/manual/cmake-properties.7.html, in the *Properties on Targets* section (not all target properties are transitive). Here are the most important ones:

- COMPILE_DEFINITIONS

- COMPILE_FEATURES

- COMPILE_OPTIONS

- INCLUDE_DIRECTORIES

- LINK_DEPENDS

- LINK_DIRECTORIES

- LINK_LIBRARIES

- LINK_OPTIONS

- POSITION_INDEPENDENT_CODE

- PRECOMPILE_HEADERS

- SOURCES

We'll discuss most of these options in the following pages, but remember that all of these options are, of course, described in the CMake manual. Find them described in detail at the following link (replace <PROPERTY> with a property that interests you): https://cmake.org/cmake/help/latest/prop_tgt/<PROPERTY>.html

The next question that comes to mind is how far this propagation goes. Are the properties set just on the first destination target, or are they sent to the very top of the dependency graph? You get to decide.

To create a dependency between targets, we use the `target_link_libraries()` command. The full signature of this command requires a propagation keyword:

```
target_link_libraries(<target>
                  <PRIVATE|PUBLIC|INTERFACE> <item>...
                  [<PRIVATE|PUBLIC|INTERFACE> <item>...]...)
```

As you can see, this signature also specifies a propagation keyword, and it controls how properties from the *source target* get stored in the *destination target*. *Figure 5.3* shows what happens to a propagated property during the generation stage (after the configuration stage is completed):

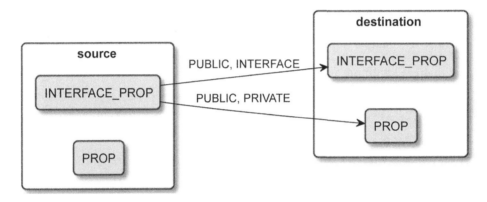

Figure 5.3: How properties are propagated to destination targets

Propagation keywords work like this:

- `PRIVATE` appends the source value to the **private** property of the *source target*.
- `INTERFACE` appends the source value to the **interface** property of the *source target*.
- `PUBLIC` appends to both properties of the *source target*.

As we discussed before, interface properties are only used to propagate the properties further down the chain (to the next *destination target*), and the *source target* won't use them in its build process.

The basic `target_link_libraries(<target> <item>...)` command that we used before implicitly specifies the `PUBLIC` keyword.

If you correctly set propagation keywords for your source targets, properties will be automatically placed on destination targets for you – unless there's a conflict...

Dealing with conflicting propagated properties

When one target depends on multiple other targets, there may be a situation where propagated properties are in outright conflict with each other. Say that one used target specifies the POSITION_INDEPENDENT_CODE property as true and the other as false. CMake understands this as a conflict and will print an error like this:

```
CMake Error: The INTERFACE_POSITION_INDEPENDENT_CODE property of "source
target" does not agree with the value of POSITION_INDEPENDENT_CODE already
determined for "destination_target".
```

It is useful to receive such a message, as we explicitly know that we introduced this conflict, and we need to resolve it. CMake has its own properties that must "agree" between source and destination targets.

On rare occasions, this may become important – for example, if you're building software using the same library in multiple targets that are then linked to a single executable. If these source targets are using different versions of the same library, you may run into problems.

To make sure that we're only using the same specific version, we can create a custom interface property, INTERFACE_LIB_VERSION, and store the version there. This is not enough to solve the problem, as CMake won't propagate custom properties by default (this mechanism works only on built-in target properties). We must explicitly add a custom property to a list of "compatible" properties.

Each target has four such lists:

- COMPATIBLE_INTERFACE_BOOL
- COMPATIBLE_INTERFACE_STRING
- COMPATIBLE_INTERFACE_NUMBER_MAX
- COMPATIBLE_INTERFACE_NUMBER_MIN

Appending your property to one of them will trigger propagation and compatibility checks. The BOOL list will check whether all properties propagated to the destination target evaluate to the same Boolean value. Analogically, STRING will evaluate to a string. NUMBER_MAX and NUMBER_MIN are a bit different – propagated values don't have to match, but the destination target will just receive the highest or the lowest value instead.

This example will help us understand how to apply this in practice:

ch05/02-propagated/CMakeLists.txt

```
cmake_minimum_required(VERSION 3.26)
project(PropagatedProperties CXX)

add_library(source1 empty.cpp)
set_property(TARGET source1 PROPERTY INTERFACE_LIB_VERSION 4)
set_property(TARGET source1 APPEND PROPERTY
             COMPATIBLE_INTERFACE_STRING LIB_VERSION)

add_library(source2 empty.cpp)
set_property(TARGET source2 PROPERTY INTERFACE_LIB_VERSION 4)

add_library(destination empty.cpp)

target_link_libraries(destination source1 source2)
```

We create three targets here; for simplicity, all are using the same empty source file. On both *source targets*, we specify our custom property with the INTERFACE_ prefix, and we set them to the same matching library version. Both *source targets* are linked to the destination target. Finally, we specify a STRING compatibility requirement as a property for source1 (we don't add the INTERFACE_ prefix here).

CMake will propagate this custom property to the *destination target* and check whether the version of all the source targets is an exact match (the compatibility property can be set on just one target).

Now that we understand what regular targets are, let's take a look at other things that look like targets, smell like targets, and sometimes act like targets but, as it turns out, aren't the real deal.

Meet the pseudo targets

The concept of a target is so useful that it would be great if some of its behaviors could be borrowed for other things too; ones that do not represent outputs of the buildsystem but rather inputs – external dependencies, aliases, and so on. These are the pseudo targets, or targets that don't make it to the generated buildsystem:

- Imported targets
- Alias targets

- Interface libraries

Let's take a look.

Imported targets

If you skimmed the table of contents of this book, you know that we'll be talking about how CMake manages external dependencies – other projects, libraries, and so on. IMPORTED targets are essentially products of this process. CMake can define them as a result of the find_package() command.

You can adjust the target properties of such a target: **compile definitions**, **compile options**, **include directories**, and so on – and they will even support Transitive Usage Requirements. However, you should treat them as immutable; don't change their sources or dependencies.

The scope of the definition of an IMPORTED target can be global or local to the directory where it was defined (visible in subdirectories but not in parent directories).

Alias targets

Alias targets do exactly what you expect – they create another reference to a target under a different name. You can create alias targets for executables and libraries with the following commands:

```
add_executable(<name> ALIAS <target>)
add_library(<name> ALIAS <target>)
```

Properties of alias targets are read only, and you cannot install or export aliases (they aren't visible in the generated buildsystem).

So, what is the reason to have aliases at all? They come in handy in scenarios where some part of a project (such as a subdirectory) requires a target with a specific name, and the actual implementation may be available under different names depending on circumstances. For example, you may wish to build a library shipped with your solution or import it based on a user's choice.

Interface libraries

This is an interesting construct – a library that doesn't compile anything but instead serves as a utility target. Its whole concept is built around propagated properties (Transitive Usage Requirements).

Interface libraries have two primary uses – to represent header-only libraries, and to bundle a bunch of propagated properties into a single logical unit.

Header-only libraries are fairly easy to create with `add_library(INTERFACE)`:

```
add_library(Eigen INTERFACE
  src/eigen.h src/vector.h src/matrix.h
)
target_include_directories(Eigen INTERFACE
  $<BUILD_INTERFACE:${CMAKE_CURRENT_SOURCE_DIR}/src>
  $<INSTALL_INTERFACE:include/Eigen>
)
```

In the preceding snippet, we created an Eigen interface library with three headers. Next, using **generator expressions** (these are indicated with dollar sign and angle brackets, $<...>$ and will be explained in the next chapter), we set its **include directories** to be `${CMAKE_CURRENT_SOURCE_DIR}/src` when a target is exported and `include/Eigen` when it's installed (which will also be explained at the end of this chapter).

To use such a library, we just must link it:

```
target_link_libraries(executable Eigen)
```

No actual linking occurs here, but CMake will understand this command as a request to propagate all the `INTERFACE` properties to the executable target.

The second use case leverages exactly the same mechanism but for a different purpose – it creates a logical target that can be a placeholder for propagated properties. We can then use this target as a dependency for other targets and set properties in a clean, convenient way. Here's an example:

```
add_library(warning_properties INTERFACE)
target_compile_options(warning_properties INTERFACE
  -Wall -Wextra -Wpedantic
)
target_link_libraries(executable warning_properties)
```

The `add_library(INTERFACE)` command creates a logical `warning_properties` target that is used to set **compile options** specified in the second command on the executable target. I recommend using these `INTERFACE` targets, as they improve the readability and reusability of your code. Think of it as refactoring a bunch of magic values to a well-named variable. I also suggest explicitly adding a suffix like `_properties` to easily differentiate interface libraries from the regular ones.

Object libraries

Object libraries are used to group multiple source files under a single logical target and are compile them into (.o) *object files* during a build. To create an *object library*, we follow the same method as with other libraries, but with the OBJECT keyword:

```
add_library(<target> OBJECT <sources>)
```

Object files produced during the build can be incorporated as compiled elements to other targets with the $<TARGET_OBJECTS:objlib> generator expression:

```
add_library(... $<TARGET_OBJECTS:objlib> ...)
add_executable(... $<TARGET_OBJECTS:objlib> ...)
```

Alternatively, you can add them as dependencies with the target_link_libraries() command.

In the context of our Calc library, *object libraries* will be useful to avoid redundant compilation of library sources for the static and shared versions of the library. It's essential to explicitly compile the *object files* with POSITION_INDEPENDENT_CODE enabled, a prerequisite for shared libraries.

Returning to the project's targets: calc_obj will supply compiled *object files*, which then will be used for both the calc_static and calc_shared libraries. Let's explore the practical distinctions between these two types of libraries and understand why one might opt to create both.

Are pseudo targets exhausting the concept of the target? Of course not! That would simply be too easy. We still need to understand how these targets are then used to generate buildsystems.

Build targets

The term "target" can have different meanings depending on the context within a project and the generated buildsystems. In the context of generating a buildsystem, CMake "compiles" the listfiles written in the CMake language into the language of the selected build tool, such as creating a Makefile for GNU Make. These generated Makefiles have their own set of targets. Some of these targets are direct conversions of the targets defined in the listfiles, while others are created implicitly as part of the buildsystem generation process.

One such buildsystem target is ALL, which CMake generates by default to contain all top-level listfile targets, such as executables and libraries (not necessarily custom targets). ALL is built when we run cmake --build <build tree> without choosing any specific target. As you might remember from the first chapter, you can choose one by adding the --target <name> parameter to the cmake build command.

Some executables or libraries might not be needed in every build, but we'd like to keep them as part of the project for those rare occasions when they come in useful. To optimize our default build, we can exclude them from the ALL target like so:

```
add_executable(<name> EXCLUDE_FROM_ALL [<source>...])
add_library(<name> EXCLUDE_FROM_ALL [<source>...])
```

Custom targets work the other way around – by default, they're excluded from the ALL target unless you explicitly add them with an ALL keyword, as we did in the BankApp example.

Another implicitly defined build target is clean, which simply removes produced artifacts from the build tree. We use it to get rid of all old files and build everything from scratch. It's important, though, to understand that it doesn't just simply delete everything in the build directory. For clean to work correctly, you need to manually specify any files that your custom targets might create as BYPRODUCTS (see the BankApp example).

This concludes our journey through targets and their different aspects: we know how to create them, configure their properties, use pseudo targets, and decide whether they should be built by default or not. There's also an interesting non-target mechanism to create custom artifacts that can be used in all actual targets – **custom commands** (not to be confused with **custom targets**).

Writing custom commands

Using custom targets has one drawback – as soon as you add them to the ALL target or start depending on them for other targets, they will be built every single time. Sometimes, this is what you want, but there are cases when custom behavior is necessary to produce files that shouldn't be recreated without reason:

- Generating a source code file that another target depends on
- Translating another language into C++
- Executing a custom action immediately before or after another target was built

There are two signatures for a custom command. The first one is an extended version of add_custom_target():

```
add_custom_command(OUTPUT output1 [output2 ...]
                   COMMAND command1 [ARGS] [args1...]
                   [COMMAND command2 [ARGS] [args2...] ...]
                   [MAIN_DEPENDENCY depend]
                   [DEPENDS [depends...]]
```

```
                    [BYPRODUCTS [files...]]
                    [IMPLICIT_DEPENDS <lang1> depend1
                                      [<lang2> depend2] ...]
                    [WORKING_DIRECTORY dir]
                    [COMMENT comment]
                    [DEPFILE depfile]
                    [JOB_POOL job_pool]
                    [VERBATIM] [APPEND] [USES_TERMINAL]
                    [COMMAND_EXPAND_LISTS])
```

As you might have guessed, a custom command doesn't create a logical target, but just like custom targets, it has to be added to a dependency graph. There are two ways of doing that – using its output artifact as a source for an executable (or library), or explicitly adding it to a DEPENDS list for a custom target.

Using a custom command as a generator

Admittedly, not every project needs to generate C++ code from other files. One such occasion might be a compilation of **Google's Protocol Buffer's (Protobuf's)** .proto files. If you're not familiar with this library, Protobuf is a platform-neutral binary serializer for structured data.

In other words: it can be used to encode objects to and from binary streams: files or network connections. To keep Protobuf cross-platform and fast at the same time, Google's engineers invented their own Protobuf language that defines models in .proto files, such as this one:

```
message Person {
  required string name = 1;
  required int32 id = 2;
  optional string email = 3;
}
```

Such a file can be then used to encode data in multiple languages – C++, Ruby, Go, Python, Java, and so on. Google provides a compiler, protoc, that reads .proto files and outputs structure and serialization source code valid for the chosen language (that later needs to be compiled or interpreted). Smart engineers don't check those generated source files into a repository but will use the original Protobuf format and add a step to generate the source files to the build chain.

We don't know yet how to detect whether (and where) a Protobuf compiler is available on the target host (we'll learn this in *Chapter 9, Managing Dependencies in CMake*). So, for now, let's just assume that the compiler's protoc command is residing in a location known to the system. We have prepared a person.proto file and we know that the Protobuf compiler will output person.pb.h and person.pb.cc files. Here's how we would define a custom command to compile them:

```
add_custom_command(OUTPUT person.pb.h person.pb.cc
        COMMAND protoc ARGS person.proto
        DEPENDS person.proto
)
```

Then, to allow serialization in our executable, we can just add output files to the sources:

```
add_executable(serializer serializer.cpp person.pb.cc)
```

Assuming we dealt correctly with the inclusion of header files and linking the Protobuf library, everything will compile and update automatically when we introduce changes to the .proto file.

A simplified (and much less practical) example would be to create the necessary header by copying it from another location:

ch05/03-command/CMakeLists.txt

```
add_executable(main main.cpp constants.h)
target_include_directories(main PRIVATE ${CMAKE_BINARY_DIR})
add_custom_command(OUTPUT constants.h COMMAND cp
                ARGS "${CMAKE_SOURCE_DIR}/template.xyz" constants.h)
```

Our "compiler", in this case, is the cp command. It fulfills a dependency of the main target by creating a constants.h file in the build tree root, simply by copying it from the source tree.

Using a custom command as a target hook

The second version of the add_custom_command() command introduces a mechanism to execute commands before or after building a target:

```
add_custom_command(TARGET <target>
                PRE_BUILD | PRE_LINK | POST_BUILD
                COMMAND command1 [ARGS] [args1...]
                [COMMAND command2 [ARGS] [args2...] ...]
                [BYPRODUCTS [files...]]
                [WORKING_DIRECTORY dir]
```

```
                    [COMMENT comment]
                    [VERBATIM] [USES_TERMINAL]
                    [COMMAND_EXPAND_LISTS])
```

We specify what target we'd like to "enhance" with the new behavior in the first argument and under the following conditions:

- `PRE_BUILD` will run before any other rules for this target (Visual Studio generators only; for others, it behaves like `PRE_LINK`).

- `PRE_LINK` binds the command to be run just after all sources have been compiled but before the linking (or archiving) of the target. It doesn't work for custom targets.

- `POST_BUILD` will run after all other rules have been executed for this target.

Using this version of `add_custom_command()`, we can replicate the generation of the checksum from the previous BankApp example:

ch05/04-command/CMakeLists.txt

```
cmake_minimum_required(VERSION 3.26)
project(Command CXX)
add_executable(main main.cpp)
add_custom_command(TARGET main POST_BUILD
                   COMMAND cksum
                   ARGS "$<TARGET_FILE:main>" > "main.ck")
```

After the build of the `main` executable completes, CMake will execute `cksum` with the provided arguments. But what is happening in the first argument? It's not a variable, as then it would be wrapped in curly braces (`${}`), not in angle brackets (`$<>`). It's a **generator expression** evaluating to a full path to the target's binary file. This mechanism is useful in the context of many target properties, which we'll explain in the next chapter.

Summary

Understanding targets is critical to writing clean, modern CMake projects. In this chapter, we have not only discussed what constitutes a target and how to define three different types of targets: executables, libraries, and custom targets. We have also explained how targets depend on each other through a dependency graph and we learned how to visualize it using the Graphviz module. With this general understanding, we were able to learn about the key feature of targets – properties. We not only went through a few commands to set regular properties on targets but we also solved the mystery of Transitive Usage Requirements also known as propagated properties.

This was a hard one to crack, as we had to not only understand how to control which properties are propagated but also how that propagation affects subsequent targets. Furthermore, we discovered how to guarantee the compatibility of properties consumed from multiple sources.

We then briefly discussed pseudo targets: imported targets, alias targets, and interface libraries. All of them will come in handy later in our projects, especially when we know how to connect them with propagated properties for our benefit. Then, we talked about generated build targets and how the configuration stage affects them. Afterward, we spent some time looking at a mechanism that is similar to targets, but not exactly it: the custom commands. We touched on how they can generate files consumed by other targets (compiled, translated, and so on) and their hooking function: executing additional steps when a target is built.

With such a solid foundation, we are ready for the next topic – compiling C++ sources into executables and libraries.

Further reading

For more information on the topics covered in this chapter, you can refer to the following:

- Graphviz module documentation:
  `https://gitlab.kitware.com/cmake/community/-/wikis/doc/cmake/Graphviz`,
  `https://cmake.org/cmake/help/latest/module/CMakeGraphVizOptions.html`

- Graphviz software:
  `https://graphviz.org`

- CMake target properties:
  `https://cmake.org/cmake/help/latest/manual/cmake-`
  `properties.7.html#properties-on-targets`

- Transitive Usage Requirements:
  `https://cmake.org/cmake/help/latest/manual/cmake-`
  `buildsystem.7.html#transitive-usage-requirements`

Join our community on Discord

Join our community's Discord space for discussions with the author and other readers:

https://discord.com/invite/vXN53A7ZcA

6

Using Generator Expressions

Many CMake users don't encounter generator expressions in their private explorations as they are quite advanced concepts. However, they are crucial for projects that are preparing for the general availability stage, or first release to the wider audience, as they play an important role in exporting, installing, and packaging. If you're trying to just learn the basics of CMake quickly and focus on the C++ aspect, feel free to skip this chapter for now and return to it later. On the other hand, we discuss generator expressions at this time, because the following chapters will reference this knowledge when explaining the more in-depth aspects of CMake.

We'll start by introducing the subject of generator expressions: what they are, what their uses are, and how they are formed and expanded. This will be followed by a short presentation of the nesting mechanism and a more thorough description of the conditional expansion, which allows the use of Boolean logic, comparison operations, and queries. Of course, we'll do a deep dive into the vastness of the available expressions.

But first, we'll study the transformations of strings, lists, and paths, as it's good to get the basics out of the way before focusing on the main subject. Ultimately, generator expressions are used in practice to fetch the information available in later stages of building and present it in the appropriate context. Determining that context is a huge part of their value. We'll discover how to parametrize our build process based on the build configuration selected by the user, the platform at hand, and the current toolchain. That is, what compiler is being used, what its version is, and which capabilities it has, that's not all: we'll figure out how to query the properties of build targets and their related information.

To make sure we can fully appreciate the value of the generator expressions, I have included a few interesting examples of use as the final part of this chapter. Oh, and there's a quick explanation of how to see the output of generator expressions as this is a bit tricky. Don't worry though, generator expressions aren't as complex as they might seem, and you will be using them in no time.

In this chapter, we're going to cover the following main topics:

- What are generator expressions?
- Learning the basic rules of general expression syntax
- Conditional expansion
- Querying and transforming
- Trying out examples

Technical requirements

You can find the code files that are present in this chapter on GitHub at `https://github.com/PacktPublishing/Modern-CMake-for-Cpp-2E/tree/main/examples/ch06`.

To build the examples provided in this book, always use the recommended commands:

```
cmake -B <build tree> -S <source tree>
cmake --build <build tree>
```

Be sure to replace the `<build tree>` and `<source tree>` placeholders with appropriate paths. As a reminder: **build tree** is the path to the target/output directory and **source tree** is the path at which your source code is located.

What are generator expressions?

CMake is building the solution in three stages: configuration, generation, and running the build tool. Generally, all the required data is available during the configuration stage. However, occasionally, we encounter a situation similar to the "chicken and the egg" paradox. Take an example from the *Using a custom command as a target hook* section in *Chapter 5, Working with Targets* – where a target needs to know the path of a binary artifact of another target. Unfortunately, this information becomes available only after all the listfiles are parsed and the configuration stage is complete.

So, how do we tackle such a problem? One solution could be to create a placeholder for the information and delay its evaluation until the next stage – the **generation stage**.

This is precisely what generator expressions (also referred to as "genexes") do. They are built around target properties such as LINK_LIBRARIES, INCLUDE_DIRECTORIES, COMPILE_DEFINITIONS, and propagated properties, although not all. They follow rules similar to the conditional statements and variable evaluation.

 Generator expressions will be evaluated at the generation stage (when the configuration is complete and the buildsystem is created), which means that capturing their output into a variable and printing it to the console is not straightforward.

There's a significant number of generator expressions, and in a way, they constitute their own, domain-specific language – language that supports conditional expressions, logical operations, comparisons, transformations, queries, and ordering. Utilizing generator expressions enables manipulation and queries of strings, lists, version numbers, shell paths, configurations, and build targets. In this chapter, we will provide brief overviews of these concepts, focusing on the essentials since they are less necessary in most cases. Our primary focus will be on the main application of generator expressions, which involves gathering information from the generated configuration of targets and the state of the build environment. For full reference, it's best to read the official CMake manual online (see the *Further reading* section for the URL).

Everything is better explained with an example, so let's jump right into it, and describe the syntax of generator expressions.

Learning the basic rules of general expression syntax

To use generator expressions, we'll need to add them to a CMake listfile through a command that supports generator expression evaluation. Most of the target-specific commands do, and there are plenty of others (review the official documentation of a particular command to learn more). A command that is often used with generator exception is target_compile_definitions(). To use a generator expression, we'll need to provide it as a command argument like so:

```
target_compile_definitions(foo PUBLIC BAR=$<TARGET_FILE:baz>)
```

This command adds a -D definition flag to the compiler's arguments (ignore PUBLIC for now) that sets the BAR preprocessor definition to *the path* at which the **binary artifact** of the foo target will be produced. This works because the generator expression is stored in the current form in a variable. The expansion is effectively postponed until the generation stage when many things are fully configured and known.

How is the generator expression formed?

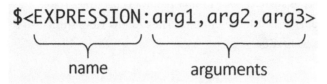

Figure 6.1: The syntax of a generator expression

As you can see in *Figure 6.1*, the structure seems fairly simple and readable:

- Open with a dollar and a bracket ($<).
- Add the EXPRESSION name.
- If an expression requires arguments, add a colon (:) and provide the arg1, arg2 … argN values, separated with a comma (,).
- Close the expression with >.

There are expressions that do not require any arguments, such as $<PLATFORM_ID>.

It's important to note that unless explicitly stated otherwise, expressions are typically evaluated in the context of the target using the expression. This association is inferred from the command in which the expression is used. In the previous example, we saw how target_compile_definitions() provides foo as the target it operates on. The target-specific generator expressions used in that command will therefore implicitly use foo. Do note, however, that the generator expression used in the example, $<TARGET_FILE>, requires the target attribute as the context to operate on. There are other generator expressions that don't accept targets as arguments (like $<COMPILE_LANGUAGE>), and will implicitly use the target of the enclosing command. These will be discussed in more detail later.

Generator expressions can quickly become very confusing and complicated when using their more advanced features, so it's important to understand their specifics beforehand.

Nesting

Let's start with the ability to pass a generator expression as an argument to another generator expression or, in other words, generator expression nesting:

```
$<UPPER_CASE:$<PLATFORM_ID>>
```

This isn't a very complex example, but it's easy to imagine what happens when we increase nesting levels and work with commands using multiple arguments.

To complicate matters even further, it's possible to add a regular variable expansion to the mix:

```
$<UPPER_CASE:${my_variable}>
```

The `my_variable` variable will be expanded first, at the configuration stage. Subsequently, the generation expression will be expanded at the generation stage. There are some rare uses for this feature, but I strongly recommend avoiding it: generator expressions provide virtually all necessary functions. Mixing regular variables into these expressions adds a layer of indirection that is hard to debug. Additionally, information collected in the config stage will often be outdated, as users will override values used in generator expressions through command-line parameters at the build or installation stage.

Having covered the syntax, let's move on to discuss the fundamental mechanisms available in generator expressions.

Conditional expansion

Determining whether an expression should be expanded is supported with Boolean logic in generator expressions. While this is a great feature, its syntax can be inconsistent and difficult to read due to legacy reasons. It's available in two forms. The first form supports both happy and sad paths:

```
$<IF:condition,true_string,false_string>
```

The `IF` expression relies on nesting to be useful: you can replace any of the arguments with another expression and produce quite complex evaluations (you can even nest one `IF` condition in another). This form requires exactly three arguments, so we can't omit anything. Our best option to skip a value in case of an unmet condition is the following:

```
$<IF:condition,true_string,>
```

There's a shorthand version that allows you to skip the `IF` keyword and the comma:

```
$<condition:true_string>
```

As you can see, it breaks the convention of providing the `EXPRESSION` name as the first token. I assume that the intention here was to shorten the expression and avoid typing those precious few characters, but the outcome can be really hard to rationalize. Here's one example from the CMake documentation:

```
$<$<AND:$<COMPILE_LANGUAGE:CXX>,$<CXX_COMPILER_ID:AppleClan
  g,Clang>>:COMPILING_CXX_WITH_CLANG>
```

This expression returns `COMPILING_CXX_WITH_CLANG` only for C++ code compiled with one of the Clang compilers. (it returns an empty string in all other cases). I wish the syntax was aligned with conditions for the regular `IF` command, but sadly that's not the case. Now, you can recognize the second form if you see it somewhere, but you should avoid it in your own projects for the sake of readability.

Evaluating to Boolean

Generator expressions are evaluated to one of two types – Boolean or string. Boolean is represented by 1 (true) and 0 (false). There are no dedicated numerical types; everything that isn't a Boolean is just a string.

It's important to remember that nested expressions passed as conditions in conditional expressions are explicitly required to evaluate to Boolean.

Boolean types can be converted to strings implicitly, but you'll need to use an explicit `BOOL` operator (explained ahead) to do the opposite.

There are three categories of expressions that get evaluated to Boolean: logical operators, comparison expressions, and queries. Let's take a quick look at these types.

Logical operators

There are four logical operators:

- `$<NOT:arg>`: This negates the Boolean argument.
- `$<AND:arg1,arg2,arg3...>`: This returns true if all the arguments are true.
- `$<OR:arg1,arg2,arg3...>`: This returns true if any of the arguments is true.
- `$<BOOL:string_arg>`: This converts arguments from a string to a Boolean type.

String conversion with `$<BOOL>` will evaluate to Boolean true (1) if none of these conditions are met:

- The string is empty.
- The string is a case-insensitive equivalent of `0`, `FALSE`, `OFF`, `N`, `NO`, `IGNORE`, or `NOTFOUND`.
- The string ends in the `-NOTFOUND` suffix (case-sensitive).

Comparisons

Comparisons will evaluate to 1 if their condition is met and 0 otherwise. Here are a few of the most common operations that you might find useful:

- `$<STREQUAL:arg1,arg2>`: This compares strings in a case-sensitive fashion.

- `$<EQUAL:arg1,arg2>`: This converts a string to a number and compares equality.

- `$<IN_LIST:arg,list>`: This checks whether the arg element is in the list list (case sensitive).

- `$<VERSION_EQUAL:v1,v2>`, `$<VERSION_LESS:v1,v2>`, `$<VERSION_GREATER:v1,v2>`, `$<VERSION_LESS_EQUAL:v1,v2>`, and `$<VERSION_GREATER_EQUAL:v1,v2>` compare versions in a component-wise fashion.

- `$<PATH_EQUAL:path1,path2>`: This compares the lexical representations of two paths without any normalization (since CMake 3.24).

Queries

Queries simply return the Boolean value directly from a variable, or as a result of an operation. One of the simplest queries is:

```
$<TARGET_EXISTS:arg>
```

As you might guess, it returns true if the target was defined in the configuration stage.

Now, you know how to apply conditional expansion, use logical operators, comparison, and basic queries to evaluate to Boolean. That is useful on its own, but generator expressions have much more to offer, especially in the context of queries: they can be used in the IF conditional expansion, or on their own as arguments to commands. It's time to introduce them in an appropriate context.

Querying and transforming

Many generator expressions are available, but to avoid getting lost in the weeds, let's focus on the most common ones. We'll start with some basic transformations of the available data.

Dealing with strings, lists, and paths

Generator expressions provide only the bare minimum of operations to transform and query data structures. Working with strings in the generator stage is possible with the following expressions:

- `$<LOWER_CASE:string>`, `$<UPPER_CASE:string>`: This converts to string to the required case.

List operations were fairly limited until recently. Since CMake 3.15, the following operations have been available:

- `$<IN_LIST:string,list>`: This returns true if list contains a string value.

- `$<JOIN:list,d>`: This joins a semicolon-separated list using a d delimiter.

- `$<REMOVE_DUPLICATES:list>`: This deduplicates list (without sorting).

- `$<FILTER:list,INCLUDE|EXCLUDE,regex>`: This includes/excludes items from `list` using a regex.

Since 3.27, the `$<LIST:OPERATION>` generator expressions were added, where `OPERATION` is one of:

- `LENGTH`
- `GET`
- `SUBLIST`
- `FIND`
- `JOIN`
- `APPEND`
- `PREPEND`
- `INSERT`
- `POP_BACK`
- `POP_FRONT`
- `REMOVE_ITEM`
- `REMOVE_AT`
- `REMOVE_DUPLICATES`
- `FILTER`
- `TRANSFORM`
- `REVERSE`
- `SORT`

It's rather rare to work with lists in generator expressions, so we're only indicating what's possible. If you find yourself in one of these cases, see the online manual for instructions on how to use these operations.

Finally, we can query and transform the system paths. It's a useful addition because of its portability across different operating systems. The following simple queries have been available since CMake 3.24:

- `$<PATH:HAS_ROOT_NAME,path>`
- `$<PATH:HAS_ROOT_DIRECTORY,path>`
- `$<PATH:HAS_ROOT_PATH,path>`
- `$<PATH:HAS_FILENAME,path>`

- `$<PATH:HAS_EXTENSION,path>`
- `$<PATH:HAS_STEM,path>`
- `$<PATH:HAS_RELATIVE_PART,path>`
- `$<PATH:HAS_PARENT_PATH,path>`
- `$<PATH:IS_ABSOLUTE,path>`
- `$<PATH:IS_RELATIVE,path>`
- `$<PATH:IS_PREFIX[,NORMALIZE],prefix,path>`: This returns true if prefix is the prefix of path

Analogically, we can retrieve all the path components we were able to check for (since CMake 3.27, it's been possible to provide a list of paths rather than just one path):

- `$<PATH:GET_ROOT_NAME,path...>`
- `$<PATH:GET_ROOT_DIRECTORY,path...>`
- `$<PATH:GET_ROOT_PATH,path...>`
- `$<PATH:GET_FILENAME,path...>`
- `$<PATH:GET_EXTENSION[,LAST_ONLY],path...>`
- `$<PATH:GET_STEM[,LAST_ONLY],path...>`
- `$<PATH:GET_RELATIVE_PART,path...>`
- `$<PATH:GET_PARENT_PATH,path...>`

Additionally, some transform operations were introduced in 3.24; we'll just list them for completeness:

- `$<PATH:CMAKE_PATH[,NORMALIZE],path...>`
- `$<PATH:APPEND,path...,input,...>`
- `$<PATH:REMOVE_FILENAME,path...>`
- `$<PATH:REPLACE_FILENAME,path...,input>`
- `$<PATH:REMOVE_EXTENSION[,LAST_ONLY],path...>`
- `$<PATH:REPLACE_EXTENSION[,LAST_ONLY],path...,input>`
- `$<PATH:NORMAL_PATH,path...>`
- `$<PATH:RELATIVE_PATH,path...,base_directory>`
- `$<PATH:ABSOLUTE_PATH[,NORMALIZE],path...,base_directory>`

There's one more path operation, which formats the provided path to the style supported by the shell of the host: `$<SHELL_PATH:path...>`.

Again, previous expressions are introduced for later reference, not as information that you need to memorize right now. The bulk of the recommended practical knowledge is detailed in the subsequent sections.

Parametrizing the build configuration and platform

One of the key pieces of information that CMake users will provide when building a project is the desired build configuration. In most cases, it will be Debug or Release. We can use the generator expressions to access these values through the following statements:

- $<CONFIG>: This returns the current build configuration as a string: Debug, Release, or another.
- $<CONFIG:configs>: This returns true if configs contains the current build configuration (case-insensitive comparison).

We discussed the platform in the *Chapter 4, Setting Up Your First CMake Project* in the *Understanding the build environment* section. We can read related information the same way as with configuration:

- $<PLATFORM_ID>: This returns the current platform ID as a string: Linux, Windows, or Darwin for macOS.
- $<PLATFORM_ID:platform> is true if platform contains the current platform ID.

Such configuration or platform-specific parametrization is a powerful addition to our toolbelt. We can use it in conjunction with the conditional expansion we discussed earlier:

```
$<IF:condition,true_string,false_string>
```

For example, we may apply one compilation flag when building test binaries, and another for production:

```
target_compile_definitions(my_target PRIVATE
                        $<IF:$<CONFIG:Debug>,Test,Production>
)
```

But this is just the beginning. There are plenty of other circumstances we can address with generator expressions. Of course, the next important aspect is the tooling present in the system.

Tuning for toolchain

Toolchains, toolkits, or, simply, compilers and linkers luckily (sadly?) aren't consistent across vendors. This has all sorts of consequences. Some of them are great (better performance in special cases), others not so much (varied configuration flavors, discrepancies in flag naming, and more).

Generator expressions help here by providing sets of queries that can be utilized to alleviate problems and opportunistically improve user experience where possible.

As with the build configurations and platform, there are multiple expressions that return information about the toolchain, both as string and Boolean. However, we're required to specify which language we're interested in (replace #LNG with one of C, CXX, CUDA, OBJC, OBJCXX, Fortran, HIP, or ISPC). Support for HIP was added in 3.21.

- `$<#LNG_COMPILER_ID>`: This returns CMake's compiler ID of the #LNG compiler used.
- `$<#LNG_COMPILER_VERSION>`: This returns CMake's compiler version of the #LNG compiler used.

To check which compiler will execute for C++, we should use the `$<CXX_COMPILER_ID>` generator expression. The returned value, the CMake's compiler ID, is a constant defined for every supported compiler. You may encounter values like AppleClang, ARMCC, Clang, GNU, Intel, and MSVC. For the full list, check the official documentation (URL in the *Further reading* section).

Similarly to the previous section, we can also utilize the toolchain information in conditional expressions. There are multiple queries that return true if any of the provided arguments matches a specific value:

- `$<#LNG_COMPILER_ID:ids>`: This returns true if ids contains CMake's #LNG compiler ID.
- `$<#LNG_COMPILER_VERSION:vers>`: This returns true if vers contains the CMake's #LNG compiler version.
- `$<COMPILE_FEATURES:features>`: This returns true if all features provided in features are supported by the compiler for this target.

Inside commands requiring a target argument, like `target_compile_definitions()`, we can use one of the target-specific expressions to get a string value:

- `$<COMPILE_LANGUAGE>`: This returns the language of source files at the compilation step.
- `$<LINK_LANGUAGE>`: This returns the language of source files at the link step.

To evaluate a simple Boolean query:

- `$<COMPILE_LANGUAGE:langs>`: This returns true if langs contains a language used for the compilation of this target. This can be used to provide language-specific flags to the compiler. For example, to compile C++ sources of the target with the `-fno-exceptions` flag:

```
target_compile_options(myapp
  PRIVATE $<$<COMPILE_LANGUAGE:CXX>:-fno-exceptions>
)
```

- `$<LINK_LANGUAGE:langs>` – It follows the same rules as `COMPILE_LANGUAGE` and returns true if `langs` contains a language used for linking of this target.

Or, to query more complex scenarios:

- `$<COMPILE_LANG_AND_ID:lang,compiler_ids...>`: This returns true if the `lang` language is used for this target, and one of the compilers in the `compiler_ids` list will be used for this compilation. This expression is useful to specify compile definitions for specific compilers:

```
target_compile_definitions(myapp PRIVATE
  $<$<COMPILE_LANG_AND_ID:CXX,AppleClang,Clang>:CXX_CLANG>
  $<$<COMPILE_LANG_AND_ID:CXX,Intel>:CXX_INTEL>
  $<$<COMPILE_LANG_AND_ID:C,Clang>:C_CLANG>
)
```

- In this example, for C++ sources (`CXX`) compiled with `AppleClang` or `Clang`, the `-DCXX_CLANG` definition will be set. For the C++ sources compiled with the `Intel` compiler, the `-DCXX_INTEL` definition flag will be set. Lastly, for the C sources (`C`) compiled with the `Clang` compiler, we'll set a `-DC_CLANG` definition.
- `$<LINK_LANG_AND_ID:lang,compiler_ids...>`: This works like `COMPILE_LANG_AND_ID`, but checks the language used for the link step instead. Use this expression to specify link libraries, link options, link directories, and link dependencies of a particular language and a linker combination in a target.

An important note to make here is that a single target can be combined from sources of multiple languages. For example, it's possible to link C artifacts with C++ (but we should declare both languages in the `project()` command). Therefore, generator expressions referencing a specific language will be used for some source files, but not for others.

Let's move on to the next important category: target-related generator expressions.

Querying target-related information

There are plenty of generator expressions that query target properties and check target-related information. Note that until CMake 3.19, many target expressions referencing another target were used to automatically create a dependency between them. This no longer happens in the latest versions of CMake.

Some generator expressions will infer the target from the command being called; the most commonly used is the basic query that returns the target's property value:

```
$<TARGET_PROPERTY:prop>
```

- Less known, but useful in the `target_link_libraries()` command, is the `$<LINK_ONLY:deps>` generator expression. It allows us to store the `PRIVATE` link dependencies, which won't be propagated through transitive usage requirements; these are used in interface libraries, which we discussed in *Chapter 5, Working with Targets*, in the *Understanding the transitive usage requirements* section.

There also is a set of install and export-related expressions, which infer their targets from the context they're being used. We'll discuss them in depth in *Chapter 14, Installing and Packaging*, so we can just have a quick introduction for now:

- `$<INSTALL_PREFIX>`: This returns the install prefix when the target is exported with `install(EXPORT)` or when evaluated in `INSTALL_NAME_DIR`; otherwise, it is empty.
- `$<INSTALL_INTERFACE:string>`: This returns `string` when the expression is exported with `install(EXPORT)`.
- `$<BUILD_INTERFACE:string>`: This returns `string` when the expression is exported with the `export()` command or by another target in the same buildsystem.
- `$<BUILD_LOCAL_INTERFACE:string>`: This returns `string` when the expression is exported by another target in the same buildsystem.

However, most queries require the target name to be explicitly provided as the first argument:

- `$<TARGET_EXISTS:target>`: This returns true if the target exists.
- `$<TARGET_NAME_IF_EXISTS:target>`: This returns the target name if the target exists and an empty string otherwise.
- `$<TARGET_PROPERTY:target,prop>`: This returns the `prop` property value for the target.
- `$<TARGET_OBJECTS:target>`: This returns a list of *object files* for an *object library* target.

You can query the path of the target artifact:

- `$<TARGET_FILE:target>`: This returns the full path.
- `$<TARGET_FILE_NAME:target>`: This returns just the filename.
- `$<TARGET_FILE_BASE_NAME:target>`: This returns the base name.
- `$<TARGET_FILE_NAME:target>`: This returns the base name without the prefix or suffix (for `libmylib.so` the base name would be `mylib`).
- `$<TARGET_FILE_PREFIX:target>`: This returns just the prefix (for example, `lib`).
- `$<TARGET_FILE_SUFFIX:target>`: This returns just the suffix (for example, `.so` or `.exe`).
- `$<TARGET_FILE_DIR:target>`: This returns the directory.

There are families of expressions that offer similar functionality as the regular TARGET_FILE expression (each expression also accepts the _NAME, _BASE_NAME or _DIR suffix):

- TARGET_LINKER_FILE: This queries the path of the file used when linking to the target. Usually, it is the library produced by the target (.a, .lib, .so). However, on platforms with **Dynamic-Link Libraries** (**DLLs**), it will be a .lib import library associated with the target's DLL.
- TARGET_PDB_FILE: This queries the path of the linker-generated program database file (.pdb).

Managing libraries is a complex topic, and CMake offers a lot of generator expressions to help. However, we'll postpone introducing them until they become relevant in *Chapter 8, Linking Executables and Libraries*.

Finally, there are some Apple package-specific expressions as well:

- $<TARGET_BUNDLE_DIR:target>: This is the full path to the bundle directory (my.app, my.framework, or my.bundle) for the target.
- $<TARGET_BUNDLE_CONTENT_DIR:target>: This is the full path to the bundle content directory for the target. On macOS, it's my.app/Contents, my.framework, or my.bundle/Contents. Other **Software Development Kits** (**SDKs**) (such as iOS) have a flat bundle structure – my.app, my.framework, or my.bundle.

These are the main generator expressions for dealing with targets. It's worth knowing, there's plenty more. I recommend referring to the official documentation for a complete list.

Escaping

On a rare occasion, you may need to pass a character to a generator expression that has a special meaning. To escape this behavior, use the following expressions:

- $<ANGLE-R>: This a literal > symbol
- $<COMMA>: This a literal , symbol
- $<SEMICOLON>: This a literal ; symbol

The last expression can be useful to prevent list expansion when an argument containing ; is used.

Now that we have introduced all the queries and transformations, we can see how they work in practice. Let's go through some examples of applications.

Trying out examples

Everything is easier to grasp when there's a good practical example to support the theory. Obviously, we'd like to write some CMake code and try it out. However, since generator expressions aren't evaluated until after the configuration is complete, we cannot use any configuration-time commands like message() to experiment. We need to use some special tricks instead. To debug generator expressions, you can use either of these methods:

- Write it to a file (this particular version of the file() command supports generator expressions): file(GENERATE OUTPUT filename CONTENT "$<...>")
- Add a custom target and build it explicitly from the command line: add_custom_target(gendbg COMMAND ${CMAKE_COMMAND} -E echo "$<...>")

I recommend the first option for simpler practice. Remember, though, that we won't be able to use all the expressions in these commands, as some are target specific. Having covered this, let's look at some of the uses for generator expressions.

Build configurations

In *Chapter 1*, *First Steps with CMake*, we discussed the build type, specifying which configuration we are building – Debug, Release, and so on. There may be cases where you'd like to act differently based on what kind of build you're making. A simple and easy way to do so is by utilizing the $<CONFIG> generator expression:

```
target_compile_options(tgt $<$<CONFIG:DEBUG>:-ginline-points>)
```

The preceding example checks whether the config equals DEBUG; if that's the case, the nested expression is evaluated to 1. The outer shorthand if expression then becomes true, and our -ginline-points debug flag gets added to the options. It's important to know this form, so you'll be able to understand such expressions in other projects, but I'd recommend using the more verbose $<IF:...> for better readability.

System-specific one liners

Generator expressions can also be used to compact verbose if commands into neat one liners. Let's suppose we have the following code:

```
if (${CMAKE_SYSTEM_NAME} STREQUAL "Linux")
    target_compile_definitions(myProject PRIVATE LINUX=1)
endif()
```

It tells the compiler to add `-DLINUX=1` to the arguments if this is the target system. While this isn't terribly long, it could be replaced with a fairly simple expression:

```
target_compile_definitions(myProject PRIVATE
                            $<$<CMAKE_SYSTEM_NAME:LINUX>:LINUX=1>)
```

Such code works well, but there's a limit to how much you can pack into a generator expression until it becomes too hard to read. On top of that, many CMake users postpone learning about generator expressions and have trouble following what happens. Luckily, we won't have such problems after completing this chapter.

Interface libraries with compiler-specific flags

Interface libraries, as we discussed in *Chapter 5*, *Working with Targets*, can be used to provide flags to match the compiler:

```
add_library(enable_rtti INTERFACE)
target_compile_options(enable_rtti INTERFACE
  $<$<OR:$<COMPILER_ID:GNU>,$<COMPILER_ID:Clang>>:-rtti>
)
```

Even in such a simple example, we can already see how difficult an expression is to understand when we nest too many generator expressions. Unfortunately, sometimes this is the only way to achieve the desired effect. Here's the explanation of the example:

- We check whether `COMPILER_ID` is `GNU`; if that's the case, we evaluate `OR` to 1.
- If it's not, we check whether `COMPILER_ID` is `Clang`, and evaluate `OR` to 1. Otherwise, evaluate `OR` to 0.
- If `OR` is evaluated to 1, add `-rtti` to the `enable_rtti` **compile options**. Otherwise, do nothing.

Next, we can link our libraries and executables with the `enable_rtti` interface library. CMake will add the `-rtti` flag if a compiler supports it. Side note: **RTTI** stands for **run-time type information** and is used in C++ with keywords like `typeid` to determine the class of an object at run time; unless your code is using this feature, the flag doesn't need to be enabled.

Nested generator expressions

Sometimes, it's not obvious what happens when we try to nest elements in a generator expression. We can debug the expressions by generating a test output to a debug file.

Let's try out a few things and see what happens:

ch06/01-nesting/CMakeLists.txt

```
set(myvar "small text")
set(myvar2 "small text >")

file(GENERATE OUTPUT nesting CONTENT "
  1 $<PLATFORM_ID>
  2 $<UPPER_CASE:$<PLATFORM_ID>>
  3 $<UPPER_CASE:hello world>
  4 $<UPPER_CASE:${myvar}>
  5 $<UPPER_CASE:${myvar2}>
")
```

After building this project as described in the *Technical requirements* section of this chapter, we can read the produced nesting file using the Unix cat command:

```
# cat nesting

  1 Linux
  2 LINUX
  3 HELLO WORLD
  4 SMALL TEXT
  5 SMALL  text>
```

This is how each line works:

1. The PLATFORM_ID output value is LINUX.
2. The output from the nested value will get transformed correctly to uppercase LINUX.
3. We can transform plain strings.
4. We can transform the content of configuration-stage variables.
5. Variables will be interpolated first, and closing angle brackets (>) will be interpreted as part of the genex, in that only part of the string will get capitalized.

In other words, be aware that the content of variables may affect the behavior of your genex expansions. If you need an angle bracket in a variable, use $<ANGLE-R>.

The difference between a conditional expression and the evaluation of a BOOL operator

Generator expressions can be a little confusing when it comes to evaluating Boolean types to strings. It is important to understand how they differ from regular conditional expressions, starting with an explicit IF keyword:

ch06/02-boolean/CMakeLists.txt

```
cmake_minimum_required(VERSION 3.26)
project(Boolean CXX)

file(GENERATE OUTPUT boolean CONTENT "
  1 $<0:TRUE>
  2 $<0:TRUE,FALSE> (won't work)
  3 $<1:TRUE,FALSE>
  4 $<IF:0,TRUE,FALSE>
  5 $<IF:0,TRUE,>
")
```

Let's read the produced file using the Linux cat command:

```
# cat boolean

1
2  (won't work)
3 TRUE,FALSE
4 FALSE
5
```

Let's examine the output for each line:

1. This is a Boolean expansion, where BOOL is 0; therefore, the TRUE string isn't written.

2. This is a typical mistake – the author intended to print TRUE or FALSE depending on the BOOL value, but since it is a Boolean false expansion as well, two arguments are treated as one and not printed.

3. This is the same mistake for a reversed value – it is a Boolean true expansion that has both arguments written in a single line.

4. This is a proper conditional expression starting with IF – it prints FALSE because the first argument is 0.

5. This is the correct usage of a conditional expression, however, when we don't need to provide values for Boolean `false`, we should use the form used in the first line.

Generator expressions are notorious for their convoluted syntax. The differences mentioned in this example can confuse even experienced builders. If in doubt, copy such an expression to another file and analyze it by adding indentation and whitespace to understand it better.

Seeing examples of how generator expressions work has prepared us to use them in practice. Upcoming chapters will discuss many topics, where generator expressions will be relevant. In time, we'll cover even more of their applications.

Summary

This chapter was all about unpacking the ins and outs of generator expressions, or "genexes." We started with the basics of forming and expanding generator expressions and looked at their nesting mechanism. We dove into the power of conditional expansion, which taps into Boolean logic, comparison operations, and queries. This aspect of generator expressions shines when adapting our build process based on factors like user-chosen build configuration, platform, and the current toolchain.

We have also covered the basic but essential transformations of strings, lists, and paths. A major highlight was using genexes to query the information gathered at the later build stages and present it when the context matches the requirements. We also now know how to check our compiler's ID, version, and capabilities. We explored querying the build target properties and extracting the related information using generator expressions. The chapter is wrapped up with practical examples and guidance on viewing the output where possible. With this, you're now ready to use the generator expressions in your projects.

In the next chapter, we'll learn how to compile programs with CMake. Specifically, we'll talk about how to configure and optimize this process.

Further reading

For more information on the topics covered in this chapter, you can refer to the following:

- Generator expressions in the official documentation:
  `https://cmake.org/cmake/help/latest/manual/cmake-generator-`
  `expressions.7.html`

- Supported compiler IDs:
  https://cmake.org/cmake/help/latest/variable/CMAKE_LANG_COMPILER_ID.html

- Mixing languages in Cmake:
  https://stackoverflow.com/questions/8096887/mixing-c-and-c-with-cmake

Leave a review!

Enjoying this book? Help readers like you by leaving an Amazon review. Scan the QR code below to get a free eBook of your choice.

7

Compiling C++ Sources with CMake

Simple compilation scenarios are usually handled by a default configuration of a toolchain or just provided out of the box by an **integrated development environment (IDE)**. However, in a professional setting, business needs often call for something more advanced. It could be a requirement for higher performance, smaller binaries, more portability, automated testing, or extensive debugging capabilities – you name it. Managing all of these in a coherent, future-proof way quickly becomes a complex, tangled mess (especially when there are multiple platforms to support).

The process of compilation is often not explained well enough in books on C++ (in-depth subjects such as virtual base classes seem to be more interesting). In this chapter, we'll fix that by going through different aspects of compilation: we'll discover how compilation works, what its internal stages are, and how they affect the binary output.

After that, we will focus on the prerequisites – we'll discuss what commands we can use to fine-tune the compilation process, how to require specific features from a compiler, and how to correctly instruct the compiler on which input files to process.

Then, we'll focus on the first stage of compilation – the preprocessor. We'll be providing paths for included headers, and we'll study how to plug in variables from CMake and the build environment with preprocessor definitions. We'll cover the most interesting use cases and learn how to expose CMake variables so they can be accessed from C++ code.

Right after that, we'll talk about the optimizer and how different flags can affect performance. We'll also discuss the costs of optimization, specifically how it affects the debuggability of produced binaries, and what to do if that isn't desired.

Lastly, we'll explain how to manage the compilation process in terms of reducing the compilation time by using precompiled headers and unity builds. We'll learn how to debug the build process and find any mistakes we might've made.

In this chapter, we're going to cover the following main topics:

- The basics of compilation
- Configuring the preprocessor
- Configuring the optimizer
- Managing the process of compilation

Technical requirements

You can find the code files that are present in this chapter on GitHub at https://github.com/PacktPublishing/Modern-CMake-for-Cpp-2E/tree/main/examples/ch07.

To build the examples provided in this book, always use the recommended commands:

```
cmake -B <build tree> -S <source tree>
cmake --build <build tree>
```

Be sure to replace the <build tree> and <source tree> placeholders with appropriate paths. As a reminder: **build tree** is the path to the target/output directory and **source tree** is the path at which your source code is located.

The basics of compilation

Compilation can be roughly described as a process of translating instructions written in a high-level programming language into low-level machine code. This allows us to create our applications using abstract concepts such as classes and objects and sparing us the tedious intricacies of processor-specific assembly languages. We don't need to work directly with CPU registers, think about short or long jumps, or manage stack frames. Compiled languages are more expressive, readable, and secure, and they encourage the creation of maintainable code, all while delivering as much performance as possible.

In C++, we use static compilation – meaning an entire program must be translated into native code before it can be executed. This is a different approach compared to languages such as Java or Python, which interpret and compile the program on the fly each time a user runs it. Each method has its own unique advantages. C++ aims to offer a multitude of high-level tools, while simultaneously delivering native performance. A C++ compiler can produce a self-contained application for almost every architecture out there.

Creating and running a C++ program involves several steps:

1. **Design your application**: This includes planning the application's functionality, structure, and behavior. Once your design is finalized, carefully write the source code following best practices for code readability and maintainability.

2. **Compile individual .cpp implementation files, also known as translation units, into object files**: This step involves converting the high-level language code that you've written into low-level machine code.

3. **Link object files together into a single executable**: During this step, all other dependencies, including dynamic and static libraries, are also linked. This process creates an executable that can be run on the intended platform.

To run the program, the **operating system (OS)** will use a tool called **loader** to map the program's machine code and all required dynamic libraries into virtual memory. The loader then reads the program headers to determine where execution should start and begins running the instructions.

At this stage, the program's start-up code comes into play. A special function called _start, provided by the system's C library, is invoked. The _start function collects command-line arguments and environment variables, initiates threading, initializes static symbols, and registers cleanup callbacks. Only after this will it call main(), the function that programmers fill with their own code.

As you can see, a considerable amount of work takes place behind the scenes. This chapter focuses on the second step from the earlier list. By considering the bigger picture, we can better understand where potential issues might originate. There's no such thing as magic in software development, despite the seeming impenetrability of the complexity involved. Everything has an explanation and a reason. We need to understand that things can go wrong during the run-time of a program due to how we compiled it, even if the compilation step itself appeared to be successful. It's simply not possible for a compiler to check all edge cases during its operation. So, let's find out what actually happens when the compiler does its job.

How compilation works

As mentioned before, compilation is the process of translating a high-level language into a low-level language. Specifically, this involves generating machine code, which are instructions that a specific processor can directly execute, in a binary **object file** format unique to a given platform. On Linux, the most commonly used format is the **Executable and Linkable Format (ELF)**. Windows uses a PE/COFF format specification, and on macOS, we'll encounter Mach objects (the Mach-O format).

Object files are the direct translation of individual source files. Each of these files must be compiled separately and subsequently combined by a linker into a single executable or library. This modular process can significantly save time when modifying code, as only the files updated by the programmer need to be recompiled.

The compiler has to execute the following stages to create an **object file:**

- Preprocessing
- Linguistic analysis
- Assembly
- Optimization
- Code emission

Let's explain them in more detail.

Preprocessing, although automatically invoked by most compilers, is considered a preparatory step prior to actual compilation. Its role is to perform rudimentary manipulations on the source code; it executes #include directives, substitutes identifiers with defined values through #define directives and -D flags, invokes simple macros, and conditionally includes or excludes parts of code based on the #if, #elif, and #endif directives. The preprocessor remains blissfully unaware of the actual C++ code. In essence, it functions as an advanced find-and-replace tool.

Nevertheless, the role of the preprocessor is vital for building advanced programs. The ability to divide code into parts and share declarations across multiple translation units is the foundation of code reusability.

Next up is **linguistic analysis**, where the compiler conducts more intricate operations. It scans the preprocessed file (which now includes all the headers inserted by the preprocessor) character by character. Through a process known as lexical analysis, it groups characters into meaningful tokens – these could be keywords, operators, variable names, and more.

The tokens are then assembled into chains and examined to verify whether their order and presence adhere to the syntax rules of C++ – a process called syntax analysis or parsing. This is typically the stage where most of the error messages are generated, as it identifies syntactical issues.

Lastly, the compiler carries out semantic analysis. In this phase, the compiler checks whether the statements in the file are logically sound. For instance, it ensures that all type correctness checks are met (you cannot assign an integer to a string variable). This analysis makes sure the program makes sense within the rules of the programming language.

The **assembly** phase is essentially a translation of these tokens into CPU-specific instructions based on the available instruction set for the platform. Some compilers actually generate an assembly output file, which is subsequently passed to a dedicated assembler program. This program produces the machine code that the CPU can execute. Other compilers produce this machine code directly in memory. Typically, such compilers also provide an option to generate a textual output of human-readable assembly code. However, just because this code can be read doesn't necessarily mean it's easy to understand or beneficial to do so.

Optimization is not confined to a single step in the compilation process but occurs incrementally at each stage. There is, however, a distinct phase after the initial assembly is produced, which focuses on minimizing register usage and eliminating redundant code.

An interesting and noteworthy optimization technique is inline expansion or *inlining*. In this process, the compiler effectively "cuts" the body of a function and "pastes" it in place of its call. The C++ standard doesn't explicitly define the circumstances under which this occurs – it is implementation dependent. Inline expansion can enhance execution speed and reduce memory usage, but it also poses significant drawbacks for debugging, as the executed code no longer corresponds to the original line in the source code.

The **code emission** phase involves writing the optimized machine code into an *object file* in a format that aligns with the target platform's specifications. However, this *object file* isn't ready for execution just yet – it needs to be passed to the next tool in the chain, the linker. The linker's job is to appropriately relocate the sections of our *object file* and resolve references to external symbols, effectively preparing the file for execution. This step marks the transformation from the **American Standard Code for Information Interchange (ASCII)** source code into *binary executable files* that can be directly processed by a CPU.

Each of these stages is significant and can be configured to meet our specific needs. Let's look at how we can manage this process with CMake.

Initial configuration

CMake provides several commands that can affect each stage of the compilation:

- `target_compile_features()`: This requires a compiler with specific features to compile this target.
- `target_sources()`: This adds sources to an already defined target.
- `target_include_directories()`: This sets up the preprocessor *include paths*.
- `target_compile_definitions()`: The sets up preprocessor definitions.

- `target_compile_options()`: This sets compiler-specific command-line options.
- `target_precompile_headers()`: This sets external header files to be optimized with precompilation.

Each of these commands accepts similar arguments in the following format:

```
target_...(<target name> <INTERFACE|PUBLIC|PRIVATE> <arguments>)
```

This means that properties set with this command propagate through transitive usage requirements, as discussed in *Chapter 5, Working with Targets,* in the *What are transitive usage requirements?* section and can be utilized for both executables and libraries. Also, it's worth noting that all these commands support generator expressions.

Requiring specific features from the compiler

As discussed in the *Checking for supported compiler features* section in *Chapter 4, Setting Up Your First CMake Project,* it's crucial to anticipate issues and aim to provide your software's users with a clear message when something goes wrong – for instance, when an available compiler, X, doesn't provide a required feature, Y. This approach is far more user friendly than having users decipher the errors produced by an incompatible toolchain they might be using. We don't want users to misattribute the incompatibility issues to our code instead of their outdated environment.

You can use the following command to specify all the features that your target needs to build:

```
target_compile_features(<target> <PRIVATE|PUBLIC|INTERFACE>
                        <feature> [...])
```

CMake understands C++ standards and supported compiler features for these `compiler_ids`:

- `AppleClang`: Apple Clang for Xcode versions 4.4+
- `Clang`: Clang Compiler versions 2.9+
- `GNU`: GNU Compiler versions 4.4+
- `MSVC`: Microsoft Visual Studio versions 2010+
- `SunPro`: Oracle Solaris Studio versions 12.4+
- `Intel`: Intel Compiler versions 12.1+

There are over 60 features supported by CMake, and you'll find a full list in the official documentation, on the page explaining the `CMAKE_CXX_KNOWN_FEATURES` variable. However, unless you're after something very specific, I recommend picking a high-level meta feature indicating the general C++ standard:

- `cxx_std_14`
- `cxx_std_17`
- `cxx_std_20`
- `cxx_std_23`
- `cxx_std_26`

Look at the following example:

```
target_compile_features(my_target PUBLIC cxx_std_26)
```

This is essentially equal to `set(CMAKE_CXX_STANDARD 26)` with `set(CMAKE_CXX_STANDARD_ REQUIRED ON)` introduced in *Chapter 4, Setting Up Your First CMake Project*. However, the difference is that `target_compile_features()` works on a per-target basis and not globally for the project, which may be cumbersome if you need to add it for all targets in the project.

Find more details on CMake's *supported compilers* in the official manual (See the *Further reading* section for the URL).

Managing sources for targets

We already know how to tell CMake which source files constitute a single target, whether it's an executable or a library. We do this by supplying a list of files when using the `add_executable()` or `add_library()` commands.

As your solution expands, the list of files for each target also grows. This can lead to some rather lengthy `add_...()` commands. How do we deal with that? A tempting approach might be to utilize the `file()` command in `GLOB` mode, which can gather all files from subdirectories and store them in a variable. We could pass it as an argument to the target declaration and not bother with the file list again:

```
file(GLOB helloworld_SRC "*.h" "*.cpp")
add_executable(helloworld ${helloworld_SRC})
```

However, this method is not recommended. Let's understand why. CMake generates buildsystems based on the changes in the listfiles. So, if no changes are detected, your builds might fail without any warning (a developer's nightmare). Besides, omitting all sources in the target declaration can disrupt code inspection in IDEs like CLion, which knows how to parse certain CMake commands to understand your project.

Using variables in target declarations is not advisable for another reason: it creates a layer of indirection, causing the developers to have to unpack the target definition when reading the project. To follow this advice, we're faced with another question: how do we conditionally add source files? This is a common scenario when dealing with platform-specific implementation files, such as gui_linux.cpp and gui_windows.cpp.

The target_sources() command allows us to append source files to a previously created target:

ch07/01-sources/CMakeLists.txt

```
add_executable(main main.cpp)
if(CMAKE_SYSTEM_NAME STREQUAL "Linux")
  target_sources(main PRIVATE gui_linux.cpp)
elseif(CMAKE_SYSTEM_NAME STREQUAL "Windows")
  target_sources(main PRIVATE gui_windows.cpp)
elseif(CMAKE_SYSTEM_NAME STREQUAL "Darwin")
  target_sources(main PRIVATE gui_macos.cpp)
else()
  message(FATAL_ERROR "CMAKE_SYSTEM_NAME=${CMAKE_SYSTEM_NAME} not
supported.")
endif()
```

This way, each platform gets its own set of compatible files. That's great, but what about long lists of sources? Well, we'll just have to accept that some things aren't perfect just yet and keep adding them manually. If you are struggling with a really long list, you're probably doing something wrong with the structure of your project: perhaps it could use partitioning sources into libraries.

Now that we've covered the essentials of compilation, let's delve into the first step – preprocessing. Like all things in computer science, the devil is in the details.

Configuring the preprocessor

The preprocessor plays a huge role in the process of building. Maybe this is a little surprising, considering its functionality appears rather straightforward and limited. In the following sections, we'll cover providing paths to included files and using the preprocessor definitions. We'll also explain how we can use CMake to configure included headers.

Providing paths to included files

The most basic feature of the preprocessor is the ability to include .h and .hpp header files with the #include directive, which exists in two forms:

- Angle-bracket form: #include <path-spec>
- Quoted form: #include "path-spec"

As we know, the preprocessor will replace these directives with the contents of the file specified in path-spec. Finding these files may be a challenge. Which directories should be searched, and in what order? Unfortunately, the C++ standard doesn't specify that exactly. We have to check the manual for the compiler in use.

Typically, the angle-bracket form will check standard *include directories*, which include the directories where standard C++ library and standard C library header files are stored in the system.

The quoted form starts by searching for the included file in the directory of the current file and then checks the directories for the angle-bracket form.

CMake provides a command to manipulate paths being searched for the included files:

```
target_include_directories(<target> [SYSTEM] [AFTER|BEFORE]
                      <INTERFACE|PUBLIC|PRIVATE> [item1...]
                     [<INTERFACE|PUBLIC|PRIVATE> [item2...]]
...])
```

This allows us to add custom paths that we want the compiler to scan. CMake will add them to compiler invocations in the generated buildsystem. They will be provided with a flag appropriate for the specific compiler (usually, it's -I).

The target_include_directories() command modifies the target's INCLUDE_DIRECTORIES property by appending or prepending directories to it, based on whether the AFTER or BEFORE keyword is used. However, it's still up to the compiler to decide whether the directories provided here will be checked before or after the default ones (usually, it's before).

The SYSTEM keyword signifies to the compiler that the given directories should be treated as standard system directories (to be used with the angle-bracket form). For many compilers, these directories are passed with the -isystem flag.

Preprocessor definitions

Recall the preprocessor's #define and #if, #elif, and #endif directives mentioned earlier when discussing the stages of compilation. Let's examine the following example:

ch07/02-definitions/definitions.cpp

```cpp
#include <iostream>
int main() {
```

```
#if defined(ABC)
    std::cout << "ABC is defined!" << std::endl;
#endif
#if (DEF > 2*4-3)
    std::cout << "DEF is greater than 5!" << std::endl;
#endif
}
```

As it stands, this example accomplishes nothing, as neither ABC nor DEF is defined (DEF would default to 0 in this example). We can easily change that by adding two lines at the top of this code:

```
#define ABC
#define DEF 8
```

After compiling and executing this code, we can see both messages in the console:

```
ABC is defined!
DEF is greater than 5!
```

This might seem simple enough, but what if we want to condition these sections based on external factors, such as an OS, architecture, or something else? The good news is that you can pass values from CMake to a C++ compiler, and it's not complicated at all.

The target_compile_definitions() command will suffice:

ch07/02-definitions/CMakeLists.txt

```
set(VAR 8)
add_executable(defined definitions.cpp)
target_compile_definitions(defined PRIVATE ABC "DEF=${VAR}")
```

The preceding code will behave exactly like the two #define statements, but we have the flexibility to use CMake's variables and generator expressions, and we can place the command in a conditional block.

Traditionally, these definitions are passed to the compiler with the -D flag (for example, -DFOO=1) and some programmers continue to use this flag in this command:

```
target_compile_definitions(hello PRIVATE -DFOO)
```

CMake recognizes this and will automatically remove any leading -D flags. It will also disregard empty strings, so the following command is perfectly valid:

```
target_compile_definitions(hello PRIVATE -D FOO)
```

In this case, -D is a separate argument that becomes an empty string after removal and is subsequently ignored, thereby ensuring correct behavior.

Avoid accessing private class fields in your unit tests

Some online resources recommend using a combination of specific -D definitions with #ifdef/ifndef directives for the purposes of unit testing. The most straightforward application of this approach is to enclose the public access specifier in conditional inclusions, effectively making all fields public when UNIT_TEST is defined (class fields are private by default):

```
class X {
#ifdef UNIT_TEST
  public:
#endif
  int x_;
}
```

While this technique offers convenience (allowing tests to directly access private members), it does not result in clean code. Ideally, unit tests should focus on verifying the functionality of methods within the public interface, treating the underlying implementation as a black box. Consequently, I suggest using this approach only as a last resort.

Using git commit to track a compiled version

Let's think about use cases that benefit from knowing details about the environment or filesystem. A prime example in professional settings might involve passing the revision or commit SHA used to build the binary. This could be achieved like so:

ch07/03-git/CMakeLists.txt

```
add_executable(print_commit print_commit.cpp)
execute_process(COMMAND git log -1 --pretty=format:%h
                OUTPUT_VARIABLE SHA)
target_compile_definitions(print_commit
                           PRIVATE "SHA=${SHA}")
```

The SHA could then be utilized in our application as follows:

ch07/03-git/print_commit.cpp

```
#include <iostream>
// special macros to convert definitions into c-strings:
#define str(s) #s
```

```
#define xstr(s) str(s)
int main()
{
#if defined(SHA)
    std::cout << "GIT commit: " << xstr(SHA) << std::endl;
#endif
}
```

Of course, the preceding code requires the user to have Git installed and accessible in their PATH. This feature is particularly useful when the programs running on production servers are the result of a continuous integration/deployment pipeline. If there's an issue with our software, we can quickly check which exact Git commit was used to build the faulty product.

Keeping track of an exact commit is extremely beneficial for debugging purposes. It's straightforward to pass a single variable to C++ code, but how would we handle the scenario where dozens of variables need to be passed to our headers?

Configuring the headers

Passing definitions through target_compile_definitions() can become tedious with numerous variables. Wouldn't it be easier to provide a header file with placeholders referencing these variables, and allow CMake to fill them in? Absolutely!

CMake's configure_file(<input> <output>) command enables you to generate new files from templates, like the following example:

ch07/04-configure/configure.h.in

```
#cmakedefine FOO_ENABLE
#cmakedefine FOO_STRING1 "@FOO_STRING1@"
#cmakedefine FOO_STRING2 "${FOO_STRING2}"
#cmakedefine FOO_UNDEFINED "@FOO_UNDEFINED@"
```

You can utilize this command as follows:

ch07/04-configure/CMakeLists.txt

```
add_executable(configure configure.cpp)
set(FOO_ENABLE ON)
set(FOO_STRING1 "abc")
set(FOO_STRING2 "def")
```

```
configure_file(configure.h.in configured/configure.h)
target_include_directories(configure PRIVATE
                           ${CMAKE_CURRENT_BINARY_DIR})
```

CMake then generates an output file like so:

ch07/04-configure/<build_tree>/configured/configure.h

```
#define FOO_ENABLE
#define FOO_STRING1 "abc"
#define FOO_STRING2 "def"
/* #undef FOO_UNDEFINED */
```

As you can see, the @VAR@ and ${VAR} variable placeholders were substituted with the values from the CMake listfile. Additionally, #cmakedefine was replaced with #define for defined variables and /* #undef VAR */ for undefined ones. If you require an explicit #define 1 or #define 0 for #if blocks, use #cmakedefine01 instead.

You can incorporate this configured header in your application by simply including it in your implementation file:

ch07/04-configure/configure.cpp

```
#include <iostream>
#include "configured/configure.h"

// special macros to convert definitions into c-strings:
#define str(s) #s
#define xstr(s) str(s)

using namespace std;
int main()
{
#ifdef FOO_ENABLE
  cout << "FOO_ENABLE: ON" << endl;
#endif
  cout << "FOO_STRING1: " << xstr(FOO_STRING1) << endl;
  cout << "FOO_STRING2: " << xstr(FOO_STRING2) << endl;
  cout << "FOO_UNDEFINED: " << xstr(FOO_UNDEFINED) << endl;
}
```

By adding the binary tree to our *include paths* with the `target_include_directories()` command, we can compile the example and receive output populated from CMake:

```
FOO_ENABLE: ON
FOO_STRING1: "abc"
FOO_STRING2: "def"
FOO_UNDEFINED: FOO_UNDEFINED
```

The `configure_file()` command also includes a range of formatting and file-permission options, which we won't delve into here due to length constraints. If you're interested, you can refer to the online documentation for further details (see the *Further reading* section in this chapter).

Having prepared a complete compilation of our headers and source files, let's discuss how the output code is shaped during the subsequent steps. While we don't have direct influence over the linguistic analysis or assembling (as these steps adhere to strict standards), we can manipulate the configuration of the optimizer. Let's explore how this can impact the end result.

Configuring the optimizer

The optimizer will analyze the output of previous stages and use a multitude of tactics, which programmers wouldn't use directly, as they don't adhere to clean-code principles. But that's fine – the optimizer's essential role is to enhance code performance, striving for low CPU usage, minimal register usage, and reduced memory footprint. As the optimizer traverses the source code, it heavily morphs it into an almost unrecognizable form, tailored specifically to the target CPU.

The optimizer will not only decide which functions could be removed or compacted; it will also move code around or even significantly duplicate it! If it can definitively ascertain that certain lines of code are redundant, it will wipe them out from the middle of an important function (and you won't even notice). It recycles memory so that numerous variables can inhabit the same slot at different times. It can even remodel your control structures into something entirely different if that translates into shaving off a few cycles here and there.

If a programmer were to manually apply the aforementioned techniques to source code, it would transmogrify it into an awful, unreadable mess, difficult to write and reason about. However, when applied by compilers, these techniques are advantageous as compilers strictly follow the provided instructions. The optimizer is a relentless beast that serves one purpose: to accelerate execution speed, regardless of how distorted the output becomes. Such output may contain some debugging information if we are running it in our test environment, or it may not, in order to make it difficult for unauthorized people to tamper with it.

Every compiler has its own unique tricks up its sleeve, consistent with the platform it supports and the philosophy it follows. We'll take a look at the most common ones, available in GNU GCC and LLVM Clang, to gain an understanding of what is practical and achievable.

Here's the thing – many compilers won't enable any optimization by default (GCC included). This is okay in some cases but not so much in others. Why go slow when you can go fast? To amend this, we can use the `target_compile_options()` command and explicitly state our expectations from the compiler.

The syntax of this command mirrors others in this chapter:

```
target_compile_options(<target> [BEFORE]
                    <INTERFACE|PUBLIC|PRIVATE> [items1...]
                    [<INTERFACE|PUBLIC|PRIVATE> [items2...]
    ...])
```

We provide command-line options to use while building the target and we also specify the propagation keyword. When executed, CMake appends the given options to the appropriate `COMPILE_OPTIONS` variable of the target. The optional `BEFORE` keyword may be used if we want to prepend them instead. The order can be significant in some scenarios, so it's beneficial to have a choice.

Note that `target_compile_options()` is a general command. It can also be used to provide other arguments to compiler-like `-D` definitions, for which CMake offers the `target_compile_definition()` command as well. It is always advisable to use the most specialized CMake commands wherever possible, as they are guaranteed to work the same way across all the supported compilers.

Time to discuss the details. The subsequent sections will introduce various kinds of optimizations that you can enable in most compilers.

General level

All the different behaviors of the optimizer can be configured in depth by specific flags that we can pass as *compile options*. Getting to know all of them is time consuming and requires a lot of knowledge about the internal workings of compilers, processors, and memory. What can we do if we just want the best possible scenario that works well in most cases? We can aim for a general solution – an optimization-level specifier.

Most compilers offer four basic levels of optimization, from 0 to 3. We specify them with the `-O<level>` option. `-O0` means *no optimization* and, usually, it's the default level for compilers. On the other hand, `-O2` is considered a *full optimization*, one that generates highly optimized code but at the cost of the slowest compilation time.

There's an in-between -O1 level, which (depending on your needs) can be a good compromise – it enables a reasonable amount of optimization mechanisms without slowing the compilation too much.

Finally, we can reach for -O3, which is *full optimization*, like -O2, but with a more aggressive approach to subprogram inlining and loop vectorization.

There are also some variants of the optimization that will optimize for the size (not necessarily the speed) of the produced file – -Os. There is a super-aggressive optimization, -Ofast, which is an -O3 optimization that doesn't strictly comply with C++ standards. The most obvious difference is the usage of -ffast-math and -ffinite-math flags, meaning that if your program is about precise calculations (as most are), you might want to avoid it.

CMake knows that not all compilers are made equal, and for that reason, it standardizes the experience for developers by providing some default flags for compilers. They are stored in system-wide (not target-specific) variables for the language used (CXX for C++) and the build configuration (DEBUG or RELEASE):

- CMAKE_CXX_FLAGS_DEBUG equals -g
- CMAKE_CXX_FLAGS_RELEASE equals -O3 -DNDEBUG

As you can see, the debug configuration doesn't enable any optimizations and the release configuration goes straight for O3. If you like, you can change them directly with the set() command or just add a target compilation option, which will override this default behavior. The other two flags (-g, -DNDEBUG) are related to debugging – we'll discuss them in the *Providing information for the debugger* section of this chapter.

Variables such as CMAKE_<LANG>_FLAGS_<CONFIG> are global – they apply to all targets. It is recommended to configure your targets through properties and commands, such as target_compile_options(), rather than relying on global variables. This way, you can control your targets at higher granularity.

By choosing an optimization level with -O<level>, we indirectly set a long list of flags, each controlling a specific optimization behavior. We can then fine-tune the optimization by appending more flags, like so:

- Enable them with an -f option: -finline-functions.
- Disable them with an -fno option: -fno-inline-functions.

Some of these flags are worth understanding better as they will often impact how your program works and how you can debug it. Let's have a look.

Function inlining

As you might recall, compilers can be encouraged to inline some functions, either by *defining* a function inside a class *declaration* block or by explicitly using the `inline` keyword:

```
struct X {
  void im_inlined(){ cout << "hi\n"; };
  void me_too();
};
inline void X::me_too() { cout << "bye\n"; };
```

The decision to inline a function ultimately rests with the compiler. If inlining is enabled and the function is used in a singular place (or a relatively small function used in a few places), inlining will most likely occur.

Function inlining is an intriguing optimization technique. It operates by extracting the code from the targeted function and embedding it in all the locations where the function was called. This process replaces the original call and conserves precious CPU cycles.

Let's consider the following example using the class we just defined:

```
int main() {
  X x;
  x.im_inlined();
  x.me_too();
  return 0;
}
```

Without inlining, the code would execute in the `main()` frame until a method call. Then, it would create a new frame for `im_inlined()`, execute in a separate scope, and return to the `main()` frame. The same would happen for the `me_too()` method.

However, when inlining takes place, the compiler will replace the calls, like so:

```
int main() {
  X x;
  cout << "hi\n";
  cout << "bye\n";
  return 0;
}
```

This isn't an exact representation because inlining happens at the level of assembly or machine code (and not the source code), but it does provide a general idea.

The compiler employs inlining to conserve time. It bypasses the creation and teardown of a new call frame and the need to look up the address of the next instruction to execute (and return to) and enhances instruction caching as they are in close proximity.

However, inlining does come with some significant side effects. If a function is used more than once, it must be copied to all locations, resulting in a larger file size and increased memory usage. While this may not be as critical today as it once was, it remains relevant, especially when developing software for low-end devices with limited RAM.

Moreover, inlining critically impacts debugging. Inlined code is no longer at the original line number, making tracking more difficult, or sometimes impossible. This is why a debugger breakpoint placed in a function that was inlined, never gets hit (even though the code is still executed somehow). To circumvent this problem, you need to disable inlining for debug builds (at the cost of not testing the exact release build version).

We can do that by specifying the -O0 (o-zero) level for the target or directly addressing the flags responsible for inlining:

- `-finline-functions-called-once`: This is only for GCC.
- `-finline-functions`: This is for both Clang and GCC.
- `-finline-hint-functions`: This is only for Clang.

Inlining can be explicitly disabled with `-fno-inline-...`, however, for detailed information, it's advisable to refer to the documentation of your specific compiler version.

Loop unrolling

Loop unrolling, also known as loop unwinding, is an optimization technique. This strategy aims to transform loops into a series of statements that accomplish the same result. Consequently, this approach exchanges the small size of the program for execution speed, as it eliminates the loop control instruction, pointer arithmetic, and end-of-loop checks.

Consider the following example:

```
void func() {
  for(int i = 0; i < 3; i++)
    cout << "hello\n";
}
```

The previous code will be transformed into something like this:

```
void func() {
    cout << "hello\n";
    cout << "hello\n";
    cout << "hello\n";
}
```

The outcome will be the same, but we no longer have to allocate the i variable, increment it, or compare it three times with a value of 3. If we call func() enough times in the lifetime of the program, unrolling even such a short and small function will make a significant difference.

However, it is important to understand two limiting factors. Firstly, loop unrolling is only effective if the compiler knows or can accurately estimate the number of iterations. Secondly, loop unrolling can lead to undesired consequences on modern CPUs, as an increased code size might hamper effective caching.

Each compiler provides a slightly different version of this flag:

- -floop-unroll: This is for GCC.
- -funroll-loops: This is for Clang.

If you're uncertain, test extensively whether this flag is affecting your particular program and explicitly enable or disable it. Do note that on GCC, it is implicitly enabled with -O3 as part of the implicitly enabled -floop-unroll-and-jam flag.

Loop vectorization

The mechanism known as **single instruction, multiple data (SIMD)** was developed in the early 1960s to achieve parallelism. As the name suggests, it is designed to carry out the same operation on multiple data simultaneously. Let's look at this in practice through the following example:

```
int a[128];
int b[128];
// initialize b
for (i = 0; i<128; i++)
    a[i] = b[i] + 5;
```

Normally, such code would loop 128 times, but with a capable CPU, the code's execution can be significantly accelerated by simultaneously calculating two or more array elements. This is possible due to the absence of dependency between consecutive elements and data overlap between arrays. Clever compilers can transform the preceding loop into something like this (which happens at the assembly level):

```
for (i = 0; i<32; i+=4) {
  a[ i ] = b[ i ] + 5;
  a[i+1] = b[i+1] + 5;
  a[i+2] = b[i+2] + 5;
  a[i+3] = b[i+3] + 5;
}
```

GCC will enable such automatic vectorization of loops at -O3. Clang enables it by default. Both compilers offer different flags to enable/disable vectorization in particular:

- `-ftree-vectorize -ftree-slp-vectorize`: This is for enabling vectorization in GCC.
- `-fno-vectorize -fno-slp-vectorize`: This is for disabling vectorization in Clang.

The efficiency of vectorization stems from the utilization of special instructions offered by CPU manufacturers, rather than merely substituting the original form of the loop with an unrolled version. Hence, it's not feasible to achieve the same performance level manually (additionally, it doesn't result in *clean code*).

The optimizer plays a vital role in enhancing a program's runtime performance. By employing its strategies effectively, we'll get more bang for our buck. Efficiency matters not only after coding completion but also during the software development process. If compilation times are lengthy, we can improve them by better managing the process.

Managing the process of compilation

As programmers and build engineers, we must also consider other aspects of compilation such as the time it takes to complete and the ease with which we can identify and rectify mistakes made during the solution-building process.

Reducing compilation time

In busy projects that require frequent recompilations (possibly several times an hour), it's paramount to ensure the compilation process is as quick as possible. This not only affects the efficiency of your code-compile-test loop but also your concentration and workflow.

Luckily, C++ is already pretty good at managing compilation time, thanks to separate translation units. CMake will take care to only recompile sources that were impacted by recent changes. However, if we need to improve things even more, there are a couple of techniques we can use: header precompilation and unity builds.

Precompilation of headers

Header files (.h) are included in the translation unit by the preprocessor before the actual compilation begins. This means they must be recompiled every time the .cpp implementation files change. Moreover, if multiple translation files are using the same shared header, it has to be compiled every time it's included. This is inefficient, but it has been the standard for a long time.

Luckily, since version 3.16, CMake offers a command to enable header precompilation. This allows the compiler to process headers separately from the implementation file, thereby speeding up the compilation process. This is the syntax for the provided command:

```
target_precompile_headers(<target>
                          <INTERFACE|PUBLIC|PRIVATE> [header1...]
                         [<INTERFACE|PUBLIC|PRIVATE> [header2...]
...])
```

The list of added headers is stored in the PRECOMPILE_HEADERS target property. As we discussed in *Chapter 5*, *Working with Targets*, in the *What are transitive usage requirements?* section, we can use the propagated properties to share the headers with any depending targets by choosing the PUBLIC or INTERFACE keyword; however, this shouldn't be done for targets exported with the install() command. Other projects shouldn't be forced to consume our precompiled headers as this is not a conventional practice.

 Use the $<BUILD_INTERFACE:...> generator expression described in *Chapter 6*, *Using Generator Expressions*, to prevent precompiled headers from appearing in the usage requirements of targets when they're installed. However, they will still be added to targets exported from the build tree with the export() command. Don't worry if this seems confusing right now – it will be fully explained in *Chapter 14*, *Installing and Packaging*.

CMake will put all headers' names in a cmake_pch.h or cmake_pch.hxx file, which will then be precompiled to a compiler-specific binary file with a .pch, .gch, or .pchi extension.

We can use it in our listfile like so:

ch07/06-precompile/CMakeLists.txt

```
add_executable(precompiled hello.cpp)
target_precompile_headers(precompiled PRIVATE <iostream>)
```

We can also use it in the corresponding source file:

ch07/06-precompile/hello.cpp

```
int main() {
  std::cout << "hello world" << std::endl;
}
```

Note that in our main.cpp file, we don't need to include cmake_pch.h or any other header – it will be included by CMake with compiler-specific command-line options.

In the previous example, I used a built-in header; however, you can easily add your own headers with class or function definitions. Use one of the two forms to reference the header:

- header.h (a direct path) is interpreted as relative to the current source directory and will be included with an absolute path.
- The [["header.h"]] (double brackets and quotes) path will be scanned according to the target's INCLUDE_DIRECTORIES property, which can be configured with target_include_directiories().

Some online references may discourage precompiling headers that aren't part of a standard library, such as <iostream>, or using precompiled headers altogether. This is because changing the list or editing a custom header will cause recompilation of all translation units in the target. With CMake, this concern is not as significant, especially if you structure your project correctly (with relatively small targets focused on a narrow domain). Each target has a separate precompiled header file, which limits the impact of the header changes.

If your headers are considered relatively stable, you might decide to reuse precompiled headers in your targets. For this purpose, CMake provides a convenient command:

```
target_precompile_headers(<target> REUSE_FROM <other_target>)
```

This sets the PRECOMPILE_HEADERS_REUSE_FROM property of the target reusing the headers and creates a dependency between these targets. Using this method, the consuming target can no longer specify its own precompiled headers. Additionally, all *compile options*, *compile flags*, and *compile definitions* must match between targets.

Pay attention to requirements, especially if you have any headers that use the double bracket format ([["header.h"]]). Both targets need to set their *include paths* appropriately to make sure those headers are found by the compiler.

Unity builds

CMake 3.16 introduced another compilation time optimization feature – unity builds, also known as *unified builds* or *jumbo builds*. Unity builds work by combining multiple implementation source files by utilizing the #include directive. This has some interesting implications, some of which are beneficial, while others could be potentially harmful.

The most obvious advantage is avoiding the recompilation of headers in different translation units when CMake creates a unified build file:

```
#include "source_a.cpp"
#include "source_b.cpp"
```

When both sources contain a #include "header.h" line, the referenced file will be parsed only once, thanks to *include guards* (assuming they have been properly added). While not as refined as precompiled headers, it is an alternative.

The second benefit of this type of build is the fact that the optimizer may now act on a greater scale and optimize interprocedural calls across all bundled sources. This is similar to link-time optimization, which we discussed in *Chapter 4, Setting Up Your First CMake Project*, in the *Interprocedural optimization* section.

However, these benefits come with trade-offs. As we reduced the number of *object files* and processing steps, we also increased the amount of memory needed to process larger files. Additionally, we reduced the amount of parallelizable work. Compilers aren't exceptionally good at multi-threaded compiling, as they don't typically need to be – the buildsystem will usually start many compilation tasks to execute all the files simultaneously on different threads. Grouping all files together complicates this, as CMake now has fewer files to compile in parallel.

With unity builds, you also need to consider some C++ semantic implications that might not be so obvious to catch – anonymous namespaces hiding symbols across files are now scoped to the unity file, rather than to an individual translation unit. The same thing happens with static global variables, functions, and macro definitions. This may cause name collisions, or incorrect function overloads to be executed.

Jumbo builds are suboptimal when recompiling, as they will compile many more files than needed. They work best when the code is meant to compile all files as fast as possible. Tests done on Qt Creator (a popular GUI library) show that you can expect an improvement anywhere between 20% to 50% (depending on the compiler used).

To enable unity builds, we have two options:

- Set the `CMAKE_UNITY_BUILD` variable to `true` – it will initialize the `UNITY_BUILD` property on every target defined thereafter.
- Manually set the `UNITY_BUILD` target property to `true` on every target that should use unity builds.

The second option is achieved by calling the following:

```
set_target_properties(<target1> <target2> ...
                      PROPERTIES UNITY_BUILD true)
```

Manually setting these properties on many targets is of course more work and increases the cost of maintenance, but you may need to do so to control this setting on a finer level.

By default, CMake will create builds containing eight source files, as specified by the `UNITY_BUILD_BATCH_SIZE` property of a target (copied at the creation of a target from the `CMAKE_UNITY_BUILD_BATCH_SIZE` variable). You can change the target property or default variable.

Starting from version 3.18, you can explicitly define how files should be bundled with named groups. To do so, change the target's `UNITY_BUILD_MODE` property to `GROUP` (the default is `BATCH`). Then, assign your source files to groups by setting their `UNITY_GROUP` property to the name of your choosing:

```
set_property(SOURCE <src1> <src2> PROPERTY UNITY_GROUP "GroupA")
```

CMake will then disregard `UNITY_BUILD_BATCH_SIZE` and add all files from the group to a single unity build.

CMake's documentation advises against enabling unity builds for public projects by default. It is recommended that the end user of your application should be able to decide whether they want jumbo builds or not by providing the `-DCMAKE_UNITY_BUILD` command-line argument. If unity builds cause issues due to the way your code is written, you should explicitly set the target's property to false. However, you are free to enable this feature for code that will be used internally, such as within a company or for your private project.

These are the most important aspects of reducing compilation time with CMake. There are other aspects of programming that often cost us a lot of time – one of the most notorious is debugging. Let's see how we can improve things there.

Finding mistakes

As programmers, we spend a substantial amount of time hunting for bugs. This, sadly, is a fact of our profession. The process of identifying errors and rectifying them can often get under our skin, especially when it requires long hours. The difficulty is amplified when we're left flying blind, without the necessary tools to help us navigate through these challenging situations. For this reason, it is crucial that we pay great attention to setting up our environment in a way that simplifies this process, making it as easy and bearable as possible. One way we can achieve this is by configuring the compiler with `target_compile_options()`. So, which *compile options* could assist us in this endeavor?

Configuring errors and warnings

There are many stressful things about software development – fixing critical bugs in the middle of the night, working on high-visibility, costly failures in large systems, and dealing with annoying compilation errors. Some errors are hard to understand, while others are tediously challenging to fix. In your quest to simplify your work and reduce the chance of failure, you'll find many recommendations on how to configure your compiler's warnings.

One such fine piece of advice is to enable the `-Werror` flag as default for all builds. On the surface, this flag's function is deceptively simple – it treats all the warnings as errors, preventing the code from compiling until you resolve each one. While it may seem like a beneficial approach, it seldom is.

You see, warnings are not classified as errors for a reason: they're designed to caution you. It's up to you to decide how to address these warnings. Having the liberty to overlook a warning, particularly when you're experimenting or prototyping your solution, is often invaluable.

On the other hand, if you have a perfect, no-warnings, all-shiny piece of code, it seems a shame to allow future modifications to tarnish this pristine state. What harm could come from enabling it and just keeping it there? Seemingly none, at least until your compiler gets upgraded, that is. New compiler versions tend to be stricter about deprecated features or more adept at offering improvement suggestions. While this is beneficial when warnings remain as warnings, it can lead to unexpected build failures with unchanged code or, even more frustratingly, when you need to quickly rectify a problem unrelated to the new warning.

So, when is it acceptable to enable all possible warnings? The short answer is when you're creating a public library. In these cases, you'll want to preempt issue tickets that fault your code for misbehavior in stricter environments than yours. If you opt to enable this setting, ensure you stay updated with the new compiler versions and the warnings they introduce. It's also important to explicitly manage this update process, separately from making any code changes.

Otherwise, let warnings be what they are, and concentrate on errors. If you feel compelled to be pedantic, use the -Wpedantic flag. This particular flag enables all warnings demanded by strict ISO C and ISO C++ standards. However, bear in mind that this flag doesn't confirm conformance with the standard; it only identifies non-ISO practices that require a diagnostic message.

More lenient and down-to-earth coders will be satisfied with -Wall, optionally coupled with -Wextra for an extra touch of sophistication, which should suffice. These warnings are considered genuinely useful, and you should address them in your code when time allows.

There are plenty of other warning flags that may be useful depending on your project type. I recommend that you read the manual for your chosen compiler to see what options are available.

Debugging the build

Occasionally, the compilation will break. This usually happens when we try to refactor a significant amount of code or clean up our buildsystem. At times, issues can be resolved easily; however, there are more complex problems that require a thorough investigation into the configuration steps. We already know how to print more verbose CMake outputs (as discussed in *Chapter 1, First Steps with CMake*), but how do we analyze what actually happens under the hood at each stage?

Debugging individual stages

The -save-temps, which can be passed to both GCC and Clang compilers, allows us to debug individual stages of compilation. This flag will instruct the compilers to store the output of certain compilation stages in files, rather than in memory.

ch07/07-debug/CMakeLists.txt

```
add_executable(debug hello.cpp)
target_compile_options(debug PRIVATE -save-temps=obj)
```

Enabling this option will produce two extra files (.ii and .s) per translation unit.

The first one, <build-tree>/CMakeFiles/<target>.dir/<source>.ii, stores the output of the preprocessing stage, with comments explaining where each part of the source code comes from:

```
# 1 "/root/examples/ch07/06-debug/hello.cpp"
# 1 "<built-in>"
# 1 "<command-line>"
# 1 "/usr/include/stdc-predef.h" 1 3 4
# / / / ... removed for brevity ... / / /
# 252 "/usr/include/x86_64-linux-
  gnu/c++/9/bits/c++config.h" 3
namespace std
{
  typedef long unsigned int size_t;
  typedef long int ptrdiff_t;
  typedef decltype(nullptr) nullptr_t;
}
...
```

The second one, `<build-tree>/CMakeFiles/<target>.dir/<source>.s`, contains the output of the linguistic analysis stage, ready for the assembler stage:

```
        .file   "hello.cpp"
        .text
        .section    .rodata
        .type   _ZStL19piecewise_construct, @object
        .size   _ZStL19piecewise_construct, 1
_ZStL19piecewise_construct:
        .zero   1
        .local  _ZStL8__ioinit
        .comm   _ZStL8__ioinit,1,1
.LC0:
        .string "hello world"
        .text
        .globl  main
        .type   main, @function
main:
( ... )
```

Depending on the type of problem, we can often uncover the actual issue. For instance, the preprocessor's output can help us identify bugs, such as incorrect *include paths* (which may provide the wrong version of libraries), or mistakes in definitions that lead to erroneous #ifdef evaluations.

Meanwhile, the output of the linguistic analysis is particularly beneficial for targeting specific processors and resolving critical optimization problems.

Debugging issues with header file inclusion

Debugging incorrectly included files can be a challenging task. I should know – in my first corporate job, I had to port an entire code base from one buildsystem to another. If you ever find yourself in a situation that requires a precise understanding of the paths used to include a requested header, consider using the -H compile option:

ch07/07-debug/CMakeLists.txt

```
add_executable(debug hello.cpp)
target_compile_options(debug PRIVATE -H)
```

The produced output will look similar to this:

```
[ 25%] Building CXX object
  CMakeFiles/inclusion.dir/hello.cpp.o
. /usr/include/c++/9/iostream
.. /usr/include/x86_64-linux-gnu/c++/9/bits/c++config.h
... /usr/include/x86_64-linux-gnu/c++/9/bits/os_defines.h
.... /usr/include/features.h
-- removed for brevity --
.. /usr/include/c++/9/ostream
```

After the name of the *object file*, each row in the output contains a path to a header. In this example, a single dot at the beginning of the line indicates a top-level inclusion (where the #include directive is in hello.cpp). Two dots signify that this file is included by the subsequent file (<iostream>). Each additional dot denotes another level of nesting.

At the end of this output, you may also find suggestions for possible improvements to your code:

```
Multiple include guards may be useful for:
/usr/include/c++/9/clocale
/usr/include/c++/9/cstdio
/usr/include/c++/9/cstdlib
```

While you're not required to address issues in the standard library, you may see some of your own headers listed. In such cases, you might want to consider making corrections.

Providing information for the debugger

Machine code is a cryptic list of instructions and data, encoded in a binary format. It doesn't convey any greater meaning or objective. This is because the CPU doesn't care what the goal of the program is or what the sense of all of the instructions is. The only requirement is the correctness of the code. The compiler will translate all of the preceding into numeric identifiers of CPU instructions, store data to initialize memory where needed, and provide tens of thousands of memory addresses. In other words, the final binary doesn't need to contain the actual source code, variable names, signatures of functions, or any other details that programmers care about. That's the default output of the compiler – raw and bare.

This is done primarily to save space and execute without too much overhead. Coincidentally, we are also somewhat protecting our application from reverse engineering. Yes, you can understand what each CPU instruction does without the source code (for example, copy this value to that register). But even basic programs contain too many of these instructions to make sense of them.

If you're a particularly driven individual, you can use a tool called a **disassembler**, and with a lot of knowledge (and a bit of luck), you'll be able to decipher what might be happening. However, this approach isn't very practical, as disassembled code doesn't have original symbols, making it incredibly hard and slow to untangle what goes where.

Instead, we can ask the compiler to store the source code in the produced binary along with the map of references between compiled and original code. Then, we can attach a debugger to a running program and see which source line is being executed at any given moment. This is indispensable when we're working on code, such as writing new functionality or correcting errors.

These two use cases are the reason for two build configs: Debug and Release. As we've seen earlier, CMake will provide some flags to the compiler by default to manage this process, storing them first in global variables:

- `CMAKE_CXX_FLAGS_DEBUG` contains -g
- `CMAKE_CXX_FLAGS_RELEASE` contains -DNDEBUG

The -g flag simply means "add debugging information." It's provided in the OS's native format: stabs, COFF, XCOFF, or DWARF. These formats can then be accessed by debuggers such as gdb (the GNU debugger). Usually, this is sufficient for IDEs such as CLion (as they use gdb under the hood). In other cases, refer to the manual of the provided debugger and check what the appropriate flag is for the compiler of your choice.

For the `Release` configuration, CMake will add the `-DNDEBUG` flag. It's a preprocessor definition, which simply means "not a debug build." Some debug-oriented macros will be deliberately disabled by this option. One of them is `assert`, available in the `<assert.h>` header file. If you decide to use assertions in your production code, they simply won't work:

```
int main(void)
{
    assert(false);
    std::cout << "This shouldn't run. \n";
    return 0;
}
```

The `assert(false)` call won't have any effect in the `Release` configuration, but it will stop the execution just fine in Debug. What do you do if you're practicing assertive programming and still need to use `assert()` for release builds? Either change the defaults that are provided by CMake (remove `NDEBUG` from `CMAKE_CXX_FLAGS_RELEASE`) or implement a hardcoded override by undefining the macro before the header inclusion:

```
#undef NDEBUG
#include <assert.h>
```

Refer to the assert reference for more information: https://en.cppreference.com/w/c/error/assert.

You can consider replacing `assert()` with `static_assert()`, which was introduced in C++11, if your assertions can be done during compilation time, as this function isn't protected with the `#ifndef(NDEBUG)` preprocessor directive like `assert()`.

With this, we have learned how to manage the process of compilation.

Summary

We have completed yet another chapter! Undoubtedly, compilation is a complex process. With all its edge cases and specific requirements, it can be difficult to manage without a robust tool. Thankfully, CMake does an excellent job supporting us here.

So, what have we learned so far? We began by discussing what compilation is and where it fits into the broader narrative of building and running applications in the OS. We then examined the stages of compilation and the internal tools that manage them. This understanding is invaluable for resolving complex issues that we might encounter in the future.

Next, we explored how to use CMake to verify whether the compiler available on the host meets all the necessary requirements for our code to build. As we have already established, it's a significantly better experience for users of our solution to see a friendly message asking them to upgrade rather than an arcane error printed by an outdated compiler that can't handle the new features of the language.

We briefly discussed how to add sources to already defined targets, then moved on to the configuration of the preprocessor. This was quite a substantial subject, as this stage brings all the bits of code together and determines which parts will be ignored. We talked about providing paths to files and adding custom definitions both individually and in bulk (along with some use cases). Then, we discussed the optimizer; we explored all the general levels of optimization and what flags they implicitly add. We also went into detail about a few of them – `finline`, `floop-unroll`, and `ftree-vectorize`.

Finally, it was time to revisit the bigger picture and study how to manage the viability of compilation. We tackled two main aspects here – reducing the compilation time (which, by extension, helps maintain the programmer's focus) and finding mistakes. The latter is extremely important for identifying what is broken and why. Setting the tools correctly and understanding why things happen greatly contributes to ensuring the quality of the code (and preserving our mental health).

In the next chapter, we'll learn about linking and everything we need to consider in order to build libraries and use them in our projects.

Further reading

For more information, you can refer to the following resources:

- CMake-supported compile features and compilers:
  `https://cmake.org/cmake/help/latest/manual/cmake-compile-features.7.html#supported-compilers`
- Managing sources for targets:
  `https://stackoverflow.com/questions/32411963/why-is-cmake-file-glob-evil`,
  `https://cmake.org/cmake/help/latest/command/target_sources.html`
- The include keyword:
  `https://en.cppreference.com/w/cpp/preprocessor/include`
- Providing paths to included files:
  `https://cmake.org/cmake/help/latest/command/target_include_directories.html`

- Configuring headers:
  https://cmake.org/cmake/help/latest/command/configure_file.html
- Pre-compilation of headers:
  https://cmake.org/cmake/help/latest/command/target_precompile_headers.html
- Unity builds:
  https://cmake.org/cmake/help/latest/prop_tgt/UNITY_BUILD.html
- Precompiled headers unity builds:
  https://www.qt.io/blog/2019/08/01/precompiled-headers-and-unity-jumbo-builds-in-upcoming-cmake
- Finding mistakes – compiler flags:
  https://interrupt.memfault.com/blog/best-and-worst-gcc-clang-compiler-flags
- Why use libraries and not object files:
  https://stackoverflow.com/questions/23615282/object-files-vs-library-files-and-why
- Separation of concerns:
  https://nalexn.github.io/separation-of-concerns/

Join our community on Discord

Join our community's Discord space for discussions with the author and other readers:

https://discord.com/invite/vXN53A7ZcA

8

Linking Executables and Libraries

You might assume that once we've successfully compiled the source code into a binary file, our role as build engineers is complete. However, that's not entirely true. While binary files do contain all the necessary code for a CPU to execute, this code can be distributed across multiple files in a complex manner. We wouldn't want the CPU to scour different files searching for individual code snippets. Instead, our goal is to consolidate these separate units into a single file. To achieve this, we use a process known as linking.

A quick look shows that CMake has few linking commands, with `target_link_libraries()` being the main one. Why dedicate a whole chapter to a single command then? Unfortunately, almost nothing is ever easy in computer science, and linking is no exception: to get the right results, we need to understand the whole story – we need to know how exactly a linker works and get the basics right. We'll talk about the internal structure of object files, how the relocation and reference resolution mechanisms work, and what are they for. We'll discuss how the final executable differs from its components and how the process image is constructed by the system when loading the program into memory.

Then, we'll introduce all kinds of libraries to you: static, shared, and shared modules. Even though they're all called "libraries," they're quite different. Creating a well-linked executable relies on having the right configuration and addressing specific details like **position-independent code (PIC)**.

We'll learn about another nuisance of linking – the **One Definition Rule (ODR)**. It's crucial to have the exact number of definitions. Managing duplicate symbols can be particularly challenging, especially with shared libraries. Additionally, we'll explore why linkers occasionally fail to locate external symbols, even if the executable is correctly linked to the relevant library.

Finally, we'll discover how to use a linker efficiently, preparing our solution for testing within specific frameworks.

In this chapter, we're going to cover the following main topics:

- Getting the basics of linking right
- Building different library types
- Solving problems with the ODR
- The order of linking and unresolved symbols
- Separating `main()` for testing

Technical requirements

You can find the code files that are present in this chapter on GitHub at `https://github.com/PacktPublishing/Modern-CMake-for-Cpp-2E/tree/main/examples/ch08`.

To build the examples provided in this book, always use the recommended commands:

```
cmake -B <build tree> -S <source tree>
cmake --build <build tree>
```

Be sure to replace the `<build tree>` and `<source tree>` placeholders with appropriate paths. As a reminder: **build tree** is the path to the target/output directory and **source tree** is the path in which your source code is located.

Getting the basics of linking right

We discussed the life cycle of a C++ program in *Chapter 7, Compiling C++ Sources with CMake*. It consists of five main stages – writing, compiling, linking, loading, and execution. After correctly compiling all the sources, we need to put them together into an executable. We said that object files produced in a compilation can't be executed by a processor directly. But why?

To answer this, let's understand that object files are a variant of the widely-used **Executable and Linkable Format** (**ELF**), common in Unix-like systems and many others. Systems like Windows or macOS have their own formats, but we'll focus on ELF to explain the principle. *Figure 8.1* shows how a compiler structures these files:

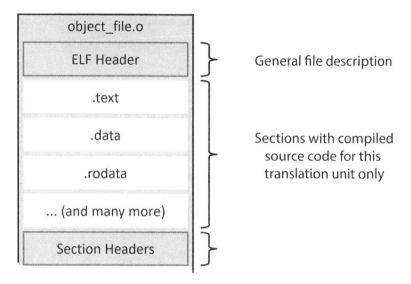

Figure 8.1: The structure of an object file

The compiler will prepare an object file for every unit of translation (for every .cpp file). These files will be used to build an in-memory image of our program. Object files consist of:

- An **ELF Header**, which identifies the target **operating system (OS)**, file type, target instruction set architecture, and details on the position and size of two header tables found in ELF files: the **Program Headers** table (which isn't present in object files) and the **Section Headers** table.

- Binary sections that group information by type.

- A **Section Headers** table, containing information about the name, the type, flags, the destination address in memory, the offset in the file, and other miscellaneous information. It is used to understand what sections are in this file and where they are, just like a table of contents.

When the compiler works through your source code, it categorizes the gathered information into distinct sections. These sections form the core of the ELF file, positioned between the **ELF Header** and the **Section Headers**. Here are some examples of such sections:

- The .text section contains machine code with all the instructions designated for processor execution.

- The .data section holds values for initialized global and static variables.

- The .bss section reserves space for uninitialized global and static variables, which get initialized to zero at the program's start.

- The .rodata section keeps values of constants, making it a read-only data segment.
- The .strtab section is a string table containing constant strings, like "Hello World" from a basic hello.cpp example.
- The .shstrtab section is a string table holding the names of all other sections.

These sections closely mirror the final version of the executable that gets placed into RAM to run our application. Yet, we can't simply concatenate object files together and load the resulting file into the memory. Merging without caution would lead to a host of complications. For one, we'd squander both space and time, consuming excessive RAM pages. Transferring instructions and data to the CPU cache would also become cumbersome. The entire system would have to deal with increased complexity, burning precious cycles, and jumping between countless .text, .data, and other sections during execution.

We'll take a more organized approach: each section of an object file will be grouped with sections of the same type as other object files. This procedure is called **relocation**, which is why the ELF file type for object files is labeled as "Relocatable." But relocation is more than just assembling matching sections. It also involves updating internal references in the file, such as addresses of variables, functions, symbol table indices, and string table indices. Each of these values is local to its own object file and starts numbering from zero. So, when merging files, it's imperative to adjust these values to ensure they reference the right addresses in the consolidated file.

Figure 8.2 shows relocation in action – the .text section is already relocated, the .data is being assembled from all linked files, and the .rodata and .strtab sections will follow the same process (for simplicity, the figure doesn't contain headers):

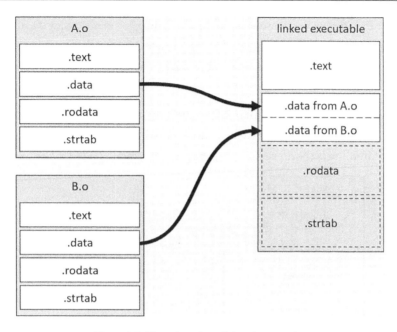

Figure 8.2: The relocation of the .data section

Next, the linker needs to resolve references. When code from one translation unit refers to a symbol defined in another, whether by including its header or using the extern keyword, the compiler acknowledges the declaration, assuming the definition will be provided later. The linker's role is mainly to gather these unresolved external symbol references, and then identify and populate the addresses where they belong in the consolidated executable. *Figure 8.3* shows a simple example of this reference resolution process:

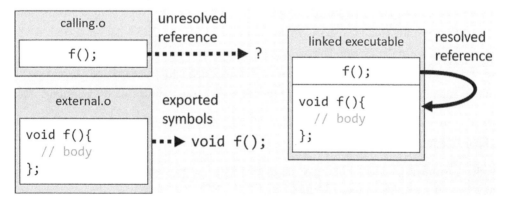

Figure 8.3: A reference resolution

This part of the linking can be a source of problems if a programmer is unaware of how it works. We may end up with unresolved references that can't locate their corresponding external symbols. Or, the opposite: we have provided too many definitions and the linker doesn't know which one to choose.

The final executable file looks very similar to the object file, as it contains relocated sections with resolved references, a **Section Headers** table, and of course, the **ELF Header** describing the whole file. The main difference is the presence of the **Program Header** depicted in the following figure:

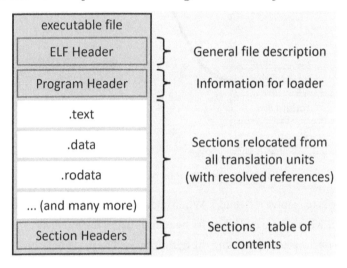

Figure 8.4: The structure of the executable file in ELF

The **Program Header** is located right after the **ELF Header**. The OS's **loader** will read this **Program Header** to set up the program, configure the memory layout, and create a process image. Entries in the **Program Header** specify which sections will be copied, in what order, and to which addresses in the virtual memory. They also contain information about their access control flags (read, write, or execute), and a few other useful details. Each named section will be represented by one fragment of memory in the created process; such a fragment is called a **segment**.

Object files may also be bundled in a library, which is an intermediate product that can be used in a final executable or another library.

Now that we understand how linking works in principle, let's move on to the next section, where we'll discuss three different types of libraries.

## Chapter 8

Building different library types

After compiling the source code, it's often desirable to sidestep recompilation for the same platform or even share the compiled output with external projects. One could distribute the individual object files as initially produced, but this comes with challenges. Distributing multiple files and integrating them one by one into a buildsystem can be a hassle, particularly when dealing with a large number. A more efficient approach is to consolidate all object files into a singular unit for sharing. CMake significantly simplifies this task. We can generate these libraries with a simple add_library() command (paired with the target_link_libraries() command).

By convention, all the libraries have a common prefix, lib, and use system-specific extensions that denote what kind of library they are:

- A static library has a .a extension on Unix-like systems and .lib on Windows.

- Shared libraries (and modules) have a .so extension on some Unix-like systems (like Linux) and .dylib on others (macOS). On Windows, their extension is .dll.

- Shared modules usually use the same extensions as shared libraries, but not always. On macOS, they can use .so, especially when the module is ported from another Unix platform.

The process of building libraries (static, shared, or shared modules) is by convention called "linking," as can be seen in the build output of the ch08/01-libraries project:

```
[ 33%] Linking CXX static library libmy_static.a
[ 66%] Linking CXX shared library libmy_shared.so
[100%] Linking CXX shared module libmy_module.so
[100%] Built target module_gui
```

However, not all of the preceding libraries necessarily use a linker for their creation. The process might skip certain steps like relocation and reference resolution for some libraries.

Let's delve into each library type to understand their respective workings.

Static libraries

Static libraries are essentially a collection of raw object files stored in an archive. Sometimes, they're extended with an index to speed up linking the process. On Unix-like systems, such archives can be created by the ar tool, and indexed with ranlib.

During the build process, only necessary symbols from the static library are imported into the final executable, optimizing its size and memory usage. This selective integration ensures the executable is self-contained, eliminating the need for external files at runtime.

To create a static library, we can simply use the command that we have already seen in the previous chapters:

```
add_library(<name> [<source>...])
```

This short-hand code will produce a static library by default. This can be overridden by setting the BUILD_SHARED_LIBS variable to ON. If we want to build a static library regardless, we can provide an explicit keyword:

```
add_library(<name> STATIC [<source>...])
```

Utilizing static libraries might not always be an ideal option, especially when we aim to share compiled code among multiple applications running on the same machine.

Shared libraries

Shared libraries differ significantly from static libraries. They are constructed using a linker, which completes both stages of linking. This results in a file complete with section headers, sections, and a section header table, as illustrated in *Figure 8.1*.

Shared libraries, often referred to as shared objects, can be utilized across multiple distinct applications simultaneously. When the first program uses a shared library, the OS loads one instance of it into the memory. Subsequent programs are then provided with the same address by the OS, courtesy of intricate virtual memory mechanisms. However, for every process that uses the library, the .data and .bss segments of the library are instantiated separately. This ensures that each process can adjust its variables without influencing other processes.

Thanks to this approach, the overall memory usage in the system is optimized. If we're using a widely recognized library, it might not be necessary to include it with our program, as it's likely already available on the target machine. However, if it's not pre-installed, users are expected to manually install it before running the application. This can lead to potential issues if the installed version of a library differs from what's expected. Such problems are referred to as "dependency hell." More details can be found in the *Further reading* section of this chapter.

We can build shared libraries by explicitly using the SHARED keyword:

```
add_library(<name> SHARED [<source>...])
```

Since shared libraries are loaded during the program initialization, there's no association between the executing program and the actual library file on disk. Instead, the linking is done indirectly. In Unix-like systems, this is achieved through a **shared object name** (**SONAME**), which can be understood as the "logical name" of the library.

This allows flexibility in library versioning and ensures that backward-compatible changes to libraries don't immediately break dependent applications.

We can query some path properties of the produced SONAME file with generator expressions (be sure to replace `target` with the name of your target):

- `$<TARGET_SONAME_FILE:target>` returns the full path (`.so.3`).
- `$<TARGET_SONAME_FILE_NAME:target>` returns only the filename.
- `$<TARGET_SONAME_FILE_DIR:target>` returns the directory.

These come in handy in more advanced scenarios that we'll cover later in the book, including:

- Correct usage of the generated library during packaging and installation.
- Writing custom CMake rules for dependency management.
- Utilizing SONAME during testing.
- Copying or renaming produced libraries in post-build commands.

You may have similar needs for other OS-specific artifacts; for that purpose, CMake offers two families of generator expressions that offer the same suffixes as SONAME. For Windows, we have:

- `$<TARGET_LINKER_FILE:target>` returns the full path to the `.lib` import library associated with the produced **dynamic-link library** (**DLL**). Note that the `.lib` extension is the same as for the static Windows library, but their application is not the same.
- `$<TARGET_RUNTIME_DLLS:target>` returns a list of DLLs that the target depends on at runtime.
- `$<TARGET_PDB_FILE:target>` returns the full path to the `.pdb` program database file (used for debugging purposes).

Since shared libraries are loaded into the OS's memory during the initialization of the program, they are applicable when knowing upfront which libraries the program will use. What about the scenarios where this needs to be determined during the runtime?

Shared modules

A shared module, or module library, is a variant of a shared library designed to be used as a plugin loaded during runtime. Unlike standard shared libraries, which load automatically when a program starts, a shared module only loads when the program explicitly requests it. This can be done through the system calls:

- `LoadLibrary` on Windows
- `dlopen()` followed by `dlsym()` on Linux and macOS

The primary reason for this approach is memory conservation. Many software applications have advanced features that aren't utilized throughout the life cycle of every process. Loading such features into memory every time would be inefficient.

Alternatively, we might want to provide an avenue for extending the main program with specialized features that can be sold, delivered, and loaded separately.

To build shared modules, we need to use the MODULE keyword:

```
add_library(<name> MODULE [<source>...])
```

You shouldn't attempt to link your executable with a module, as the module is designed to be deployed separately from the executable that will utilize it.

Position-independent code (PIC)

Programs today are inherently somewhat position-independent because of the use of virtual memory. This technology abstracts physical addresses. When calling a function, the CPU uses the **memory management unit (MMU)** to translate a virtual address (starting from 0 for every process) to the corresponding physical address (determined at the time of allocation). Interestingly, these mappings don't always follow a specific order.

Compiling a library introduces uncertainty: it's unclear which processes might use the library or where it will be located in virtual memory. We also can't predict the addresses of the symbols or their locations relative to the library's machine code. To handle this, we need another level of indirection.

PIC was introduced to map symbols (like references to functions and global variables) to their runtime addresses. PIC introduces a new section to the binary file: the **Global Offset Table (GOT)**. During the linking, the relative position of the GOT section to the .text section (the program code) is calculated. All symbol references will be pointed through an offset to a placeholder in the GOT.

When the program is loaded, the GOT section transforms into a memory segment. Over time, this segment accumulates the runtime addresses of the symbols. This method, termed "lazy loading," ensures that the loader populates specific GOT entries only when required.

All sources for shared libraries and modules must be compiled with a PIC flag activated. By setting the POSITION_INDEPENDENT_CODE target property to ON, we'll tell CMake to appropriately add compiler-specific flags such as -fPIC for GCC or Clang.

This property is automatically enabled for shared libraries. However, if a shared library depends on another target, such as a static or object library, you must also apply this property to the dependent target:

```
set_target_properties(dependency
                        PROPERTIES POSITION_INDEPENDENT_CODE ON)
```

Overlooking this step will cause conflicts in CMake, since it checks this property for inconsistencies. You can find a more thorough exploration of this in the *Dealing with conflicting propagated properties* section of *Chapter 5, Working with Targets*.

Our next discussion point pivots to symbols. Specifically, the subsequent section will explore the challenges of name collisions, which can lead to ambiguity and definition inconsistencies.

Solving problems with the ODR

Phil Karlton, Netscape's principal curmudgeon and tech visionary, was right when he said the following:

> "*There are two hard things in computer science: cache invalidation and naming things.*"

Names are difficult for several reasons. They must be precise yet simple, brief yet expressive. This not only gives them meaning but also enables programmers to grasp the concepts underlying the raw implementation. C++ and many other languages add another stipulation: most names must be unique.

This requirement manifests in the form of the ODR: within the scope of a single translation unit (a single .cpp file), you are required to define a symbol exactly once, even if the same name (whether for a variable, function, class type, enumeration, concept, or template) is declared multiple times. To clarify, "declaring" introduces the symbol, while "defining" provides all its details, such as a value for a variable or a body for a function.

During linking, this rule is extended to the entire program, covering all non-inlined functions and variables you effectively use in your code. Consider the following example comprising three source files:

ch08/02-odr-fail/shared.h

```
int i;
```

ch08/02-odr-fail/one.cpp

```
#include <iostream>
#include "shared.h"

int main() {
  std::cout << i << std::endl;
}
```

ch08/02-odr-fail/two.cpp

```
#include "shared.h"
```

It also comprises a listfile:

ch08/02-odr-fail/CMakeLists.txt

```
cmake_minimum_required(VERSION 3.26)
project(ODR CXX)
set(CMAKE_CXX_STANDARD 20)
add_executable(odr one.cpp two.cpp)
```

As you can see, the example is very simple – we created a shared.h header file defining the i variable, which is used in two separate translation units:

- one.cpp simply printing i to the screen
- two.cpp only including the header

But when we try to build the example, the linker produces the following error:

```
/usr/bin/ld:
CMakeFiles/odr.dir/two.cpp.o:(.bss+0x0): multiple definition of 'i';
CMakeFiles/odr.dir/one.cpp.o:(.bss+0x0): first defined here
collect2: error: ld returned 1 exit status
```

Symbols cannot be defined more than once. Yet, there's a significant exception. Types, templates, and extern inline functions can have repeated definitions across multiple translation units, but only if these definitions are identical (meaning they have the exact same sequence of tokens).

To demonstrate this, let's replace the definition of a variable with a definition of a type:

ch08/03-odr-success/shared.h

```
struct shared {
  static inline int i = 1;
};
```

Then, we use it like so:

ch08/03-odr-success/one.cpp

```
#include <iostream>
#include "shared.h"
int main() {
  std::cout << shared::i << std::endl;
}
```

The other two files, two.cpp and CMakeLists.txt, remain the same as in the 02-odr-fail example. Such a change will allow the linking to succeed:

```
[ 33%] Building CXX object CMakeFiles/odr.dir/one.cpp.o
[ 66%] Building CXX object CMakeFiles/odr.dir/two.cpp.o
[100%] Linking CXX executable odr
[100%] Built target odr
```

Alternatively, we can mark the variable as local to a translation unit (it won't be exported outside of the object file). To do so, we'll use the static keyword (this keyword is context specific, so don't confuse it with static keyword in classes), like so:

ch08/04-odr-success/shared.h

```
static int i;
```

If you try linking this example, you will see it works, which implies that the static variables are stored separately for each translation unit. Therefore, modifications to one will not impact the other.

The ODR rule works exactly the same for static libraries as it does for object files, but things aren't so clear when we build our code with shared libraries – let's take a look.

Sorting out dynamically linked duplicated symbols

The linker will allow duplicated symbols here. In the following example, we'll create two shared libraries, A and B, with one `duplicated()` function and two unique `a()` and `b()` functions:

ch08/05-dynamic/a.cpp

```
#include <iostream>
void a() {
  std::cout << "A" << std::endl;
}
void duplicated() {
  std::cout << "duplicated A" << std::endl;
}
```

The second implementation file is almost an exact copy of the first:

ch08/05-dynamic/b.cpp

```
#include <iostream>
void b() {
  std::cout << "B" << std::endl;
}
void duplicated() {
  std::cout << "duplicated B" << std::endl;
}
```

Now, let's use each function to see what happens (we'll declare them locally with extern for simplicity):

ch08/05-dynamic/main.cpp

```
extern void a();
extern void b();
extern void duplicated();
int main() {
  a();
  b();
  duplicated();
}
```

The preceding code will run unique functions from each library and then call a function defined with the same signature in both dynamic libraries. What do you think will happen? Would the linking order matter in this case? Let's test it for two cases:

- `main_1` target will be linked with the a library first
- `main_2` target will be linked with the b library first

The listfile looks like this:

ch08/05-dynamic/CMakeLists.txt

```
cmake_minimum_required(VERSION 3.26)
project(Dynamic CXX)
add_library(a SHARED a.cpp)
add_library(b SHARED b.cpp)
add_executable(main_1 main.cpp)
target_link_libraries(main_1 a b)
add_executable(main_2 main.cpp)
target_link_libraries(main_2 b a)
```

After building and running both executables, we'll see the following output:

```
root@ce492a7cd64b:/root/examples/ch08/05-dynamic# b/main_1
A
B
duplicated A

root@ce492a7cd64b:/root/examples/ch08/05-dynamic# b/main_2
A
B
duplicated B
```

Aha! Clearly, the order in which the libraries are linked matters to the linker. This can lead to confusion if we aren't vigilant. Contrary to what one might think, naming collisions are not that uncommon in practice.

If we define locally visible symbols, they will take precedence over those available from DLLs. Defining the `duplicated()` function in `main.cpp` will override the behavior of both targets.

Always take great care when exporting names from libraries, as you're bound to encounter name collisions sooner or later.

Use namespaces – don't count on the linker

C++ namespaces were invented to avoid such weird problems and deal with the ODR more effectively. The best practice is to wrap your library code in a namespace named after the library. This tactic helps to prevent the complications arising from duplicated symbols.

In our projects we might come across cases where one shared library links to another, forming a long chain. Such situations are not as uncommon as they might seem, especially in intricate configurations. However, it's crucial to understand that simply linking one library to another doesn't introduce any sort of namespace inheritance. Symbols at each link of this chain stay in their original namespaces, as they were when compiled.

While the intricacies of linkers are intriguing and occasionally essential, another pressing issue often crops up: the mysterious disappearance of properly defined symbols. Let's delve into that in the next section.

The order of linking and unresolved symbols

The behavior of the linker can sometimes seem capricious, throwing complaints seemingly without cause. This often becomes a particularly vexing challenge for novice programmers unfamiliar with the intricacies of this tool. Understandably, they often try to steer clear of build configurations for as long as possible. But there comes a time when they need to make a change – perhaps integrating a library they've developed – and all hell breaks loose.

Consider this: a relatively straightforward dependency chain where the main executable relies on an "outer" library. In turn, this outer library depends on a "nested" library that contains the essential int b variable. Out of the blue, a cryptic error message confronts the programmer:

```
outer.cpp:(.text+0x1f): undefined reference to 'b'
```

Such errors are not particularly uncommon. Typically, they indicate a forgotten library in the linker. Yet, in this scenario, the library seems to have been correctly added to the target_link_libraries() command:

ch08/06-unresolved/CMakeLists.txt

```
cmake_minimum_required(VERSION 3.26)
project(Order CXX)
add_library(outer outer.cpp)
add_library(nested nested.cpp)
add_executable(main main.cpp)
target_link_libraries(main nested outer)
```

What then!? Very few errors can be as infuriating to debug and understand. What we're seeing here is an incorrect order of linking. Let's dive into the source code to figure out the reason:

ch08/06-unresolved/main.cpp

```
#include <iostream>
extern int a;
int main() {
  std::cout << a << std::endl;
}
```

The code seems easy enough – we'll print an external variable a, which can be found in the outer library. We're declaring it ahead of time with the extern keyword. Here is the source for that library:

ch08/06-unresolved/outer.cpp

```
extern int b;
int a = b;
```

This is quite simple too – outer depends on the nested library to provide the external variable, b, which gets assigned to the a variable. Let's see the source of nested to confirm that we're not missing the definition:

ch08/06-unresolved/nested.cpp

```
int b = 123;
```

Indeed, we have provided the definition for b, and since it's not marked as local with the static keyword, it's correctly exported from the nested target. As we saw previously, this target is linked with the main executable in CMakeLists.txt:

```
target_link_libraries(main nested outer)
```

So, where does the undefined reference to 'b' error come from?

Resolving undefined symbols works like this – a linker processes the binaries from left to right. As the linker iterates through the binaries, it will do the following:

1. Collect all undefined symbols exported from this binary and store them for later.
2. Try to resolve undefined symbols (collected from all binaries processed so far) with symbols defined in this binary.
3. Repeat this process for the next binary.

If any symbols remain undefined after the whole operation is completed, the linking fails. This is the case in our example (CMake prepends the object files of the executable target in front of the libraries):

1. The linker processed main.o, found an undefined reference to the a variable, and collected it for future resolution.

2. The linker processed libnested.a, no undefined references were found, and there was nothing to resolve.

3. The linker processed libouter.a, found an undefined reference to the b variable, and resolved the reference to the a variable.

We did correctly resolve the reference to the a variable, but not to the b variable. To correct this, we need to reverse the order of linking so that nested comes after outer:

```
target_link_libraries(main outer nested)
```

Sometimes, we'll encounter cyclic references, where translation units define symbols for each other, and there's no single valid order where all references can be satisfied. The only way to solve this is to process some targets twice:

```
target_link_libraries(main nested outer nested)
```

This is a common practice, however slightly inelegant in use. If you have the privilege of using CMake 3.24 or newer, you can utilize the $<LINK_GROUP> generator expression with the RESCAN feature that adds linker-specific flags, like --start-group or --end-group, to ensure all symbols are evaluated:

```
target_link_libraries(main "$<LINK_GROUP:RESCAN,nested,outer>")
```

Bear in mind that this mechanism introduces additional processing steps and should be used only if necessary. There are very rare cases where cyclic references are needed (and justified). Encountering this issue usually indicates poor design. It's supported on Linux, BSD, SunOS, and Windows with a GNU toolchain.

We're now prepared to deal with ODR issues. What other problems we can encounter? Suspiciously missing symbols during linking. Let's find out what that's about.

Dealing with unreferenced symbols

When libraries, especially static libraries, are created, they are essentially archives that consist of multiple object files bundled together. We mentioned that some archiving tools might also create symbol indexes to expedite the linking process. Those indexes provide a mapping between each symbol and the object files in which they are defined. When a symbol is resolved, the object file containing it is incorporated into the resulting binary (some linkers further optimize this by only including specific sections of the file). If no symbols from an object file within a static library are referenced, that object file might be entirely omitted. Hence, only portions of a static library that are actually used could appear in the final binary.

However, there are several scenarios where you might need some of the unreferenced symbols:

- **Static initialization**: If your library has global objects requiring initialization (i.e., their constructors are executed) before `main()`, and these objects aren't directly referenced elsewhere; the linker might exclude them from the final binary.

- **Plugin architectures**: If you're developing a plugin system (with module libraries) where code needs to be identified and loaded at runtime without direct referencing.

- **Unused code in static libraries**: If you're developing a static library containing utility functions or code that isn't always directly referenced but you still want it in the final binary.

- **Template instantiations**: For libraries relying heavily on templates; some template instantiations might be overlooked during linking if not explicitly mentioned.

- **Linking Issues**: Particularly with intricate buildsystems or elaborate codebases, linking might yield unpredictable outcomes where some symbols or code sections appear to be absent.

In these instances, forcing the inclusion of all object files during the linking process might be beneficial. This is often achieved via a mode called `whole-archive` linking.

Specific compiler linking flags are:

- `--whole-archive` for GCC
- `--force-load` for Clang
- `/WHOLEARCHIVE` for MSVC

To do so, we can use the `target_link_options()` command:

```
target_link_options(tgt INTERFACE
  -Wl,--whole-archive $<TARGET_FILE:lib1> -Wl,--no-whole-archive
)
```

However, this command is linker specific, so incorporating generator expressions to detect different compilers and provide respective flags is essential. Fortunately, CMake 3.24 introduced a new generator expression for this purpose:

```
target_link_libraries(tgt INTERFACE
  "$<LINK_LIBRARY:WHOLE_ARCHIVE,lib1>"
)
```

Utilizing this method ensures that the `tgt` target incorporates all object files from the `lib1` library.

Nevertheless, a few potential drawbacks need consideration:

- **Increased binary size:** This flag can substantially enlarge your final binary since all objects from the specified library are incorporated, whether they're utilized or not.
- **Potential for symbol clashes:** Introducing all symbols might cause clashes with others, leading to linker errors.
- **Maintenance overhead:** Over-relying on such flags can obscure underlying issues in the design or structure of your code.

With an understanding of how to address common linking challenges, we can now progress to preparing our project for tests.

Separating main() for testing

As we've established, the linker enforces the ODR and ensures that all external symbols provide their definitions during the linking process. Another linker-related challenge we might face is the elegant and efficient testing of the project.

In an ideal scenario, we should be testing the exact same source code that runs in production. A comprehensive testing pipeline would build the source code, run tests on the resulting binary, and then package and distribute the executable (optionally excluding the tests themselves).

But how can we implement this? Executables typically have a precise execution flow, often involving the reading of command-line arguments. The compiled nature of C++ doesn't readily support pluggable units that can be temporarily injected into the binary just for testing. This suggests that we may need a nuanced approach to tackle this challenge.

Luckily, we can use a linker to help us deal with this in an elegant manner. Consider extracting all logic from your program's main() to an external function, start_program(), like so:

ch08/07-testing/main.cpp

```
extern int start_program(int, const char**);
int main(int argc, const char** argv) {
  return start_program(argc, argv);
}
```

It's reasonable to skip testing this new main() function when it's written in such form; it is only forwarding arguments to a function defined elsewhere (in another file). We can then create a library containing the original source from main() wrapped in a new function – start_program(). In this example, the code checks whether the command-line argument count is higher than 1:

ch08/07-testing/program.cpp

```
#include <iostream>
int start_program(int argc, const char** argv) {
  if (argc <= 1) {
    std::cout << "Not enough arguments" << std::endl;
    return 1;
  }
  return 0;
}
```

We can now prepare a project that builds this application and links together those two translation units:

ch08/07-testing/CMakeLists.txt

```
cmake_minimum_required(VERSION 3.26)
project(Testing CXX)
add_library(program program.cpp)
add_executable(main main.cpp)
target_link_libraries(main program)
```

The main target is just providing the required main() function. The command-line argument verification logic is contained in the program target. We can now test it by creating another executable with its own main() function, which will host the test cases.

In a real-world scenario, frameworks such as **GoogleTest** or **Catch2** will provide their own main() method that can be used to replace your program's entry point and run all the defined tests. We'll dive deep into the subject of actual testing in *Chapter 11, Testing Frameworks*. For now, let's focus on the general principle and write our own test cases directly in the main() function:

ch08/07-testing/test.cpp

```cpp
#include <iostream>
extern int start_program(int, const char**);
using namespace std;
int main()
{
  cout << "Test 1: Passing zero arguments to start_program:\n";
  auto exit_code = start_program(0, nullptr);
  if (exit_code == 0)
    cout << "Test FAILED: Unexpected zero exit code.\n";
  else
    cout << "Test PASSED: Non-zero exit code returned.\n";
  cout << endl;

  cout << "Test 2: Passing 2 arguments to start_program:\n";
  const char *arguments[2] = {"hello", "world"};
  exit_code = start_program(2, arguments);
  if (exit_code != 0)
    cout << "Test FAILED: Unexpected non-zero exit code\n";
  else
    cout << "Test PASSED\n";
}
```

The preceding code will call start_program twice, with and without arguments, and check whether the returned exit codes are correct. Here's the output you'll see if tests execute correctly:

```
./test
Test 1: Passing zero arguments to start_program:
Not enough arguments
Test PASSED: Non-zero exit code returned

Test 2: Passing 2 arguments to start_program:
Test PASSED
```

The Not enough arguments line is coming from start_program(), and is an expected error message (we're checking whether the program is failing correctly).

This unit test leaves much to be desired in terms of clean code and elegant testing practices, but it's a start.

We have now defined main() twice:

- In main.cpp for production use
- In test.cpp for test purposes

Let's define the testing executable at the bottom of our CMakeLists.txt now:

```
add_executable(test test.cpp)
target_link_libraries(test program)
```

This addition creates a new target that links against the same binary code as our production code. Yet, it gives us the flexibility to call all exported functions as needed. Thanks to this, we can run all code paths automatically and check whether they work as expected. Great!

Summary

Linking in CMake might initially appear straightforward, but as we dig deeper, we see there's much more beneath the surface. After all, linking executables isn't as simple as piecing puzzle parts together. When we delve deep into the structure of object files and libraries, it's clear that sections, which store various types of data, instructions, symbol names, and the like, need some reordering. Before a program is runnable, these sections undergo what's known as relocation.

It's also crucial to resolve symbols. The linker must sort through references across all translation units, ensuring nothing's left out. Once this is settled, the linker then creates the program header and places it into the final executable. This header offers instructions to the system loader, detailing how to transform consolidated sections into segments that will make up the runtime memory image of the process. We also discussed the three kinds of libraries: static, shared, and shared modules. We examined how they differ and which scenarios some might be better suited for than others. Additionally, we touched on PIC – a powerful concept that facilitates the lazy binding of symbols.

The ODR is a C++ concept, but as we've seen, it's strongly enforced by linkers. We looked at how to tackle the most basic symbol duplication in both static and dynamic libraries. We also highlighted the value of using namespaces whenever possible and advised against depending too much on a linker to prevent symbol collisions.

For a step that might seem straightforward (given CMake's limited commands dedicated to linking), it certainly has its complexities. One of the trickier aspects is the order of linking, especially when dealing with libraries that have nested and cyclical dependencies. We now understand how the linker selects symbols that end up in the final binary file, and how we can override this behavior if needed.

Lastly, we investigated how to take advantage of a linker to prepare our program for testing – by separating the main() function into another translation unit. This enabled us to introduce another executable, which ran tests against the exact same machine code that will be executed in production.

With our newfound knowledge of linking, we're ready to bring external libraries into our CMake projects. In the next chapter, we'll look at how to manage dependencies in CMake.

Further reading

For more information on the topics covered in this chapter, you can refer to the following:

- The structure of ELF files:
  https://en.wikipedia.org/wiki/Executable_and_Linkable_Format
- The CMake manual for add_library():
  https://cmake.org/cmake/help/latest/command/add_library.html
- Dependency hell:
  https://en.wikipedia.org/wiki/Dependency_hell
- The differences between modules and shared libraries:
  https://stackoverflow.com/questions/4845984/difference-between-modules-and-shared-libraries

Join our community on Discord

Join our community's Discord space for discussions with the author and other readers:

https://discord.com/invite/vXN53A7ZcA

9

Managing Dependencies in CMake

It doesn't really matter if your solution is large or small; as it grows, you'll likely choose to rely on other projects. Avoiding the effort of creating and maintaining boilerplate code is crucial. This frees up your time for what truly matters: the business logic. External dependencies serve multiple purposes. They offer frameworks and features, solve complex issues, and play a key role in building and ensuring code quality. These dependencies can vary, ranging from specialized compilers like **Protocol Buffers (Protobuf)** to testing frameworks like Google Test.

When working with open-source projects or in-house code, managing external dependencies efficiently is essential. Doing this manually would require a lot of setup time and ongoing support. Luckily, CMake excels at handling various approaches to dependency management while staying current with industry standards.

We will first learn how to identify and utilize dependencies already present on the host system, thereby avoiding unnecessary downloads and extended compilation times. This task is relatively straightforward, as many packages are either CMake-compatible or supported by CMake right out of the box. We'll also explore how to instruct CMake to locate and include dependencies that lack this native support. For legacy packages, an alternative approach can be beneficial in specific situations: we can employ the once-popular `pkg-config` tool to handle the more cumbersome tasks.

Additionally, we will delve into managing dependencies that are available online but not yet installed on the system. We'll examine how to fetch these from HTTP servers, Git, and other types of repositories. We will also discuss how to choose the optimal approach: first, searching within the system and then resorting to fetching if the package is not found. Finally, we'll review an older technique for downloading external projects that may be applicable in special cases.

In this chapter, we're going to cover the following main topics:

- Using already installed dependencies
- Using dependencies not present in the system

Technical requirements

You can find the code files that are present in this chapter on GitHub at `https://github.com/ PacktPublishing/Modern-CMake-for-Cpp-2E/tree/main/examples/ch09`.

To build the examples provided in this book, always use the recommended commands:

```
cmake -B <build tree> -S <source tree>
cmake --build <build tree>
```

Be sure to replace the `<build tree>` and `<source tree>` placeholders with appropriate paths. As a reminder: **build tree** is the path to the target/output directory and **source tree** is the path at which your source code is located.

Using already installed dependencies

When our project depends on a popular library, it's likely that the operating system already has the right package installed. We just have to connect it to our project's build process. How do we do that? We need to find out where the package is on the system so CMake can use its files. Doing this by hand is possible, but every environment is a little different. A path that works on one system might not work on another. So, we should automatically find these paths when building. There are different ways to do this, but the best method is usually CMake's built-in `find_package()` command, which knows how to find many commonly used packages.

If our package isn't supported, we have two options:

- We can write a small plugin called a `find-module` to help `find_package()`
- We can use an older method called `pkg-config`

Let's start with the recommended option first.

Finding packages with CMake's find_package()

Let's start by looking at the following scenario: you want to improve the way you're doing network communication or data storage. Simple plain-text files or open-text formats like JSON and XML are too verbose in terms of size. Using a binary format would help things, and a well-known library like Google's Protobuf looks like the answer.

You've read the instructions and installed what you need on your system. Now what? How do you get CMake's find_package() to find and use this new library?

To execute this example, we have to install the dependencies we want to use because the find_package() command only looks for packages that are already on your system. It assumes you've got everything installed, or that users know how to install what's needed if they're told to. If you want to handle other situations, you'll need a backup plan. You can find more about this in the *Using dependencies not present in the system* section.

In the case of Protobuf, the situation is fairly straightforward: you can either download, compile, and install the library yourself from the official repository (https://github.com/protocolbuffers/protobuf) or use the package manager in your operating system. If you're following these examples using the Docker image mentioned in *Chapter 1*, *First Steps with CMake*, your dependencies are already installed and you don't need to do anything. However, if you'd like to try installing by yourself, the commands to install the Protobuf library and compiler for Debian Linux are as follows:

```
$ apt update
$ apt install protobuf-compiler libprotobuf-dev
```

Many projects these days choose to support CMake. They do this by creating a **config file** and putting it in the appropriate system directory during installation. Config files are an inherent part of projects opting in to support CMake.

If you want to use a library that doesn't have a config file, don't worry. CMake supports an external mechanism to find such libraries called **find modules**. Unlike config files, find modules are not part of the project they're helping to locate. In fact, CMake itself often comes with these find modules for many popular libraries.

If you're stuck and without either a config file or a find module, you have other choices:

- Write your own find modules for the specific package and include them in your project
- Use a FindPkgConfig module to leverage legacy Unix package definition files
- Write a config file and ask package maintainers to include it

You might think that you're not quite ready to create such merge requests yourself. That's okay because you most likely won't have to. CMake comes with over 150 find modules that can find libraries such as Boost, bzip2, curl, curses, GIF, GTK, iconv, ImageMagick, JPEG, Lua, OpenGL, OpenSSL, PNG, PostgreSQL, Qt, SDL, Threads, XML-RPC, X11, and zlib, as well as the Protobuf file that we're going to use in this example. A full list is available in the CMake documentation (see the *Further reading* section).

Both find modules and config files can be used with CMake's `find_package()` command. CMake starts by checking its built-in find modules. If it doesn't find what it needs, it moves on to checking the config files provided by different packages. CMake scans paths where packages are usually installed (depending on the operating system). It looks for files that match these patterns:

- `<CamelCasePackageName>Config.cmake`
- `<kebab-case-package-name>-config.cmake`

If you want to add external find modules to your project, set the `CMAKE_MODULE_PATH` variable. CMake will scan this directory first.

Going back to our example, the goal is simple: I want to show that I can build a project that uses Protobuf effectively. Don't worry, you don't need to know Protobuf to understand what happens. In basic terms, Protobuf is a library that saves data in a specific binary format. This makes it easy to write and read C++ objects to and from files or over a network. To set this up, we use a `.proto` file to give Protobuf the data structure:

ch09/01-find-package-variables/message.proto

```
syntax = "proto3";
message Message {
    int32 id = 1;
}
```

This code is a simple schema definition that includes a single 32-bit integer. The Protobuf package comes with a binary that will compile these `.proto` files into C++ sources and headers that our application can use. We'll need to add this compilation step to our build process, but we'll get back to that later. For now, let's see how our `main.cpp` file uses the output generated by Protobuf:

ch09/01-find-package-variables/main.cpp

```
#include "message.pb.h"
#include <fstream>
using namespace std;
int main()
{
  Message m;
  m.set_id(123);
  m.PrintDebugString();
  fstream fo("./hello.data", ios::binary | ios::out);
  m.SerializeToOstream(&fo);
```

```
    fo.close();
    return 0;
}
```

I've included a `message.pb.h` header that I expect Protobuf to generate. This header will have the definition for the `Message` object, as configured in `message.proto`. In the `main()` function, I'm creating a simple `Message` object. I set its `id` field to 123 as a random example and then print its debug information to the standard output. Next, a binary version of this object is written to the file stream. This is the most basic use case for a serialization library like Protobuf.

The `message.pb.h` header has to be generated before `main.cpp` is compiled. This is done by `protoc`, the Protobuf compiler, which takes `message.proto` as input. Managing this process sounds complicated, but it's really not!

This is where the CMake magic happens:

ch09/01-find-package-variables/CMakeLists.txt

```
cmake_minimum_required(VERSION 3.26.0)
project(FindPackageProtobufVariables CXX)
find_package(Protobuf REQUIRED)
protobuf_generate_cpp(GENERATED_SRC GENERATED_HEADER
                      message.proto)
add_executable(main main.cpp ${GENERATED_SRC} ${GENERATED_HEADER})
target_link_libraries(main PRIVATE ${Protobuf_LIBRARIES})
target_include_directories(main PRIVATE
  ${Protobuf_INCLUDE_DIRS} ${CMAKE_CURRENT_BINARY_DIR}
)
```

Let's break this down:

- The first two lines are straightforward: they set up the project and specify that it will use the C++ language.

- `find_package(Protobuf REQUIRED)` tells CMake to find the Protobuf library (by executing the bundled `FindProtobuf.cmake` find module) and prepare it for use in our project. If it can't find the library, the build will stop because we used the `REQUIRED` keyword.

- `protobuf_generate_cpp` is a custom function defined in the Protobuf find module. It automates the process of invoking the `protoc` compiler. After successful compilation, it will store paths to the generated sources in variables provided as the first two arguments: `GENERATED_SRC` and `GENERATED_HEADER`. All subsequent arguments will be treated as a list of files to compile (`message.proto`).

- add_executable creates our executable using main.cpp and Protobuf-generated files.
- target_link_libraries tells CMake to link the Protobuf libraries to our executable.
- target_include_directories() adds to include paths the necessary INCLUDE_DIRS provided by the package and CMAKE_CURRENT_BINARY_DIR. The latter tells the compiler where to find the message.pb.h header.

The Protobuf find module provides the following functionalities:

- It finds the Protobuf library and its compiler.
- It provides helper functions to compile the .proto files.
- It sets variables with paths for inclusion and linking.

While not every module comes with convenient helper functions like Protobuf, most modules do set up a few key variables for you. These are useful for managing the dependency in your project. Whether you're using a built-in find module or a config file, after the package is successfully found, you can expect some or all of the following variables to be set:

- <PKG_NAME>_FOUND: This indicates whether the package was successfully found.
- <PKG_NAME>_INCLUDE_DIRS or <PKG_NAME>_INCLUDES: This points to the directories where the package's header files are located.
- <PKG_NAME>_LIBRARIES or <PKG_NAME>_LIBS: These are lists of libraries that you'll need to link against.
- <PKG_NAME>_DEFINITIONS: This contains any compiler definitions needed for the package.

After running find_package(), you can immediately check the <PKG_NAME>_FOUND variable to see whether CMake was successful in locating the package.

If a package module is written for CMake 3.10 or newer, it will also likely provide target definitions. These targets will be designated as IMPORTED targets to distinguish them as originating from an external dependency.

Protobuf is a great example to explore when learning about dependencies in CMake, as it defines module-specific variables and IMPORTED targets. Such targets allow us to write even more concise code:

ch09/02-find-package-targets/CMakeLists.txt

```
cmake_minimum_required(VERSION 3.26.0)
project(FindPackageProtobufTargets CXX)
find_package(Protobuf REQUIRED)
```

```
protobuf_generate_cpp(GENERATED_SRC GENERATED_HEADER
  message.proto)
add_executable(main main.cpp ${GENERATED_SRC} ${GENERATED_HEADER})
target_link_libraries(main PRIVATE protobuf::libprotobuf)
target_include_directories(main PRIVATE
                                ${CMAKE_CURRENT_BINARY_DIR})
```

Look at how the highlighted code compares with the previous version of this example: instead of using variables that listfiles and directories, it's a good idea to use IMPORTED targets. This approach simplifies the listfile. It also automatically takes care of transient usage requirements, or propagated properties, as illustrated here with protobuf::libprotobuf target.

 If you want to know exactly what a specific find module provides, your best resource is its online documentation. For example, you can find detailed information for Protobuf on the CMake official website at this link: https://cmake.org/cmake/help/latest/module/FindProtobuf.html.

To keep things simple, examples in this section will simply fail if the Protobuf library is not found in the user's system. But a really robust solution should verify the Protobuf_FOUND variable, and present a clear diagnostic message for the user (so they can install it) or perform the installation automatically. We'll learn how to do this later in this chapter.

The find_package() command has several arguments you can use. While there's a longer list of them, we'll focus on the key ones here. The basic format of the command is:

```
find_package(<Name> [version] [EXACT] [QUIET] [REQUIRED])
```

Let's break down what each of these optional arguments means:

- [version] This specifies the minimum version of the package you need in the major.minor.patch.tweak format (such as 1.22). You can also specify a range, like 1.22...1.40.1, using three dots as a separator.

- EXACT: Use this with a non-range [version] to tell CMake you want an exact version and not a newer one.

- QUIET: This suppresses all messages about whether the package was found or not.

- REQUIRED: This will stop the build if a package is not found and a diagnostic message will be shown even if QUIET is used.

If you're pretty sure that a package should be on your system but find_package() isn't locating it, there's a way to dig deeper. Starting with CMake 3.24, you can run the configure stage in debug mode to get more information. Use the following command:

```
cmake -B <build tree> -S <source tree> --debug-find-pkg=<pkg>
```

Be cautious with this command. Make sure you type the package name exactly as it is because it's case-sensitive.

More information on the find_package() command can be found on the documentation page here: https://cmake.org/cmake/help/latest/command/find_package.html.

Find modules are meant as a very convenient way of providing CMake with information on installed dependencies. Most popular libraries are widely supported by CMake on all major platforms. What can we do, though, when we want to use a third-party library that doesn't have a dedicated find module yet?

Writing your own find modules

On a rare occasion, the library that you really want to use in your project doesn't provide a config file and there's no find module readily available in CMake yet. You can then write a custom find module for that library and ship it with your project. This situation is not ideal, but in the interest of taking care of the users of your project, it has to be done.

We can try writing a custom find module for the libpqxx library, a client for the PostgreSQL database. libpqxx is preinstalled in the Docker image for this book, so there's no need to worry if you're using that. Debian users can install it using the libpqxx-dev package (other operating systems may require different commands):

```
apt-get install libpqxx-dev
```

We'll begin by writing a new file named FindPQXX.cmake and storing it in the cmake/module directory within our project's source tree. To ensure that CMake discovers this find module when find_package() is called, we'll add its path to the CMAKE_MODULE_PATH variable in our CMakeLists. txt using list(APPEND). Just a quick reminder: CMake will first check the directories listed in CMAKE_MODULE_PATH to find the find modules before searching in other locations. Your complete listfile should look like this:

ch09/03-find-package-custom/CMakeLists.txt

```
cmake_minimum_required(VERSION 3.26.0)
project(FindPackageCustom CXX)
```

```
list(APPEND CMAKE_MODULE_PATH
            "${CMAKE_SOURCE_DIR}/cmake/module/")
find_package(PQXX REQUIRED)
add_executable(main main.cpp)
target_link_libraries(main PRIVATE PQXX::PQXX)
```

With that in place, let's move on to writing the actual find module. If the FindPQXX.cmake file is empty, CMake won't raise any errors, even if you use find_package() with REQUIRED. It's the responsibility of the find module's author to set the correct variables and follow best practices (like raising errors). According to CMake's guidelines, here are some key points to note:

- When find_package(<PKG_NAME> REQUIRED) is called, CMake sets a <PKG_NAME>_FIND_REQUIRED variable to 1. The find module should then use message(FATAL_ERROR) if the library isn't found.

- When find_package(<PKG_NAME> QUIET) is used, CMake sets <PKG_NAME>_FIND_QUIETLY to 1. The find module should avoid displaying any extra messages.

- CMake sets a <PKG_NAME>_FIND_VERSION variable to the version specified in the listfiles. If the find module can't locate the right version, it should trigger a FATAL_ERROR.

Of course, it's best to follow the preceding rules for consistency with other find modules.

To create an elegant find module for PQXX, let's follow these steps:

1. If the paths to the library and headers are already known (supplied by the user or retrieved from the cache of a previous run), use these paths to create an IMPORTED target. If this is done, you can stop here.

2. If the paths are not known, begin by finding the library and headers for the underlying dependency, which, in this case, is PostgreSQL.

3. Next, search the well-known paths to locate the binary version of the PostgreSQL client library.

4. Similarly, scan the known paths to find the PostgreSQL client's include headers.

5. Finally, confirm whether both the library and include headers are located. If they are, create an IMPORTED target.

To create a robust find module for PQXX, let's focus on a couple of important tasks. First, the creation of an IMPORTED target can happen in two scenarios – either the user specifies the library's paths or the paths are automatically detected. To keep our code clean and avoid duplication, we'll write a function that manages the outcome of our search process.

Defining IMPORTED targets

To set up an IMPORTED target, all we really need is a library defined with the IMPORTED keyword. This will enable us to use the target_link_libraries() command in the calling CMakeLists. txt listfile. We need to specify the type of the library, and for simplicity, we'll mark it as UNKNOWN. This means we're not concerned about whether the library is static or dynamic; we just want to pass an argument to the linker.

Next, we set the essential properties for our target – namely, IMPORTED_LOCATION and INTERFACE_ INCLUDE_DIRECTORIES. We use the arguments provided to the function for these settings. It's possible to specify additional properties like COMPILE_DEFINITIONS, but they are not needed for PQXX.

After that, to make our find module more efficient, we'll store the found paths in cache variables. This way, we won't have to repeat the search in future runs. It's worth noting that we explicitly set PQXX_FOUND in the cache, making it globally accessible and allowing the user's CMakeLists. txt to reference it.

Finally, we mark these cache variables as advanced, hiding them in the CMake GUI unless the advanced option is activated. This is a common best practice that we'll also adopt.

Here's how the code looks for these operations:

ch09/03-find-package-custom/cmake/module/FindPQXX.cmake

```
# Defining IMPORTED targets
function(define_imported_target library headers)
  add_library(PQXX::PQXX UNKNOWN IMPORTED)
  set_target_properties(PQXX::PQXX PROPERTIES
    IMPORTED_LOCATION ${library}
    INTERFACE_INCLUDE_DIRECTORIES ${headers}
  )
  set(PQXX_FOUND 1 CACHE INTERNAL "PQXX found" FORCE)
  set(PQXX_LIBRARIES ${library}
      CACHE STRING "Path to pqxx library" FORCE)
  set(PQXX_INCLUDES ${headers}
      CACHE STRING "Path to pqxx headers" FORCE)
  mark_as_advanced(FORCE PQXX_LIBRARIES)
  mark_as_advanced(FORCE PQXX_INCLUDES)
endfunction()
```

Now, we'll discuss how to use custom or previously stored paths for quicker setup.

Accepting user-provided paths and reusing cached values

Let's address the situation where a user has installed PQXX in a non-standard location and provides the needed paths via command-line arguments using -D. If that's the case, we immediately call the function we defined earlier and stop the search by using return(). We assume that the user has provided accurate paths to both the library and its dependencies, like PostgreSQL:

ch09/03-find-package-custom/cmake/module/FindPQXX.cmake (continued)

```
...

# Accepting user-provided paths and reusing cached values
if (PQXX_LIBRARIES AND PQXX_INCLUDES)
  define_imported_target(${PQXX_LIBRARIES} ${PQXX_INCLUDES})
  return()
endif()
```

This condition will hold true if a configuration was carried out previously, as the variables PQXX_LIBRARIES and PQXX_INCLUDES are stored in the cache.

It's time to see how to handle finding the additional libraries that PQXX relies on.

Searching for nested dependencies

To utilize PQXX, the host system must also have PostgreSQL installed. While it's perfectly fine to use another find module within our current find module, we should pass along the REQUIRED and QUIET flags to ensure consistent behavior between the nested search and the main search. To do so, we'll set two helper variables to store the keywords we need to pass and fill them according to arguments received from CMake: PQXX_FIND_QUIETLY and PQXX_FIND_REQUIRED.

```
# Searching for nested dependencies
set(QUIET_ARG)
if(PQXX_FIND_QUIETLY)
  set(QUIET_ARG QUIET)
endif()

set(REQUIRED_ARG)
if(PQXX_FIND_REQUIRED)
  set(REQUIRED_ARG REQUIRED)
endif()
find_package(PostgreSQL ${QUIET_ARG} ${REQUIRED_ARG})
```

Having this done, we'll dive into the specifics of pinpointing where the PQXX library resides in the operating system.

Searching for library files

CMake offers the find_library() command to help find library files. This command will accept the filenames to look for and a list of possible paths, formatted in CMake's path style:

```
find_library(<VAR_NAME> NAMES <NAMES> PATHS <PATHS> <...>)
```

<VAR_NAME> will serve as the name for variables that store the command's output. If a matching file is found, its path will be stored in the <VAR_NAME> variable. Otherwise, the <VAR_NAME>-NOTFOUND variable will be set to 1. We'll use PQXX_LIBRARY_PATH as our VAR_NAME, so we'll end up with either a path in PQXX_LIBRARY_PATH or 1 in PQXX_LIBRARY_PATH-NOTFOUND.

The PQXX library often exports its location to an $ENV{PQXX_DIR} environment variable, meaning the system may already know its whereabouts. We can include this path in our search by first formatting it using file(TO_CMAKE_PATH):

ch09/03-find-package-custom/cmake/module/FindPQXX.cmake (continued)

```
...

# Searching for library files
file(TO_CMAKE_PATH "$ENV{PQXX_DIR}" _PQXX_DIR)
find_library(PQXX_LIBRARY_PATH NAMES libpqxx pqxx
  PATHS
    ${_PQXX_DIR}/lib/${CMAKE_LIBRARY_ARCHITECTURE}
    # (...) many other paths - removed for brevity
    /usr/lib
  NO_DEFAULT_PATH
)
```

The NO_DEFAULT_PATH keyword instructs CMake to bypass its standard list of search paths. While you generally wouldn't want to do this (since the default paths are often correct), using NO_DEFAULT_PATH allows you to explicitly specify your own search locations if needed.

Let's move on to finding the required header files that can be included by users of the library.

Searching for header files

To search for all known header files, we'll use the find_path() command, which works very similarly to find_library(). The main difference is that find_library() automatically appends system-specific extensions for libraries, whereas with find_path(), we need to specify exact names.

Also, don't get confused here with pqxx/pqxx. It's an actual header file, but its extension was intentionally left off by the library creators to align with C++ #include directives. This allows it to be used with angle brackets, like so: #include <pqxx/pqxx>.

Here's the snippet:

ch09/03-find-package-custom/cmake/module/FindPQXX.cmake (continued)

```
...

# Searching for header files
find_path(PQXX_HEADER_PATH NAMES pqxx/pqxx
  PATHS
    ${_PQXX_DIR}/include
    # (...) many other paths - removed for brevity
    /usr/include
  NO_DEFAULT_PATH
)
```

Next, we'll look at how to finalize the search process, handle any missing paths, and call the function defining imported targets.

Returning the final results

Now, it's time to check whether we have any PQXX_LIBRARY_PATH-NOTFOUND or PQXX_HEADER_PATH-NOTFOUND variables set. We can either manually print diagnostic messages and halt the build, or we can use the find_package_handle_standard_args() helper function from CMake. This function sets the <PKG_NAME>_FOUND variable to 1 if the path variables are correctly filled. It also provides appropriate diagnostic messages (it will respect the QUIET keyword) and will halt execution with a FATAL_ERROR if a REQUIRED keyword is provided in the find_package() invocation.

If a library is found, we'll call the function we wrote earlier to define the IMPORTED targets and store the paths in the cache:

ch09/03-find-package-custom/cmake/module/FindPQXX.cmake (continued)

```
...

# Returning the final results
include(FindPackageHandleStandardArgs)
find_package_handle_standard_args(
  PQXX DEFAULT_MSG PQXX_LIBRARY_PATH PQXX_HEADER_PATH
)
if (PQXX_FOUND)
  define_imported_target(
    "${PQXX_LIBRARY_PATH};${POSTGRES_LIBRARIES}"
    "${PQXX_HEADER_PATH};${POSTGRES_INCLUDE_DIRECTORIES}"
  )
elseif(PQXX_FIND_REQUIRED)
  message(FATAL_ERROR "Required PQXX library not found")
endif()
```

That's it! This find module will find PQXX and create the appropriate PQXX::PQXX targets. The complete file is available in the book's examples repository.

For libraries that are well supported and likely already installed, this method is very effective. But what if you're dealing with older, less-supported packages? Unix-like systems have a tool called pkg-config, and CMake has a useful wrapper module to support it as well.

Discovering legacy packages with FindPkgConfig

Managing dependencies and figuring out the necessary compile flags is a challenge as old as C++ libraries themselves. Various tools have been developed to tackle this issue, from simple mechanisms to comprehensive solutions integrated into buildsystems and IDEs. PkgConfig (freedesktop.org/wiki/Software/pkg-config) is one such tool, once very popular and commonly found on Unix-like systems, although it's also available on macOS and Windows.

However, PkgConfig is gradually being replaced by more modern solutions. So, should you still consider supporting it? Chances are, you probably don't need to. Here's why:

- If your library doesn't provide the .pc PkgConfig files, there's little value in writing definition files for an aging tool; opt for newer alternatives instead

- If you can pick a newer version of the library that supports CMake (we'll discuss how to download dependencies from the internet later in this chapter)

- If the package is widely used, the latest version of CMake might already include a find module for it

- If a community-created find module is available online and its license allows you to use it, that's another good option

- If you can write and maintain a find module yourself

Use PkgConfig only if you're working with a library version that already provides a PkgConfig .pc file, and no config module or find module is available. Also, there should be a strong reason why creating a find module yourself isn't a viable option. If you're convinced that you don't need PkgConfig, go ahead and skip this section.

Sadly, not all environments can be quickly updated to the latest versions of a library. Many companies are still using legacy systems in production, which are no longer receiving the latest packages. If you have a .pc file for a specific library in your system, it will look something like the one for foobar shown here:

```
prefix=/usr/local
exec_prefix=${prefix}
includedir=${prefix}/include
libdir=${exec_prefix}/lib
Name: foobar
Description: A foobar library
Version: 1.0.0
Cflags: -I${includedir}/foobar
Libs: -L${libdir} -lfoobar
```

The format of PkgConfig is simple, and many developers familiar with this tool prefer using it out of habit over learning more advanced systems like CMake. Despite its simplicity, PkgConfig can check whether a specific library and its version are available, and it can also get linking flags and directory information for the library.

To use it with CMake, you need to find the pkg-config tool on your system, run specific commands, and then store the results for later use by the compiler. Doing all these steps each time you use PkgConfig can feel like a lot of work. Luckily, CMake provides a FindPkgConfig find module. If PkgConfig is found, PKG_CONFIG_FOUND will be set. We can then use pkg_check_modules() to look for the package we need.

We have already become familiar with libpqxx in the previous section, and since it offers a .pc file, let's try and find it using PkgConfig. To put this in action, let's write a simple main.cpp file, which utilizes a placeholder connection class:

ch09/04-find-pkg-config/main.cpp

```cpp
#include <pqxx/pqxx>
int main()
{
  // We're not actually connecting, but
  // just proving that pqxx is available.
  pqxx::nullconnection connection;
}
```

In a typical listfile, we usually start with the find_package() function and switch to PkgConfig if the library isn't detected. This approach is useful when the environment gets updated, as we can keep using the main method without altering the code. We'll skip this part for this example to keep it short.

ch09/04-find-pkg-config/CMakeLists.txt

```cmake
cmake_minimum_required(VERSION 3.26.0)
project(FindPkgConfig CXX)
find_package(PkgConfig REQUIRED)
pkg_check_modules(PQXX REQUIRED IMPORTED_TARGET libpqxx)
message("PQXX_FOUND: ${PQXX_FOUND}")
add_executable(main main.cpp)
target_link_libraries(main PRIVATE PkgConfig::PQXX)
```

Let's break down what happens:

1. The find_package() command is used to locate PkgConfig. If pkg-config is missing, the process stops due to the REQUIRED keyword.

2. The pkg_check_modules() custom macro from the FindPkgConfig find module sets up a new IMPORTED target named PQXX. The find module looks for a libpqxx dependency and will fail if it's not there, again because of the REQUIRED keyword. The IMPORTED_TARGET keyword is crucial; otherwise, we'd need to define the target manually.

3. We validate the setup with a message() function, displaying PQXX_FOUND. If we hadn't used REQUIRED earlier, this is where we could check whether the variable was set, maybe to activate other fallbacks.

4. The `main` executable is declared with `add_executable()`.

5. Finally, we use `target_link_libraries()` to link the `PkgConfig::PQXX` target, imported by `pkg_check_modules()`. Note that `PkgConfig::` is a fixed prefix and PQXX is derived from the first argument we passed to the macro.

Using this option is faster than creating a find module for dependencies that don't have CMake support. However, it does come with some downsides. One issue is that it relies on the older `pkg-config` tool, which may not be available in the operating system that builds the project. Additionally, this approach creates a special case that needs to be maintained differently from other methods.

We've discussed how to work with dependencies that are already installed on your computer. However, that's only part of the story. Many times, your project will go to users who might not have all the required dependencies on their systems. Let's see how to handle this situation.

Using dependencies not present in the system

CMake excels at managing dependencies, particularly when they're not already installed on the system. There are several approaches you can take. If you're using CMake version 3.14 or newer, the `FetchContent` module is your best choice for managing dependencies. Essentially, `FetchContent` is a user-friendly wrapper around another module called `ExternalProject`. It not only simplifies the process but also adds some extra features. We'll dive deeper into `ExternalProject` later in this chapter. For now, just know that the main difference between the two is the order of execution:

• `FetchContent` brings dependencies in during the *configuration stage*.

• `ExternalProject` brings dependencies in during the *build stage*.

This order is significant, as targets defined by `FetchContent` during the configuration stage will be in the same namespace, and as such can be easily used by our project. We can link them with other targets, just as if we had defined them ourselves. There are rare cases when this is not desirable, and that's when `ExternalProject` is the necessary choice.

Let's see how to deal with the majority of the cases first.

FetchContent

The `FetchContent` module is extremely useful; it offers the following features:

• Management of directory structure for an external project

• Downloading of sources from a URL (and extracting from archives if needed)

- Support for Git, Subversion, Mercurial, and CVS (Concurrent Versions System) repositories
- Fetching updates if needed
- Configuring and building the project with CMake, Make, or with a user-specified tool
- Providing nested dependencies on other targets

The usage of the `FetchContent` module involves three main steps:

1. Add the module to your project with `include(FetchContent)`.
2. Configure the dependencies with the `FetchContent_Declare()` command. This will instruct FetchContent where the dependencies are and which version should be used.
3. Complete the dependency setup using the `FetchContent_MakeAvailable()` command. This will download, build, install, and add the listfiles to your main project for parsing.

You might wonder why *steps 2* and *3* are separate. The reason is to allow for **configuration overrides** in multi-layered projects. For example, consider a project that depends on external libraries, A and B. Library A also depends on B, but its authors are using an older version that differs from the parent project's version (*Figure 9.1*):

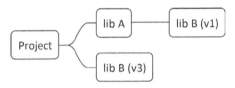

Figure 9.1: The hierarchical project

If configuration and download were to occur in the same command, the parent project wouldn't be able to use a newer version, even if it's backward compatible, because the dependency has already configured the *imported targets* for the older version introducing conflicts to target names and files of the library.

To specify what version is needed, the top-most project has to call the `FetchContent_Declare()` command and provide overridden configuration for B, before library A is fully set up. The subsequent call to `FetchContent_Declare()` in A will be ignored, as the B dependency was already configured.

Let's take a look at the signature of the `FetchContent_Declare()` command:

```
FetchContent_Declare(<depName> <contentOptions>...)
```

The `depName` is a unique identifier of the dependency and will be later used by the `FetchContent_MakeAvailable()` command.

The contentOptions provides a detailed configuration of the dependency, which can get quite complex. It's important to realize that, under the hood, FetchContent_Declare() uses the older ExternalProject_Add() command. As a matter of fact, many arguments provided to FetchContent_Declare are directly forwarded to that internal call. Before explaining all the arguments in detail, let's see a working example that downloads a dependency from GitHub.

Basic example with a YAML reader

I've written a tiny program that reads a username from a YAML file and prints it out in a welcome message. YAML is a great, simple format to store human-readable configuration, but it's quite complex to parse by machines. I've found a neat, small project that solves this problem called yaml-cpp by Jesse Beder (https://github.com/jbeder/yaml-cpp).

The example is fairly straightforward. It's a greeting program that prints a Welcome <name> message. The default value of name will be Guest, but we can specify a different name in a YAML configuration file. Here's the C++ code:

ch09/05-fetch-content/main.cpp

```cpp
#include <string>
#include <iostream>
#include "yaml-cpp/yaml.h"

using namespace std;
int main() {
  string name = "Guest";

  YAML::Node config = YAML::LoadFile("config.yaml");
  if (config["name"])
    name = config["name"].as<string>();

  cout << "Welcome " << name << endl;
  return 0;
}
```

The configuration file for this example is just a single line:

ch09/05-fetch-content/config.yaml

```yaml
name: Rafal
```

We'll reuse this example in other sections, so take a second to understand how it works. Now that we have the code ready, let's see how we can build it and get the dependency in:

ch09/05-fetch-content/CMakeLists.txt

```
cmake_minimum_required(VERSION 3.26.0)
project(ExternalProjectGit CXX)
add_executable(welcome main.cpp)
configure_file(config.yaml config.yaml COPYONLY)
include(FetchContent)
FetchContent_Declare(external-yaml-cpp
  GIT_REPOSITORY    https://github.com/jbeder/yaml-cpp.git
  GIT_TAG           0.8.0
)
FetchContent_MakeAvailable(external-yaml-cpp)
target_link_libraries(welcome PRIVATE yaml-cpp::yaml-cpp)
```

We can explicitly access the targets created by the yaml-cpp library. To prove it, we'll use a CMakePrintHelpers helper module:

```
include(CMakePrintHelpers)
cmake_print_properties(TARGETS yaml-cpp::yaml-cpp
                       PROPERTIES TYPE SOURCE_DIR)
```

When we build such a project, the configuration stage will print the following output:

```
Properties for TARGET yaml-cpp::yaml-cpp:
   yaml-cpp.TYPE = "STATIC_LIBRARY"
   yaml-cpp.SOURCE_DIR = "/tmp/b/_deps/external-yaml-cpp-src"
```

This tells us that the target defined by the external-yaml-cpp dependency exists; it's a static library, and its source directory resides inside the build tree. This printout isn't necessary for real-life projects, but it helps to debug things if you're not sure how to correctly include an imported target.

Since we already copied the .yaml file to the output with the configure_file() command, we can run the program:

```
~/examples/ch09/05-fetch-content$ /tmp/b/welcome
Welcome Rafal
```

Everything works like a charm! With hardly any work, we have introduced an external dependency and used it in our project.

If we need more than one dependency, we should write multiple calls to the `FetchContent_Declare()` command, each time selecting a unique identifier. But there's no need to call `FetchContent_MakeAvailable()` more than once because it supports multiple identifiers (these are case-insensitive):

```
FetchContent_MakeAvailable(lib-A lib-B lib-C)
```

Now, we'll learn how to write declarations of dependencies.

Downloading the dependencies

The `FetchContent_Declare()` command offers a wide range of options, which come from the `ExternalProject` module. Essentially, you can perform three main actions:

- Downloading dependencies
- Updating dependencies
- Patching dependencies

Let's begin by looking at the most common scenario: fetching files from the internet. There are many download sources supported by CMake:

- HTTP Server (URL)
- Git
- Subversion
- Mercurial
- CVS

Going from the top of the list, we'll first explore how to download dependencies from URLs and customize the process to fit our needs.

Downloading from a URL

We can provide a list of URLs to be scanned in sequence until a download succeeds. CMake will recognize whether the downloaded file is an archive and will unpack it by default.

Basic declaration:

```
FetchContent_Declare(dependency-id
                    URL <url1> [<url2>...]
)
```

Here are some additional options to further customize this method:

- `URL_HASH <algo>=<hashValue>`: This checks whether a downloaded file's checksum generated by `<algo>` matches the provided `<hashValue>`. It is recommended to guarantee the integrity of downloads. The following algorithms are supported: `MD5`, `SHA1`, `SHA224`, `SHA256`, `SHA384`, `SHA512`, `SHA3_224`, `SHA3_256`, `SHA3_384`, and `SHA3_512`

- `DOWNLOAD_NO_EXTRACT <bool>`: This explicitly disables extraction after downloading. We may consume the filename of downloaded files in the follow-up steps by accessing the `<DOWNLOADED_FILE>` variable.

- `DOWNLOAD_NO_PROGRESS <bool>`: This explicitly disables logging of the download progress.

- `TIMEOUT <seconds>` and `INACTIVITY_TIMEOUT <seconds>`: These set timeouts to terminate the download after a fixed total time or period of inactivity.

- `HTTP_USERNAME <username>` and `HTTP_PASSWORD <password>`: These configure HTTP authentication. Be cautious not to hardcode credentials.

- `HTTP_HEADER <header1> [<header2>...]`: This adds extra headers to your HTTP request, which is useful for AWS or custom tokens.

- `TLS_VERIFY <bool>`: This verifies the SSL certificate. If this is not set, CMake will read this setting from the `CMAKE_TLS_VERIFY` variable, which is set to `false` by default. Skipping TLS verification is an unsafe, bad practice and should be avoided, especially in production environments.

- `TLS_CAINFO <file>`: This provides a path to the authority file; if it isn't specified, CMake will read this setting from the `CMAKE_TLS_CAINFO` variable. It is useful if your company is issuing self-signed SSL certificates.

The majority of programmers will refer to online repositories like GitHub to grab the latest versions of libraries. Here's how.

Downloading from Git

To download dependencies from Git, ensure that the host system has Git version 1.6.5 or later. The following options are essential for cloning the project from Git:

```
FetchContent_Declare(dependency-id
                GIT_REPOSITORY <url>
                GIT_TAG <tag>
)
```

Both <url> and <tag> should be compatible with the git command. In a production environment, it's advisable to use a specific git hash (rather than tag) to ensure traceability of the produced binaries and to avoid unnecessary git fetch operations. If you prefer using a branch, stick to remote names such as origin/main. This ensures the proper synchronization of the local clone.

Additional options include:

- GIT_REMOTE_NAME <name>: This sets the remote name (origin is the default).
- GIT_SUBMODULES <module>...: This specifies which submodules to update; since 3.16, this value defaults to none (previously, all submodules were updated).
- GIT_SUBMODULES_RECURSE 1: This enables the recursive updating of submodules.
- GIT_SHALLOW 1: This performs a shallow clone, which is faster as it skips downloading historical commits.
- TLS_VERIFY <bool>: This verifies the SSL certificate. If this is not set, CMake will read this setting from the CMAKE_TLS_VERIFY variable, which is set to false by default; skipping TLS verification is an unsafe, bad practice and should be avoided, especially in production environments.

If your dependency is stored in Subversion, you can also fetch it with CMake.

Downloading from Subversion

To download from Subversion, we should specify the following options:

```
FetchContent_Declare(dependency-id
                     SVN_REPOSITORY <url>
                     SVN_REVISION -r<rev>
)
```

Additionally, we may provide the following:

- SVN_USERNAME <user> and SVN_PASSWORD <password>: These provide credentials for checkout and update. Avoid hardcoding these in your projects.
- SVN_TRUST_CERT <bool>: This skips the verification of the Subversion server site certificate. Use this option only if the network path to the server and its integrity are trustworthy.

Subversion is very easy to use with CMake. So is Mercurial.

Downloading from Mercurial

This mode is very straightforward. We need to provide two arguments and we're done:

```
FetchContent_Declare(dependency-id
                     HG_REPOSITORY <url>
                     HG_TAG <tag>
)
```

Lastly, we can use CVS to provide dependencies.

Downloading from CVS

To check out modules from CVS, we need to provide the following three arguments:

```
FetchContent_Declare(dependency-id
                     CVS_REPOSITORY <cvsroot>
                     CVS_MODULE <module>
                     CVS_TAG <tag>
)
```

With that, we covered all the download options for `FetchContent_Declare()`. CMake supports additional steps that can be executed after a successful download.

Updating and patching

By default, the update step will re-download the external project's files if the download method supports updates, for example, if we configure the Git dependency pointing to the main or master branch. We can override this behavior in two ways:

- Provide a custom command to be executed during the update with `UPDATE_COMMAND <cmd>`.
- Completely disable the update step (to allow building with a disconnected network) – `UPDATE_DISCONNECTED <bool>`. Do note that dependency will still be downloaded during the first build.

Patch, on the other hand, is an optional step that will execute after the update is fetched. To enable it, we need to specify the exact command we want to execute with `PATCH_COMMAND <cmd>`.

CMake documentation warns that some patches may be more "sticky" than others. For example, in Git, changed files don't get restored to the original state during the update, and we need to be careful to avoid incorrectly patching the file twice. Ideally, the patch command should be robust and idempotent.

You can chain update and patch commands:

```
FetchContent_Declare(dependency-id
                     GIT_REPOSITORY <url>
                     GIT_TAG <tag>
                     UPDATE_COMMAND <cmd>
                     PATCH_COMMAND <cmd>
)
```

Downloading dependencies is helpful when they're not already on the system. But what if they are? How can we use the local version instead?

Using the installed dependency where possible

Starting with version 3.24, CMake introduced a feature that allows FetchContent to skip downloading if the dependencies are already available locally. To enable this, simply add the FIND_PACKAGE_ARGS keyword to your declaration:

```
FetchContent_Declare(dependency-id
                     GIT_REPOSITORY <url>
                     GIT_TAG <tag>
                     FIND_PACKAGE_ARGS <args>
)
```

As you can guess, this keyword instructs the FetchContent module to use the find_package() function before initiating any downloads. If the package is found locally, it will be used, and no download or build will occur. Note that this keyword should be the last one in the command, as it will consume all subsequent arguments.

Here's how to update the previous example:

ch09/06-fetch-content-find-package/CMakeLists.txt

```
cmake_minimum_required(VERSION 3.26)
project(ExternalProjectGit CXX)

add_executable(welcome main.cpp)
configure_file(config.yaml config.yaml COPYONLY)

include(FetchContent)
FetchContent_Declare(external-yaml-cpp
  GIT_REPOSITORY    https://github.com/jbeder/yaml-cpp.git
```

```
  GIT_TAG           0.8.0
  FIND_PACKAGE_ARGS NAMES yaml-cpp
)
FetchContent_MakeAvailable(external-yaml-cpp)
target_link_libraries(welcome PRIVATE yaml-cpp::yaml-cpp)
include(CMakePrintHelpers)
cmake_print_properties(TARGETS yaml-cpp::yaml-cpp
                        PROPERTIES TYPE SOURCE_DIR
                        INTERFACE_INCLUDE_DIRECTORIES
                        )
```

We made two key changes:

1. We added `FIND_PACKAGE_ARGS` with the `NAMES` keyword to specify that we're looking for the yaml-cpp package. Without `NAMES`, CMake would default to using the dependency-id, which, in this case, is external-yaml-cpp.

2. We added `INTERFACE_INCLUDE_DIRECTORIES` in the printed properties. This is a one-off check so we can manually verify whether we're using the installed package or if a new one was downloaded.

Before testing, make sure the package is actually installed on your system. If it's not, you can install it using the following commands:

```
git clone https://github.com/jbeder/yaml-cpp.git
cmake -S yaml-cpp -B build-dir
cmake --build build-dir
cmake --install build-dir
```

With this setup, we can now build our project. If all goes well, you should see debug output from the cmake_print_properties() command. This will indicate that we're using the local version, as shown in the `INTERFACE_INCLUDE_DIRECTORIES` property. Keep in mind that this output is specific to your environment, your mileage may vary.

```
 --
  Properties for TARGET yaml-cpp::yaml-cpp:
    yaml-cpp::yaml-cpp.TYPE = "STATIC_LIBRARY"
    yaml-cpp::yaml-cpp.INTERFACE_INCLUDE_DIRECTORIES =
                                          "/usr/local/include"
```

If you're not using CMake 3.24, or if you want to support users with older versions, you might consider running the find_package() command manually. This way, you'll only download packages that aren't already installed:

```
find_package(yaml-cpp QUIET)
if (NOT TARGET yaml-cpp::yaml-cpp)
  # download missing dependency
endif()
```

Whichever method you choose, trying to use the local version first and downloading only if the dependency isn't found is a thoughtful approach that offers the best user experience.

Before the introduction of FetchContent, CMake had a simpler module called ExternalProject. Although FetchContent is the recommended choice for most situations, ExternalProject still has its own set of advantages and can be useful in certain cases.

ExternalProject

As mentioned, before FetchContent was introduced to CMake, another module was serving a similar purpose: ExternalProject (added in 3.0.0). As you can guess, it was used to fetch external projects from online repositories. Over the years, the module was gradually extended for different needs, resulting in quite a complicated command: ExternalProject_Add().

The ExternalProject module populates the dependencies during the build stage. That's quite different from FetchContent, which executes in the configuration stage. Because of this difference, ExternalProject cannot import targets into the project like FetchContent does. On the other hand, ExternalProject can install dependencies directly into the system, execute their tests, and do other interesting things, like overriding the commands used for configuration and the build.

There is a small set of use cases where this may be necessary. Since there's a lot of overhead needed to use this legacy module effectively, treat it as a curiosity. We're mostly introducing it here to show how the current method evolved from it.

ExternalProject offers an ExternalProject_Add command that configures the dependency. Here's an example:

```
include(ExternalProject)
ExternalProject_Add(external-yaml-cpp
  GIT_REPOSITORY    https://github.com/jbeder/yaml-cpp.git
  GIT_TAG           0.8.0
  INSTALL_COMMAND   ""
```

```
    TEST_COMMAND            " "
  )
```

As mentioned, it closely resembles the FetchContent_Declare from FetchContent. You'll notice that there are two additional keywords in the example: INSTALL_COMMAND and TEST_COMMAND. In this case, they are used to suppress the installation and tests of the dependency, as they would normally execute during the build. ExternalProject executes many steps that are deeply configurable, and they execute in the following order:

1. mkdir: Create a subdirectory for the external project.

2. download: Download the project files from a repository or URL.

3. update: Download updates if supported by the fetch method.

4. patch: Execute a patch command that alters downloaded files.

5. configure: Execute the configure stage.

6. build: Perform the build stage for CMake projects.

7. install: Install CMake projects.

8. test: Execute the tests.

For each of the steps, excluding mkdir, you can override the default behavior by adding a <STEP>_ COMMAND keyword. There are plenty of other options – please refer to the online documentation for the full reference. If, for some reason, you'd like to use this method over the recommended FetchContent, there's an ugly hack that can be applied to import the targets anyway by executing CMake within CMake. For more details, check out the ch09/05-external-project code example in the repository for this book.

Typically, we would rely on the library being available in the system. If it's not, we'd resort to FetchContent, an approach that is particularly suitable for dependencies that are small and quick to compile.

However, for more substantial libraries like Qt, this method could be time consuming. In such cases, package managers offering precompiled libraries tailored to the user's environment become advisable. While tools like Apt or Conan provide solutions, they are either too system-specific or complex to be covered in this book. The good news is that most users can install the dependencies your project may require, as long as clear installation instructions are provided.

Summary

This chapter has equipped you with the knowledge to identify system-installed packages using CMake's find modules and how to utilize the config files that come with the library. For older libraries that don't support CMake but include `.pc` files, the PkgConfig tool and CMake's bundled `FindPkgConfig` find module can be used.

We also explored the capabilities of the `FetchContent` module. This module allows us to download dependencies from various sources while configuring CMake to first scan the system, thereby avoiding unnecessary downloads. We touched upon the historical context of these modules and discussed the option of using the `ExternalProject` module for special cases.

CMake is designed to automatically generate build targets when a library is located through most of the methods we've discussed. This adds a layer of convenience and elegance to the process. With this foundation in place, you're ready to incorporate standard libraries into your projects.

In the next chapter, we'll learn how to provide reusable code on a smaller scale with C++20 modules.

Further reading

For more information on the topics covered in this chapter, you can refer to the following:

- CMake documentation – provided find modules:
  `https://cmake.org/cmake/help/latest/manual/cmake-modules.7.html#find modules`

- CMake documentation – *Using Dependencies Guide*:
  `https://cmake.org/cmake/help/latest/guide/using-dependencies/index.html`

- *CMake and using git-submodule for dependence projects*:
  `https://stackoverflow.com/questions/43761594/`

- Piggybacking on PkgConfig:
  `https://gitlab.kitware.com/cmake/community/-/wikis/doc/tutorials/How-To-Find-Libraries#piggybacking-on-pkg-config`

- How to use ExternalProject:
  `https://www.jwlawson.co.uk/interest/2020/02/23/cmake-external-project.html`

- *CMake FetchContent vs. ExternalProject*:
  `https://www.scivision.dev/cmake-fetchcontent-vs-external-project/`

- *Using CMake with External Projects*:
  `http://www.saoe.net/blog/using-cmake-with-external-projects/`

Join our community on Discord

Join our community's Discord space for discussions with the author and other readers:

`https://discord.com/invite/vXN53A7ZcA`

10

Using the C++20 Modules

C++20 introduces a new feature to the language: modules. They replace the plain-text symbol declarations in header files with a module file that will be precompiled to an intermediary binary format, greatly reducing the build time.

We will discuss the most essential topics for C++20 modules in CMake, starting with a general introduction to C++20 modules as a concept: their advantages over standard header files and how they simplify the management of units in source code. Although the promise of streamlining the build process is exciting, this chapter highlights how difficult and long the road to their adoption is.

With the theory out of the way, we'll move on to the practical aspects of implementing the modules in our projects: we'll discuss enabling their experimental support in earlier versions of CMake, and the full release in CMake 3.28.

Our journey through C++20 modules is not just about understanding a new feature—it's about rethinking how components interact in large C++ projects. By the end of this chapter, you'll not only grasp the theoretical aspects of modules but also gain practical insights through examples, enhancing your ability to leverage this feature for better project outcomes.

In this chapter, we're going to cover the following main topics:

- What are the C++20 modules?
- Writing projects with C++20 module support
- Configuring the toolchain

 This chapter has different technical requirements than others. Make sure you read the next section thoroughly.

Technical requirements

You can find the code files that are present in this chapter on GitHub at `https://github.com/PacktPublishing/Modern-CMake-for-Cpp-2E/tree/main/examples/ch10`.

The following toolchain utilities are required to try out the examples in this chapter:

- CMake 3.26 or newer (3.28 recommended)
- Any of the supported generators:
  - Ninja 1.11 and newer (Ninja and Ninja Multi-Config)
  - Visual Studio 17 2022 and newer
- Any of the supported compilers:
  - MSVC toolset 14.34 and newer
  - Clang 16 and newer
  - GCC 14 (for the in-development branch, after 2023-09-20) and newer

If you're familiar with Docker, you can use a fully tooled image introduced in the *Installing CMake on different platforms* section from *Chapter 1, First Steps with CMake*.

To build the examples provided in this chapter, use the following command:

```
cmake -B <build tree> -S <source tree> -G "Ninja" -D CMAKE_CXX_
COMPILER=clang++-18 && cmake --build <build tree>
```

Be sure to replace the placeholders <build tree> and <source tree> with appropriate paths.

What are the C++20 modules?

I wanted to write about how to use C++ modules over three years ago. Despite the fact that modules were already accepted as part of the C++20 specification, the support of the C++ ecosystem was still nowhere near ready to use this feature. Fortunately, a lot has changed since the first edition of this book, and with the release of CMake 3.28, the C++20 modules are officially supported (although experimental support has been available since 3.26).

Three years may seem like a long time to implement a single feature, but we need to remember that it's not only up to CMake. Many pieces of the puzzle have to come together and work well. First, we need compilers to understand how to deal with modules, then buildsystems like GNU Make or Ninja have to be able to work with modules, and only then can CMake use these new mechanisms to provide its support for modules.

This tells us one thing: not everyone will have the latest compatible tooling, and even then, the current support is still in an early phase. These limitations make modules unsuitable for a wide audience. So maybe don't build production-grade projects depending on them just yet.

Nevertheless, if you are an enthusiast of cutting-edge solutions, you're in for a treat! If you can strictly control the build environment of your project, for example, with dedicated machines or build containerization (Docker et al.), you can effectively use modules internally. Just proceed with caution and understand that your mileage may vary. There may be a point at which you'll need to back out of the modules altogether because of a missing or incorrectly implemented feature in any of the utilities.

"Module" is quite an overloaded word in the context of C++ builds. We previously discussed modules in this book in the context of CMake: find modules, utility modules, and such. To clarify, C++ modules have nothing to do with CMake modules. Instead, they are a native feature of the language added in the C++20 version.

At its core, a C++ module is a single source file that encapsulates the functionality of headers and implementation files into one coherent unit of code. It comprises two primary components:

- The **Binary Module Interface** (**BMI**) serves a similar purpose to a header file but is in a binary format, significantly reducing the need for recompilation when consumed by other translation units.

- The **Module Implementation Unit** provides the implementation, definitions, and internal details of the module. Its contents are not directly accessible from outside the module, effectively encapsulating the implementation details.

Modules were introduced to reduce compilation time and address some problematic aspects of the preprocessor and traditional header files. Let's see how multiple translation units are glued together in a typical, legacy project.

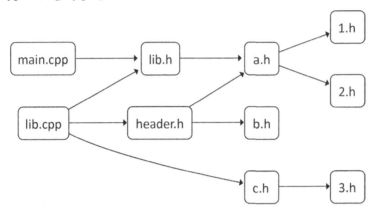

Figure 10.1: Project structure using traditional headers

The preceding figure shows how the preprocessor would traverse the project tree to build the program. As we learned in *Chapter 7, Compiling C++ Sources with CMake*, to build each translation unit, the preprocessor mechanically stitches files together. This means producing a long file containing all the headers included by preprocessor directives. That way, main.cpp would first include its own source, then the contents of lib.h, a.h, 1.h, and 2.h. Only then will the compiler kick in and start parsing every single character to produce binary object files. There's nothing wrong with that until we realize that to compile lib.cpp, headers included in main.cpp have to be compiled again. And this redundancy keeps growing with every translation unit added.

There are other complications with traditional headers:

- **Include guards** are required, leading to problems when forgotten.
- Symbols with circular references need **forward declarations.**
- Small changes to headers are required for the recompilation of all translation units.
- Preprocessor macros can be difficult to debug and maintain.

Modules solve many of these problems right off the bat, but some still remain relevant: modules, like headers, can depend on each other. When one module imports another, we still need to compile them in the right order, starting from the most nested one first. This usually isn't a significant issue, as modules tend to be much larger in size. In many cases, an entire library can be stored in a single module.

Let's take a look at how modules are written and used in practice. In this simple example, we'll just return the sum of two arguments:

ch10/01-cxx-modules/math.cppm

```
export module math;
export int add(int a, int b) {
    return a + b;
}
```

Such a module is self-explanatory: we start with a statement that tells the rest of the program that this is indeed a module called math. We then follow with a regular function definition that has been designated with the export keyword as available from outside the module.

> You'll notice the extension of module files is different than of regular C++ source code. This is a matter of convention and shouldn't affect how this code is treated. My advice is to pick based on the toolchain you'll be using:
>
> - .ixx is an MSVC extension.
> - .cppm is a Clang extension.
> - .cxx is a GCC extension.

To use this module, we need to import it in our program:

ch10/01-cxx-modules/main.cpp

```
import math;

#include <iostream>

int main() {
    std::cout << "Addition 2 + 2 = " << add(2, 2) << std::endl;
    return 0;
}
```

The import math statement is enough to bring the symbols exported from the module directly into the main program. We can now use the add() function in the body of the main() function. On the surface, modules look very similar to headers. But if we tried to write our CMake listfile as usual, we wouldn't have much success with building the project. Time to introduce the necessary steps to use the C++ modules.

Writing projects with C++20 module support

This book mainly discusses CMake 3.26, but it's worth noting that CMake frequently updates, and version 3.28 was released just before this chapter went to press. If you're using this version or newer, you can access the latest features by setting the `cmake_minimum_required()` command to `VERSION 3.28.0`.

On the other hand, if you need to stick with an older version or want to cater to a broader audience who might not have upgraded, you'll need to enable experimental support to use C++20 modules in CMake.

Let's explore how to do that.

Enabling the experimental support in CMake 3.26 and 3.27

Experimental support represents a form of agreement: you, as the developer, acknowledge that this feature is not yet production-ready and should be used solely for testing purposes. To *sign* such an agreement, you'll need to set the `CMAKE_EXPERIMENTAL_CXX_MODULE_CMAKE_API` variable in the project's listfile to a specific value for the CMake version you're using.

 The official Kitware repository for CMake hosts an issue tracker, where you can search for the label `area:cxxmodules`. Until 3.28 was released, only one issue was reported (in 3.25.0), which is a good indicator of a potentially stable feature. If you decide to enable the experiment, build your project to confirm it will work for your users.

Here are flags that can be found in the repository and documentation of CMake:

- `3c375311-a3c9-4396-a187-3227ef642046` for 3.25 (undocumented)
- `2182bf5c-ef0d-489a-91da-49dbc3090d2a` for 3.26
- `aa1f7df0-828a-4fcd-9afc-2dc80491aca7` for 3.27

Unfortunately, if you don't have access to at least CMake 3.25, you're out of luck. Modules weren't available before that version. Additionally, if CMake is older than 3.27, you'll need to set one more variable to enable dynamic dependencies for modules:

```
set(CMAKE_EXPERIMENTAL_CXX_MODULE_DYNDEP 1)
```

Here's how you might automatically pick the correct API key for the current version, and explicitly disable builds for versions you don't support (in this example, we'll only support CMake 3.26 and above).

ch10/01-cxx-modules/CMakeLists.txt

```
cmake_minimum_required(VERSION 3.26.0)
project(CXXModules CXX)

# turn on the experimental API
if(CMAKE_VERSION VERSION_GREATER_EQUAL 3.28.0)
  # Assume that C++ sources do import modules
  cmake_policy(SET CMP0155 NEW)
elseif(CMAKE_VERSION VERSION_GREATER_EQUAL 3.27.0)
  set(CMAKE_EXPERIMENTAL_CXX_MODULE_CMAKE_API
      "aa1f7df0-828a-4fcd-9afc-2dc80491aca7")
elseif(CMAKE_VERSION VERSION_GREATER_EQUAL 3.26.0)
  set(CMAKE_EXPERIMENTAL_CXX_MODULE_CMAKE_API
      "2182bf5c-ef0d-489a-91da-49dbc3090d2a")
  set(CMAKE_EXPERIMENTAL_CXX_MODULE_DYNDEP 1)
else()
  message(FATAL_ERROR "Version lower than 3.26 not supported")
endif()
```

Let's break it down statement by statement:

1. First, we check if the version is 3.28 or newer. This allows us to enable the CMP0155 policy, with cmake_policy( ). This is required if we want to support versions older than 3.28.

2. If that's not the case, we'll check if the version is above 3.27. If so, we'll set the appropriate API key.

3. If it's not above 3.27, we'll check if it's above 3.26. If that's the case, set the appropriate API key and enable the experimental C++20 module dynamic dependency flag.

4. If the version is lower than 3.26, it's not supported by our project, and a fatal error message will be printed informing the user.

This allows us to support the range of CMake versions, starting from 3.26. If we have the benefit of running CMake 3.28 in every environment the project is going to be built in, the above if( ) block is not necessary. So, what is?

Enabling support for CMake 3.28 and up

To use C++20 modules since 3.28, you explicitly have to declare this version as minimal. Use a project header like this:

```
cmake_minimum_required(VERSION 3.28.0)
project(CXXModules CXX)
```

It will enable the CMP0155 policy by default if the minimum required version is set to 3.28 or above. Read on to learn what other aspects we need to configure before defining a module. If you require 3.27 or lower, your build will likely fail, even if the project is being built with CMake 3.28 or newer.

The next thing to consider is the compiler requirements.

Setting the compiler requirements

Regardless of whether we're building with CMake 3.26, 3.27, 3.28, or newer, to create solutions using C++ modules, there are two global variables that we need to set. The first disables unsupported C++ extensions, and the second ensures that the compiler supports the required standard.

ch10/01-cxx-modules/CMakeLists.txt (continued)

```
# Libc++ has no support compiler extensions for modules.
set(CMAKE_CXX_EXTENSIONS OFF)
set(CMAKE_CXX_STANDARD 20)
```

Setting the standard may seem redundant, given that there's a very limited number of compilers that support modules. Nonetheless, it's good practice for future-proofing projects.

The general configuration is quite straightforward and concludes here. We can now proceed to define a module within CMake.

Declaring a C++ module

CMake module definition leverages the target_sources() command and the FILE_SET keyword:

```
target_sources(math
  PUBLIC FILE_SET CXX_MODULES TYPE CXX_MODULES FILES math.cppm
)
```

In the highlighted line above, we introduce a new file set type: CXX_MODULES. This type is supported by default only since CMake 3.28. For 3.26, the experimental API has to be enabled. Without proper support, an error message like the following will occur:

```
CMake Error at CMakeLists.txt:25 (target_sources):
  target_sources File set TYPE may only be "HEADERS"
```

If you see this in the build output, check if your code is correct. This message will also appear if the API key value is incorrect for the version used.

Defining modules within the same binary where they are used offers benefits, as discussed earlier. However, the advantages are more pronounced when creating a library. Such libraries can be utilized in other projects or within the same project by other libraries, further enhancing modularity.

To declare the module and link it with the main program, the following CMake configuration is used:

ch10/01-cxx-modules/CMakeLists.txt (continued)

```
add_library(math)
target_sources(math
  PUBLIC FILE_SET CXX_MODULES FILES math.cppm
)
target_compile_features(math PUBLIC cxx_std_20)
set_target_properties(math PROPERTIES CXX_EXTENSIONS OFF)

add_executable(main main.cpp)
target_link_libraries(main PRIVATE math)
```

To ensure that this library can be used in other projects, we must use the `target_compile_features()` command and explicitly require `cxx_std_20`. Additionally, we have to repeat setting the `CXX_EXTENSIONS OFF` on the target level. Without this, CMake will generate an error and halt the build. This seems redundant and will likely be solved in future versions of CMake.

With the project setup complete, it's time to finally build it.

Configuring the toolchain

According to a blog post on Kitware's page (see the *Further reading* section), CMake supports modules as early as version 3.25. Despite the fact that 3.28 makes the feature officially supported, this isn't the only piece of the puzzle that we have to get right to enjoy the convenience of modules.

The next requirement focuses on the buildsystem: it needs to support dynamic dependencies. As of now, you have only two choices:

- Ninja 1.11 and newer (Ninja and Ninja Multi-Config)

- Visual Studio 17 2022 and newer

Similarly, your compiler needs to produce files that map source dependencies for CMake in a specific format. This format is described in a paper written by Kitware developers known as p1589r5. This paper has been submitted to all major compilers for implementation. Currently, only three compilers have managed to implement the required format:

- Clang 16
- MSVC in Visual Studio 2022 17.4 (19.34)
- GCC 14 (for the in-development branch, after 2023-09-20) and newer

Assuming you have all the necessary tools in your environment (you may use the Docker image we're providing for this book), and your CMake project is ready for building, all that remains is to configure CMake to use the required toolchain. As you may recall from the first chapter, you can select the buildsystem generator using the -G command-line argument:

```
cmake -B <build tree> -S <source tree> -G "Ninja"
```

This command will configure the project to use the Ninja buildsystem. The next step is to set the compiler. If your default compiler doesn't support the modules and you have another one installed to try things out, you can do this by defining the global variable CMAKE_CXX_COMPILER like this:

```
cmake -B <build tree> -S <source tree> -G "Ninja" -D CMAKE_CXX_
COMPILER=clang++-18
```

We chose Clang 18 in our example because it's the latest version available at the time of writing (bundled in the Docker image). After successfully configuring (you might see some warnings about experimental features), you need to build the project:

```
cmake --build <build tree>
```

As always, be sure to replace the placeholders <build tree> and <source tree> with appropriate paths. If everything goes smoothly, you can run your program and observe the module function working as expected:

```
$ ./main
Addition 2 + 2 = 4
```

There you have it, C++20 modules working in practice.

The Further reading section includes a blog post from Kitware and a proposal on the source dependency format for C++ compilers, providing more insights into the implementation and usage of C++20 modules.

Summary

In this chapter, we've delved into C++20 modules, clarifying that they are distinct from CMake modules and represent a significant advancement in C++ to streamline compilation and address challenges associated with redundant header compilation and problematic preprocessor macros. We demonstrated how to write and import a C++20 module using a simple example. We then explored setting up CMake for C++20 modules. Since this feature is experimental, specific variables need to be set, and we provided a series of conditional statements to ensure your project is configured correctly for the CMake version in use.

Regarding the necessary tools, we emphasized that the buildsystem must support dynamic dependencies, with Ninja 1.11 or newer being the current option. For compiler support, Clang 16 and MSVC in Visual Studio 2022 17.4 (19.34) are suitable for full C++20 module support, while GCC support is still pending. We additionally guided you through configuring CMake to use the selected toolchain, involving choosing a buildsystem generator and setting the compiler version. After configuring and building the project, you can run your program to see the C++20 module in action.

In the next chapter, we'll learn about importance and application of automated testing, and the available CMake support for testing frameworks.

Further reading

For more information, you can refer to the following resources:

- Blog post describing the new feature:
  https://www.kitware.com/import-cmake-c20-modules/
- Proposed source dependency format for C++ compilers:
  https://www.open-std.org/jtc1/sc22/wg21/docs/papers/2022/p1689r5.html

Leave a review!

Enjoying this book? Help readers like you by leaving an Amazon review. Scan the QR code below to get a free eBook of your choice.

11

Testing Frameworks

Tenured professionals know that testing must be automated. Someone explained this to them years ago or they learned it the hard way. This practice isn't as obvious to inexperienced programmers; it seems like unnecessary, extra work that doesn't bring much value. It's understandable: when someone is just starting to write code, they have yet to create really complex solutions and work on large code bases. Most likely, they are the sole developer of their pet project. These early projects rarely take more than a few months to complete, so there's little chance to see how code deteriorates over a longer period.

All these factors contribute to the belief that writing tests is a waste of time and effort. The programming novice may tell themselves that they actually do test their code each time they go through the *build-and-run* routine. After all, they have manually confirmed that their code works and does what's expected. So, it's time to move on to the next task, right?

Automated testing ensures that new changes don't unintentionally break our program. In this chapter, we'll learn why tests are important and how to use CTest, a tool bundled with CMake, to coordinate test execution. CTest can query available tests, filter execution, shuffle, repeat, and set time limits. We'll explore how to use these features, control CTest's output, and handle test failures.

Next, we'll modify our project's structure to accommodate testing and create our own test runner. After covering the basic principles, we'll proceed to add popular testing frameworks: Catch2 and GoogleTest, also known as GTest, along with its mocking library. Finally, we'll introduce detailed test coverage reporting with LCOV.

In this chapter, we're going to cover the following main topics:

- Why are automated tests worth the trouble?
- Using CTest to standardize testing in CMake
- Creating the most basic unit test for CTest
- Unit testing frameworks
- Generating test coverage reports

Technical requirements

You can find the code files that are present in this chapter on GitHub at `https://github.com/PacktPublishing/Modern-CMake-for-Cpp-2E/tree/main/examples/ch11`.

To build the examples provided in this book, always use the recommended commands:

```
cmake -B <build tree> -S <source tree>
cmake --build <build tree>
```

Be sure to replace the placeholders `<build tree>` and `<source tree>` with appropriate paths. As a reminder, **build tree** is the path to the target/output directory, and **source tree** is the path at which your source code is located.

Why are automated tests worth the trouble?

Imagine a factory line where a machine puts holes in sheets of steel. These holes need to be a specific size and shape to house bolts for the finished product. The designer of the factory line will set up the machine, test the holes, and move on. Eventually, something will change: the steel might be thicker, a worker could adjust the hole size, or more holes may need to be punched because the design has changed. A smart designer will install quality control checks at key points to ensure that the product meets the specifications. It doesn't matter how the holes are made: drilled, punched, or laser cut, they must meet certain requirements.

The same principle applies to software development. It's hard to predict which code will remain stable for years and which will undergo multiple revisions. As software functionality expands, we must ensure that we don't inadvertently break things. And we will make mistakes. Even the best programmers can't foresee the implications of every change. Developers often work on code they didn't originally write and may not understand all the assumptions behind it. They'll read the code, form a mental model, make changes, and hope for the best. When this doesn't work, fixing the bug can take hours or days and will negatively impact the product and its users.

At times, you'll find code that's hard to understand. You might even start blaming others for the mess, only to discover you're the culprit. This happens when code is written quickly, without fully grasping the problem.

As developers, we're not just under pressure from project deadlines or limited budgets; sometimes we're awakened at night to fix a critical issue. It's surprising how some less obvious errors can slip through code review.

Automated tests can prevent most of these issues. They are code snippets that verify whether another piece of code behaves correctly. As the name suggests, these tests run automatically whenever someone makes a change, typically as part of the build process. They're often added as a step to ensure code quality before merging it into the repository.

You might be tempted to skip creating automated tests to save time, but that's a costly mistake. As Steven Wright said, *"Experience is something you don't get until just after you need it."* Unless you're writing a one-use script or experimenting, don't skip tests. You might initially be frustrated that your carefully crafted code keeps failing tests. But remember that a failed test means that you just avoided introducing a major issue into the production environment. The time spent on tests now will save you time on bug fixes later—and let you sleep better at night. Tests are not as difficult to add and maintain as you might think.

Using CTest to standardize testing in CMake

Ultimately, automated testing is simply about running an executable that puts your **System Under Test (SUT)** in a specific state, performs the operations you want to test, and checks whether the results meet expectations. You can think of them as a structured way to complete the sentence `GIVEN_<CONDITION>_WHEN_<SCENARIO>_THEN_<EXPECTED-OUTCOME>` and verify whether it holds true for the SUT. Some resources suggest naming your test functions in this very fashion: for example, `GIVEN_4_and_2_WHEN_Sum_THEN_returns_6`.

There are many ways to implement and execute these tests, depending on the framework you choose, how you connect it to your SUT, and its exact setup. For a user who is interacting with your project for the first time, even small details like the filename of your testing binary will impact their experience. Because there's no standard naming convention, one developer might name their test executable `test_my_app`, another might choose `unit_tests`, and a third might opt for something less straightforward or skip tests entirely. Figuring out which file to run, which framework is in use, what arguments to pass, and how to collect results are hassles that users would rather avoid.

CMake addresses this with a separate `ctest` command-line tool. Configured by the project's author through listfiles, it offers a standardized way to run tests. This uniform interface applies to every project built with CMake. By following this standard, you'll enjoy other benefits: integrating the project into a **Continuous Integration/Continuous Deployment (CI/CD)** pipeline becomes easier, and tests will show up more conveniently in IDEs like Visual Studio or CLion. Most importantly, you get a robust test-running utility with minimal effort.

So, how do you run tests with CTest in an already configured project? You'll need to choose one of the following three modes of operation:

- Dashboard
- Test
- Build-and-test

The **Dashboard mode** allows you to send the test results to a separate tool called CDash, also from Kitware. CDash collects and presents software quality test results in an easy-to-navigate dashboard. It's a topic useful for very large projects, but outside of the scope of this book.

The command line for **Test mode** is as follows:

```
ctest [<options>]
```

In this mode, CTest should be run in the build tree after you've built the project with CMake. There are many options available, but before we dive into them, there's a minor inconvenience to address: the `ctest` binary must be run in the build tree, and only after the project has been built. This can be a bit awkward during the development cycle as you'll need to run multiple commands and toggle between directories.

To make things easier, CTest offers a **Build-and-Test mode**. We'll explore this mode first, so we can give our full attention to the **Test mode** later.

Build-and-test mode

To use this mode, we need to execute `ctest` followed with `--build-and-test`:

```
ctest --build-and-test <source-tree> <build-tree>
      --build-generator <generator> [<options>...]
      [--build-options <opts>...]
      [--test-command <command> [<args>...]]
```

Essentially, this is a simple wrapper around the **Test mode**. It accepts build configuration options and a test command after the --test-command argument. It's important to note that no tests will be run unless you include the ctest keyword after --test-command, as shown here:

```
ctest --build-and-test project/source-tree /tmp/build-tree --build-
generator "Unix Makefiles" --test-command ctest
```

In this command, we specify source and build paths, and select a build generator. All three are required and follow the rules for the cmake command, described in detail in *Chapter 1, First Steps with CMake.*

You can add more arguments, which generally fall into one of three categories: configuration control, build process, or test settings.

Arguments for the configuration stage are as follows:

- --build-options—Include extra options for the cmake configuration. Place them just before --test-command, which must be last.
- --build-two-config—Run the configuration stage for CMake twice.
- --build-nocmake—Skip the configuration stage.
- --build-generator-platform—Provide a generator-specific platform.
- --build-generator-toolset—Provide a generator-specific toolset.
- --build-makeprogram—Specify a make executable for Make- or Ninja-based generators.

Arguments for the build stage are as follows:

- --build-target—Specify which target to build.
- --build-noclean—Build without building the clean target first.
- --build-project—Name the project that is being built.

The argument for the test stage is as follows:

- --test-timeout—Set a time limit for the tests, in seconds.

Now we can configure Test mode, either by adding arguments after the --test-command cmake or by running Test mode directly.

Test mode

After building your project, you can use the ctest command within the build directory to run your tests. If you're using Build-and-test mode, this will be done for you. Running ctest without any extra flags is usually sufficient for most situations. If all tests are successful, ctest will return an exit code of 0 (on Unix-like systems), which you can verify in your CI/CD pipeline to prevent merging faulty changes into your production branch.

Writing good tests can be as challenging as writing the production code itself. We set up our SUT to be in a specific state, run a single test, and then tear down the SUT instance. This process is rather complex and can generate all sorts of issues: cross-test pollution, timing and concurrency disruptions, resource contention, frozen execution due to deadlocks, and many others.

Fortunately, CTest offers various options to mitigate these issues. You can control aspects like which tests to run, their execution order, the output they generate, time constraints, and repetition rates, among other things. The following sections will provide the necessary context and a brief overview of the most useful options.

Querying tests

The first thing we might need to do is to understand which tests are actually written for the project. CTest offers the -N option, which disables execution and only prints a list, as follows:

```
# ctest -N
Test project /tmp/b
  Test #1: SumAddsTwoInts
  Test #2: MultiplyMultipliesTwoInts
Total Tests: 2
```

You might want to use -N with the filters described in the next section to check which tests would be executed when a filter is applied.

If you need a JSON format that can be consumed by automated tooling, execute ctest with --show-only=json-v1.

CTest also offers a mechanism to group tests with the LABELS keyword. To list all available labels (without actually executing any tests), use --print-labels. This option is helpful when tests are defined manually with the add_test(<name> <test-command>) command in your listfile, as you are then able to specify individual labels through test properties, like this:

```
set_tests_properties(<name> PROPERTIES LABELS "<label>")
```

However, keep in mind that automated test discovery methods from various frameworks may not support this level of labeling detail.

Filtering tests

Sometimes you may want to run only specific tests instead of the entire suite. For example, if you're debugging a single failing test, there's no need to run all the others. You can also use this mechanism to distribute tests across multiple machines for large projects.

These flags will filter tests according to the provided `<r>` **regular expression** (**regex**), as follows:

- `-R <r>, --tests-regex <r>` - Only run tests with names matching `<r>`
- `-E <r>, --exclude-regex <r>` - Skip tests with names matching `<r>`
- `-L <r>, --label-regex <r>` - Only run tests with labels matching `<r>`
- `-LE <r>, --label-exclude <regex>` - Skip tests with labels matching `<r>`

Advanced scenarios can be achieved with the `--tests-information` option (or the shorter form, `-I`). This option takes a range in the comma-separated format `<start>,<end>,<step>,<test-IDs>`. You can omit any field but keep the commas. The `<Test IDs>` option is a comma-separated list of an ordinal number of tests to run. For example:

- `-I 3,,` will skip tests 1 and 2 (execution starts from the third test)
- `-I ,2,` will only run the first and second test
- `-I 2,,3` will run every third test, starting from the second test in the row
- `-I ,0,,3,9,7` will only run the third, ninth, and seventh test

You can also specify these ranges in a file to execute tests on multiple machines in a distributed fashion for really large test suites. When using `-I` along with `-R`, only tests that meet both criteria will run. If you want to run tests that meet either condition, use the `-U` option. As mentioned before, you can use the `-N` option to check the outcome of filtering.

Shuffling tests

Writing unit tests can be tricky. One of the more surprising problems to encounter is test coupling, which is a situation where one test affects another by incompletely setting or clearing the state of the SUT. In other words, the first test to execute can "leak" its state and pollute the second test. Such coupling is bad news because it introduces unknown, implicit relations between tests.

What's worse, this kind of error is known to hide really well in the complexities of testing scenarios. We might detect it when it causes one of the tests to randomly fail, but the opposite is equally possible: an incorrect state causes the test to pass when it shouldn't. Such falsely passing tests give developers an illusion of security, which is even worse than not having tests at all. The assumption that the code is correctly tested may encourage bolder actions, leading to unexpected outcomes.

One way of discovering such problems is by running each test in isolation. Usually, this is not the case when executing test runners straight from the testing framework without CTest. To run a single test, you'll need to pass a framework-specific argument to the test executable. This allows you to detect tests that are passing in the suite but are failing when executed on their own.

CTest, on the other hand, effectively removes all memory-based cross-contamination of tests by implicitly executing every test case in a child CTest instance. You may even go further and add the `--force-new-ctest-process` option to enforce separate processes.

Unfortunately, this alone won't work if your tests are using external, contested resources such as GPUs, databases, or files. An additional precaution we can take is to simply randomize the order of test execution. Introducing such variation is often enough to eventually detect spuriously passing tests. CTest supports this strategy with the `--schedule-random` option.

Handling failures

Here's a famous quote from John C. Maxwell: *"Fail early, fail often, but always fail forward."* Failing forward means learning from our mistakes. This is exactly what we want to do when running unit tests (and perhaps in other areas of life). Unless you're running your tests with a debugger attached, it's not easy to detect where you made a mistake, as CTest will keep things brief and only list tests that failed, without actually printing any of their output.

Messages printed to stdout by the test case or the SUT might be invaluable to determine exactly what was wrong. To see them, we can run `ctest` with `--output-on-failure`. Alternatively, setting the `CTEST_OUTPUT_ON_FAILURE` environment variable will have the same effect.

Depending on the size of the solution, it might make sense to stop execution after any of the tests fail. This can be done by providing the `--stop-on-failure` argument to `ctest`.

CTest stores the names of failed tests. To save time in lengthy test suites, we can focus on these failed tests and skip running the passing tests until the problem is solved. This feature is enabled with the `--rerun-failed` option (any other filters will be ignored). Remember to run all tests after solving all issues to make sure that no regression has been introduced in the meantime.

When CTest doesn't detect any tests, it may mean two things: either tests aren't there or there's an issue with the project. By default, `ctest` will print a warning message and return a 0 exit code, to avoid muddying the waters. Most users will have enough context to understand which case they encountered and what to do next. However, in some environments, `ctest` will always be executed as part of an automated pipeline. Then, we might need to explicitly say that a lack of tests should be interpreted as an error (and return a nonzero exit code). We can configure this behavior by providing the `--no-tests=error` argument. For the opposite behavior (no warning), use the `--no-tests=ignore` option.

Repeating tests

Sooner or later in your career, you'll encounter tests that work correctly most of the time. I want to emphasize the word "most." Once in a blue moon, these tests will fail for environmental reasons: because of incorrectly mocked time, issues with event loops, poor handling of asynchronous execution, parallelism, hash collisions, and other really complicated scenarios that don't occur on every run. These unreliable tests are called *flaky tests*.

Such inconsistency seems a not-so-important problem. We might say that tests aren't a real production environment and this is the ultimate reason why they sometimes fail. There is a grain of truth in this: tests aren't meant to replicate every little detail, because it's not viable. Tests are a simulation, an approximation of what might happen, and that's usually good enough. Does it hurt to rerun tests if they'll pass on the next execution?

Actually, it does. There are three main concerns, as outlined here:

- If you have gathered enough flaky tests in your code base, they will become a serious obstacle to the smooth delivery of code changes. It's especially frustrating when you're in a hurry: either getting ready to go home on a Friday afternoon or delivering a critical fix to a severe issue impacting your customers.

- You can't be truly sure that your flaky tests are failing because of the inadequacy of the testing environment. It may be the opposite: they fail because they replicated a rare scenario that already occurs in production. It's just not obvious enough to raise an alert... yet.

- It's not the test that's flaky—it's your code! The environment is wonky from time to time—as programmers, we deal with that in a deterministic manner. If the SUT behaves this way, it's a sign of a serious error—for example, the code might be reading from uninitialized memory.

There isn't a perfect way to address all of the preceding cases—the multitude of possible reasons is simply too great. However, we might increase our chance of identifying flaky tests by running them repeatedly with the `-repeat <mode>:<#>` option. Three modes are available, as outlined here:

- `until-fail`—Run test `<#>` times; all runs have to pass.
- `until-pass`—Run test up to `<#>` times; it has to pass at least once. This is useful when dealing with tests that are known to be flaky but are too difficult and important to debug or disable.
- `after-timeout`—Run test up to `<#>` times but retry only if the test is timing out. Use it in busy test environments.

A general recommendation is to debug flaky tests as quickly as possible or get rid of them if they can't be trusted to produce consistent results.

Controlling output

Printing every piece of information to the screen every time would get incredibly busy. CTest reduces the noise and collects the outputs of tests it executes to the log files, providing only the most useful information on regular runs. When things go bad and tests fail, you can expect a summary and possibly some logs if you enabled `--output-on-failure`, as mentioned earlier.

I know from experience that "enough information" is enough until it isn't. Sometimes, we may want to see the output of passed tests too, perhaps to check if they're truly working (and not just silently stopping without an error). To get access to more verbose output, add the `-V` option (or `--verbose` if you want to be explicit in your automated pipelines). If that's not enough, you might want `-VV` or `--extra-verbose`. For extremely in-depth debugging, use `--debug` (but be prepared for walls of text with all the details).

If you're looking for the opposite, CTest also offers "Zen mode," enabled with `-Q` or `--quiet`. No output will be printed then (you can stop worrying and learn to love the bug). It seems that this option has no other use than to confuse people, but be aware that the output will still be stored in test files (in `./Testing/Temporary` by default). Automated pipelines can check if the exit code is a nonzero value and collect the log files for further processing without littering the main output with details that may confuse developers not familiar with the product.

To store the logs in a specific path, use the `-O <file>, --output-log <file>` option. If you're suffering from lengthy outputs, there are two limit options to cap them to the given number of bytes per test: `--test-output-size-passed <size>` and `--test-output-size-failed <size>`.

Miscellaneous

There are a few other options that can be useful for your everyday testing needs, as outlined here:

- `-C <cfg>`, `--build-config <cfg>`—Specify which configuration to test. The Debug configuration usually has debugging symbols, making things easier to understand, but Release should be tested too, as heavy optimization options could potentially affect the behavior of SUT. This option is for multi-configuration generators only.

- `-j <jobs>`, `--parallel <jobs>`—Sets the number of tests executed in parallel. It's very useful to speed up the execution of long tests during development. Be mindful that in a busy environment (on a shared test runner), it might have an adverse effect due to scheduling. This can be slightly mitigated with the next option.

- `--test-load <level>`—Schedule parallel tests in a fashion that CPU load doesn't exceed the `<level>` value (on a best-effort basis).

- `--timeout <seconds>`—Specify the default limit of time for a single test.

Now that we understand how to execute `ctest` in many different scenarios, let's learn how to add a simple test.

Creating the most basic unit test for CTest

Writing unit tests is technically possible without any kind of framework. All we have to do is create an instance of the class we want to test, execute one of its methods, and check if the new state or value returned meets our expectations. Then, we report the result and delete the object under test. Let's try it out.

We'll use the following structure:

```
- CMakeLists.txt
- src
  |- CMakeLists.txt
  |- calc.cpp
  |- calc.h
  |- main.cpp
- test
  |- CMakeLists.txt
  |- calc_test.cpp
```

Starting from `main.cpp`, we see that it uses a `Calc` class:

ch11/01-no-framework/src/main.cpp

```
#include <iostream>
#include "calc.h"
using namespace std;
int main() {
  Calc c;
  cout << "2 + 2 = " << c.Sum(2, 2) << endl;
  cout << "3 * 3 = " << c.Multiply(3, 3) << endl;
}
```

Nothing too fancy—`main.cpp` simply includes the `calc.h` header and calls two methods of the `Calc` object. Let's quickly glance at the interface of `Calc`, our SUT:

ch11/01-no-framework/src/calc.h

```
#pragma once
class Calc {
public:
    int Sum(int a, int b);
    int Multiply(int a, int b);
};
```

The interface is as simple as possible. We're using `#pragma once` here—it works exactly like common preprocessor **include guards** and is understood by almost all modern compilers, despite not being part of the official standard.

 Include guards are short lines in header files that prevent multiple inclusions in the same parent file.

Let's see the class implementation:

ch11/01-no-framework/src/calc.cpp

```
#include "calc.h"
int Calc::Sum(int a, int b) {
  return a + b;
}
int Calc::Multiply(int a, int b) {
```

```
    return a * a; // a mistake!
  }
```

Uh-oh! We introduced a mistake! `Multiply` is ignoring the b argument and returning a square of a instead. That should be detected by correctly written unit tests. So, let's write some! Here we go:

ch11/01-no-framework/test/calc_test.cpp

```cpp
#include "calc.h"
#include <cstdlib>
void SumAddsTwoIntegers() {
  Calc sut;
  if (4 != sut.Sum(2, 2))
    std::exit(1);
}
void MultiplyMultipliesTwoIntegers() {
  Calc sut;
  if(3 != sut.Multiply(1, 3))
    std::exit(1);
}
```

We start our `calc_test.cpp` file by writing two test methods, one for each tested method of SUT. If the value returned from the called method doesn't match expectations, each function will call `std::exit(1)`. We could use `assert()`, `abort()`, or `terminate()` here, but that would result in a less explicit `Subprocess aborted` message in the output of `ctest`, instead of the more readable `Failed` message.

Time to create a test runner. Ours will be as simple as possible to avoid introducing ridiculous amounts of work. Just look at the `main()` function we had to write in order to run just two tests:

ch11/01-no-framework/test/unit_tests.cpp

```cpp
#include <string>
void SumAddsTwoIntegers();
void MultiplyMultipliesTwoIntegers();
int main(int argc, char *argv[]) {
  if (argc < 2 || argv[1] == std::string("1"))
    SumAddsTwoIntegers();
  if (argc < 2 || argv[1] == std::string("2"))
    MultiplyMultipliesTwoIntegers();
}
```

Here's a breakdown of what happens:

1. We declare two external functions that will be linked from another translation unit.
2. If no arguments were provided, execute both tests (the zeroth element in argv[] is always the program name).
3. If the first argument is an identifier of the test, execute it.
4. If any of the tests fail, it internally calls exit() and returns with a 1 exit code.
5. If no tests were executed or all passed, it implicitly returns with a 0 exit code.

To run the first test, execute:

```
./unit_tests 1
```

To run the second, execute:

```
./unit_tests 2
```

We simplified the code as much as possible, but it's still hard to read. Anyone who might need to maintain this section isn't going to have an easy time after adding a few more tests. The functionality is pretty raw—debugging such a test suite will be difficult. Nevertheless, let's see how we can use it with CTest:

ch11/01-no-framework/CMakeLists.txt

```
cmake_minimum_required(VERSION 3.26.0)
project(NoFrameworkTests CXX)
include(CTest)
add_subdirectory(src bin)
add_subdirectory(test)
```

We start with the usual header and include(CTest). This enables CTest and should be always done in the top-level CMakeLists.txt. Next, we include two nested listfiles in each of the subdirectories: src and test. The specified bin value indicates that we want the binary output from the src subdirectory to be placed in <build_tree>/bin. Otherwise, binary files would end up in <build_tree>/src, which could be confusing for the user, since build artifacts are not source files.

For the src directory, the listfile is straightforward and contains a simple main target definition:

ch11/01-no-framework/src/CMakeLists.txt

```
add_executable(main main.cpp calc.cpp)
```

We also need a listfile for the test directory:

ch11/01-no-framework/test/CMakeLists.txt

```
add_executable(unit_tests
               unit_tests.cpp
               calc_test.cpp
               ../src/calc.cpp)
target_include_directories(unit_tests PRIVATE ../src)
add_test(NAME SumAddsTwoInts COMMAND unit_tests 1)
add_test(NAME MultiplyMultipliesTwoInts COMMAND unit_tests 2)
```

We have now defined a second unit_tests target that also uses the src/calc.cpp implementation file and its respective header. Finally, we explicitly add two tests:

- SumAddsTwoInts
- MultiplyMultipliesTwoInts

Each provides its ID as an argument to the add_test() command. CTest will simply take anything provided after the COMMAND keyword and execute it in a subshell, collecting the output and exit code. Don't get too attached to the add_test() method; in the *Unit-testing frameworks* section later, we'll discover a much better way of dealing with test cases.

To run the tests, execute ctest in the build tree:

```
# ctest
Test project /tmp/b
    Start 1: SumAddsTwoInts
1/2 Test #1: SumAddsTwoInts ...................   Passed    0.00 sec
    Start 2: MultiplyMultipliesTwoInts
2/2 Test #2: MultiplyMultipliesTwoInts ........***Failed    0.00 sec
50% tests passed, 1 tests failed out of 2
Total Test time (real) =   0.00 sec
The following tests FAILED:
         2 - MultiplyMultipliesTwoInts (Failed)
Errors while running CTest
Output from these tests are in: /tmp/b/Testing/Temporary/LastTest.log
Use "--rerun-failed --output-on-failure" to re-run the failed cases
verbosely.
```

CTest executed both tests and reported that one of them is failing—the returned value from `Calc::Multiply` didn't meet expectations. Very good. We now know that our code has a bug, and someone should fix it.

 You may have noticed that in most examples so far, we didn't necessarily employ the project structure described in *Chapter 4, Setting Up Your First CMake Project*. This was done to keep things brief. This chapter discusses more advanced concepts; therefore, using a full structure is warranted. In your projects (no matter how small), it's best to follow this structure from the start. As a wise man once said: "*You step onto the road, and if you don't keep your feet, there's no knowing where you might be swept off to.*"

I hope it's now clear that building a testing framework from scratch for your own project is not advisable. Even the most basic example is hard on the eyes, has a lot of overhead, and doesn't add any value. However, before we can adopt a unit-testing framework, we'll need to rethink the structure of the project.

Structuring our projects for testing

C++ has some limited introspection capabilities but can't offer as powerful retrospection features as Java can. This could be why writing tests and unit-testing frameworks for C++ code is more challenging than in other, more feature-rich environments. One result of this limited approach is that the programmer needs to be more involved in crafting testable code. We'll need to design our interfaces carefully and consider practical aspects. For example, how can we avoid compiling code twice and reuse artifacts between tests and production?

Compilation time may not be a big issue for smaller projects, but as projects grow, the need for short compilation loops remains. In the previous example, we included all the SUT sources in the unit test executable except the `main.cpp` file. If you paid close attention, you would have noticed that some code in that file wasn't tested (the contents of `main()` itself). Compiling the code twice introduces a slight chance that the produced artifacts *won't be identical*. These discrepancies can gradually increase over time, particularly when adding compilation flags and preprocessor directives, and may be risky when contributors are rushed, inexperienced, or unfamiliar with the project.

Multiple solutions exist for this problem, but the most straightforward is to build your entire solution as a library and link it with unit tests. You might wonder how to run it then. The answer is to create a bootstrap executable that links with the library and executes its code.

Begin by renaming your current main() function to something like run() or start_program().
Then, create another implementation file (bootstrap.cpp) containing only a new main() function. This function serves as an adapter: its only role is to provide an entry point and call run(),
passing along any command-line arguments. After linking everything together, you end up with
a testable project.

By renaming main(), you can now link the SUT with tests and test its main functionality as well.
Otherwise, you'd violate the **One Definition Rule** (**ODR**) discussed in *Chapter 8*, *Linking Executables and Libraries*, because the test runner also needs its own main() function. As we promised
in the *Separating main() for testing* section of *Chapter 8*, we'll delve into this topic in detail here.

Note also that the testing framework might provide its own main() function by default, so writing
one may not be necessary. Typically, it will automatically detect all linked tests and run them
according to your configuration.

Artifacts produced by this approach can be grouped into the following targets:

- A sut library with production code
- bootstrap with a main() wrapper calling run() from sut
- unit tests with a main() wrapper that runs all the tests on sut

The following diagram shows the symbol relations between targets:

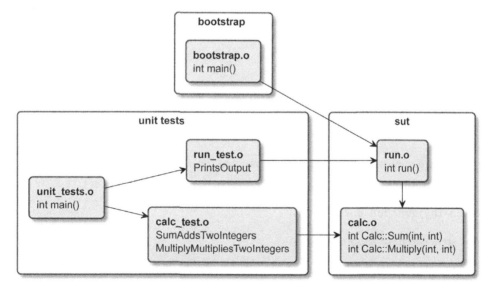

Figure 11.1: Sharing artifacts between test and production executables

We end up with six implementation files that will produce their respective (.o) *object files*, as follows:

- `calc.cpp`: The `Calc` class to be unit-tested. This is called a **unit under test** (**UUT**) because UUT is a specialization of SUT.
- `run.cpp`: Original entry point renamed `run()`, which can be now tested.
- `bootstrap.cpp`: New `main()` entry point calling `run()`.
- `calc_test.cpp`: Tests the `Calc` class.
- `run_test.cpp`: New tests for `run()` can go here.
- `unit_tests.o`: Entry point for unit tests, extended to call tests for `run()`.

The library we're about to build doesn't necessarily have to be a static or shared library. By opting for an object library, we can avoid unnecessary archiving or linking. Technically, it's possible to save some time by using dynamic linking for the SUT, but we often find ourselves making changes in both targets: tests and SUT, which negates any time saved.

Let's examine how our files have changed, starting with the file previously named `main.cpp`:

ch11/02-structured/src/run.cpp

```cpp
#include <iostream>
#include "calc.h"
using namespace std;
int run() {
  Calc c;
  cout << "2 + 2 = " << c.Sum(2, 2) << endl;
  cout << "3 * 3 = " << c.Multiply(3, 3) << endl;
  return 0;
}
```

The changes are minor: the file and function are renamed, and we've added a `return` statement because the compiler won't add one implicitly for functions other than `main()`.

The new `main()` function looks like this:

ch11/02-structured/src/bootstrap.cpp

```cpp
int run(); // declaration
int main() {
  run();
}
```

Keeping it simple, we declare that the linker will provide the run() function from another translation unit, and we call it.

Next up is the src listfile:

ch11/02-structured/src/CMakeLists.txt

```
add_library(sut STATIC calc.cpp run.cpp)
target_include_directories(sut PUBLIC .)
add_executable(bootstrap bootstrap.cpp)
target_link_libraries(bootstrap PRIVATE sut)
```

First, we create a SUT library and mark . as a PUBLIC *include directory* so it will be propagated to all targets that link with SUT (i.e., bootstrap and unit_tests). Note that *include directories* are relative to the listfile, allowing us to use a dot (.) to refer to the current <source_tree>/src directory.

Time to update our unit_tests target. We'll replace the direct reference to the ../src/calc.cpp file with a linking reference to sut for the unit_tests target. We'll also add a new test for the primary function in the run_test.cpp file. We'll skip discussing that for brevity, but if you're interested, check out the examples in the repository for this book.

Meanwhile, here's the whole test listfile:

ch11/02-structured/test/CMakeLists.txt

```
add_executable(unit_tests
               unit_tests.cpp
               calc_test.cpp
               run_test.cpp)
target_link_libraries(unit_tests PRIVATE sut)
```

ch11/02-structured/test/CMakeLists.txt (continued)

```
add_test(NAME SumAddsTwoInts COMMAND unit_tests 1)
add_test(NAME MultiplyMultipliesTwoInts COMMAND unit_tests 2)
add_test(NAME RunOutputsCorrectEquations COMMAND unit_tests 3)
```

Done! We registered the new test, as necessary. By following this practice, you can be sure that your tests are executed on the very machine code that will be used in production.

The target names we're using here, sut and bootstrap, are chosen to make it very clear what they're about from the perspective of testing. In real-life projects, you should pick names that match the context of the production code (rather than tests). For example, for a FooApp, name your target foo instead of bootstrap, and lib_foo instead of sut.

Now that we know how to structure a testable project in appropriate targets, let's shift our focus to the testing frameworks themselves. We don't want to add every test case to our listfiles manually, do we?

Unit-testing frameworks

The previous section shows that writing a small unit-testing driver isn't overly complicated. It may not have been pretty, but believe it or not, some professional developers *do like* to reinvent the wheel, thinking their version will be better in every way. Avoid this pitfall: you'll end up creating so much boilerplate code that it could become its own project. Using a popular unit-testing framework aligns your solution with a standard that's recognized across multiple projects and companies, and often comes with free updates and extensions. You can't lose.

How do you incorporate a unit-testing framework into your project? Of course, by implementing tests according to the rules of the chosen framework, then linking these tests with a test runner provided by the framework. Test runners initiate the execution of selected tests and collect the results. Unlike the basic unit_tests.cpp file we looked at earlier, many frameworks will automatically detect all the tests and make them visible for CTest. It's a much smoother process.

In this chapter, I've chosen to introduce two unit-testing frameworks for specific reasons:

- **Catch2** is relatively easy to learn and comes with good support and documentation. While it offers basic test cases, it also includes elegant macros for **behavior-driven development (BDD)**. While it may lack some features, it can be supplemented with external tools when needed. Visit its home page here: https://github.com/catchorg/Catch2.
- **GoogleTest (GTest)** is convenient but also more advanced. It offers a rich set of features like various assertions, death tests, as well as value- and type-parametrized tests. It even supports XML test report generation and mocking through its GMock module. Find it here: https://github.com/google/googletest.

The choice of framework depends on your learning preference and project size. If you like to ease into things and don't require a full feature set, Catch2 is a good choice. Those who prefer to dive in headfirst and need a comprehensive toolset will find GoogleTest more suitable.

Catch2

This framework, maintained by Martin Hořeňovský, is well-suited for beginners and smaller projects. That's not to say it can't accommodate larger applications, but be aware that you may need additional tools in some areas (exploring this in detail would take us too far off-topic). To begin, let's examine a simple unit test implementation for our Calc class:

ch11/03-catch2/test/calc_test.cpp

```
#include <catch2/catch_test_macros.hpp>
#include "calc.h"

TEST_CASE("SumAddsTwoInts", "[calc]") {
  Calc sut;
  CHECK(4 == sut.Sum(2, 2));
}

TEST_CASE("MultiplyMultipliesTwoInts", "[calc]") {
  Calc sut;
  CHECK(12 == sut.Multiply(3, 4));
}
```

That's it. These few lines are more powerful than our previous examples. The CHECK() macros do more than just verify expectations; they collect all failed assertions and present them together, helping you avoid constant recompilation.

The best part? You don't need to manually add these tests to listfiles to inform CMake about them. Forget about add_test(); you won't need it anymore. Catch2 will automatically register your tests with CTest if you allow it. Adding the framework is straightforward once you've configured your project as discussed in the previous section. Use FetchContent() to bring it into your project.

You can choose between two major versions: Catch2 v2 and Catch2 v3. Version 2 is a legacy option available as a single-header library for C++11. Version 3 compiles as a static library and requires C++14. It's recommended to opt for the latest release.

When working with Catch2, make sure to pick a Git tag and pin it in your listfile. Upgrading through the main branch isn't guaranteed to be seamless.

In a business setting, you're likely to be running tests in a CI pipeline. In such cases, remember to set up your environment so it already has the dependencies installed in the system, and each build doesn't need to fetch them every time it runs. As mentioned in the section *Using the installed dependency where possible* in *Chapter 9, Managing Dependencies in CMake*, you'll want to extend your FetchContent_Declare() command with the FIND_PACKAGE_ARGS keyword to use packages from the system.

We'll include version 3.4.0 in our listfile like so:

ch11/03-catch2/test/CMakeLists.txt

```
include(FetchContent)
FetchContent_Declare(
  Catch2
  GIT_REPOSITORY https://github.com/catchorg/Catch2.git
  GIT_TAG        v3.4.0
)
FetchContent_MakeAvailable(Catch2)
```

Then, we need to define our unit_tests target and link it with sut and with a framework-provided entry point and Catch2::Catch2WithMain library. Since Catch2 provides its own main() function, we no longer use the unit_tests.cpp file (this file can be removed). The code is illustrated in the following snippet:

ch11/03-catch2/test/CMakeLists.txt (continued)

```
add_executable(unit_tests calc_test.cpp run_test.cpp)
target_link_libraries(unit_tests PRIVATE
                      sut Catch2::Catch2WithMain)
```

Lastly, we use a catch_discover_tests() command defined in the module provided by Catch2 to automatically detect all test cases from unit_tests and register them with CTest, as follows:

ch11/03-catch2/test/CMakeLists.txt (continued)

```
list(APPEND CMAKE_MODULE_PATH ${catch2_SOURCE_DIR}/extras)
include(Catch)
catch_discover_tests(unit_tests)
```

Done. We just added a unit-testing framework to our solution. Let's now see it in practice. The output from the test runner looks like this:

```
# ./test/unit_tests
unit_tests is a Catch2 v3.4.0 host application.
Run with -? for options
-----------------------------------------------------------------
MultiplyMultipliesTwoInts
-----------------------------------------------------------------
/root/examples/ch11/03-catch2/test/calc_test.cpp:9
.................................................................
/root/examples/ch11/03-catch2/test/calc_test.cpp:11: FAILED:
  CHECK( 12 == sut.Multiply(3, 4) )
with expansion:
  12 == 9
=================================================================
test cases: 3 | 2 passed | 1 failed
assertions: 3 | 2 passed | 1 failed
```

Catch2 was able to expand the sut.Multiply(3, 4) expression to 9, giving us more context, which is really helpful in debugging.

Note that the direct execution of the runner binary (the compiled unit_test executable) may be slightly faster than using ctest, but the additional advantages offered by CTest are worth the trade-off.

This wraps up the Catch2 setup. If you need to add more tests in the future, simply create new implementation files and add their paths to the list of sources for the unit_tests target.

Catch2 offers various features like event listeners, data generators, and micro-benchmarking, but it lacks built-in mocking functionality. If you're not familiar with mocks, we'll cover that in the next section. You can add mocks to Catch2 with one of the following mocking frameworks:

- FakeIt (https://github.com/eranpeer/FakeIt)
- Hippomocks (https://github.com/dascandy/hippomocks)
- Trompeloeil (https://github.com/rollbear/trompeloeil)

That said, for a more streamlined, advanced experience, there is another framework worth looking at, GoogleTest.

GoogleTest

There are several important advantages to using GoogleTest: it's been around for a long time and is highly recognized in the C++ community, so multiple IDEs support it natively. The company behind the world's largest search engine maintains and uses it extensively, making it unlikely to become obsolete or abandoned. It can test C++11 and up, which is good news if you're working in an older environment.

The GoogleTest repository contains two projects: GTest (the main testing framework) and GMock (a library that adds mocking functionality). This means you can download both with a single `FetchContent()` call.

Using GTest

To use GTest, our project needs to follow the directions from the *Structuring our projects for testing* section. This is how we'd write a unit test in this framework:

ch11/04-gtest/test/calc_test.cpp

```cpp
#include <gtest/gtest.h>
#include "calc.h"


class CalcTestSuite : public ::testing::Test {
protected:
  Calc sut_;
};


TEST_F(CalcTestSuite, SumAddsTwoInts) {
  EXPECT_EQ(4, sut_.Sum(2, 2));
}


TEST_F(CalcTestSuite, MultiplyMultipliesTwoInts) {
  EXPECT_EQ(12, sut_.Multiply(3, 4));
}
```

Because this example will also be used in GMock, I chose to place the tests in a single `CalcTestSuite` class. Test suites group related tests so they can reuse the same fields, methods, setup, and teardown steps. To create a test suite, declare a new class that inherits from `::testing::Test` and place reusable elements in its protected section.

Each test case within a test suite is declared with the TEST_F() macro. A simpler TEST() macro exists for standalone tests. Since we defined Calc sut_ in the class, each test case can access it as if test cases were methods of CalcTestSuite. In reality, each test case runs in its own instance that inherits from CalcTestSuite, which is why the protected keyword is necessary. Note that reusable fields aren't meant to share data between consecutive tests; their purpose is to keep the code DRY.

GTest does not offer the natural syntax for assertions like Catch2. Instead, you use explicit comparisons such as EXPECT_EQ(). By convention, the expected value goes first, followed by the actual value. There are many other types of assertions, helpers, and macros worth exploring. For detailed information on GTest, see the official reference material (https://google.github.io/googletest/).

To add this dependency to our project, we need to decide which version to use. Unlike Catch2, GoogleTest is leaning toward a "live at head" philosophy (originating from the Abseil project that GTest depends on). It states: *"If you build our dependency from source and follow our API, you shouldn't have any issues."* (Refer to the *Further reading* section for more details.) If you're comfortable following this rule (and building from source isn't an issue), set your Git tag to the master branch. Otherwise, pick a release from the GoogleTest repository.

In a business setting, you're likely to be running tests in a CI pipeline. In such cases, remember to set up your environment so it already has the dependencies installed in the system, and each build doesn't need to fetch them every time it runs. As mentioned in the section *Using the installed dependency where possible* in *Chapter 9, Managing Dependencies in CMake*, you'll want to extend your FetchContent_Declare() command with the FIND_PACKAGE_ARGS keyword to use packages from the system.

In any case, adding a dependency on GTest looks like this:

ch11/04-gtest/test/CMakeLists.txt

```
include(FetchContent)
FetchContent_Declare(
  googletest
  GIT_REPOSITORY https://github.com/google/googletest.git
  GIT_TAG v1.14.0
)
set(gtest_force_shared_crt ON CACHE BOOL "" FORCE)
FetchContent_MakeAvailable(googletest)
```

We're following the same method as with Catch2—execute FetchContent() and build the framework from source. The only difference is the addition of the set(gtest...) command, as recommended by GoogleTest authors to prevent overriding the parent project's compiler and linker settings on Windows.

Finally, we can declare our test runner executable, link it with gtest_main, and have our test cases automatically discovered thanks to the built-in CMake GoogleTest module, as illustrated here:

ch11/04-gtest/test/CMakeLists.txt (continued)

```
add_executable(unit_tests
               calc_test.cpp
               run_test.cpp)
target_link_libraries(unit_tests PRIVATE sut gtest_main)
include(GoogleTest)
gtest_discover_tests(unit_tests)
```

This completes the setup of GTest. The output of the directly executed test runner is much more verbose than that from Catch2, but we can pass --gtest_brief=1 to limit it to failures only, as follows:

```
# ./test/unit_tests --gtest_brief=1
~/examples/ch11/04-gtest/test/calc_test.cpp:15: Failure
Expected equality of these values:
  12
  sut_.Multiply(3, 4)
    Which is: 9
[  FAILED  ] CalcTestSuite.MultiplyMultipliesTwoInts (0 ms)
[==========] 3 tests from 2 test suites ran. (0 ms total)
[  PASSED  ] 2 tests.
```

Fortunately, even the noisy output will be suppressed when running from CTest (unless we explicitly enable it with the ctest --output-on-failure command line).

Now that we have the framework in place, let's discuss mocking. After all, no test can be truly "unit test" when it's tightly coupled with other elements.

GMock

Writing pure unit tests is about executing a piece of code in isolation from other pieces of code. Such a tested unit has to be a self-contained element, either a class or a component. Of course, hardly any programs written in C++ have all of their units in clear isolation from others.

Most likely, your code will rely heavily on some form of association relationship between classes. There's only one problem with that: objects of such a class will require objects of another class, and those will require yet another. Before you know it, your entire solution is participating in a "unit test." Even worse, your code might be coupled to an external system and be dependent on its state. For example, it might rely closely on specific records in a database, network packets coming in, or specific files stored on the disk.

To decouple units for the purpose of testing, developers use **test doubles** or a special version of classes that are used by a unit under test. Some examples include fakes, stubs, and mocks. Here are some rough definitions of these terms:

- A **fake** is a limited implementation of a more complex mechanism. An example could be an in-memory map instead of an actual database client.

- A **stub** provides specific, canned answers to method calls, limited to responses used by tests. It can also record which methods were called and how many times this occurred.

- A **mock** is a slightly more extended version of a stub. It will additionally verify if methods were called during the test as expected.

Such a test double is created at the beginning of a test and provided as an argument to the constructor of a tested class to be used instead of a real object. This mechanism is called **dependency injesction**.

The problem with simple test doubles is that they are *too simple*. To simulate behaviors for different test scenarios, we would have to provide many different doubles, one for every state in which the coupled object can be. This isn't very practical and would scatter testing code across too many files. This is where GMock comes in: it allows developers to create a generic test double for a specific class and define its behavior for every test in line. GMock calls these doubles "mocks," but in reality, they're a mixture of all the aforementioned test doubles, depending on the occasion.

Consider the following example: let's add a functionality to our `Calc` class that would add a random number to the provided argument. It will be represented by an `AddRandomNumber()` method that returns this sum as an `int`. How would we confirm the fact that the returned value is really an exact sum of something random and the value provided to the class? As we know, randomly generated numbers are key to many important processes, and if we're using them incorrectly, we might suffer all kinds of consequences. Checking all random numbers until we exhaust all possibilities isn't very practical.

To test it, we need to wrap a random number generator in a class that could be mocked (or, in other words, replaced with a mock). Mocks will allow us to force a specific response, which is used to "fake" the generation of a random number. Calc will use that value in AddRandomNumber() and allow us to check if the returned value from that method meets expectations. The clean separation of random number generation from another unit is an added value (as we'll be able to exchange one type of generator for another).

Let's start with the public interface for the abstract generator. This header will allow us to implement it in the actual generator and a mock, enabling us to use them interchangeably:

ch11/05-gmock/src/rng.h

```
#pragma once
class RandomNumberGenerator {
public:
  virtual int Get() = 0;
  virtual ~RandomNumberGenerator() = default;
};
```

Classes implementing this interface will provide us with a random number from the Get() method. Note the virtual keyword—it has to be on all methods to be mocked unless we'd like to get involved with more complex template-based mocking. We also need to remember to add a virtual destructor.

Next, we have to extend our Calc class to accept and store the generator, so we can either provide the real generator for the release build or a mock for tests:

ch11/05-gmock/src/calc.h

```
#pragma once
#include "rng.h"
class Calc {
  RandomNumberGenerator* rng_;
public:
  Calc(RandomNumberGenerator* rng);
  int Sum(int a, int b);
  int Multiply(int a, int b);
  int AddRandomNumber(int a);
};
```

We included the header and added a method to provide random additions. Additionally, a field to store the pointer to the generator was created, along with a parameterized constructor. This is how dependency injection works in practice. Now, we implement these methods, as follows:

ch11/05-gmock/src/calc.cpp

```
#include "calc.h"
Calc::Calc(RandomNumberGenerator* rng) {
  rng_ = rng;
}
int Calc::Sum(int a, int b) {
  return a + b;
}
int Calc::Multiply(int a, int b) {
  return a * b; // now corrected
}
int Calc::AddRandomNumber(int a) {
  return a + rng_->Get();
}
```

In the constructor, we're assigning the provided pointer to a class field. We're then using this field in AddRandomNumber() to fetch the generated value. The production code will use a real number generator; the tests will use mocks. Remember that we need to dereference pointers to enable polymorphism. As a bonus, we could possibly create different generator classes for different implementations. I just need one: a Mersenne Twister pseudo-random generator with uniform distribution, as illustrated in the following code snippet:

ch11/05-gmock/src/rng_mt19937.cpp

```
#include <random>
#include "rng_mt19937.h"
int RandomNumberGeneratorMt19937::Get() {
  std::random_device rd;
  std::mt19937 gen(rd());
  std::uniform_int_distribution<> distrib(1, 6);
  return distrib(gen);
}
```

Creating a new instance on every call isn't very efficient, but it will suffice for this simple example. The purpose is to generate numbers from 1 to 6 and return them to the caller.

The header for this class simply provides the signature of one method:

ch11/05-gmock/src/rng_mt19937.h

```
#include "rng.h"
class RandomNumberGeneratorMt19937
        : public RandomNumberGenerator {
public:
  int Get() override;
};
```

And this is how we're using it in the production code:

ch11/05-gmock/src/run.cpp

```
#include <iostream>
#include "calc.h"
#include "rng_mt19937.h"
using namespace std;
int run() {
  auto rng = new RandomNumberGeneratorMt19937();
  Calc c(rng);
  cout << "Random dice throw + 1 = "
        << c.AddRandomNumber(1) << endl;
  delete rng;
  return 0;
}
```

We have created a generator and passed a pointer to it to the constructor of `Calc`. Everything is ready and we can start writing our mock. To keep things organized, developers usually put mocks in a separate test/mocks directory. To prevent ambiguity, the header name has a _mock suffix.

Here is the code:

ch11/05-gmock/test/mocks/rng_mock.h

```
#pragma once
#include "gmock/gmock.h"
class RandomNumberGeneratorMock : public
RandomNumberGenerator {
public:
  MOCK_METHOD(int, Get, (), (override));
};
```

After adding the gmock.h header, we can declare our mock. As planned, it's a class implementing the RandomNumberGenerator interface. Instead of writing methods ourselves, we need to use MOCK_METHOD macros provided by GMock. These inform the framework which methods from the interface should be mocked. Use the following format (the extensive parentheses are required):

```
MOCK_METHOD(<return type>, <method name>,
            (<argument list>), (<keywords>))
```

We're ready to use the mock in our test suite (previous test cases are omitted for brevity), as follows:

ch11/05-gmock/test/calc_test.cpp

```
#include <gtest/gtest.h>
#include "calc.h"
#include "mocks/rng_mock.h"
using namespace ::testing;
class CalcTestSuite : public Test {
protected:
  RandomNumberGeneratorMock rng_mock_;
  Calc sut_{&rng_mock_};
};
TEST_F(CalcTestSuite, AddRandomNumberAddsThree) {
  EXPECT_CALL(rng_mock_, Get()).Times(1).WillOnce(Return(3));
  EXPECT_EQ(4, sut_.AddRandomNumber(1));
}
```

Let's break down the changes: we added the new header and created a new field for rng_mock_ in the test suite. Next, the mock's address is passed to the constructor of sut_. We can do that because fields are initialized in the order of declaration (rng_mock_ precedes sut_).

In our test case, we call GMock's EXPECT_CALL macro on the Get() method of rng_mock_. This tells the framework to fail the test if the Get() method isn't called during execution. The chained Times call explicitly states how many calls must happen for the test to pass. WillOnce determines what the mocking framework does after the method is called (it returns 3).

By virtue of using GMock, we're able to express mocked behavior alongside the expected outcome. This greatly improves readability and eases the maintenance of tests. Most importantly, though, it provides flexibility in each test case, as we get to differentiate what happens with a single expressive statement.

Finally, to build the project, we need to make sure that the gmock library is linked with a test runner. To achieve that, we add it to the `target_link_libraries()` list:

ch11/05-gmock/test/CMakeLists.txt

```
include(FetchContent)
FetchContent_Declare(
  googletest
  GIT_REPOSITORY https://github.com/google/googletest.git
  GIT_TAG release-1.14.0
)
# For Windows: Prevent overriding the parent project's
  compiler/linker settings
set(gtest_force_shared_crt ON CACHE BOOL "" FORCE)
FetchContent_MakeAvailable(googletest)
add_executable(unit_tests
               calc_test.cpp
               run_test.cpp)
target_link_libraries(unit_tests PRIVATE sut gtest_main gmock)
include(GoogleTest)
gtest_discover_tests(unit_tests)
```

Now, we can enjoy all the benefits of the GoogleTest framework. Both GTest and GMock are advanced tools with a multitude of concepts, utilities, and helpers for different situations. This example (despite being a bit lengthy) only scratches the surface of what's possible. I encourage you to incorporate them into your projects as they will greatly improve the quality of your work. A good place to start with GMock is the "Mocking for Dummies" page in the official documentation (you can find a link to this in the *Further reading* section).

Having tests in place, we should somehow measure what's tested and what isn't and strive to improve the situation. It's best to use automated tools that will collect and report this information.

Generating test coverage reports

Adding tests to such a small solution isn't incredibly challenging. The real difficulty comes with slightly more advanced and longer programs. Over the years, I have found that as I approach over 1,000 lines of code, it slowly becomes hard to track which lines and branches are executed during tests and which aren't. After crossing 3,000 lines, it is nearly impossible. Most professional applications will have much more code than that. What's more, one of the key metrics many managers use to negotiate addressing tech debt is code coverage percentage, so knowing how to generate useful reports is helpful to get the actual data for those discussions. To deal with this problem, we can use a utility to understand which code lines are "covered" by test cases. Such code coverage tools hook up to the SUT and gather information on the execution of each line during tests to present it in a convenient report like the one shown here:

LCOV - code coverage report

			Hit	Total	Coverage
Current view:	top level - src				
Test:	coverage.info	**Lines:**	20	21	**95.2 %**
Date:	2021-08-30 16:33:33	**Functions:**	6	8	**75.0 %**
Legend:	Rating: low: < 75 % medium: >= 75 % high: >= 90 %				

Filename	Line Coverage (show details) ⬍			Functions ⬍	
calc.cpp		100.0 %	9 / 9	100.0 %	4 / 4
rng.h		0.0 %	0 / 1	0.0 %	0 / 2
rng_mt19937.cpp		100.0 %	5 / 5	100.0 %	1 / 1
run.cpp		100.0 %	6 / 6	100.0 %	1 / 1

Generated by: LCOV version 1.14

Figure 11.2: Code coverage report generated by LCOV

These reports will show you which files are covered by tests and which aren't. More than that, you can also take a peek inside the details of each file and see exactly which lines of code are executed and how many times this occurs. In the following screenshot, the **Line data** column says that the Calc constructor was run 4 times, one time for each of the tests:

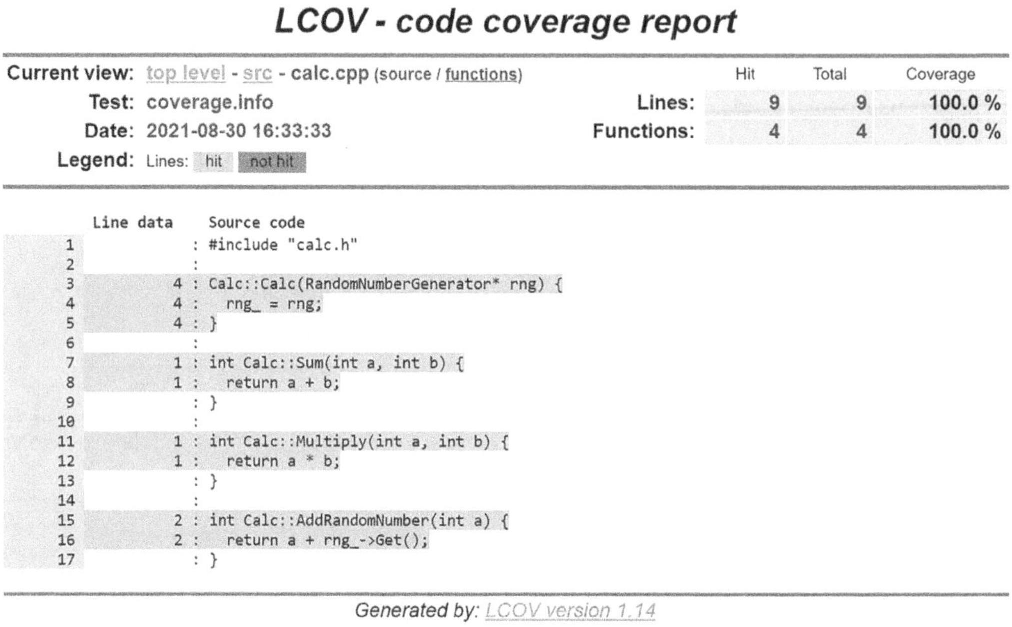

LCOV - code coverage report

Current view:	top level - src - **calc.cpp** (source / functions)		Hit	Total	Coverage
Test:	coverage.info	**Lines:**	9	9	**100.0 %**
Date:	2021-08-30 16:33:33	**Functions:**	4	4	**100.0 %**
Legend:	Lines: hit not hit				

```
     Line data    Source code
  1            : #include "calc.h"
  2            :
  3         4  : Calc::Calc(RandomNumberGenerator* rng) {
  4         4  :   rng_ = rng;
  5         4  : }
  6            :
  7         1  : int Calc::Sum(int a, int b) {
  8         1  :   return a + b;
  9            : }
 10            :
 11         1  : int Calc::Multiply(int a, int b) {
 12         1  :   return a * b;
 13            : }
 14            :
 15         2  : int Calc::AddRandomNumber(int a) {
 16         2  :   return a + rng_->Get();
 17            : }
```

Generated by: LCOV version 1.14

Figure 11.3: Detailed view of a code coverage report

There are multiple ways of generating similar reports and they differ across platforms and compilers, but they generally follow the same procedure: prepare the SUT to be measured and get the baseline, measure, and report.

The simplest tool for the job is called **LCOV**. Rather than being an acronym, it's a graphical frontend for gcov, a coverage utility from the **GNU Compiler Collection (GCC)**. Let's see how to use it in practice.

Using LCOV for coverage reports

LCOV will generate HTML coverage reports and internally use gcov to measure coverage. If you're using Clang, don't worry—Clang supports producing metrics in this format. You can get LCOV from the official repository maintained by the **Linux Test Project** (https://github.com/linux-test-project/lcov) or simply use a package manager. As the name suggests, it is a Linux-targeted utility.

It's possible to run it on macOS, but the Windows platform is not supported. End users often don't care about test coverage, so it's usually fine to install LCOV manually in your own build environment instead of incorporating it into the project.

To measure coverage, we'll need to do the following:

1. Compile in the Debug configuration with compiler flags enabling code coverage. This will generate coverage note (.gcno) files.
2. Link the test executable with the gcov library.
3. Gather coverage metrics for the baseline, without any tests being run.
4. Run the tests. This will create coverage data (.gcda) files.
5. Collect the metrics into an aggregated information file.
6. Generate a (.html) report.

We should start by explaining why the code has to be compiled in the Debug configuration. The most important reason is the fact that, usually, Debug configurations have disabled any optimization with a -O0 flag. CMake does this by default in the CMAKE_CXX_FLAGS_DEBUG variable (despite not stating this anywhere in the documentation). Unless you decide to override this variable, your Debug build should be unoptimized. This is desired to prevent any inlining and other kinds of implicit code simplification. Otherwise, it would be hard to trace which machine instruction came from which line of source code.

In the first step, we need to instruct the compiler to add the necessary instrumentation to our SUT. The exact flag to add is compiler-specific; however, two major compilers (GCC and Clang) offer the same --coverage flag to enable the coverage instrumentation, producing data in a GCC-compatible gcov format.

This is how we can add the coverage instrumentation to our exemplary SUT from the previous section:

ch11/06-coverage/src/CMakeLists.txt

```
add_library(sut STATIC calc.cpp run.cpp rng_mt19937.cpp)
target_include_directories(sut PUBLIC .)
if (CMAKE_BUILD_TYPE STREQUAL Debug)
  target_compile_options(sut PRIVATE --coverage)
  target_link_options(sut PUBLIC --coverage)
  add_custom_command(TARGET sut PRE_BUILD COMMAND
                     find ${CMAKE_BINARY_DIR} -type f
```

```
                           -name '*.gcda' -exec rm {} +)
endif()
add_executable(bootstrap bootstrap.cpp)
target_link_libraries(bootstrap PRIVATE sut)
```

Let's break this down step by step, as follows:

1. Ensure that we're running in the Debug configuration with the if(STREQUAL) command. Remember that you won't be able to get any coverage unless you run cmake with the -DCMAKE_BUILD_TYPE=Debug option.

2. Add --coverage to the PRIVATE *compile options* for all *object files* that are part of the sut library.

3. Add --coverage to the PUBLIC linker options: both GCC and Clang interpret this as a request to link the gcov (or compatible) library with all targets that depend on sut (due to propagated properties).

4. The add_custom_command() command is introduced to clean any stale .gcda files. Reasons to add this command are discussed in detail in the *Avoiding the SEGFAULT gotcha* section.

This is enough to produce code coverage. If you're using an IDE such as CLion, you'll be able to run your unit tests with coverage and get the results in a built-in report view. However, this won't work in any automated pipeline that might be run in your CI/CD. To get reports, we'll need to generate them ourselves with LCOV.

For this purpose, it's best to define a new target called coverage. To keep things clean, we'll define a separate function, AddCoverage, in another file to be used in the test listfile, as follows:

ch11/06-coverage/cmake/Coverage.cmake

```
function(AddCoverage target)
  find_program(LCOV_PATH lcov REQUIRED)
  find_program(GENHTML_PATH genhtml REQUIRED)
  add_custom_target(coverage
    COMMENT "Running coverage for ${target}..."
    COMMAND ${LCOV_PATH} -d . --zerocounters
    COMMAND $<TARGET_FILE:${target}>
    COMMAND ${LCOV_PATH} -d . --capture -o coverage.info
    COMMAND ${LCOV_PATH} -r coverage.info '/usr/include/*'
                         -o filtered.info
    COMMAND ${GENHTML_PATH} -o coverage filtered.info
      --legend
```

```
      COMMAND rm -rf coverage.info filtered.info
      WORKING_DIRECTORY ${CMAKE_BINARY_DIR}
  )
endfunction()
```

In the preceding snippet, we first detect the paths for lcov and genhtml (two command-line tools from the LCOV package). The REQUIRED keyword instructs CMake to throw an error when they're not found. Next, we add a custom coverage target with the following steps:

1. Clear the counters from any previous runs.

2. Run the target executable (using generator expressions to get its path). $<TARGET_ FILE:target> is an exceptional generator expression, and it will implicitly add a dependency on target in this case, causing it to be built before executing all commands. We'll provide target as an argument to this function.

3. Collect metrics for the solution from the current directory (-d .) and output to a file (-o coverage.info).

4. Remove (-r) unwanted coverage data on system headers ('/usr/include/*') and output to another file (-o filtered.info).

5. Generate an HTML report in the coverage directory, and add a --legend color.

6. Remove temporary .info files.

7. Specifying the WORKING_DIRECTORY keyword sets the binary tree as the working directory for all commands.

These are the general steps for both GCC and Clang. It's important to know that the gcov tool's version has to match the version of the compiler: you can't use GCC's gcov tool for Clang-compiled code. To point lcov to Clang's gcov tool, we can use the --gcov-tool argument. The only problem here is that it has to be a single executable. To deal with that, we can provide a simple wrapper script (remember to mark it as an executable with chmod +x), as follows:

```
# cmake/gcov-llvm-wrapper.sh
#!/bin/bash
exec llvm-cov gcov "$@"
```

Doing so will mean that all of our calls to ${LCOV_PATH} in the previous function will receive the following flag:

```
--gcov-tool ${CMAKE_SOURCE_DIR}/cmake/gcov-llvm-wrapper.sh
```

Make sure that this function is available for inclusion in the test listfile. We can do this by extending the *include search path* in the main listfile, as follows:

ch11/06-coverage/CMakeLists.txt

```
cmake_minimum_required(VERSION 3.26.0)
project(Coverage CXX)
include(CTest)
list(APPEND CMAKE_MODULE_PATH "${CMAKE_SOURCE_DIR}/cmake")
add_subdirectory(src bin)
add_subdirectory(test)
```

The highlighted line allows us to include all .cmake files from the cmake directory in our project. We can now use Coverage.cmake in the test listfile, like so:

ch11/06-coverage/test/CMakeLists.txt (fragment)

```
# ... skipped unit_tests target declaration for brevity
include(Coverage)
AddCoverage(unit_tests)
include(GoogleTest)
gtest_discover_tests(unit_tests)
```

To build the coverage target, use the following commands (notice that the first command ends with a -DCMAKE_BUILD_TYPE=Debug build type selection):

```
# cmake -B <binary_tree> -S <source_tree> -DCMAKE_BUILD_TYPE=Debug
# cmake --build <binary_tree> -t coverage
```

After executing all of the mentioned steps, you will see a short summary like this:

```
Writing directory view page.
Overall coverage rate:
  lines......: 95.7% (22 of 23 lines)
  functions..: 75.0% (6 of 8 functions)
[100%] Built target coverage
```

Next, open the coverage/index.html file in your browser and enjoy the reports! There's only one small issue though...

Avoiding the SEGFAULT gotcha

We may get ourselves into trouble when we start editing sources in such a built solution. This is because the coverage information is split into two parts:

- gcno files, or **GNU Coverage Notes**, generated during the compilation of the SUT
- gcda files, or **GNU Coverage Data**, generated and **updated** during test runs

The "update" functionality is a potential source of segmentation faults. After we run our tests initially, we're left with a bunch of gcda files that don't get removed at any point. If we make some changes to the source code and recompile the *object files*, new gcno files will be created. However, there's no wipe step—the gcda files from previous test runs follow the stale source. When we execute the unit_tests binary (it happens in the gtest_discover_tests macro), the coverage information files won't match, and we'll receive a SEGFAULT (segmentation fault) error.

To avoid this problem, we should erase any stale gcda files. Since our sut instance is a STATIC library, we can hook the add_custom_command(TARGET) command to building events. The clean will be executed before the rebuild starts.

Find links to more information in the *Further reading* section.

Summary

On the surface, it may seem that the complexities associated with proper testing are so great that they aren't worth the effort. It's striking how much code out there is running without any tests at all, the primary argument being that testing your software is a daunting endeavor. I'll add: even more so if done manually. Unfortunately, without rigorous automated testing, visibility of any issues in the code is incomplete or non-existent. Untested code is maybe quicker to write (but not always); however, it's definitely much slower to read, refactor, and fix.

In this chapter, we outlined some key reasons for working with tests from the get-go. One of the most compelling is mental health and a good night's sleep. Not one developer lies in bed thinking: *I can't wait to be woken up in a few hours to put out some production fires and fix bugs*. But seriously, catching errors before deploying them to production can be a lifesaver for you (and the company).

When it comes to testing utilities, CMake really shows its true strength here. CTest can do wonders in detecting faulty tests: isolation, shuffling, repetition, and timeouts. All these techniques are extremely handy and available through a convenient command-line flag. We learned how we can use CTest to list tests, filter them, and control the output of test cases, but most importantly, we now know the true power of adopting a standard solution across the board. Any project built with CMake can be tested exactly the same, without investigating any details about its internals.

Next, we structured our project to simplify the process of testing and reuse the same *object files* between production code and test runners. It was interesting to write our own test runner, but maybe let's focus on the actual problem our program should solve and invest time in embracing a popular third-party testing framework.

Speaking of which, we learned the very basics of Catch2 and GoogleTest. We further dove into details of the GMock library and understood how test doubles work to make true unit tests possible. Lastly, we set up some reporting with LCOV. After all, there's nothing better than hard data to prove that our solution is, in fact, fully tested.

In the next chapter, we'll discuss more useful tooling to improve the quality of our source code and find issues we didn't even know existed.

Further reading

For more information, you can refer to the following links:

- CMake documentation on CTest:
  https://cmake.org/cmake/help/latest/manual/ctest.1.html
- Catch2 documentation:
  https://github.com/catchorg/Catch2/blob/devel/docs/
- GMock tutorial:
  https://google.github.io/googletest/gmock_for_dummies.html
- Abseil:
  https://abseil.io/
- Live at head with Abseil:
  https://abseil.io/about/philosophy#we-recommend-that-you-choose-to-live-at-head
- Why Abseil is becoming a dependency of GTest:
  https://github.com/google/googletest/issues/2883
- Coverage in GCC:
  https://gcc.gnu.org/onlinedocs/gcc/Instrumentation-Options.html
  https://gcc.gnu.org/onlinedocs/gcc/Invoking-Gcov.html
  https://gcc.gnu.org/onlinedocs/gcc/Gcov-Data-Files.html
- Coverage in Clang:
  https://clang.llvm.org/docs/SourceBasedCodeCoverage.html

- LCOV documentation for command-line tools:
  `https://helpmanual.io/man1/lcov/`

- LCOV project repository:
  `https://github.com/linux-test-project/lcov`

- GCOV update functionality:
  `https://gcc.gnu.org/onlinedocs/gcc/Invoking-Gcov.html#Invoking-Gcov`

Join our community on Discord

Join our community's Discord space for discussions with the author and other readers:

`https://discord.com/invite/vXN53A7ZcA`

12

Program Analysis Tools

Producing high-quality code is not an easy task, even for highly experienced developers. By including tests in our solution, we lower the chance of making basic mistakes in the main code. But that won't be enough to avoid more intricate problems. Every piece of software consists of so many details that keeping track of them all becomes a full-time job. Various conventions and specific design practices are established by teams responsible for maintaining the product.

Some questions relate to consistent coding style: should we use 80 or 120 columns in our code? Should we allow `std::bind` or stick to lambda functions? Is it acceptable to use C-style arrays? Should small functions be written in a single line? Should we always use auto, or only when it improves readability? Ideally, we should steer clear of statements known to be generally incorrect: infinite loops, the use of identifiers reserved by a standard library, unintended data loss, unnecessary `if` statements, and anything else that is not a "best practice" (see the *Further reading* section for more information).

Another aspect to consider is code modernization. As C++ evolves, it introduces new features. Keeping track of all the spots where we can update to the latest standard can be challenging. Moreover, doing this manually takes time and increases the risk of introducing errors, especially in a large code base. Finally, we should check how things operate when set into motion: running the program and checking its memory. Is the memory properly released after use? Are we accessing data that was correctly initialized? Or does the code attempt to access non-existent pointers?

Managing all these challenges and questions manually is both time-consuming and prone to errors. Fortunately, we can use automated tools to inspect and enforce rules, correct mistakes, and bring our code up to date. It's time to explore tools for program analysis. Our code will be scrutinized during every build to make sure it meets industry standards.

In this chapter, we're going to cover the following main topics:

- Enforcing formatting
- Using static checkers
- Dynamic analysis with Valgrind

Technical requirements

You can find the code files that are present in this chapter on GitHub at `https://github.com/PacktPublishing/Modern-CMake-for-Cpp-2E/tree/main/examples/ch12`.

To build the examples provided in this book, always use these recommended commands:

```
cmake -B <build tree> -S <source tree>
cmake --build <build tree>
```

Be sure to replace the placeholders `<build tree>` and `<source tree>` with appropriate paths. As a reminder, **build tree** is the path to target/output directory, and **source tree** is the path where your source code is located.

Enforcing formatting

Professional developers usually follow rules. It's said that senior developers know when to break them because they can justify the need. On the flip side, very senior developers often avoid breaking rules to save time explaining their choices. The key is to focus on issues that genuinely affect a product, rather than getting caught up in minor details.

When it comes to coding style and formatting, developers face many options: should we use tabs or spaces for indentation? If spaces, how many? What should be the character limit in a column or a file? These choices typically don't change the program's behavior but can trigger lengthy discussions that add little value.

Common practices do exist, but debates often center on personal preference and anecdotal evidence. For instance, choosing 80 characters per column over 120 is arbitrary. What matters is maintaining a consistent style, as inconsistency can hinder the code's readability. To ensure consistency, it's advisable to use a formatting tool like `clang-format`. This tool can notify us if the code isn't formatted correctly and even make corrections. Here's an example command for formatting code:

```
clang-format -i --style=LLVM filename1.cpp filename2.cpp
```

The -i option instructs clang-format to edit files directly, while --style specifies the formatting style to use, such as LLVM, Google, Chromium, Mozilla, WebKit, or a custom style provided in a file (more details are available in the *Further reading* section).

Of course, we don't want to execute this command manually every time we make a change; CMake should handle this as part of the building process. We already know how to locate clang-format on the system (we'll need to install it manually beforehand). What we haven't covered is how to apply this external tool to all our source files. To do it, we'll create a convenient function that can be included from the cmake directory:

ch12/01-formatting/cmake/Format.cmake

```
function(Format target directory)
  find_program(CLANG-FORMAT_PATH clang-format REQUIRED)
  set(EXPRESSION h hpp hh c cc cxx cpp)
  list(TRANSFORM EXPRESSION PREPEND "${directory}/*.")
  file(GLOB_RECURSE SOURCE_FILES FOLLOW_SYMLINKS
      LIST_DIRECTORIES false ${EXPRESSION}
  )
  add_custom_command(TARGET ${target} PRE_BUILD COMMAND
    ${CLANG-FORMAT_PATH} -i --style=file ${SOURCE_FILES}
  )
endfunction()
```

The Format function accepts two arguments: target and directory. It will format all source files from the directory, right before the target is built.

Technically, not all files in the directory must belong to the target, and the target's sources could be spread across multiple directories. However, tracking down all the source files and headers related to the target is complicated, especially when we need to exclude headers from external libraries. In this case, it's easier to focus on directories than on logical targets. We can call the function for each directory that needs formatting.

This function has the following steps:

1. Find the installed clang-format binary. The REQUIRED keyword will halt the configuration with an error if the binary wasn't found.

2. Create a list of file extensions to format (to be used as a **globbing expression**).

3. Prepend each expression with a path to directory.

4. Search recursively for sources and headers (using the previously created list), put found file paths into the SOURCE_FILES variable (but skip any directory paths found)

5. Attach the formatting command to the PRE_BUILD step of target.

This approach works well for small to medium-sized code bases. For larger code bases, we might need to convert absolute file paths to relative ones and run the formatting command, using the directory as a working directory. This could be necessary due to character limits in shell commands, which usually cap at around 13,000 characters.

Let's explore how to use this function in practice. Here's our project structure:

```
- CMakeLists.txt
- .clang-format
- cmake
  |- Format.cmake
- src
  |- CMakeLists.txt
  |- header.h
  |- main.cpp
```

First, we set up the project and add the cmake directory to the module path for later inclusion:

ch12/01-formatting/CMakeLists.txt

```
cmake_minimum_required(VERSION 3.26)
project(Formatting CXX)
enable_testing()
list(APPEND CMAKE_MODULE_PATH "${CMAKE_SOURCE_DIR}/cmake")
add_subdirectory(src bin)
```

Next, we populate the listfile for the src directory:

ch12/01-formatting/src/CMakeLists.txt

```
add_executable(main main.cpp)
include(Format)
Format(main .)
```

This is straightforward. We create an executable target named main, include the Format.cmake module, and call the Format() function for the main target in the current directory (src).

Now, we need some unformatted source files. The header contains a simple unused function:

ch12/01-formatting/src/header.h

```
int unused() { return 2 + 2; }
```

We'll also include a source file with excessive, incorrect whitespace:

ch12/01-formatting/src/main.cpp

```
#include <iostream>

                                using namespace std;
                      int main() {
     cout << "Hello, world!" << endl;
                                        }
```

Almost there. We just need the formatter's configuration file, enabled via the `--style=file` command-line argument:

ch12/01-formatting/.clang-format

```
BasedOnStyle: Google
ColumnLimit: 140
UseTab: Never
AllowShortLoopsOnASingleLine: false
AllowShortFunctionsOnASingleLine: false
AllowShortIfStatementsOnASingleLine: false
```

ClangFormat will scan the parent directories for the `.clang-format` file, which specifies the exact formatting rules. This lets us customize every detail. In my case, I've started with Google's coding style and made a few adjustments: a 140-character column limit, no tabs, and no short loops, functions, or `if` statements on a single line.

After building the project (formatting occurs automatically before compilation), our files look like this:

ch12/01-formatting/src/header.h (formatted)

```
int unused() {
  return 2 + 2;
}
```

The header file was formatted, even though it isn't used by the target. Short functions can't be on a single line, and as expected, new lines were added. The `main.cpp` file also looks pretty slick now. Unneeded whitespace is gone, and indentations are standardized:

ch12/01-formatting/src/main.cpp (formatted)

```
#include <iostream>
using namespace std;
int main() {
```

```
    cout << "Hello, world!" << endl;
}
```

Automating formatting saves time during code reviews. If you've ever had to amend a commit just because of whitespace issues, you know the relief this brings. Consistent formatting keeps your code clean effortlessly.

 Applying formatting to an entire code base will most likely introduce a big one-off change to the majority of the files in the repository. This may cause *a lot* of merge conflicts if you (or your teammates) have some ongoing work. It's best to coordinate such efforts to happen after all pending changes are done. If this isn't possible, consider gradual adoption, perhaps on a per-directory basis. Your teammates will appreciate it.

Although the formatter excels in making code visually consistent, it's not a comprehensive program analysis tool. For more advanced needs, other utilities designed for static analysis are necessary.

Using static checkers

Static program analysis involves examining source code without running the compiled version. Consistently using static checkers can significantly improve code quality by making it more consistent and less susceptible to bugs and known security vulnerabilities. The C++ community offers a wide range of static checkers like Astrée, clang-tidy, CLazy, CMetrics, Cppcheck, Cpplint, CQMetrics, ESBMC, FlawFinder, Flint, IKOS, Joern, PC-Lint, Scan-Build, Vera++, and more.

Many of these tools recognize CMake as an industry standard and offer ready-to-use support or integration tutorials. Some build engineers prefer not to write CMake code and instead include static checkers through external modules available online. An example is the collection by Lars Bilke on his GitHub repository: https://github.com/bilke/cmake-modules.

A common belief is that setting up static checkers is complicated. This perception exists because static checkers often emulate the behavior of a real compiler to understand the code. But it doesn't have to be difficult.

Cppcheck outlines the following simple steps in its manual:

1. Locate the static checker's executable.

2. Generate a *compile database* with the following:

    *   `cmake -DCMAKE_EXPORT_COMPILE_COMMANDS=ON.`

3. Run the checker using the generated JSON file:

- `<path-to-cppcheck> --project=compile_commands.json`

These steps should be integrated into the build process to ensure they are not overlooked.

Since CMake knows how to build our targets, can it also support any static checkers? Absolutely, and it's easier than you might think. CMake allows you to enable checkers on a per-target basis for the following tools:

- include-what-you-use (https://include-what-you-use.org)
- clang-tidy (https://clang.llvm.org/extra/clang-tidy)
- Link What You Use (a built-in CMake checker)
- Cpplint (https://github.com/cpplint/cpplint)
- Cppcheck (https://cppcheck.sourceforge.io)

To enable these checkers, set a target property to a semicolon-separated list containing the path to the checker's executable and any command-line options to forward:

- `<LANG>_CLANG_TIDY`
- `<LANG>_CPPCHECK`
- `<LANG>_CPPLINT`
- `<LANG>_INCLUDE_WHAT_YOU_USE`
- `LINK_WHAT_YOU_USE`

Replace `<LANG>` with C for C sources and CXX for C++. If you want to enable a checker for all project targets, set a global variable prefixed with CMAKE_ – for example:

```
set(CMAKE_CXX_CLANG_TIDY /usr/bin/clang-tidy-3.9;-checks=*)
```

Any target defined after this statement will have its `CXX_CLANG_TIDY` property set to this value. Remember that enabling this analysis may slightly extend your build time. On the other hand, having more detailed control over how targets are tested by the checker can be useful. We can create a straightforward function to handle this:

ch12/02-clang-tidy/cmake/ClangTidy.cmake

```
function(AddClangTidy target)
  find_program(CLANG-TIDY_PATH clang-tidy REQUIRED)
  set_target_properties(${target}
    PROPERTIES CXX_CLANG_TIDY
    "${CLANG-TIDY_PATH};-checks=*;--warnings-as-errors=*"
```

```
    )
endfunction()
```

The `AddClangTidy` function follows two basic steps:

1. Locate the `clang-tidy` binary and store its path in `CLANG-TIDY_PATH`. The `REQUIRED` keyword ensures that configuration stops with an error if the binary is not found.

2. Enable `clang-tidy` for the target by providing the binary path and specific options to activate all checks and treat warnings as errors.

To use this function, we just need to include the module and call it for the chosen target:

ch12/02-clang-tidy/src/CMakeLists.txt

```
add_library(sut STATIC calc.cpp run.cpp)
target_include_directories(sut PUBLIC .)
add_executable(bootstrap bootstrap.cpp)
target_link_libraries(bootstrap PRIVATE sut)
include(ClangTidy)
AddClangTidy(sut)
```

This approach is concise and very effective. When building the solution, the `clang-tidy` output will appear as follows:

```
[  6%] Building CXX object bin/CMakeFiles/sut.dir/calc.cpp.o
/root/examples/ch12/04-clang-tidy/src/calc.cpp:3:11: warning: method 'Sum'
can be made static [readability-convert-member-functions-to-static]
int Calc::Sum(int a, int b) {
          ^
[ 12%] Building CXX object bin/CMakeFiles/sut.dir/run.cpp.o
/root/examples/ch12/04-clang-tidy/src/run.cpp:1:1: warning: #includes are
not sorted properly [llvm-include-order]
#include <iostream>
^        ~~~~~~~~~~
/root/examples/ch12/04-clang-tidy/src/run.cpp:3:1: warning: do not use
namespace using-directives; use using-declarations instead [google-build-
using-namespace]
using namespace std;
^
/root/examples/ch12/04-clang-tidy/src/run.cpp:6:3: warning: initializing
non-owner 'Calc *' with a newly created 'gsl::owner<>' [cppcoreguidelines-
owning-memory]
```

```
auto c = new Calc();
    ^
```

Note that unless you add the --warnings-as-errors=* option to the command-line arguments, the build will succeed. Organizations should decide on a set of rules that must be strictly followed to prevent non-compliant code from entering the repository.

clang-tidy also offers a useful --fix option that automatically corrects your code when possible. This feature is a valuable time-saver and is particularly helpful when expanding the list of checks. Just like with formatting, be cautious of merge conflicts when adding changes made by static analysis tools to existing code bases.

Depending on your situation, the repository size, and team preferences, you should select a handful of checkers that best suit your needs. Including too many can become disruptive. Here's a brief overview of the checkers supported by CMake right out of the box.

clang-tidy

Here's what the official website says about clang-tidy:

> *clang-tidy is a clang-based C++ "linter" tool. Its purpose is to provide an extensible framework for diagnosing and fixing typical programming errors, like style violations, interface misuse, or bugs that can be deduced via static analysis. clang-tidy is modular and provides a convenient interface for writing new checks.*

The tool is quite versatile, offering more than 400 checks. It pairs well with ClangFormat, enabling automatically applied fixes (over 150 are available) to conform to the same format file. The checks it offers cover performance, readability, modernization, C++ core guidelines, and bug-prone areas.

Cpplint

Here's a description of Cpplint from its official website:

> *Cpplint is a command-line tool to check C/C++ files for style issues following Google's C++ style guide. Cpplint is developed and maintained by Google Inc. at google/styleguide.*

This linter aims to align your code with Google's style guide. Written in Python, it may introduce an unwanted dependency for some projects. The fixes are offered in formats consumable by Emacs, Eclipse, VS7, Junit, and as sed commands.

Cppcheck

Here's what the official website says about Cppcheck:

> *Cppcheck is a static analysis tool for C/C++ code. It provides unique code analysis to detect bugs and focuses on detecting undefined behaviour and dangerous coding constructs. The goal is to have very few false positives. Cppcheck is designed to be able to analyze your C/C++ code even if it has non-standard syntax (common in embedded projects).*

This tool is particularly good for minimizing false positives, making it a reliable option for code analysis. It has been around for over 14 years and is still actively maintained. It's especially useful if your code is not compatible with Clang.

include-what-you-use

Here's a description of include-what-you-use from its official website:

> *The main goal of include-what-you-use is to remove superfluous #includes. It does this both by figuring out what #includes are not actually needed for this file (for both .cc and .h files), and replacing #includes with forward-declares when possible.*

While having too many included headers may not seem like a significant issue in small projects, the time saved from avoiding needless compilation of header files can quickly accumulate in larger projects.

Link What You Use

Here is a description of "Link what you use" on CMake's blog:

> *This is a built in CMake feature that uses options of ld and ldd to print out if executables link more libraries than they actually require.*

Static analysis plays a crucial role in industries like medicine, nuclear power, aviation, automotive, and machinery, where software errors could be life-threatening. Wise developers also adopt these practices in less critical environments, especially when the costs are low. Using static analysis during the build process is not only more cost-effective than manual bug finding and fixing, but it's also easy to enable with CMake. I'd go as far as to say that there's almost no reason to skip these checks in any quality-sensitive software, which includes any software involving people other than just the developer.

This feature also helps speed up the build time by focusing on eliminating unneeded binary artifacts. Unfortunately, not all bugs can be detected before running a program. Luckily, we can take additional steps to gain a deeper understanding of our projects, like using Valgrind.

Dynamic analysis with Valgrind

Valgrind (https://www.valgrind.org) is an *nix instrumentation framework for building dynamic analysis utilities, which means it performs analysis during a program's runtime. It comes with a wide range of tools for various types of investigations and checks. Some of the tools include:

- Memcheck: detects memory management problems
- Cachegrind: profiles CPU caches, and identifies cache misses and other issues
- Callgrind: an extension of Cachegrind that provides extra information on call graphs
- Massif: a heap profiler that shows how different parts of the program use the heap over time
- Helgrind: a thread debugger for data race issues
- DRD: a lighter, more limited version of Helgrind

Each tool on this list is highly useful when the situation calls for it. Most system package managers know Valgrind and can install it on your OS with ease. If you're using Linux, it may already be installed. Additionally, the official website provides the source code for those who prefer to build it themselves.

Our discussion will primarily focus on Memcheck, the most commonly used tool in the Valgrind suite (when developers refer to Valgrind, they often mean Valgrind's Memcheck). We'll explore how to use it with CMake, which will make it easier to adopt other tools from the suite if you find them necessary later on.

Memcheck

Memcheck is invaluable for debugging memory issues, a topic that can be especially complex in C++. Programmers have extensive control over memory management, making various mistakes possible. These can range from reading unallocated or already freed memory to freeing memory multiple times, and even writing to incorrect addresses. These bugs can easily go unnoticed and creep into even straightforward programs. Sometimes, a single forgotten variable initialization is all it takes to run into trouble.

Invoking Memcheck looks like this:

```
valgrind [valgrind-options] tested-binary [binary-options]
```

Memcheck is Valgrind's default tool, but you can also explicitly specify it like so:

```
valgrind --tool=memcheck tested-binary
```

Running Memcheck can slow down your program considerably; the manual (see the link in *Further reading*) says that programs instrumented with it can be 10–15 times slower. To avoid waiting for Valgrind every time we run tests, we'll create a separate target that will be called from the command line whenever we need to test our code. Ideally, this will be done before any new code is merged into the main code base. You can include this step in an early Git hook or as part of your **Continuous Integration (CI)** pipeline.

To create a custom target for Valgrind, you can use this command after the CMake generation stage:

```
cmake --build <build-tree> -t valgrind
```

Here's how you can add such a target in CMake:

ch12/03-valgrind/cmake/Valgrind.cmake

```
function(AddValgrind target)
  find_program(VALGRIND_PATH valgrind REQUIRED)
  add_custom_target(valgrind
    COMMAND ${VALGRIND_PATH} --leak-check=yes
            $<TARGET_FILE:${target}>
    WORKING_DIRECTORY ${CMAKE_BINARY_DIR}
  )
endfunction()
```

In this example, we define a CMake function named AddValgrind that takes the target to be tested (we'll be able to reuse it across projects). Two main things occur here:

1. CMake checks default system paths for the valgrind executable and stores its path in the VALGRIND_PATH variable. The REQUIRED keyword will halt the configuration with an error if the binary isn't found.

2. A custom target, valgrind, is created. It runs Memcheck on the specified binary, with an option to always check for memory leaks.

Valgrind options can be set in various ways:

- In the ~/.valgrindrc file (in your home directory)
- Through the $VALGRIND_OPTS environment variable
- In the ./.valgrindrc file (in the working directory)

These are checked in that order. Also, note that the last file will only be considered if it belongs to the current user, is a regular file, and isn't marked as world-writable. This is a safety mechanism, as options given to Valgrind can be potentially harmful.

To use the AddValgrind function, we provide it with a unit_tests target, as we want to run it in a finely controlled environment like unit tests:

ch12/03-valgrind/test/CMakeLists.txt (fragment)

```
# ...
add_executable(unit_tests calc_test.cpp run_test.cpp)
# ...
include(Valgrind)
AddValgrind(unit_tests)
```

Remember that generating build trees with the Debug config allows Valgrind to tap into the debug information, making its output much clearer.

Let's see how this works in practice:

```
# cmake -B <build tree> -S <source tree> -DCMAKE_BUILD_TYPE=Debug
# cmake --build <build-tree> -t valgrind
```

This configures the project, builds the `sut` and `unit_tests` targets, and starts the execution of Memcheck, which will provide us with general information:

```
[100%] Built target unit_tests
==954== Memcheck, a memory error detector
==954== Copyright (C) 2002-2017, and GNU GPL'd, by Julian Seward et al.
==954== Using Valgrind-3.18.1 and LibVEX; rerun with -h for copyright info
==954== Command: ./unit_tests
```

The ==954== prefix contains the process ID, helping to distinguish Valgrind commentary from the output of the tested process.

Next, tests are run as usual with gtest:

```
[==========] Running 3 tests from 2 test suites.
[----------] Global test environment set-up.
...
[==========] 3 tests from 2 test suites ran. (42 ms total)
[  PASSED  ] 3 tests.
```

At the end, a summary is presented:

```
==954==
==954== HEAP SUMMARY:
==954==     in use at exit: 1 bytes in 1 blocks
==954==   total heap usage: 209 allocs, 208 frees, 115,555 bytes allocated
```

Uh-oh! We are still using at least 1 byte. Allocations made with `malloc()` and new aren't matched with the appropriate `free()` and delete operations. It seems we have a memory leak in our program. Valgrind provides more details to find it:

```
==954== 1 bytes in 1 blocks are definitely lost in loss record 1 of 1
==954==     at 0x483BE63: operator new(unsigned long) (in /usr/lib/x86_64-
linux-gnu/valgrind/vgpreload_memcheck-amd64-linux.so)
==954==     by 0x114FC5: run() (run.cpp:6)
==954==     by 0x1142B9: RunTest_RunOutputsCorrectEquations_
Test::TestBody() (run_test.cpp:14)
```

Lines starting with by 0x<address> indicate individual functions in a call stack. I've truncated the output (it had some noise from GTest) to focus on the interesting bit – the topmost function and source reference, run()(run.cpp:6):

Finally, the summary is found at the bottom:

```
==954== LEAK SUMMARY:
==954==    definitely lost: 1 bytes in 1 blocks
==954==    indirectly lost: 0 bytes in 0 blocks
==954==      possibly lost: 0 bytes in 0 blocks
==954==    still reachable: 0 bytes in 0 blocks
==954==         suppressed: 0 bytes in 0 blocks
==954==
==954== ERROR SUMMARY: 1 errors from 1 contexts (suppressed: 0 from 0)
```

Valgrind is excellent at finding complex issues. Sometimes, it can dig even deeper to find issues that aren't easily categorized. These will show up in the "possibly lost" row.

Let's see what the issue found by Memcheck was in this case:

ch12/03-valgrind/src/run.cpp

```cpp
#include <iostream>
#include "calc.h"
using namespace std;
int run() {
  auto c = new Calc();
  cout << "2 + 2 = " << c->Sum(2, 2) << endl;
  cout << "3 * 3 = " << c->Multiply(3, 3) << endl;
  return 0;
}
```

That's right: the highlighted code is faulty. We do, in fact, create an object that isn't deleted before the test ends. This is the exact reason why having extensive test coverage is so important.

Valgrind is a helpful tool, but its output can become overwhelming in complex programs. There is a way to manage this information more efficiently – it's the Memcheck-Cover project.

Memcheck-Cover

Commercial IDEs like CLion can directly parse `Valgrind`'s output, making it easier to navigate through a graphical interface without having to scroll in the console. If your editor lacks this feature, a third-party report generator can offer a clearer view. `Memcheck-Cover`, developed by *David Garcin*, gives a better experience by creating an HTML file, as shown in the following figure:

Figure 12.1: A report generated by Memcheck-Cover

This neat little project is available on GitHub (`https://github.com/Farigh/memcheck-cover`); it requires `Valgrind` and `gawk` (the GNU AWK tool). To use it, we'll prepare a setup function in a separate `CMake` module. It will consist of two parts:

1. Fetching and configuring the tool
2. Adding a custom target to run `Valgrind` and generate a report

Here's how the configuration looks:

ch12/04-memcheck/cmake/Memcheck.cmake

```
function(AddMemcheck target)
  include(FetchContent)
  FetchContent_Declare(
   memcheck-cover
   GIT_REPOSITORY https://github.com/Farigh/memcheck-cover.git
   GIT_TAG        release-1.2
  )
  FetchContent_MakeAvailable(memcheck-cover)
  set(MEMCHECK_PATH ${memcheck-cover_SOURCE_DIR}/bin)
```

In the first part, we follow the same practices as with a regular dependency: include the FetchContent module, and specify the project's repository and desired Git tag with FetchContent_ Declare. Next, we initiate the fetch process and configure the binary path, using the memcheck- cover_SOURCE_DIR variable set by FetchContent_Populate (called implicitly by FetchContent_ MakeAvailable).

The second part of the function is creating the target to generate reports. We'll call it memcheck (so that it doesn't overlap with the previous valgrind target if we want to keep both options for some reason):

ch12/04-memcheck/cmake/Memcheck.cmake (continued)

```
  add_custom_target(memcheck
    COMMAND ${MEMCHECK_PATH}/memcheck_runner.sh -o
      "${CMAKE_BINARY_DIR}/valgrind/report"
      -- $<TARGET_FILE:${target}>
    COMMAND ${MEMCHECK_PATH}/generate_html_report.sh
      -i "${CMAKE_BINARY_DIR}/valgrind"
      -o "${CMAKE_BINARY_DIR}/valgrind"
    WORKING_DIRECTORY ${CMAKE_BINARY_DIR}
  )
endfunction()
```

This happens in two commands:

1. First, we'll run the memcheck_runner.sh wrapper script, which will execute Valgrind's Memcheck and collect the output to the file provided with the -o argument.

2. Then, we'll parse the output and create the report with `generate_html_report.sh`. This script requires input and output directories provided with the `-i` and `-o` arguments.

Both steps should be executed in the `CMAKE_BINARY_DIR` working directory so that the unit test binary can access files through relative paths if needed.

The last thing we need to add to our listfiles is, of course, a call to this function:

ch12/04-memcheck/test/CMakeLists.txt (fragment)

```
include(Memcheck)
AddMemcheck(unit_tests)
```

After generating a buildsystem with the Debug config, we can build the target with the following:

```
# cmake -B <build tree> -S <source tree> -DCMAKE_BUILD_TYPE=Debug
# cmake --build <build-tree> -t memcheck
```

Then, we can enjoy our formatted report, generated as an HTML page.

Summary

"You'll spend more time reading code than writing it, so optimize for readability over writability." This principle is often echoed in various books on clean code. It's supported by the experiences of many software developers, which is why even small details like the number of spaces, newlines, and the order of `#import` statements are standardized. This standardization isn't just for the sake of being meticulous; it's about saving time. Following the practices in this chapter, you can forget about manually formatting code. It gets automatically formatted when you build, a step you'd do anyway to test the code. With `ClangFormat`, you can make sure the formatting is up to the standard of your choosing.

Going beyond simple whitespace adjustments, code should also meet numerous other guidelines. That's where clang-tidy comes in. It helps enforce coding that your team or organization agreed on. We discussed this static checker in depth and also touched on other options like `Cpplint`, `Cppcheck`, include-what-you-use, and Link What You Use. Since static linkers are relatively fast, we can add them to our builds with little investment, and it will usually be well worth the price.

We also examined `Valgrind` utilities, focusing on `Memcheck` to identify issues with memory management, such as incorrect reads and writes. This tool is invaluable for avoiding hours of manual debugging and keeping bugs out of a production environment. We introduced a way to make `Valgrind`'s output more user-friendly with `Memcheck-Cover`, an HTML report generator. This is especially useful in environments where running an IDE is not possible, like CI pipelines.

This chapter is just a starting point. Many other tools, both free and commercial, are available to help you with code quality. Explore them to find what suits you best. In the next chapter, we'll dive into generating documentation.

Further reading

For more information, you can refer to the following links:

- C++ Core guidelines, curated by Bjarne Stroustrup, author of C++: `https://github.com/isocpp/CppCoreGuidelines`

- The `ClangFormat` reference: `https://clang.llvm.org/docs/ClangFormat.html`

- Static analyzers for C++ – a curated list: `https://github.com/analysis-tools-dev/static-analysis#cpp`

- Built-in static checker support in CMake: `https://blog.kitware.com/static-checks-with-cmake-cdash-iwyu-clang-tidy-lwyu-cpplint-and-cppcheck/`

- A target property enabling `clang-tidy`: `https://cmake.org/cmake/help/latest/prop_tgt/LANG_CLANG_TIDY.html`

- The `Valgrind` manual: `https://www.valgrind.org/docs/manual/manual-core.html`

Leave a review!

Enjoying this book? Help readers like you by leaving an Amazon review. Scan the QR code below to get a free eBook of your choice.

13
Generating Documentation

High-quality code is not only well written, working, and tested—it is also thoroughly document-ed. Documentation allows us to share information that might otherwise get lost, draw a bigger picture, give context, reveal intent, and—finally—educate both external users and maintainers.

Do you remember the last time you joined a new project and got lost for hours in a maze of direc-tories and files? This can be avoided. Truly excellent documentation leads a complete newcomer to the exact line of code they're looking for in seconds. Sadly, the issue of missing documentation is often overlooked. No wonder—it takes considerable skill, and many of us aren't very good at it. Furthermore, documentation and code can quickly become outdated. Unless a strict update and review process is implemented, it's easy to forget that documentation needs attention too.

Some teams (in the interest of time or because they are encouraged to do so by managers) follow a practice of writing *self-documenting code*. By choosing meaningful, readable identifiers for file-names, functions, variables, and so on, they hope to avoid the chore of documenting. Even the best function signatures don't ensure that all necessary information is conveyed—for example, `int removeDuplicates();` is descriptive, but it doesn't reveal what is returned. It could be the number of duplicates found, the number of items remaining, or something else—it's unclear. While the habit of good naming is absolutely correct, it cannot replace the act of conscientious documentation. Remember: there's no such thing as a free lunch.

To make things easier, professionals use automatic documentation generators that analyze code and comments in source files to produce comprehensive documentation in various formats. Add-ing such generators to a CMake project is very simple—let's see how!

In this chapter, we're going to cover the following main topics:

- Adding Doxygen to your project
- Generating documentation with a modern look
- Enhancing output with custom HTML

Technical requirements

You can find the code files that are present in this chapter on GitHub at `https://github.com/PacktPublishing/Modern-CMake-for-Cpp-2E/tree/main/examples/ch13`.

To build the examples provided in this book, always use the recommended commands:

```
cmake -B <build tree> -S <source tree>
cmake --build <build tree>
```

Be sure to replace the placeholders `<build tree>` and `<source tree>` with appropriate paths. As a reminder: **build tree** is the path to the target/output directory, and **source tree** is the path at which your source code is located.

Adding Doxygen to your project

One of the most established and popular tools for generating documentation from C++ sources is Doxygen. And when I say "established," I mean it: the first version was released by Dimitri van Heesch in October 1997. Since then, it has grown immensely and is actively supported by almost 250 contributors to its repository (`https://github.com/doxygen/doxygen`).

You might be concerned about the challenge of incorporating Doxygen into larger projects that haven't used documentation generation from the start. Indeed, the task of annotating every function can appear overwhelming. However, I encourage you to start small. Focus on documenting elements you've recently worked on in your latest commits. Remember, even partially complete documentation is a step forward compared to none at all, and it gradually helps in building a more comprehensive understanding of your project.

Doxygen can produce documentation in the following formats:

- **HyperText Markup Language (HTML)**
- **Rich Text Format (RTF)**
- **Portable Document Format (PDF)**
- **Lamport TeX (LaTeX)**
- **PostScript (PS)**

- Unix manual (man pages)
- **Microsoft Compiled HTML** Help (.CHM)

If you annotate your code with comments providing additional information in the format specified by Doxygen, it will parse them to enrich the output file. Moreover, the code structure will be analyzed to produce helpful charts and diagrams. The latter is optional, as it requires the external Graphviz tool (`https://graphviz.org/`).

The developer should first consider the following question: *Will the users of the project only receive the documentation, or will they generate it themselves (perhaps when building from source)?* The first option implies that documentation is distributed with the binaries, available online, or (less elegantly) checked in with the source code into the repository.

This consideration matters because if you want users to generate documentation during the build, they will need the dependencies present in their system. This isn't a significant problem since Doxygen and Graphviz are available through most package managers, and all that's required is a simple command, such as this one for Debian:

```
apt-get install doxygen graphviz
```

Binaries are also available for Windows (check the project's website in the *Further reading* section).

However, some users might not be comfortable installing this tooling. We must decide whether to generate documentation for users or have them add the dependencies if needed. The project could automatically add them for users as well, as described in *Chapter 9, Managing Dependencies in CMake*. Note that Doxygen is built with CMake, so you already know how to compile it from sources if needed.

When Doxygen and Graphviz are installed in the system, we can add the generation to our project. Contrary to what some online sources suggest, this isn't as difficult or involved as it might seem. We don't need to create external configuration files, provide paths to the Doxygen executable, or add custom targets. Since CMake 3.9, we can use the `doxygen_add_docs()` function from the `FindDoxygen` find-module, which sets up the documentation target.

The signature looks like this:

```
doxygen_add_docs(targetName [sourceFilesOrDirs...]
    [ALL] [WORKING_DIRECTORY dir] [COMMENT comment])
```

The first argument specifies the target name, which we need to build explicitly with the `-t` argument to `cmake` (after generating a build tree), as follows:

```
# cmake --build <build-tree> -t targetName
```

Or, we can ensure that the documentation is always built by adding the ALL argument, although this is usually not necessary. The WORKING_DIRECTORY option is straightforward; it specifies the directory where the command should be run. The value set by the COMMENT option is displayed before the documentation generation starts, providing useful information or instructions.

We'll follow the practice from previous chapters and create a utility module with a helper function (so it can be reused in other projects), as follows:

ch13/01-doxygen/cmake/Doxygen.cmake

```
function(Doxygen input output)
  find_package(Doxygen)
  if (NOT DOXYGEN_FOUND)
    add_custom_target(doxygen COMMAND false
      COMMENT "Doxygen not found")
    return()
  endif()
  set(DOXYGEN_GENERATE_HTML YES)
  set(DOXYGEN_HTML_OUTPUT
    ${PROJECT_BINARY_DIR}/${output})
  doxygen_add_docs(doxygen
      ${PROJECT_SOURCE_DIR}/${input}
      COMMENT "Generate HTML documentation"
  )
endfunction()
```

The function accepts two arguments—input and output directories—and creates a custom doxygen target. Here's what happens:

1. First, we use CMake's built-in Doxygen find-module to determine whether Doxygen is available in the system.

2. If it isn't available, we create a dummy doxygen target that informs the user and runs a false command, which (on Unix-like systems) returns 1, causing the build to fail. We terminate the function at that point with return().

3. If Doxygen is available, we configure it to generate HTML output in the provided output directory. Doxygen is extremely configurable (find out more in the official documentation). To set any option, simply follow the example by calling set() and prepend its name with DOXYGEN_.

4. Set up the actual doxygen target. All the DOXYGEN_ variables will be forwarded to Doxygen's configuration file, and documentation will be generated from the provided input directory in the source tree.

If your documentation is to be generated by users, *step 2* should probably involve installing Doxygen instead.

To use this function, we can incorporate it into the main listfile of our project as follows:

ch13/01-doxygen/CMakeLists.txt

```
cmake_minimum_required(VERSION 3.26)
project(Doxygen CXX)
enable_testing()
list(APPEND CMAKE_MODULE_PATH "${CMAKE_SOURCE_DIR}/cmake")
add_subdirectory(src bin)
include(Doxygen)
Doxygen(src docs)
```

Not difficult at all! Building the doxygen target generates HTML documentation that looks like this:

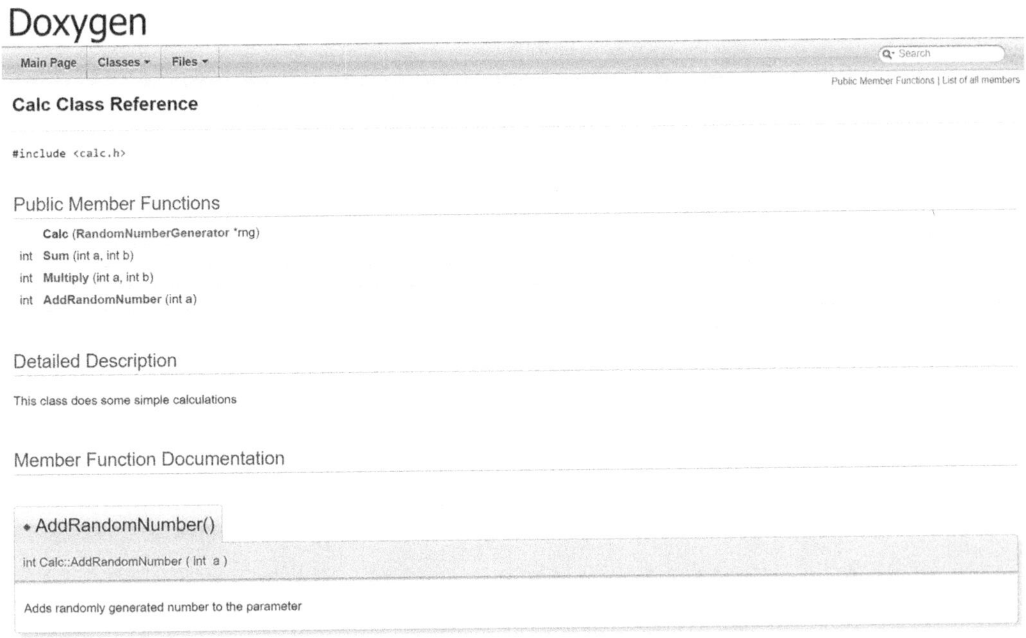

Figure 13.1: Class reference generated with Doxygen

To add important details in **Member Function Documentation**, we can precede the C++ method declaration with an appropriate comment in the header file, like so:

ch13/01-doxygen/src/calc.h (fragment)

```
/**
 Multiply... Who would have thought?
 @param a the first factor
 @param b the second factor
 @result The product
*/
int Multiply(int a, int b);
```

This format is known as Javadoc. It is important to begin the comment block with double asterisks: /**. More information can be found in the description of Doxygen's docblocks (see the link in the *Further reading* section). The Multiply function with such annotations will be rendered as shown in the following figure:

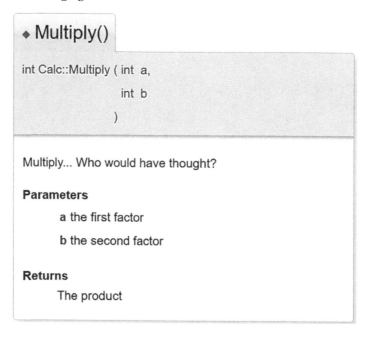

Figure 13.2: Annotations of the parameters and result

As mentioned earlier, if Graphviz is installed, Doxygen will detect it and generate dependency diagrams, as illustrated here:

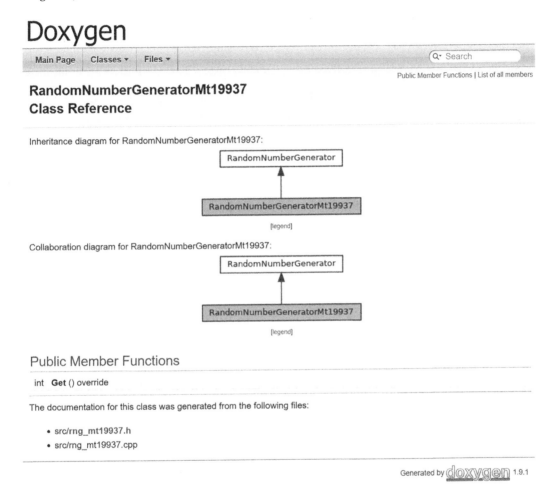

Figure 13.3: Inheritance and collaboration diagrams generated by Doxygen

By generating documentation directly from the source code, we establish a process that enables quick updates in tandem with any code changes during the development cycle. Also, any overlooked updates in the comments are likely to be noticed during code review.

Many developers express concerns that the design provided by Doxygen appears dated, making them hesitant to showcase the generated documentation to their clients. However, there is a simple solution to this issue.

Generating documentation with a modern look

Having your project documented with a clean, fresh design is important. After all, if we put all this work into writing high-quality documentation for our cutting-edge project, it is imperative that the user perceives it as such. Although Doxygen is feature-rich, it isn't renowned for adhering to the latest visual trends. However, revamping its appearance doesn't require substantial effort.

Luckily, a developer named jothepro created a theme called doxygen-awesome-css, which offers a modern, customizable design. This theme is presented in the following screenshot:

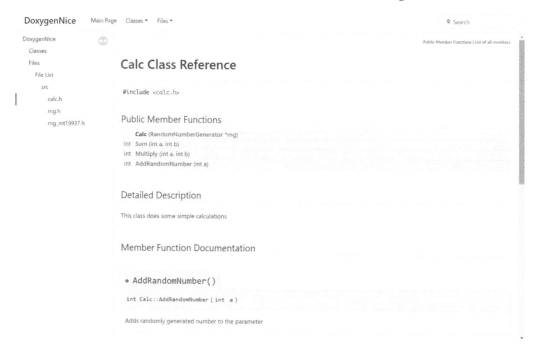

Figure 13.4: HTML documentation in doxygen-awesome-css theme

The theme doesn't require any additional dependencies and can be easily fetched from its GitHub page at https://github.com/jothepro/doxygen-awesome-css.

 While some online sources recommend using a combination of applications, like transforming Doxygen's output with Sphinx via Breathe and Exhale extensions, this method can be complex and dependency-heavy (requiring Python, for example). A simpler approach is usually more practical, particularly for teams where not all members are deeply familiar with CMake.

We can efficiently implement this theme with an automated process. Let's see how we can extend our Doxygen.cmake file to use it by adding a new macro:

ch13/02-doxygen-nice/cmake/Doxygen.cmake (fragment)

```
macro(UseDoxygenAwesomeCss)
  include(FetchContent)
  FetchContent_Declare(doxygen-awesome-css
    GIT_REPOSITORY
      https://github.com/jothepro/doxygen-awesome-css.git
    GIT_TAG
      V2.3.1
  )
  FetchContent_MakeAvailable(doxygen-awesome-css)
  set(DOXYGEN_GENERATE_TREEVIEW     YES)
  set(DOXYGEN_HAVE_DOT              YES)
  set(DOXYGEN_DOT_IMAGE_FORMAT      svg)
  set(DOXYGEN_DOT_TRANSPARENT       YES)
  set(DOXYGEN_HTML_EXTRA_STYLESHEET
    ${doxygen-awesome-css_SOURCE_DIR}/doxygen-awesome.css)
endmacro()
```

We already know all of these commands from previous chapters of the book, but let's reiterate what happens for perfect clarity:

1. Fetching doxygen-awesome-css from Git using the FetchContent module
2. Configuring extra options for Doxygen (these are specifically recommended by the theme's README file)
3. Copying the theme's css file to Doxygen's output directory

As you can imagine, it's best to call this macro in the Doxygen function right before doxygen_add_docs(), like this:

ch13/02-doxygen-nice/cmake/Doxygen.cmake (fragment)

```
function(Doxygen input output)
# ...
  UseDoxygenAwesomeCss()
  doxygen_add_docs (...)
endfunction()
```

```
macro(UseDoxygenAwesomeCss)
# ...
endmacro()
```

Remember, all variables in macros are set in the scope of the calling function.

We can now enjoy a modern style in our generated HTML documentation and share it proudly with the world. However, our theme offers some JavaScript modules to enhance the experience. How do we include them?

Enhancing output with custom HTML

Doxygen Awesome offers a few additional features that can be enabled by including a few JavaScript snippets in the documentation header, within the HTML <head> tags. They can be quite useful, as they allow switching between light and dark mode, adding a **Copy** button for code snippets, paragraph-header permalinks, and an interactive table of contents.

However, implementing these features requires copying additional code to the output directory and including it in the generated HTML files.

Here is the JavaScript code to be included just before the </head> tag:

ch13/cmake/extra_headers

```
<script type="text/javascript" src="$relpath^doxygen-awesome-darkmode-
toggle.js"></script>
<script type="text/javascript" src="$relpath^doxygen-awesome-fragment-
copy-button.js"></script>
<script type="text/javascript" src="$relpath^doxygen-awesome-paragraph-
link.js"></script>
<script type="text/javascript" src="$relpath^doxygen-awesome-interactive-
toc.js"></script>

<script type="text/javascript">
    DoxygenAwesomeDarkModeToggle.init()
    DoxygenAwesomeFragmentCopyButton.init()
    DoxygenAwesomeParagraphLink.init()
    DoxygenAwesomeInteractiveToc.init()
</script>
```

As you can see, this code will first include a few JavaScript files and then initialize different extensions. Unfortunately, this code cannot be simply added to a variable somewhere. Instead, we'll need to override the default header with a custom file. Such an override can be done by providing a path to this file in the Doxygen's HTML_HEADER configuration variable.

To create a custom header without hardcoding the entire content, you can use Doxygen's command-line tool to generate a default header file and edit it before generating the documentation:

```
doxygen -w html header.html footer.html style.css
```

Although we won't be using or changing the footer.html or style.css, they are required arguments, so we need to create them anyway.

Finally, we need to automatically prepend the </head> tag with the contents of the ch13/cmake/extra_headers file to include the required JavaScript. This can be done with the Unix command-line tool sed, which will edit the header.html file in place:

```
sed -i '/<\/head>/r ch13/cmake/extra_headers' header.html
```

Now we need to codify those steps in CMake language. Here's the macro that achieves that:

ch13/02-doxygen-nice/cmake/Doxygen.cmake (fragment)

```
macro(UseDoxygenAwesomeExtensions)
  set(DOXYGEN_HTML_EXTRA_FILES
    ${doxygen-awesome-css_SOURCE_DIR}/doxygen-awesome-darkmode-toggle.js
    ${doxygen-awesome-css_SOURCE_DIR}/doxygen-awesome-fragment-copy-
button.js
    ${doxygen-awesome-css_SOURCE_DIR}/doxygen-awesome-paragraph-link.js
    ${doxygen-awesome-css_SOURCE_DIR}/doxygen-awesome-interactive-toc.js
  )

  execute_process(
   COMMAND doxygen -w html header.html footer.html style.css
   WORKING_DIRECTORY ${PROJECT_BINARY_DIR}
  )
  execute_process(
   COMMAND sed -i
   "/<\\/head>/r ${PROJECT_SOURCE_DIR}/cmake/extra_headers"
   header.html
   WORKING_DIRECTORY ${PROJECT_BINARY_DIR}
  )
```

```
    set(DOXYGEN_HTML_HEADER ${PROJECT_BINARY_DIR}/header.html)
  endmacro()
```

This code looks complex, but after a close inspection, you'll find it's actually quite straightforward. Here's what it does:

1. Copies the four JavaScript files to the output directory
2. Executes the doxygen command to generate the default HTML files
3. Executes the sed command to inject the required JavaScript into the header
4. Overrides the default header with the custom version

To complete the integration, call this macro right after enabling the basic stylesheet:

ch13/02-doxygen-nice/cmake/Doxygen.cmake (fragment)

```
function(Doxygen input output)
  # …
  UseDoxygenAwesomeCss()
  UseDoxygenAwesomeExtensions()
  # …
endfunction()
```

The complete code for this example, along with practical examples, is available in the online repository for the book. As always, I recommend reviewing and exploring these examples in a practical environment.

Other documentation generation utilities

There are dozens of other tools that are not covered in this book, as we're focusing on projects supported by CMake. Nevertheless, some of them may be more appropriate for your use case. If you're feeling adventurous, visit the websites of two projects I found interesting:

- Adobe's Hyde (https://github.com/adobe/hyde): Aimed at the Clang compiler, Hyde produces Markdown files that can be consumed by tools such as Jekyll (https://jekyllrb.com/), a static page generator supported by GitHub

- Standardese (https://github.com/standardese/standardese): This uses libclang to compile your code and provides output in HTML, Markdown, LaTex, and man pages. It aims (quite boldly) to be the next Doxygen.

Summary

In this chapter, we delved into the practicalities of adding Doxygen, a powerful documentation generation tool, to your CMake project and enhancing its appeal. This task, though seemingly daunting, is quite manageable and significantly enhances the flow and clarity of information within your solution. As you'll find, the time invested in adding and maintaining documentation is a worthwhile effort, especially when you or your teammates grapple with understanding complex relationships in the application.

After exploring how to use CMake's built-in Doxygen support to generate documentation in practice, we took a slight turn, to ensure not only the readability of the documentation but also its legibility.

Since dated design can be difficult on the eye, we explored alternative looks of the produced HTML. This was done using the Doxygen Awesome extension. To enable enhancements it comes with, we customized the standard header by adding the necessary javascript.

By generating documentation, you ensure its proximity to the actual code, making it easier to maintain written explanations in sync with the logic, especially if they're both in the same file. Also, as a programmer, you're likely juggling numerous tasks and details. Documentation acts as a memory aid, helping you retain and recall project intricacies. Keep in mind that even "the shortest pencil is longer than the longest memory." Do yourself a favor—write long things down, and prosper.

Wrapping up, this chapter emphasizes the value of Doxygen in your project management toolkit, aiding both understanding and communication within your team.

In the next chapter, I'll take you through automating packaging and the installation of projects with CMake, further enhancing your project management skills.

Further reading

- Official website of Doxygen:
  `https://www.doxygen.nl/`
- `FindDoxygen` find-module documentation:
  `https://cmake.org/cmake/help/latest/module/FindDoxygen.html`
- Doxygen's docblocks:
  `https://www.doxygen.nl/manual/docblocks.html#specialblock`

Join our community on Discord

Join our community's Discord space for discussions with the author and other readers:

`https://discord.com/invite/vXN53A7ZcA`

14

Installing and Packaging

Our project has been built, tested, and documented. Now, it's finally time to release it to our users. This chapter primarily focuses on the final two steps we need to take: installation and packaging. These are advanced techniques that build on top of everything we've learned so far: managing targets and their dependencies, transient usage requirements, generator expressions, and much more.

Installation allows our project to be discoverable and accessible system-wide. We will cover how to export targets for use by other projects without needing installation and how to install our projects for easy system-wide accessibility. We'll learn how to configure our project to automatically place various artifact types in their appropriate directories. To handle more advanced scenarios, we'll introduce low-level commands for installing files and directories, as well as for executing custom scripts and CMake commands.

Next, we'll explore setting up reusable CMake packages that other projects can discover using the find_package() command. We'll explain how to ensure that targets and their definitions are not restricted to a specific file system location. We'll also discuss how to write basic and advanced **config files**, along with the **version files** associated with packages. Then, to make things modular, we'll briefly introduce the concept of components, both in terms of CMake packages and the install() command. All this preparation will pave the way for the final aspect we'll be covering in this chapter: using CPack to generate archives, installers, bundles, and packages that are recognized by all kinds of package managers in different operating systems. These packages can distribute pre-built artifacts, executables, and libraries. It's the easiest way for end users to start using our software.

In this chapter, we're going to cover the following main topics:

- Exporting without installation
- Installing projects on the system
- Creating reusable packages
- Defining components
- Packaging with CPack

Technical requirements

You can find the code files that are present in this chapter on GitHub at `https://github.com/PacktPublishing/Modern-CMake-for-Cpp-2E/tree/main/examples/ch14`.

To build the examples provided in this book, always use the recommended commands:

```
cmake -B <build tree> -S <source tree>
cmake --build <build tree>
```

To install examples, use the following command:

```
cmake --install <build tree>
```

Be sure to replace the `<build tree>` and `<source tree>` placeholders with appropriate paths. As a reminder: **build tree** is the path to the target/output directory and **source tree** is the path at which your source code is located.

Exporting without installation

How can we make the targets of project A available to the consuming project, B? Usually, we'd use the `find_package()` command, but that requires creating a package and installing it on the system. While useful, this approach involves some work. Sometimes, we just need a quick way to build a project and make its targets available for other projects.

One time-saving method is to include in project B the main listfile of A, which already contains all the target definitions. However, this file might also include global configuration, CMake commands with side effects, additional dependencies, and perhaps unwanted targets for B (like unit tests). So, this is not the best approach. Instead, we can provide a **target export file** for the consuming project, B, to include with the `include()` command:

```
cmake_minimum_required(VERSION 3.26.0)
project(B)
include(/path/to/A/TargetsOfA.cmake)
```

This will define all targets of A with the correct properties set, using commands such as add_library() and add_executable().

You must specify all targets to export after the TARGETS keyword and provide the destination filename after FILE. The other arguments are optional:

```
export(TARGETS [target1 [target2 [...]]]
       [NAMESPACE <namespace>] [APPEND] FILE <path>
       [EXPORT_LINK_INTERFACE_LIBRARIES]
)
```

Here's the explanation of the individual arguments:

- NAMESPACE is recommended to indicate that the target has been imported from other projects.
- APPEND prevents CMake from erasing the file's contents before writing.
- EXPORT_LINK_INTERFACE_LIBRARIES exports target link dependencies (including imported and config-specific variants).

Let's apply this exporting method to the Calc library example, which provides two simple methods:

ch14/01-export/src/include/calc/basic.h

```
#pragma once
int Sum(int a, int b);
int Multiply(int a, int b);
```

We need to declare the Calc target so we have something to export:

ch14/01-export/src/CMakeLists.txt

```
add_library(calc STATIC basic.cpp)
target_include_directories(calc INTERFACE include)
```

Then, to generate the export file, we are using the export(TARGETS) command:

ch14/01-export/CMakeLists.txt (fragment)

```
cmake_minimum_required(VERSION 3.26)
project(ExportCalcCXX)
add_subdirectory(src bin)
set(EXPORT_DIR "${CMAKE_CURRENT_BINARY_DIR}/cmake")
export(TARGETS calc
```

```
    FILE "${EXPORT_DIR}/CalcTargets.cmake"
    NAMESPACE Calc::
)
```

Our exported target declaration file will be located in the cmake subdirectory of the build tree (following the convention for .cmake files). To avoid repeating this path later, we're setting it in the EXPORT_DIR variable. Then, we call export() to generate the target declaration file, CalcTargets. cmake, with the calc target. For projects including this file, it will be visible as Calc::calc.

Note that this export file isn't *a package* yet. More importantly, all paths in this file are absolute and hardcoded to the build tree, making them non-relocatable (discussed in the *Understanding the issues with relocatable targets* section).

The export() command also has a shorter version using the EXPORT keyword:

```
    export(EXPORT <export> [NAMESPACE <namespace>] [FILE <path>])
```

However, it requires the name of a predefined export rather than a list of exported targets. Such <export> instances are named lists of targets that are created by install(TARGETS) (we'll cover this command in the *Installing logical targets* section).

Here's a tiny example demonstrating how this shorthand is used in practice:

ch14/01-export/CMakeLists.txt (continued)

```
    install(TARGETS calc EXPORT CalcTargets)
    export(EXPORT CalcTargets
      FILE "${EXPORT_DIR}/CalcTargets2.cmake"
      NAMESPACE Calc::
    )
```

This code works similarly to the previous example, but now it shares a single target list between the export() and install() commands.

Both methods of generating export files yield similar results. They include some boilerplate code and a few lines defining the target. With <build-tree> set to the build tree path, they'll create a **target export file** similar to this:

<build-tree>/cmake/CalcTargets.cmake (fragment)

```
    # Create imported target Calc::calc
    add_library(Calc::calc STATIC IMPORTED)
    set_target_properties(Calc::calc PROPERTIES
```

```
    INTERFACE_INCLUDE_DIRECTORIES
    "/<source-tree>/include"
)
# Import target "Calc::calc" for configuration ""
set_property(TARGET Calc::calc APPEND PROPERTY
    IMPORTED_CONFIGURATIONS NOCONFIG
)
set_target_properties(Calc::calc PROPERTIES
    IMPORTED_LINK_INTERFACE_LANGUAGES_NOCONFIG "CXX"
    IMPORTED_LOCATION_NOCONFIG "/<build-tree>/libcalc.a"
)
```

Normally, we wouldn't edit or even open this file, but it's important to note that the paths will be hardcoded in it (see the highlighted lines). In its current form, the built project isn't relocatable. To change that, some additional steps are required. In the next section, we'll explain what relocation is and why it is important.

Installing projects on the system

In *Chapter 1*, *First Steps with CMake*, we indicated that CMake offers a command-line mode for installing built projects on the system:

```
cmake --install <dir> [<options>]
```

Here, <dir> is the path to the generated build tree (required). The <options> include:

- --config <cfg>: This selects the build configuration for multi-configuration generators.
- --component <comp>: This limits the installation to the given component.
- --default-directory-permissions <permissions>: This sets the default permissions for the installed directories (in <u=rwx,g=rx,o=rx> format).
- --install-prefix <prefix>: This specifies the non-default installation path (stored in the CMAKE_INSTALL_PREFIX variable). It defaults to /usr/local on Unix-like systems and to c:/Program Files/${PROJECT_NAME} on Windows. Before CMake 3.21, you'll have to use a less-explicit option: --prefix <prefix>.
- -v, --verbose: This increases the verbosity of the output (achievable also by setting the VERBOSE environment variable).

Installations typically involve copying generated artifacts and necessary dependencies to a system directory. Using CMake introduces a convenient installation standard to all CMake projects and offers several additional benefits:

- It provides platform-specific installation paths for artifacts, depending on their types (by following *GNU coding standards*).

- It enhances the installation process by generating target export files, allowing direct reuse of project targets by other projects.

- It creates discoverable packages through **config files**, wrapping the target export files and package-specific CMake macros and functions defined by the author.

These features are quite powerful as they save a lot of time and simplify the usage of projects that are prepared this way. The first step in performing a basic installation is copying the built artifacts to their destination directory. This brings us to the install() command and its various modes:

- install(TARGETS): This installs output artifacts such as libraries and executables.

- install(FILES|PROGRAMS): This installs individual files and sets their permissions. These files don't need to be part of any logical targets.

- install(DIRECTORY): This installs entire directories.

- install(SCRIPT|CODE): This runs a CMake script or a snippet during installation.

- install(EXPORT): This generates and installs a target export file.

- install(RUNTIME_DEPENDENCY_SET <set-name> [...]): This installs runtime dependency sets defined in the project.

- install(IMPORTED_RUNTIME_ARTIFACTS <target>... [...]): This queries imported targets for runtime artifacts and installs them.

Adding these commands to your listfile generates a cmake_install.cmake file in your build tree. While it's possible to manually invoke this script with cmake -P, this is not recommended. The file is intended for internal use by CMake when cmake --install is executed.

Every install() mode has a comprehensive set of options, with a few shared across modes:

- DESTINATION: This specifies the installation path. Relative paths are prepended with CMAKE_INSTALL_PREFIX, while absolute paths are used verbatim (and not supported by cpack).

- PERMISSIONS: This sets file permissions on supported platforms. The available values include OWNER_READ, OWNER_WRITE, OWNER_EXECUTE, GROUP_READ, GROUP_WRITE, GROUP_EXECUTE, WORLD_READ, WORLD_WRITE, WORLD_EXECUTE, SETUID, and SETGID. Default directory permissions created during installation time can be set with the CMAKE_INSTALL_DEFAULT_DIRECTORY_PERMISSIONS variable.

- CONFIGURATIONS: This specifies configurations (Debug, Release). Options following this keyword apply only if the current build configuration is in the list.
- OPTIONAL: This prevents errors when the installed files don't exist.

Two shared options, COMPONENT and EXCLUDE_FROM_ALL, are used in component-specific installations. These will be discussed in the *Defining components* section later in the chapter. For now, let's take a look at the first installation mode: install(TARGETS).

Installing logical targets

Targets defined by add_library() and add_executable() can easily be installed with the install(TARGETS) command. This means copying the artifacts that have been produced by the buildsystem to the appropriate destination directories and setting suitable file permissions for them. The general signature for this mode is as follows:

```
install(TARGETS <target>... [EXPORT <export-name>]
        [<output-artifact-configuration> ...]
        [INCLUDES DESTINATION [<dir> ...]]
)
```

After the initial mode specifier, that is, TARGETS, we must provide a list of targets we'd like to install. Here, we may optionally assign them to a **named export** with the EXPORT option, which can be used in export(EXPORT) and install(EXPORT) to produce a target export file. Then, we must configure the installation of output artifacts (grouped by type). Optionally, we can provide a list of directories that will be added to the target export file for each target in its INTERFACE_INCLUDE_DIRECTORIES property.

[<output-artifact-configuration>...] provides a list of configuration blocks. The full syntax of a single block is as follows:

```
<TYPE> [DESTINATION <dir>]
       [PERMISSIONS permissions...]
       [CONFIGURATIONS [Debug|Release|...]]
       [COMPONENT <component>]
       [NAMELINK_COMPONENT <component>]
       [OPTIONAL] [EXCLUDE_FROM_ALL]
       [NAMELINK_ONLY|NAMELINK_SKIP]
```

The command mandates that every output artifact block starts with `<TYPE>` (this is the only required element). CMake recognizes several of them:

- `ARCHIVE`: Static libraries (`.a`) and DLL import libraries for Windows-based systems (`.lib`).
- `LIBRARY`: Shared libraries (`.so`), but not DLLs.
- `RUNTIME`: Executables and DLLs.
- `OBJECTS`: *Object files* from `OBJECT` libraries.
- `FRAMEWORK`: Static and shared libraries that have the `FRAMEWORK` property set (this excludes them from `ARCHIVE` and `LIBRARY`). This is macOS-specific.
- `BUNDLE`: Executables marked with `MACOSX_BUNDLE` (also not part of `RUNTIME`).
- `FILE_SET <set>`: Files in the `<set>` file set specified for the target. Either C++ header files or C++ module headers (since CMake 3.23).
- `PUBLIC_HEADER`, `PRIVATE_HEADER`, `RESOURCE`: Files specified in the target properties with the same name (on Apple platforms, they should be set on the `FRAMEWORK` or `BUNDLE` targets).

The CMake documentation claims that if you only configure one artifact type (for example, `LIBRARY`), only this type will be installed. For CMake version 3.26.0, this is not true: all the artifacts will be installed as if they were configured with the default options. This can be solved by specifying `<TYPE> EXCLUDE_FROM_ALL` for all unwanted artifact types.

A single `install(TARGETS)` command can have multiple artifact configuration blocks. However, be aware that you may only specify one of each type per call. That is, if you'd like to configure different destinations of `ARCHIVE` artifacts for the `Debug` and `Release` configurations, then you must make two separate `install(TARGETS ... ARCHIVE)` calls.

You may also omit the type name and specify options for all the artifacts. Installation would then be then performed for every file that's produced by these targets, regardless of their type:

```
install(TARGETS executable, static_lib1
  DESTINATION /tmp
)
```

In many cases, you don't need to provide the `DESTINATION` explicitly, thanks to the built-in defaults, but there are a few caveats to keep in mind when dealing with different platforms.

Utilizing the default destination for different platforms

When CMake installs your project's files, it copies them into a specific directory in the system. Different file types belong in different directories. This directory is determined by the following formula:

```
${CMAKE_INSTALL_PREFIX} + ${DESTINATION}
```

As mentioned in the previous section, you can explicitly provide the DESTINATION component for installation, or let CMake use a built-in default based on the type of the artifact:

Artifact type	Built-in default	Install directory variable
RUNTIME	bin	CMAKE_INSTALL_BINDIR
LIBRARY ARCHIVE	lib	CMAKE_INSTALL_LIBDIR
PUBLIC_HEADER PRIVATE_HEADER FILE_SET (type HEADERS)	include	CMAKE_INSTALL_INCLUDEDIR

Table 14.1: Default destinations per artifact type

While default paths are useful, they aren't always appropriate. For example, CMake defaults the DESTINATION for libraries to lib. The full path for libraries is then computed as /usr/local/lib for Unix-like systems and something like C:\Program Files (x86)\<project-name>\lib on Windows. However, this is not ideal for Debian with multi-arch support, which requires an architecture-specific path (e.g., i386-linux-gnu) when INSTALL_PREFIX is /usr. Determining the correct path for each platform is a common challenge for Unix-like systems. To address this, follow the *GNU Coding Standards*, the link to which is added in the *Further reading* section at the end of this chapter.

We can override the default destinations for each value by setting a CMAKE_INSTALL_<DIRTYPE>DIR variable. Instead of developing an algorithm to detect the platform and assign appropriate paths to the install directory variables, use the CMake GNUInstallDirs utility module. This module handles most platforms by setting the install directory variables accordingly. Just include it using include() before any install() commands, and you'll be set.

Users needing custom configurations can override the install directory variables via the command-line argument like so:

```
-DCMAKE_INSTALL_BINDIR=/path/in/the/system
```

However, installing the public headers of libraries still presents challenges. Let's explore why.

Dealing with public headers

When managing public headers in CMake, it's best practice to store them in a directory that indicates their origin and introduces namespacing, such as /usr/local/include/calc. This enables their use in C++ projects with the inclusion directive:

```
#include <calc/basic.h>
```

Most preprocessors interpret angle-bracketed directives as requests to scan standard system directories. We can use the GNUInstallDirs module to automatically populate the DESTINATION part of the installation path, ensuring headers end up in the include directory.

Since CMake 3.23.0, we can explicitly add headers to be installed to the appropriate target with the target_sources() command and the FILE_SET keyword. This method is preferred, as it takes care of the *relocation* of headers. Here's the syntax:

```
target_sources(<target>
  [<PUBLIC|PRIVATE|INTERFACE>
   [FILE_SET <name> TYPE <type> [BASE_DIR <dir>] FILES]
   <files>...
  ]...
)
```

Assuming our headers are in the src/include/calc directory, here's a practical example:

ch14/02-install-targets/src/CMakeLists.txt (fragment)

```
add_library(calc STATIC basic.cpp)
target_include_directories(calc INTERFACE include)
target_sources(calc PUBLIC FILE_SET HEADERS
                          BASE_DIRS include
                          FILES include/calc/basic.h
)
```

The preceding snippet defines a new target file set called HEADERS. We're using a special case here: if the name of the file set matches one of the available types, CMake will assume we want the file set to be of such type, eliminating the need to define the type explicitly. If you use a different name, remember to define the FILE_SET's type with the appropriate TYPE <TYPE> keyword.

Having defined the file set, we can use it in the installation command like so:

ch14/02-install-targets/src/CMakeLists.txt (continued)

```
...

include(GNUInstallDirs)
install(TARGETS calc ARCHIVE FILE_SET HEADERS)
```

We include the GNUInstallDirs module and configure the installation of the calc static library and its headers. Running cmake in install mode works as expected:

```
# cmake -S <source-tree> -B <build-tree>
# cmake --build <build-tree>
# cmake --install <build-tree>
-- Install configuration: ""
-- Installing: /usr/local/lib/libcalc.a
-- Installing: /usr/local/include/calc/basic.h
```

Support for the FILE_SET HEADERS keyword is a relatively recent update, and unfortunately, not all environments will provide the newer version of CMake.

If you're stuck on a version older than 3.23, you'll need to specify public headers (as a semicolon-separated list) in the PUBLIC_HEADER property of the library target, and deal with the relocation manually (more on this in the *Understanding the issues with relocatable targets* section):

ch14/03-install-targets-legacy/src/CMakeLists.txt (fragment)

```
add_library(calc STATIC basic.cpp)
target_include_directories(calc INTERFACE include)
set_target_properties(calc PROPERTIES
  PUBLIC_HEADER src/include/calc/basic.h
)
```

You'll also need to change the destination directory to include the library name in the include path:

ch14/02-install-targets-legacy/src/CMakeLists.txt (continued)

```
...

include(GNUInstallDirs)
install(TARGETS calc
  ARCHIVE
```

```
    PUBLIC_HEADER
    DESTINATION ${CMAKE_INSTALL_INCLUDEDIR}/calc
)
```

Explicitly inserting /calc in the path is necessary because files specified in the PUBLIC_HEADER property don't retain their directory structure. They will all be installed in the same destination, even if nested in different base directories. This significant drawback led to the development of FILE_SET.

Now, you know how to address most installation cases, but how should you approach more advanced scenarios?

Low-level installation

Modern CMake is moving away from directly manipulating files. Ideally, we should add files to a logical target, using it as a higher level of abstraction to represent all underlying assets: source files, headers, resources, configuration, and so on. The main advantage is the code's dryness; usually, adding a file to the target requires changing no more than one line.

Unfortunately, adding every installed file to a target isn't always possible or convenient. In such cases, three options are available: install(FILES), install(PROGRAMS), and install(DIRECTORY).

Installing with install(FILES) and install(PROGRAMS)

The FILES and PROGRAMS modes are very similar. They can be used to install various assets, including public header files, documentation, shell scripts, configuration, and runtime assets like images, audio files, and datasets.

Here's the command signature:

```
install(<FILES|PROGRAMS> files...
        TYPE <type> | DESTINATION <dir>
        [PERMISSIONS permissions...]
        [CONFIGURATIONS [Debug|Release|...]]
        [COMPONENT <component>]
        [RENAME <name>] [OPTIONAL] [EXCLUDE_FROM_ALL]
)
```

The main difference between FILES and PROGRAMS is the default file permissions set on the copied files. install(PROGRAMS) sets EXECUTE for all users, whereas install(FILES) does not (though both will set OWNER_WRITE, OWNER_READ, GROUP_READ, and WORLD_READ).

You can modify this behavior by using the optional PERMISSIONS keyword, and then choosing the leading keyword (FILES or PROGRAMS) as an indicator of what's installed. We've already covered how PERMISSIONS, CONFIGURATIONS, and OPTIONAL work. COMPONENT and EXCLUDE_FROM_ALL will be discussed later in the *Defining components* section.

After the initial keyword, we need to list all the files we want to install. CMake supports relative and absolute paths, as well as generator expressions. Remember that if your file path starts with a generator expression, it must be absolute.

The next required keyword is TYPE or DESTINATION. You can either explicitly provide the DESTINATION path or ask CMake to look it up for a specific TYPE file. Unlike in install(TARGETS), TYPE in this context does not select any subset of the provided files to be installed. Nevertheless, the computation of the installation path follows the same pattern (where the + symbol denotes a platform-specific path separator):

${CMAKE_INSTALL_PREFIX} + ${DESTINATION}

Similarly, every TYPE will have built-in defaults:

File Type	Built-In Default	Installation Directory Variable
BIN	bin	CMAKE_INSTALL_BINDIR
SBIN	sbin	CMAKE_INSTALL_SBINDIR
LIB	lib	CMAKE_INSTALL_LIBDIR
INCLUDE	include	CMAKE_INSTALL_INCLUDEDIR
SYSCONF	etc	CMAKE_INSTALL_SYSCONFDIR
SHAREDSTATE	com	CMAKE_INSTALL_SHARESTATEDIR
LOCALSTATE	var	CMAKE_INSTALL_LOCALSTATEDIR
RUNSTATE	$LOCALSTATE/run	CMAKE_INSTALL_RUNSTATEDIR
DATA	$DATAROOT	CMAKE_INSTALL_DATADIR
INFO	$DATAROOT/info	CMAKE_INSTALL_INFODIR
LOCALE	$DATAROOT/locale	CMAKE_INSTALL_LOCALEDIR
MAN	$DATAROOT/man	CMAKE_INSTALL_MANDIR
DOC	$DATAROOT/doc	CMAKE_INSTALL_DOCDIR

Table 14.2: Built-in defaults per file type

The behavior here follows the same principle that was described in the *Utilizing the default destination for different platforms* subsection: if no installation directory variable for this TYPE of file is set, CMake will provide a built-in default path. Again, for portability, we can use the GNUInstallDirs module.

Some of the built-in guesses in the table are prefixed with installation directory variables:

- $LOCALSTATE is CMAKE_INSTALL_LOCALSTATEDIR or defaults to var
- $DATAROOT is CMAKE_INSTALL_DATAROOTDIR or defaults to share

As with install(TARGETS), the GNUInstallDirs module will provide platform-specific installation directory variables. Let's look at an example:

ch14/04-install-files/CMakeLists.txt

```
cmake_minimum_required(VERSION 3.26)
project(InstallFiles CXX)
include(GNUInstallDirs)
install(FILES
  src/include/calc/basic.h
  src/include/calc/nested/calc_extended.h
  DESTINATION ${CMAKE_INSTALL_INCLUDEDIR}/calc
)
```

In this case, CMake installs the two header-only libraries, basic.h and nested/calc_extended.h, into the project-specific subdirectory within the system-wide include directory.

From the GNUInstallDirs source, we know that CMAKE_INSTALL_INCLUDEDIR is the same for all supported platforms. However, using it is still recommended for readability and consistency with more dynamic variables. For instance, CMAKE_INSTALL_LIBDIR varies by architecture and distribution – lib, lib64, or lib/<multiarch-tuple>.

Since CMake 3.20, you can use the RENAME keyword with the install(FILES) and install(PROGRAMS) commands. This keyword has to be followed by a new filename and only works if the command installs a single file.

The example in this section demonstrates the ease of installing files in the appropriate directory. However, there's one issue – observe the installation output:

```
# cmake -S <source-tree> -B <build-tree>
# cmake --build <build-tree>
# cmake --install <build-tree>
-- Install configuration: ""
```

```
-- Installing: /usr/local/include/calc/basic.h
-- Installing: /usr/local/include/calc/calc_extended.h
```

Both files are installed in the same directory, regardless of their original nesting. Sometimes, this isn't desirable. In the next section, we'll explore how to handle this situation.

Working with entire directories

If adding individual files to your installation command isn't suitable, you can opt for a broader approach and work with entire directories. The install(DIRECTORY) mode is designed for this, copying the specified directories verbatim to the chosen destination. Here's how it looks:

```
install(DIRECTORY dirs...
        TYPE <type> | DESTINATION <dir>
        [FILE_PERMISSIONS permissions...]
        [DIRECTORY_PERMISSIONS permissions...]
        [USE_SOURCE_PERMISSIONS] [OPTIONAL] [MESSAGE_NEVER]
        [CONFIGURATIONS [Debug|Release|...]]
        [COMPONENT <component>] [EXCLUDE_FROM_ALL]
        [FILES_MATCHING]
        [[PATTERN <pattern> | REGEX <regex>] [EXCLUDE]
        [PERMISSIONS permissions...]] [...]
)
```

Many options here are similar to those in install(FILES) and install(PROGRAMS) and function in the same manner. One key detail is that if the paths provided after the DIRECTORY keyword don't end with /, the last directory of the path is appended to the destination. For example:

```
install(DIRECTORY aaa DESTINATION /xxx)
```

This command creates a directory, /xxx/aaa, and copies the contents of aaa to it. In contrast, the following command copies the contents of aaa directly to /xxx:

```
install(DIRECTORY aaa/ DESTINATION /xxx)
```

install(DIRECTORY) also introduces other mechanisms that are not available for files:

- Output silencing
- Extended permission control
- File/directory filtering

Let's start with the output silencing option, `MESSAGE_NEVER`. It disables output diagnostics during installation. It is very useful when we have many files in the directories we're installing and it would be too noisy to print them all.

Regarding permissions, `install(DIRECTORY)` supports three options:

- `USE_SOURCE_PERMISSIONS` sets the permissions on installed files that follow the original files. This only works when `FILE_PERMISSIONS` is not set.

- `FILE_PERMISSIONS` allows us to specify the permissions we want to set on installed files and directories. The default permissions are `OWNER_WRITE`, `OWNER_READ`, `GROUP_READ`, and `WORLD_READ`.

- `DIRECTORY_PERMISSIONS` works similarly to `FILE_PERMISSIONS`, but it will set additional `EXECUTE` permissions for all users (this is because `EXECUTE` on directories in Unix-like systems denotes permission to list their contents).

Note that CMake ignores permissions options on platforms that don't support them. More nuanced permission control is achievable by adding the `PERMISSIONS` keyword after each filtering expression. Files or directories matched by this will receive the specified permissions.

Let's talk about filters or "globbing" expressions. They control which files/directories from source directories are installed and follow this syntax:

```
PATTERN <pat> | REGEX <reg> [EXCLUDE] [PERMISSIONS <perm>]
```

There are two matching methods to choose from:

- With `PATTERN`, which is the simpler option, you can provide a pattern with the ? placeholders (matching any character) and the * wildcards (matching any string). Only paths that end with `<pat>` will be matched.

- The `REGEX` option is more advanced, supporting regular expressions. It allows the matching of any part of the path, although the ^ and $ anchors can still denote the beginning and end of the path.

Optionally, the `FILES_MATCHING` keyword can be set before the first filter, specifying that the filters will apply to files and not directories.

Remember two caveats:

- `FILES_MATCHING` requires an inclusive filter. You may exclude some files, but no files will be copied unless you also include some. However, all directories will be created, regardless of filtering.

- All subdirectories are included by default; you can only filter out.

For each filter method, you can choose to exclude matched paths with the EXCLUDE command (this only works when FILES_MATCHING isn't used).

Specific permissions for all matched paths can be set by adding the PERMISSIONS keyword and a list of desired permissions after any filter. Let's explore this with an example where we install three directories in different ways. We have some static data files for runtime use:

```
data
- data.csv
```

We also need some public headers located in the src directory among other unrelated files:

```
src
- include
  - calc
    - basic.h
    - ignored
      - empty.file
    - nested
      - calc_extended.h
```

Finally, we need two configuration files at two levels of nesting. To make things more interesting, we'll make /etc/calc/ contents accessible only to the file owner:

```
etc
- calc
  - nested.conf
- sample.conf
```

To install the directory with static data files, we start our project with the most basic form of the install(DIRECTORY) command:

ch14/05-install-directories/CMakeLists.txt (fragment)

```
cmake_minimum_required(VERSION 3.26)
project(InstallDirectories CXX)
install(DIRECTORY data/ DESTINATION share/calc)
```

This command will simply take all the contents of our data directory and put it in ${CMAKE_INSTALL_PREFIX} and share/calc. Note that our source path ends with a / symbol to indicate we don't want to copy the data directory itself, only its contents.

The second case is the opposite: we don't add the trailing / because the directory should be included. This is because we're relying on a system-specific path for the INCLUDE file type, which is provided by GNUInstallDirs (note how the INCLUDE and EXCLUDE keywords represent unrelated concepts):

ch14/05-install-directories/CMakeLists.txt (fragment)

```
...
include(GNUInstallDirs)
install(DIRECTORY src/include/calc TYPE INCLUDE
  PATTERN "ignored" EXCLUDE
  PATTERN "calc_extended.h" EXCLUDE
)
```

Additionally, we have excluded two paths from this operation: the entire ignored directory and all files ending with calc_extended.h (remember how PATTERN works).

The third case installs some default configuration files and sets their permissions:

ch14/05-install-directories/CMakeLists.txt (fragment)

```
install(DIRECTORY etc/ TYPE SYSCONF
  DIRECTORY_PERMISSIONS
    OWNER_READ OWNER_WRITE OWNER_EXECUTE
  PATTERN "nested.conf"
    PERMISSIONS OWNER_READ OWNER_WRITE
)
```

We avoid appending etc from the source path to the SYSCONF path (as GNUInstallDirs has already provided this) to prevent duplication. We set two permission rules: subdirectories are editable and listable only by the owner, and files ending with nested.conf are editable only by the owner.

Installing directories covers various use cases, but for other advanced scenarios (like post-install configuration), external tools may be required. How do we integrate them?

Invoking scripts during installation

If you have ever installed a shared library on a Unix-like system, you might recall needing to instruct the dynamic linker to scan trusted directories and build its cache using ldconfig (refer to the *Further reading* section for references). To facilitate fully automatic installations, CMake provides the install(SCRIPT) and install(CODE) modes. Here is the complete syntax:

```
install([[SCRIPT <file>] [CODE <code>]]
        [ALL_COMPONENTS | COMPONENT <component>]
        [EXCLUDE_FROM_ALL] [...]
)
```

Choose between the SCRIPT and CODE modes and provide the necessary arguments – a path to a CMake script to run or a CMake snippet to execute during installation. To illustrate, let's modify the 02-install-targets example to build a shared library:

ch14/06-install-code/src/CMakeLists.txt

```
add_library(calc SHARED basic.cpp)
target_include_directories(calc INTERFACE include)
target_sources(calc PUBLIC FILE_SET HEADERS
                           BASE_DIRS include
                           FILES include/calc/basic.h
)
```

Change the artifact type from ARCHIVE to LIBRARY in the installation script and then add logic to run ldconfig afterward:

ch14/06-install-code/CMakeLists.txt (fragment)

```
install(TARGETS calc LIBRARY FILE_SET HEADERS))
if (UNIX)
  install(CODE "execute_process(COMMAND ldconfig)")
endif()
```

The if() condition ensures the command is appropriate for the operating system (ldconfig should not be executed on Windows or macOS). The provided code must be syntactically valid in CMake (errors will only surface during installation).

After running the installation command, confirm its success by printing the cached libraries:

```
# cmake -S <source-tree> -B <build-tree>
# cmake --build <build-tree>
# cmake --install <build-tree>
-- Install configuration: ""
-- Installing: /usr/local/lib/libcalc.so
-- Installing: /usr/local/include/calc/basic.h
# ldconfig -p | grep libcalc
        libcalc.so (libc6,x86-64) => /usr/local/lib/libcalc.so
```

Both SCRIPT and CODE modes support generator expressions, adding versatility to this command. It can be used for various purposes: printing user messages, verifying successful installations, extensive configuration, file signing, and more.

Next, let's delve into the aspect of managing runtime dependencies in CMake installations, one of the newest features of CMake.

Installing runtime dependencies

We've covered almost all kinds of installable artifacts and their respective commands. The final subject to discuss is runtime dependencies. Executables and shared libraries often depend on other libraries that must be present in the system and are dynamically loaded at program initialization. Since version 3.21, CMake can build a list of these required libraries for each target and capture their location at build time by referencing the appropriate sections of the binary file. This list can then be used to install these runtime artifacts in the system for future use.

For a target defined in the project, this can be achieved in two steps:

```
install(TARGETS ... RUNTIME_DEPENDENCY_SET <set-name>)
install(RUNTIME_DEPENDENCY_SET <set-name> <arg>...)
```

Alternatively, this can be accomplished with a single command with the same effect:

```
install(TARGETS ... RUNTIME_DEPENDENCIES <arg>...)
```

If a target is imported, rather than defined in the project, its runtime dependencies can be installed as follows:

```
install(IMPORTED_RUNTIME_ARTIFACTS <target>...)
```

The preceding snippet can be extended with the RUNTIME_DEPENDENCY_SET <set-name> argument to create a named reference that can be later used in the install(RUNTIME_DEPENDENCY_SET) command.

If this feature sounds beneficial for your project, I recommend checking the official documentation of the install() command to learn more.

Now that we understand all the different ways we can install files on the system, let's explore how to turn them into a natively available package for other CMake projects.

Creating reusable packages

We've extensively used find_package() in previous chapters and observed its convenience and simplicity. To make our project accessible through this command, we need to complete a few steps so CMake can treat our project as a coherent package:

1. Make our targets relocatable.
2. Install the *target export file* to a standard location.
3. Create a *config file for the package*.
4. Generate a *version file* for the package.

Let's start from the beginning: why do targets need to be relocatable and how can we do this?

Understanding the issues with relocatable targets

Installation solves many problems but also introduces some complexity. The CMAKE_INSTALL_ PREFIX is platform specific and can be set by the user at the installation stage with the --install-prefix command-line argument. The challenge is that target export files are generated before installation, during the build stage, when the final destination of the installed artifacts is unknown. Consider this code:

ch14/03-install-targets-legacy/src/CMakeLists.txt

```
add_library(calc STATIC basic.cpp)
target_include_directories(calc INTERFACE include)
set_target_properties(calc PROPERTIES
  PUBLIC_HEADER src/include/calc/basic.h
)
```

In this example, we specifically add the include directory to the include directories of calc. Since this is a relative path, CMake's exported target generation implicitly prepends this path with the contents of the CMAKE_CURRENT_SOURCE_DIR variable, pointing to the directory where this listfile is located.

Here's the problem: after installation, the project mustn't rely on files from the source or build tree. Everything, including library headers, is copied to a shared location, like /usr/lib/calc/ on Linux. The target that has been defined in this snippet isn't suitable for use in another project since its include directory path still points to its source tree.

CMake addresses this *carriage-before-the-horse* problem with generator expressions that are replaced with their argument or an empty string, depending on the context:

- `$<BUILD_INTERFACE:...>`: This evaluates to the '...' argument for regular builds but excludes it for installation.
- `$<INSTALL_INTERFACE:...>`: This evaluates to the '...' argument for installation but excludes it for regular builds.
- `$<BUILD_LOCAL_INTERFACE:...>`: This evaluates to the '...' argument when used by another target in the same buildsystem (added in CMake 3.26).

These expressions allow the deferment of the decision of which path to use to the later stages of the process: building and installation. Here's how to use them in practice:

ch14/07-install-export-legacy/src/CMakeLists.txt (fragment)

```
add_library(calc STATIC basic.cpp)
target_include_directories(calc INTERFACE
  "$<BUILD_INTERFACE:${CMAKE_CURRENT_SOURCE_DIR}/include>"
  "$<INSTALL_INTERFACE:${CMAKE_INSTALL_INCLUDEDIR}>"
)
set_target_properties(calc PROPERTIES
  PUBLIC_HEADER "include/calc/basic.h"
)
```

In `target_include_directories()`, we focus on the last two arguments. The used generator expressions are mutually exclusive, meaning only one of the arguments will be used in the final step, and the other will be erased.

For regular builds, the `INTERFACE_INCLUDE_DIRECTORIES` property of the `calc` target will be expanded, using the first argument:

```
"/root/examples/ch14/07-install-export/src/include" ""
```

On the other hand, when installing, the value will expand with the second argument:

```
"" "/usr/lib/calc/include"
```

 Quotes are not present in the final value; they're added here to express empty text values for clarity.

Regarding CMAKE_INSTALL_PREFIX: it should not be used as a component in paths specified in targets. It would be evaluated during the build stage, making the path absolute and potentially different from the one provided during installation (if the --install-prefix option is used). Instead, use the $<INSTALL_PREFIX> generator expression:

```
target_include_directories(my_target PUBLIC
  $<INSTALL_INTERFACE:$<INSTALL_PREFIX>/include/MyTarget>
)
```

Or, even better, you can use relative paths, which will be prepended with the correct installation prefix:

```
target_include_directories(my_target PUBLIC
  $<INSTALL_INTERFACE:include/MyTarget>
)
```

For more examples and information, please consult the official documentation (a link to this can be found in the *Further reading* section).

Now that our targets are *installation compatible*, we can safely generate and install their target export files.

Installing target export files

We previously touched on target export files in the *Exporting without installation* section. The process for installing target export files is quite similar, and so is the command syntax for creating them:

```
install(EXPORT <export-name> DESTINATION <dir>
        [NAMESPACE <namespace>] [[FILE <name>.cmake]|
        [PERMISSIONS permissions...]
        [CONFIGURATIONS [Debug|Release|...]]
        [EXPORT_LINK_INTERFACE_LIBRARIES]
        [COMPONENT <component>]
        [EXCLUDE_FROM_ALL])
```

It's a blend of the plain export(EXPORT) and other install() commands (its options function similarly). Remember, it will create and install a target export file for a named export that must be defined with the install(TARGETS) command. The key difference here is that the generated export file will contain target paths evaluated in the INSTALL_INTERFACE generator expression, unlike export(EXPORT), which uses BUILD_INTERFACE. This means we need to be careful about our include files and other relatively referenced files.

Again, with CMake 3.23 or newer this won't be a problem if `FILE_SET HEADERS` is used correctly. Let's see how we can generate and install the export file for the targets from the `ch14/02-install-export` example. To do this, we must call `install(EXPORT)` after the `install(TARGETS)` command:

ch14/07-install-export/src/CMakeLists.txt

```
add_library(calc STATIC basic.cpp)
target_sources(calc
  PUBLIC FILE_SET HEADERS BASE_DIRS include
  FILES "include/calc/basic.h"
)


include(GNUInstallDirs)
install(TARGETS calc EXPORT CalcTargets ARCHIVE FILE_SET HEADERS)
install(EXPORT CalcTargets
  DESTINATION ${CMAKE_INSTALL_LIBDIR}/calc/cmake
  NAMESPACE Calc::
)
```

Note the reference to the `CalcTargets` export name in `install(EXPORT)`. Running `cmake --install` in the build tree will result in the export file being generated in the specified destination:

```
...
-- Installing: /usr/local/lib/calc/cmake/CalcTargets.cmake
-- Installing: /usr/local/lib/calc/cmake/CalcTargets-noconfig.cmake
```

If you need to override the default target export filename (`<export name>.cmake`), add the `FILE new-name.cmake` argument to change it (the filename must end with `.cmake`).

Don't confuse this – the *target export file* isn't a *config file*, so you can't use `find_package()` to consume installed targets just yet. However, it's possible to `include()` export files directly if necessary. So, how do we define a package that can be consumed by other projects? Let's find out!

Writing basic config files

A complete package definition consists of the target export files, the package's *config file*, and the package's *version file*. However, technically, all that's needed for `find_package()` to work is a config file. It acts as a package definition, responsible for providing any package functions and macros, checking requirements, finding dependencies, and including target export files.

As we mentioned earlier, users can install your package anywhere on their system by using:

```
# cmake --install <build tree> --install-prefix=<path>
```

This prefix determines where the installed files will be copied. To support this, you must ensure the following:

- The paths on the target properties are relocatable (as described in the *Understanding the issues with relocatable targets* section).
- The paths that are used in your config file are relative to it.

To use such packages that have been installed in non-default locations, the consuming projects need to provide <installation path> through the CMAKE_PREFIX_PATH variable during the configuration stage:

```
# cmake -B <build tree> -DCMAKE_PREFIX_PATH=<installation path>
```

The find_package() command will scan the list of paths that are outlined in the documentation (see the *Further reading* section) in a platform-specific manner. One pattern checked on Windows and Unix-like systems is:

```
<prefix>/<name>*/(lib/<arch>|lib*|share)/<name>*/(cmake|CMake)
```

This indicates that installing the config file in a path such as lib/calc/cmake should work. Additionally, CMake requires that config files be named <PackageName>-config.cmake or <PackageName>Config.cmake to be found.

Let's add the installation of the config file to the 06-install-export example:

ch14/09-config-file/CMakeLists.txt (fragment)

```
...
install(EXPORT CalcTargets
  DESTINATION ${CMAKE_INSTALL_LIBDIR}/calc/cmake
  NAMESPACE Calc::
)
install(FILES "CalcConfig.cmake"
  DESTINATION ${CMAKE_INSTALL_LIBDIR}/calc/cmake
)
```

This command installs CalcConfig.cmake from the same source directory (CMAKE_INSTALL_LIBDIR will be evaluated to the correct lib path for the platform).

The simplest config file consists of a single line including the target export file:

ch14/09-config-file/CalcConfig.cmake

```
include("${CMAKE_CURRENT_LIST_DIR}/CalcTargets.cmake")
```

CMAKE_CURRENT_LIST_DIR refers to the directory where the config file resides. Since CalcConfig. cmake and CalcTargets.cmake are installed in the same directory in our example (as set by install(EXPORT)), the target export file will be included correctly.

To verify our package's usability, we'll create a simple project with one listfile:

ch14/10-find-package/CMakeLists.txt

```
cmake_minimum_required(VERSION 3.26)
project(FindCalcPackage CXX)
find_package(Calc REQUIRED)
include(CMakePrintHelpers)
message("CMAKE_PREFIX_PATH: ${CMAKE_PREFIX_PATH}")
message("CALC_FOUND: ${Calc_FOUND}")
cmake_print_properties(TARGETS "Calc::calc" PROPERTIES
  IMPORTED_CONFIGURATIONS
  INTERFACE_INCLUDE_DIRECTORIES
)
```

To test this, build and install the 09-config-file example to one directory, and then build 10-find-package while referencing it with the DCMAKE_PREFIX_PATH argument:

```
# cmake -S <source-tree-of-08> -B <build-tree-of-08>
# cmake --build <build-tree-of-08>
# cmake --install <build-tree-of-08>
# cmake -S <source-tree-of-09> -B <build-tree-of-09>
        -DCMAKE_PREFIX_PATH=<build-tree-of-08>
```

This will produce the following output (all the <*_tree-of_> placeholders will be replaced with real paths):

```
CMAKE_PREFIX_PATH: <build-tree-of-08>
CALC_FOUND: 1
--
Properties for TARGET Calc::calc:
   Calc::calc.IMPORTED_CONFIGURATIONS = "NOCONFIG"
```

```
    Calc::calc.INTERFACE_INCLUDE_DIRECTORIES = "<build-tree-of-08>/include"
-- Configuring done
-- Generating done
-- Build files have been written to: <build-tree-of-09>
```

This output indicates that the CalcTargets.cmake file was found and included correctly, and the path to the include directory follows the chosen prefix. This solution is suitable for basic packaging cases. Now, let's learn how to handle more advanced scenarios.

Creating advanced config files

If you need to manage more than a single *target export file*, including a few macros in your *config file* can be useful. The CMakePackageConfigHelpers utility module provides access to the configure_package_config_file() command. To use it, supply a template file that will be interpolated with CMake variables to generate a *config file* with two embedded macro definitions:

- set_and_check(<variable> <path>): This works like set(), but it checks that <path> actually exists and fails with FATAL_ERROR otherwise. This is recommended for use in your config files to detect incorrect paths early.
- check_required_components(<PackageName>): This is added to the end of the config file. It verifies whether all components required by the user in find_package(<package> REQUIRED <component>) have been found.

Paths for complex directory trees can be prepared for installation during *config file* generation. Here's the command signature:

```
configure_package_config_file(<template> <output>
   INSTALL_DESTINATION <path>
   [PATH_VARS <var1> <var2> ... <varN>]
   [NO_SET_AND_CHECK_MACRO]
   [NO_CHECK_REQUIRED_COMPONENTS_MACRO]
   [INSTALL_PREFIX <path>]
)
```

The <template> file will be interpolated with variables and stored in the <output> path. The INSTALL_DESTINATION path is used to transform the paths stored in the PATH_VARS to be relative to the install destination. The INSTALL_PREFIX can be provided as a base path to indicate that INSTALL_DESTINATION is relative to it.

The NO_SET_AND_CHECK_MACRO and NO_CHECK_REQUIRED_COMPONENTS_MACRO options tell CMake not to add these macro definitions to the generated *config file*. Let's see this generation in practice, extending the 07-install-export example:

ch14/11-advanced-config/CMakeLists.txt (fragment)

```
...
install(EXPORT CalcTargets
  DESTINATION ${CMAKE_INSTALL_LIBDIR}/calc/cmake
  NAMESPACE Calc::
)
include(CMakePackageConfigHelpers)
set(LIB_INSTALL_DIR ${CMAKE_INSTALL_LIBDIR}/calc)
configure_package_config_file(
  ${CMAKE_CURRENT_SOURCE_DIR}/CalcConfig.cmake.in
  "${CMAKE_CURRENT_BINARY_DIR}/CalcConfig.cmake"
  INSTALL_DESTINATION ${CMAKE_INSTALL_LIBDIR}/calc/cmake
  PATH_VARS LIB_INSTALL_DIR
)
install(FILES "${CMAKE_CURRENT_BINARY_DIR}/CalcConfig.cmake"
  DESTINATION ${CMAKE_INSTALL_LIBDIR}/calc/cmake
)
```

In the preceding code, we:

1. Use include() to include the utility module with helpers.

2. Use set() to set a variable that will be used to make a relocatable path.

3. Generate the CalcConfig.cmake config file for the build tree using the CalcConfig.cmake.in template, and provide LIB_INSTALL_DIR as a variable name to be computed as relative to INSTALL_DESTINATION or ${CMAKE_INSTALL_LIBDIR}/calc/cmake.

4. Pass the config file that was generated for the build tree to install(FILE).

Note that the path in DESTINATION in install(FILES) and the path in INSTALL_DESTINATION in configure_package_config_file() are equal, which ensures correct relative path computation inside of the configuration file.

Finally, we'll need a config file template (their names are usually suffixed with .in):

ch14/11-advanced-config/CalcConfig.cmake.in

```
@PACKAGE_INIT@
set_and_check(CALC_LIB_DIR "@PACKAGE_LIB_INSTALL_DIR@")
include("${CALC_LIB_DIR}/cmake/CalcTargets.cmake")
check_required_components(Calc)
```

This template begins with a @PACKAGE_INIT@ placeholder. The generator will fill it with the definitions of the set_and_check and check_required_components macros.

The next line sets CALC_LIB_DIR to the path passed in the @PACKAGE_LIB_INSTALL_DIR@ placeholder. CMake will fill it with $LIB_INSTALL_DIR, provided in the listfile, but calculated relative to the installation path. Subsequently, that path is used in the include() command to include the *target export file*. Finally, check_required_components() verifies whether all of the components required by the project using this package have been found. This command is recommended, even if the package doesn't have any components to ensure the users are using only supported requirements. Otherwise, they may incorrectly think they've successfully added components (perhaps only present in newer versions of the package).

The CalcConfig.cmake *config file*, when generated this way, looks like this:

```
#### Expanded from @PACKAGE_INIT@ by
  configure_package_config_file() #######
#### Any changes to this file will be overwritten by the
  next CMake run ####
#### The input file was CalcConfig.cmake.in  #####

get_filename_component(PACKAGE_PREFIX_DIR
  "${CMAKE_CURRENT_LIST_DIR}/../../../" ABSOLUTE)

macro(set_and_check _var _file)
  # ... removed for brevity
endmacro()
macro(check_required_components _NAME)
  # ... removed for brevity
endmacro()
```

```
##################################################################
set_and_check(CALC_LIB_DIR "${PACKAGE_PREFIX_DIR}/lib/calc")
include("${CALC_LIB_DIR}/cmake/CalcTargets.cmake")
check_required_components(Calc)
```

The following diagram, which shows how the various package files are related to each other, puts this into perspective:

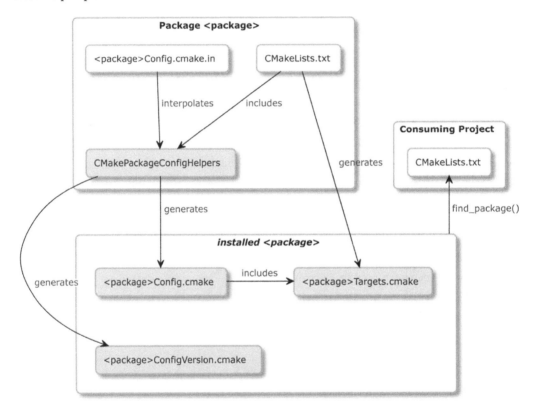

Figure 14.1: The file structure for advanced packages

All the required sub-dependencies of a package must also be found in the package config file. This can be done by calling the find_dependency() macro from the CMakeFindDependencyMacro helper. We learned how to use it in *Chapter 9, Managing Dependencies in CMake*.

Definitions for any macros or functions exposed to the consuming project should be in a separate file included from the package's *config file*. Interestingly, CMakePackageConfigHelpers also helps generate package version files. Let's explore this next.

Generating package version files

As your package evolves, gaining new features and phasing out older ones, it's vital to track these changes in a changelog accessible to developers using your package. When a specific feature is required, a developer that is using your package can specify the minimum version that supports it in find_package(), like so:

```
find_package(Calc 1.2.3 REQUIRED)
```

CMake will then search for Calc's config file and check whether a *version file* named <config-file>-version.cmake or <config-file>Version.cmake is present in the same directory (e.g., CalcConfigVersion.cmake). This file contains version information and specifies compatibility with other versions. For instance, even if you don't have the exact version 1.2.3 installed, you might have 1.3.5, which is marked as compatible with older versions. CMake will accept this package, knowing it's backward compatible.

You can use the CMakePackageConfigHelpers utility module to generate package *version files* by calling write_basic_package_version_file():

```
write_basic_package_version_file(
    <filename> [VERSION <ver>]
    COMPATIBILITY <AnyNewerVersion | SameMajorVersion |
                   SameMinorVersion | ExactVersion>
    [ARCH_INDEPENDENT]
)
```

First, provide the <filename> for the artifact; ensure it follows the naming rules previously discussed. Optionally, you can pass an explicit VERSION (in major.minor.patch format). If not provided, the version specified in the project() command is used (an error will occur if the project doesn't specify one).

The COMPATIBILITY keyword indicates:

- ExactVersion must match all three components of the version and doesn't support ranged versions: (e.g., find_package(<package> 1.2.8...1.3.4)).
- SameMinorVersion matches if the first two components are the same (ignores patch).
- SameMajorVersion matches if the first component is the same (ignores minor and patch).
- AnyNewerVersion, contrary to its name, matches any older version (e.g., version 1.4.2 is compatible with find_package(<package> 1.2.8)).

For architecture-dependent packages, an exact architecture match is required. However, for architecture-agnostic packages (like header-only libraries or macro packages), you can specify the ARCH_INDEPENDENT keyword to skip this check.

The following code shows a practical example of how to provide the *version file* for the project that we started in the 07-install-export:

ch14/12-version-file/CMakeLists.txt (fragment)

```
cmake_minimum_required(VERSION 3.26)
project(VersionFile VERSION 1.2.3 LANGUAGES CXX)
...
include(CMakePackageConfigHelpers)
write_basic_package_version_file(
  "${CMAKE_CURRENT_BINARY_DIR}/CalcConfigVersion.cmake"
  COMPATIBILITY AnyNewerVersion
)
install(FILES "CalcConfig.cmake"
  "${CMAKE_CURRENT_BINARY_DIR}/CalcConfigVersion.cmake"
  DESTINATION ${CMAKE_INSTALL_LIBDIR}/calc/cmake
)
```

For convenience, we configure the version of the package at the top of the file, in the project() command, switching from the short project(<name> <languages>) syntax to an explicit, full syntax by adding the LANGUAGE keyword.

After including the helper module, we generate the version file and install it alongside CalcConfig.cmake. By skipping the VERSION keyword, we use the PROJECT_VERSION variable. The package is marked as fully backward compatible with COMPATIBILITY AnyNewerVersion. This installs the package *version file* to the same destination as CalcConfig.cmake. That's it – our package is fully configured.

With this, we concluded the subject of package creation. We now know how to deal with relocation and why it is important, how to install *target export files*, and how to write *config* and *version files*.

In the next section, we'll explore components and their use with packages.

Defining components

We'll begin by addressing potential confusion surrounding the term **component**. Consider the full signature for find_package():

```
find_package(<PackageName>
             [version] [EXACT] [QUIET] [MODULE] [REQUIRED]
             [[COMPONENTS] [components...]]
             [OPTIONAL_COMPONENTS components...]
             [NO_POLICY_SCOPE]
)
```

It's important not to confuse the components mentioned here with the COMPONENT keyword that's used in the install() command. Despite sharing the same name, they are distinct concepts and must be understood separately. We'll explore this further in the following subsections.

How to use components in find_package()

When calling find_package() with a list of COMPONENTS or OPTIONAL_COMPONENTS, we indicate to CMake that we are only interested in packages that provide these components. However, it's crucial to understand that verifying this requirement is the responsibility of the package. If the package vendor doesn't implement the necessary checks in the config file, as mentioned in the *Creating advanced config files* section, the process will not proceed as expected.

Requested components are passed to the config file via the <package>_FIND_COMPONENTS variable (both optional and non-optional). For every non-optional component, a <package>_FIND_REQUIRED_<component> variable is set. Package authors could write a macro to scan this list and verify the provision of all required components, but this is unnecessary. The check_required_components() function serves this purpose. The *config file* should set the <package>_<component>_FOUND variable when a necessary component is found. A macro at the file's end will then verify whether all required variables are set.

How to use components in the install() command

Not all produced artifacts need installation in every scenario. For instance, a project might install static libraries and public headers for development, but by default, it may only need to install a shared library for runtime. To enable this dual behavior, artifacts can be grouped under a common name using the COMPONENT keyword, available in all install() commands. Users interested in limiting installation to specific components can do so by executing the following case-sensitive command:

```
cmake --install <build tree>
      --component=<component1 name> --component=<component2 name>
```

Assigning the COMPONENT keyword to an artifact doesn't automatically exclude it from the default installation. To achieve this exclusion, the EXCLUDE_FROM_ALL keyword must be added.

Let's explore this concept in a code example:

ch14/13-components/CMakeLists.txt (fragment)

```
install(TARGETS calc EXPORT CalcTargets
  ARCHIVE
    COMPONENT lib
  FILE_SET HEADERS
    COMPONENT headers
)
install(EXPORT CalcTargets
  DESTINATION ${CMAKE_INSTALL_LIBDIR}/calc/cmake
  NAMESPACE Calc::
  COMPONENT lib
)
install(CODE "MESSAGE(\"Installing 'extra' component\")"
  COMPONENT extra
  EXCLUDE_FROM_ALL
)
```

The preceding install commands define the following components:

- lib: This contains the static library and target export files. It's installed by default.
- headers: This contains C++ header files. Also installed by default.
- extra: This executes a piece of code to print a message. Not installed by default.

Let's reiterate:

- cmake --install without the --component argument will install both the lib and headers components.
- cmake --install --component headers will only install public headers.
- cmake --install --component extra will print a message that's inaccessible otherwise (the EXCLUDE_FROM_ALL keyword prevents that).

If the COMPONENT keyword isn't specified for an installed artifact, it defaults to Unspecified, as defined by the CMAKE_INSTALL_DEFAULT_COMPONENT_NAME variable.

Since there's no way to list all available components from the cmake command line, thoroughly documenting your package's components can be extremely helpful for users. An INSTALL "READM" file is a good place for this information.

If cmake is invoked with the --component argument for a non-existent component, the command will complete successfully without warnings or errors, but it won't install anything.

Partitioning our installation into components allows users to selectively install parts of the package. Let's now turn to managing symbolic links for versioned shared libraries, a useful feature for optimizing your installation processes.

Managing symbolic links for versioned shared libraries

The target platform for your installation may use symbolic links to help linkers discover the currently installed version of a shared library. After creating a lib<name>.so symlink to the lib<name>.so.1 file, it's possible to link this library by passing the -l<name> argument to the linker.

CMake's install(TARGETS <target> LIBRARY) block handles the creation of such symlinks when needed. However, we may decide to move that step to another install() command by adding NAMELINK_SKIP to this block:

```
install(TARGETS <target> LIBRARY
        COMPONENT cmp NAMELINK_SKIP)
```

To assign symlinking to another component (instead of disabling it altogether), we can repeat the install() command for the same target and specify a different component, followed by the NAMELINK_ONLY keyword:

```
install(TARGETS <target> LIBRARY
        COMPONENT lnk NAMELINK_ONLY)
```

The same effect can be achieved with the NAMELINK_COMPONENT keyword:

```
install(TARGETS <target> LIBRARY
        COMPONENT cmp NAMELINK_COMPONENT lnk)
```

Now that we have configured automatic installation, we can provide pre-built artifacts for our users using the CPack tool, which is included with CMake.

Packaging with CPack

While building projects from source has its benefits, it can be time-consuming and complex, which isn't ideal for end users, especially non-developers. A more convenient distribution method is using binary packages, containing compiled artifacts and other necessary static files. CMake supports generating such packages with a command-line tool called cpack.

To generate a package, select an appropriate package generator for your target platform and package type. Don't confuse package generators with buildsystem generators like Unix Makefiles or Visual Studio.

The following table lists the available package generators:

Generator Name	Produced File Types	Platform
Archive	7Z, 7zip - (.7z) TBZ2 (.tar.bz2) TGZ (.tar.gz) TXZ (.tar.xz) TZ (.tar.Z) TZST (.tar.zst) ZIP (.zip)	Cross-platform
Bundle	macOs Bundle (.bundle)	macOS
Cygwin	Cygwin packages	Cygwin
DEB	Debian packages (.deb)	Linux
External	JSON (.json) file for 3rd party packagers	Cross-platform
FreeBSD	PKG (.pkg)	*BSD, Linux, macOS
IFW	QT installer binary	Linux, Windows, macOS
NSIS	Binary (.exe)	Windows
NuGet	NuGet package (.nupkg)	Windows
productbuild	PKG (.pkg)	macOS
RPM	RPM (.rpm)	Linux
WIX	Microsoft Installer (.msi)	Windows

Table 14.3: Available package generators

Most of these generators have extensive configurations. While it's beyond this book's scope to delve into all their details, you can find more information in the *Further reading* section. We'll focus on a general use case.

To use CPack, configure your project's installation with the necessary install() commands and build your project. The resulting cmake_install.cmake in the build tree is used by CPack to prepare binary packages based on the CPackConfig.cmake file. While you can create this file manually, using include(CPack) in your project's listfile is easier. It generates the configuration in the build tree and supplies default values where needed.

Let's extend the 13-components example for CPack use:

ch14/14-cpack/CMakeLists.txt (fragment)

```
cmake_minimum_required(VERSION 3.26)
project(CPackPackage VERSION 1.2.3 LANGUAGES CXX)
include(GNUInstallDirs)
add_subdirectory(src bin)
install(...)
install(...)
install(...)
set(CPACK_PACKAGE_VENDOR "Rafal Swidzinski")
set(CPACK_PACKAGE_CONTACT "email@example.com")
set(CPACK_PACKAGE_DESCRIPTION "Simple Calculator")
include(CPack)
```

The CPack module extracts the following variables from the project() command:

- CPACK_PACKAGE_NAME
- CPACK_PACKAGE_VERSION
- CPACK_PACKAGE_FILE_NAME

The CPACK_PACKAGE_FILE_NAME stores the structure of the package name:

```
$CPACK_PACKAGE_NAME-$CPACK_PACKAGE_VERSION-$CPACK_SYSTEM_NAME
```

Here, CPACK_SYSTEM_NAME is the target OS name, like Linux or win32. For example, by executing a ZIP generator on Debian, CPack will generate a file named CPackPackage-1.2.3-Linux.zip.

To generate packages after building your project, go to the build tree of your project and run:

```
cpack [<options>]
```

CPack reads options from the CPackConfig.cmake file, but you can override these settings:

- -G <generators>: Semicolon-separated list of package generators. The default value can be specified in the CPackConfig.cmake in the CPACK_GENERATOR variable.
- -C <configs>: Semicolon-separated list of build configurations (debug, release) to generate packages for (required for multi-configuration buildsystem generators).
- -D <var>=<value>: This overrides a variable that's set in the CPackConfig.cmake file.
- --config <config-file>: This uses a specified config file instead of the default CPackConfig.cmake.
- --verbose, -V: This provides verbose output.
- -P <packageName>: This overrides the package name.
- -R <packageVersion>: This overrides the package version.
- --vendor <vendorName>: This overrides the package vendor.
- -B <packageDirectory>: This specifies the output directory for cpack (by default, this will be the current working directory).

Let's try generating packages for our 14-cpack example project. We're going to use ZIP, 7Z, and the Debian package generator:

```
cpack -G "ZIP;7Z;DEB" -B packages
```

You should get these packages:

- CPackPackage-1.2.3-Linux.7z
- CPackPackage-1.2.3-Linux.deb
- CPackPackage-1.2.3-Linux.zip

These binary packages are ready for publication on your project's website, a GitHub release, or a package repository for end users.

Summary

Navigating the intricacies of writing cross-platform installation scripts can be daunting, but CMake significantly simplifies this task. Although it requires some initial setup, CMake streamlines the process, integrating seamlessly with the concepts and techniques we've explored throughout this book.

We began by understanding how to export CMake targets from projects, enabling their use in other projects without installation. This was followed by insights into installing projects that are already configured for export. Delving into installation basics, we focused on a crucial aspect: installing CMake targets. We now have a grasp of how CMake allocates different destinations for various artifact types and the special considerations for public headers. We also examined other modes of the install() command, encompassing the installation of files, programs, and directories, and executing scripts during installation.

Our journey then led us to CMake's reusable packages. We explored how to make project targets relocatable, facilitating user-defined installation locations. This included creating fully defined packages consumable via find_package(), entailing the preparation of *target export files*, *config files*, and *version files*. Acknowledging diverse user needs, we learned how to group artifacts and actions into installation components, distinguishing them from the components of CMake packages. Our exploration culminated in an introduction to CPack. We discovered how to prepare basic binary packages, offering an efficient method to distribute pre-compiled software. While mastering the nuances of installation and packaging in CMake is an ongoing journey, this chapter lays a robust foundation. It equips us to handle common scenarios and delve deeper with confidence.

In the next chapter, we'll apply our accumulated knowledge by crafting a cohesive, professional project, showcasing practical applications of these CMake techniques.

Further reading

- GNU coding standards for destinations:
  https://www.gnu.org/prep/standards/html_node/Directory-Variables.html

- Discussion on new public header management with the FILE_SET keyword:
  https://gitlab.kitware.com/cmake/cmake/-/issues/22468#note_991860

- How to install a shared library:
  https://tldp.org/HOWTO/Program-Library-HOWTO/shared-libraries.html

- Creating relocatable packages:
  https://cmake.org/cmake/help/latest/guide/importing-exporting/index.html#creating-relocatable-packages

- List of paths scanned by find_package() to find the config file:
  https://cmake.org/cmake/help/latest/command/find_package.html#config-mode-search-procedure

- Full documentation of CMakePackageConfigHelpers:
  https://cmake.org/cmake/help/latest/module/CMakePackageConfigHelpers.html

- CPack package generators:

  `https://cmake.org/cmake/help/latest/manual/cpack-generators.7.html`

- On preferred package generators for different platforms:

  `https://stackoverflow.com/a/46013099`

- CPack utility module documentation:

  `https://cmake.org/cmake/help/latest/module/CPack.html`

Join our community on Discord

Join our community's Discord space for discussions with the author and other readers:

`https://discord.com/invite/vXN53A7ZcA`

15

Creating Your Professional Project

We have gathered all the necessary knowledge to build professional projects, including structuring, building, dependency management, testing, analyzing, installing, and packaging. Now, it's time to apply these skills by creating a coherent, professional project. It's important to understand that even trivial programs benefit from automated quality checks and a seamless process that transforms raw code into a complete solution. It's true that implementing these checks and processes is a significant investment, as it requires many steps to set up everything correctly. This is especially true when adding these mechanisms to existing code bases, which are often large and complex. That's why it's beneficial to use CMake from the start and establish all the necessary processes early on. It's easier to configure and more efficient, as such quality controls and build automation will eventually need to be integrated into long-term projects anyway.

In this chapter, we will develop a new solution that is as small as possible, while making the most of the CMake practices we discussed in the book so far. To keep it simple, we will implement only a single practical function – adding two numbers. Such basic business code will allow us to focus on the build-related aspects of the project we learned in previous chapters. To tackle a more challenging problem related to building, this project will include both a library and an executable. The library will handle the internal business logic and be available as a CMake package for other projects. The executable, intended for end users, will provide a user interface demonstrating the library's functionality.

To sum that up, in this chapter, we're going to cover the following main topics:

- Planning our work

- Project layout
- Building and managing dependencies
- Testing and program analysis
- Installing and packaging
- Providing the documentation

Technical requirements

You can find the code files that are present in this chapter on GitHub at `https://github.com/PacktPublishing/Modern-CMake-for-Cpp-2E/tree/main/examples/ch15`.

To build the examples provided in this book, always use the recommended commands:

```
cmake -B <build tree> -S <source tree>
cmake --build <build tree>
```

Be sure to replace the placeholders `<build tree>` and `<source tree>` with appropriate paths. As a reminder: the **build tree** is the path to the target/output directory, and the **source tree** is the path at which your source code is located.

This chapter is compiled with GCC to provide compatibility between code coverage instrumentation with the `lcov` tool used to collect the results. If you want to compile with `llvm` or another toolchain, be sure to adapt the coverage processing as needed.

To run tests, execute the following command:

```
ctest --test-dir <build tree>
```

Or simply execute it from the build tree directory:

```
ctest
```

Note that, in this chapter, the tests will be outputted to the `test` subdirectory.

Planning our work

The software we'll be building in this chapter isn't meant to be extremely complex – we'll create a simple calculator that adds two numbers together (*Figure 15.1*). It will be a console application with a text user interface, utilizing a third-party library and a separate calculation library that could be used in other projects. Although this project may not have significant practical applications, its simplicity is perfect for demonstrating the application of various techniques discussed throughout the book.

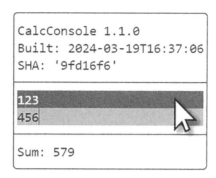

Figure 15.1: The text user interface of our project executed in a terminal with mouse support

Usually, projects either generate a user-facing executable or a library for developers. It's less common for projects to produce both, though it does happen. For instance, some applications come with standalone SDKs or libraries to help develop plugins. Another example is a library bundled with usage examples. Our project falls into the latter category, showcasing the library's functionalities.

We'll start planning by reviewing the chapter list, recalling the contents of each chapter, and selecting the techniques and tools described that we'll use to build our application:

- *Chapter 1, First Steps with CMake*:

  This chapter provided basic details about CMake, including installation and command-line usage for building projects. It also covered essential information about project files, such as their roles, typical naming conventions, and peculiarities.

- *Chapter 2, The CMake Language*:

  We introduced the necessary tools for writing correct CMake listfiles and scripts, covering code basics like comments, command invocations, and arguments. We explained variables, lists, and control structures, introducing several useful commands. This foundation will be crucial throughout our project.

- *Chapter 3, Using CMake in Popular IDEs*:

  We discussed three IDEs – CLion, VS Code, and Visual Studio IDE – highlighting their strengths. In our final project, choosing an IDE (or not) is up to you. Once decided, you can start this project in a Dev container to enjoy a fully prepared environment with just a few steps to build a Docker image (or just get it from the Docker Hub). Running the image in a container ensures that the development environment mirrors production.

- *Chapter 4, Setting Up Your First CMake Project*:

  Configuring the project is crucial as it determines the CMake policies that will be in effect, naming, versioning, and programming language. We'll use this chapter to influence the fundamental behavior of the build process.

  We'll also follow established project partitioning and structuring to determine the layout of directories and files, and utilize system discovery variables to adapt to different build environments. Toolchain configuration is another critical aspect that allows us to mandate a specific C++ version and the standards supported by the compiler. Following the chapter's advice, we will disable in-source builds to maintain a clean workspace.

- *Chapter 5, Working with Targets*:

  Here, we learned how every modern CMake project makes extensive use of targets. We'll, of course, apply targets as well to define a few libraries and executables (both for test and production) that will keep the project organized and ensure we comply with the principle of **DRY (Don't Repeat Yourself)**. The acquired knowledge of target properties and transitive usage requirements (propagated properties) will allow us to keep the configuration close to target definitions.

- *Chapter 6, Using Generator Expressions*:

  Generator expressions are heavily used throughout our project. We'll aim to keep these expressions as straightforward as possible. The project will incorporate custom commands to generate files for Valgrind and coverage reports. Additionally, we'll employ target hooks, specifically PRE_BUILD, to clean up the .gcda files that are produced by the coverage instrumentation process.

- *Chapter 7, Compiling C++ Sources with CMake*:

  There's no C++ project without compilation. The basics are quite simple, but CMake allows us to tweak this process in so many ways: extend the sources of a target, configure the optimizer, and provide debugging information. For this project, the default compilation flags will do just fine, but we'll go ahead and play a bit with the preprocessor:

  - We'll store build metadata (the project version, build time, and the Git commit SHA) in the compiled executable and show it to the user.
  - We'll enable the precompilation of headers. It's not really a necessity in such a small project, but it will help us practice this concept.

Unity builds won't be necessary – this project won't be big enough to make adding them worthwhile.

- *Chapter 8, Linking Executables and Libraries*:

We will obtain general information on linking, useful in any project by default. Additionally, since this project includes a library, we will explicitly reference some specific building instructions for the following:

  - Static libraries for testing and development
  - Shared libraries for release

This chapter also outlines how to isolate the `main()` function for testing purposes, a practice we will adopt.

- *Chapter 9, Managing Dependencies in CMake*:

To enhance the project's appeal, we will introduce an external dependency: a text-based UI library. *Chapter 9* explores various methods for managing dependencies. The choice will be simple: the `FetchContent` utility module is generally recommended and most convenient.

- *Chapter 10, Using C++20 Modules*:

Although we have explored the use of C++20 modules and the environment requirements to support this feature (CMake 3.28, latest compilers), its wide support is still lacking. To ensure the project's accessibility, we will not incorporate modules yet.

- *Chapter 11, Testing Frameworks*:

Implementing proper automated tests is imperative to ensuring the quality of our solution remains consistent over time. We will integrate CTest and organize our project to facilitate testing, applying the `main()` function separation mentioned previously.

This chapter discusses two testing frameworks: Catch2 and GTest with GMock; we will use the latter. To obtain detailed information on our coverage, we will generate HTML reports with LCOV.

- *Chapter 12, Program Analysis Tools*:

For static analysis, we can select from a range of tools: Clang-Tidy, Cpplint, Cppcheck, include-what-you-use, and link-what-you-use. We will opt for Cppcheck, as Clang-Tidy is less compatible with precompiled headers built using GCC.

Dynamic analysis will be conducted using Valgrind's Memcheck tool, complemented by the Memcheck-cover wrapper to produce HTML reports. Additionally, our source code will be automatically formatted during the build process with ClangFormat.

- *Chapter 13, Generating Documentation:*

  Providing documentation is essential when offering a library as part of our project. CMake facilitates the automation of documentation generation using Doxygen. We will adopt this approach in a refreshed design by incorporating the doxygen-awesome-css theme.

- *Chapter 14, Installing and Packaging*:

  Finally, we'll configure the installation and packaging of our solution and prepare files to form the package as described, along with target definitions. We'll install that and the artifacts from build targets to appropriate directories by including the GNUInstallDirs module. We will additionally configure a few components to modularize the solution and prepare it for use with CPack.

Professional projects also come with a few text files: README, LICENSE, INSTALL, and so on. We will briefly cover these at the end of the chapter.

To make things simpler, we won't implement custom logic that checks whether all the required utilities and dependencies are available. We'll rely on CMake to show its diagnostics and tell users what's missing. If your projects get significant traction, you might want to consider adding these mechanisms to improve the user experience.

Having formed a clear plan, let's discuss how to actually structure the project, both in terms of logical targets and directory structure.

Project layout

To build any project, we should start with a clear understanding of what logical targets are going to be created within it. In this case, we'll follow the structure shown in the following figure:

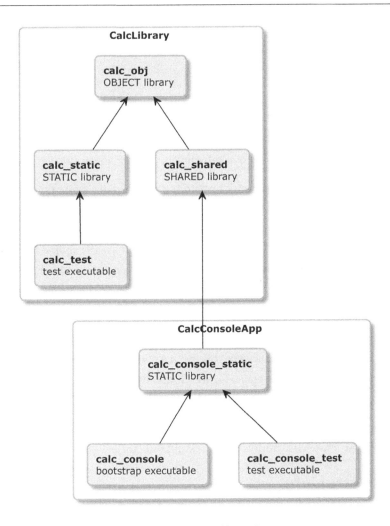

Figure 15.2: A structure of logical targets

Let's explore the structure by following the build order. First, we compile `calc_obj`, an **object library**. For a refresher on object libraries, please check *Chapter 5, Working with Targets*. We should then turn our attention to **static libraries** and **shared libraries**.

Shared libraries versus static libraries

In *Chapter 8, Linking Executables and Libraries*, we introduced both shared and static libraries. We noted that shared libraries can reduce overall memory usage when multiple programs use the same library. Also, it's common for users to already have popular libraries installed or to know how to install them quickly.

More importantly, **shared libraries** are separate files that must be placed in specific paths for the dynamic linker to locate them. In contrast, **static libraries** are embedded directly into the executable file, which leads to faster usage as there are no additional steps required to locate the code in memory.

As library authors, we can decide whether we're providing a static or a shared version of the library, or we can simply ship both versions and leave this decision to the programmer using our library in their project. Since we're exercising our knowledge, we will deliver two versions.

The `calc_test` target, which includes unit tests to verify the library's core functionality, will utilize the static library. Although we are building both types of libraries from the same *object files*, testing with either library type is acceptable since their functionalities should be identical. The console app associated with `calc_console_static` target will use the shared library. This target also links against an external dependency, the Functional Terminal (X) User Interface (FTXUI) library by Arthur Sonzogni (there is a link to the GitHub project in the *Further reading* section).

The last two targets, `calc_console` and `calc_console_test`, are designed to tackle a common issue in testing executables: the clash of multiple entry points provided by both the test frameworks and the executables. To circumvent this, we have intentionally isolated the `main()` function into a bootstrap target, `calc_console`, which merely invokes the primary function from `calc_console_static`.

With an understanding of the necessary targets and their interrelations, our next step is to organize the project's structure with appropriate files and directories.

Project file structure

The project consists of two key elements: the `calc` libraries and the `calc_console` executable. To organize our project effectively, we will employ the following directory structure:

- `src` contains sources for all released targets and library header files.
- `test` contains tests for the above libraries and executables.
- `cmake` contains utility modules and helper files used by CMake to build and install the project.
- *root directory* contains top-level configuration and documentation files.

This structure (shown in *Figure 15.3*) ensures a clear separation of concerns, facilitating easier navigation and maintenance of the project:

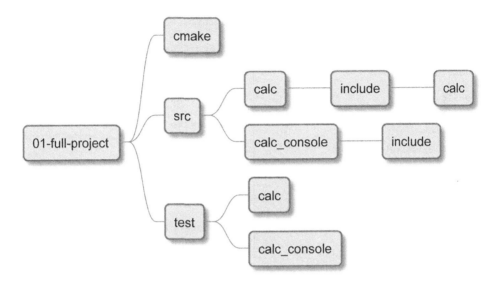

Figure 15.3: The directory structure of the project

Here's the full list of files in each of the four main directories:

Root directory	./test
CHANGELOG	CMakeLists.txt
CMakeLists.txt	**calc/CMakeLists.txt**
INSTALL	calc/calc_test.cpp
LICENSE	calc_console/CMakeLists.txt
README.md	calc_console/tui_test.cpp
./src	**./cmake**

CMakeLists.txt	BuildInfo.cmake
calc/CMakeLists.txt	Coverage.cmake
calc/CalcConfig.cmake	CppCheck.cmake
calc/basic.cpp	Doxygen.cmake
calc/include/calc/basic.h	Format.cmake
calc_console/CMakeLists.txt	GetFTXUI.cmake
calc_console/bootstrap.cpp	Packaging.cmake
calc_console/include/tui.h	Memcheck.cmake
calc_console/tui.cpp	NoInSourceBuilds.cmake
	Testing.cmake
	buildinfo.h.in
	doxygen_extra_headers

Table 15.1: File structure of the project

While it may appear that CMake introduces considerable overhead, with the cmake directory initially containing more content than the actual business code, this dynamic will shift as the project expands in functionality. The initial effort to establish a clean and organized project structure is substantial, but rest assured, this investment will yield significant benefits in the future.

We'll go through all the files mentioned in *Table 15.1* throughout the chapter and see in detail what they do and what role they play in the project. This will happen in four steps: building, testing, installing, and providing documentation.

Building and managing dependencies

All build processes follow the same procedure. We begin with the top-level listfile and progress downward through the project's source tree. *Figure 15.4* illustrates the project files involved in the build process, with numbers in parentheses indicating the order of CMake script execution.

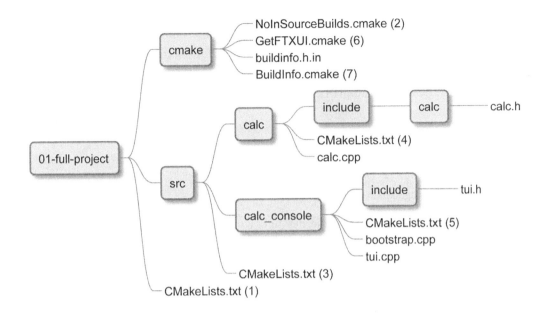

Figure 15.4: Files used in the build stage

The top-level CMakeLists.txt (1) listfile configures the project:

ch15/01-full-project/CMakeLists.txt

```
cmake_minimum_required(VERSION 3.26)
project(Calc VERSION 1.1.0 LANGUAGES CXX)
list(APPEND CMAKE_MODULE_PATH "${CMAKE_SOURCE_DIR}/cmake")

include(NoInSourceBuilds)

include(CTest)

add_subdirectory(src bin)
add_subdirectory(test)

include(Packaging)
```

We start by specifying essential project details and setting the path to the CMake utility modules (the cmake directory in our project). We then prevent in-source builds using a custom module. Following that, we enable testing with the CTest module (built into CMake). This should be done at the project's root level because this command creates the CTestTestfile.cmake file in the binary tree relative to its location in the source tree. Placing it elsewhere would prevent ctest from finding it.

Next, we include two key directories:

- src, containing the project source (to be named bin in the build tree)
- test, containing all the testing utilities

Finally, we include the Packaging module, details of which will be discussed in the *Installing and packaging* section.

Let's examine the NoInSourceBuilds utility module to understand its function:

ch15/01-full-project/cmake/NoInSourceBuilds.cmake

```
if(PROJECT_SOURCE_DIR STREQUAL PROJECT_BINARY_DIR)
  message(FATAL_ERROR
    "\n"
    "In-source builds are not allowed.\n"
    "Instead, provide a path to build tree like so:\n"
    "cmake -B <destination>\n"
    "\n"
    "To remove files you accidentally created execute:\n"
    "rm -rf CMakeFiles CMakeCache.txt\n"
  )
endif()
```

No surprises here, we check if the user has provided a separate destination directory for generated files using the cmake command. It must differ from the project's source tree path. If not, we instruct the user on how to specify it and how to clean up the repository if they made a mistake.

Our top-level listfile then includes the src subdirectory, instructing CMake to process the listfile within it:

ch15/01-full-project/src/CMakeLists.txt

```
include(Coverage)
include(Format)
```

```
include(CppCheck)
include(Doxygen)

add_subdirectory(calc)
add_subdirectory(calc_console)
```

This file is straightforward – it includes all the modules from the ./cmake directory we will be using and directs CMake to the nested directories to execute the listfiles found there.

Next, let's examine the listfile for the calc library. It's somewhat complex, so we'll break it down and discuss it in sections.

Building the Calc library

The listfile in the calc directory configures various aspects of this library but, for now, we'll focus only on the building:

ch15/01-full-project/src/calc/CMakeLists.txt (fragment)

```
add_library(calc_obj OBJECT basic.cpp)
target_sources(calc_obj
                PUBLIC FILE_SET HEADERS
                BASE_DIRS include
                FILES include/calc/basic.h
)
set_target_properties(calc_obj PROPERTIES
    POSITION_INDEPENDENT_CODE 1
)

# ... instrumentation of calc_obj for coverage

add_library(calc_shared SHARED)
target_link_libraries(calc_shared calc_obj)

add_library(calc_static STATIC)
target_link_libraries(calc_static calc_obj)

# ... testing and program analysis modules
# ... documentation generation
# ... installation
```

We define three targets:

- `calc_obj`, an *object library* compiling the `basic.cpp` implementation file. Its `basic.h` header file is included using the `FILE_SET` keyword in the `target_sources()` command. This implicitly configures appropriate include directories to be exported correctly for both building and installation modes. By creating an *object library*, we prevent redundant compilation for the two library versions, but it's essential to enable `POSITION_INDEPENDENT_CODE` so that the shared library can depend on this target.
- `calc_shared`, a shared library that depends on `calc_obj`.
- `calc_static`, a static library that also depends on `calc_obj`.

For context, here's the C++ header for the basic library. This header file simply declares two functions within the `Calc` namespace, which helps avoid name collisions:

ch15/01-full-project/src/calc/include/calc/basic.h

```
#pragma once
namespace Calc {
    int Add(int a, int b);
    int Subtract(int a, int b);
}  // namespace Calc
```

The implementation file is straightforward as well:

ch15/01-full-project/src/calc/basic.cpp

```
namespace Calc {
  int Add(int a, int b) {
    return a + b;
  }

  int Subtract(int a, int b) {
    return a - b;
  }
} // namespace Calc
```

This wraps up the explanation of files in the `src/calc` directory. Next up is the `src/calc_console` and building the executable of the console calculator using this library.

Building the Calc console executable

The calc_console directory contains several files: a listfile, two implementation files (the business logic and a bootstrap file), and a header file. The listfile looks as follows:

ch15/01-full-project/src/calc_console/CMakeLists.txt (fragment)

```
add_library(calc_console_static STATIC tui.cpp)
target_include_directories(calc_console_static PUBLIC include)
target_precompile_headers(calc_console_static PUBLIC <string>)

include(GetFTXUI)
target_link_libraries(calc_console_static PUBLIC calc_shared
                      ftxui::screen ftxui::dom ftxui::component)

include(BuildInfo)
BuildInfo(calc_console_static)

# ... instrumentation of calc_console_static for coverage
# ... testing and program analysis modules
# ... documentation generation

add_executable(calc_console bootstrap.cpp)
target_link_libraries(calc_console calc_console_static)

# ... installation
```

Though the listfile appears complex, as seasoned CMake users, we can now easily decipher its contents:

1. Define the calc_console_static target, containing the business code without the main() function to allow linking with GTest, which has its own entry point.
2. Configure the *include directories*. We could add headers individually with FILE_SET, but since they are internal, we simplify this step.
3. Implement header precompilation, here demonstrated with just the <string> header as an example, though larger projects might include many more.
4. Include a custom CMake module to fetch the FTXUI dependency.
5. Link the business code with the shared calc_shared library and the FTXUI components.

6. Add a custom module to generate build information and embed it into the artifact.

7. Outline additional steps for this target: coverage instrumentation, testing, program analysis, and documentation.

8. Create and link the `calc_console` bootstrap executable, establishing the entry point.

9. Outline the installation.

We will explore testing, documentation, and installation processes in their respective sections later in this chapter.

We're including the `GetFTXUI` utility module rather than looking for `config-module` in the system because it's not very likely that most users have it installed. We'll just fetch and build it:

ch15/01-full-project/cmake/GetFTXUI.cmake

```
include(FetchContent)
FetchContent_Declare(
FTXTUI
GIT_REPOSITORY https://github.com/ArthurSonzogni/FTXUI.git
GIT_TAG        v0.11
)
option(FTXUI_ENABLE_INSTALL "" OFF)
option(FTXUI_BUILD_EXAMPLES "" OFF)
option(FTXUI_BUILD_DOCS "" OFF)
FetchContent_MakeAvailable(FTXTUI)
```

We're using the recommended `FetchContent` method, described in detail in *Chapter 9, Managing Dependencies in CMake*. The only unusual addition is the calls of the `option()` command, which lets us bypass the lengthy build steps for FTXUI and prevents its installation steps from affecting this project's installation process. For more details, refer to the *Further reading* section.

The listfile for the `calc_console` directory includes another custom utility module that is build-related: `BuildInfo`. This module will capture three pieces of information to be displayed in the executable:

*   The current Git commit SHA
*   The build timestamp
*   The project version specified in the top-level listfile

As we learned in *Chapter 7, Compiling C++ Sources with CMake*, CMake can capture build-time values and pass them to C++ code via template files, for example, with a struct:

ch15/01-full-project/cmake/buildinfo.h.in

```
struct BuildInfo {
  static inline const std::string CommitSHA = "@COMMIT_SHA@";
  static inline const std::string Timestamp = "@TIMESTAMP@";
  static inline const std::string Version = "@PROJECT_VERSION@";
};
```

To fill that structure during the configuration stage, we'll use the following code:

ch15/01-full-project/cmake/BuildInfo.cmake

```
set(BUILDINFO_TEMPLATE_DIR ${CMAKE_CURRENT_LIST_DIR})
set(DESTINATION "${CMAKE_CURRENT_BINARY_DIR}/buildinfo")
string(TIMESTAMP TIMESTAMP)

find_program(GIT_PATH git REQUIRED)
execute_process(COMMAND ${GIT_PATH} log --pretty=format:'%h' -n 1
                OUTPUT_VARIABLE COMMIT_SHA)

configure_file(
  "${BUILDINFO_TEMPLATE_DIR}/buildinfo.h.in"
  "${DESTINATION}/buildinfo.h" @ONLY
)

function(BuildInfo target)
  target_include_directories(${target} PRIVATE ${DESTINATION})
endfunction()
```

After including the module, we have set variables to capture the desired information and use `configure_file()` to generate `buildinfo.h`. The final step was to invoke the `BuildInfo` function to include the generated file's directory in the target's `include` directories.

The produced header file can be then shared with multiple different consumers if needed. In such a case, you'll probably want to add `include_guard(GLOBAL)` at the top of the listfile to avoid running the `git` command for every target.

Before looking into the implementation of the console calculator, I'd like to emphasize that you don't need to deeply understand the intricacies of the `tui.cpp` file or the FXTUI library, as this isn't essential for our purposes. Instead, let's focus on the highlighted parts of the code:

ch15/01-full-project/src/calc_console/tui.cpp

```cpp
#include "tui.h"
#include <ftxui/dom/elements.hpp>
#include "buildinfo.h"
#include "calc/basic.h"

using namespace ftxui;
using namespace std;

string a{"12"}, b{"90"};
auto input_a = Input(&a, "");
auto input_b = Input(&b, "");
auto component = Container::Vertical({input_a, input_b});

Component getTui() {
  return Renderer(component, [&] {
    auto sum = Calc::Add(stoi(a), stoi(b));
    return vbox({
      text("CalcConsole " + BuildInfo::Version),
      text("Built: " + BuildInfo::Timestamp),
      text("SHA: " + BuildInfo::CommitSHA),
      separator(),
      input_a->Render(),
      input_b->Render(),
      separator(),
      text("Sum: " + to_string(sum)),
    }) |
    border;
  });
}
```

This piece of code provides the getTui() function, which returns a ftxui::Component, an object that encapsulates interactive UI elements like labels, text fields, separators, and a border. For those curious about the detailed workings of these elements, further materials are available in the *Further reading* section.

More importantly, the *include directives* link to the headers from the calc_obj target and the BuildInfo module. The interaction begins with the lambda function, invoking Calc::Sum, and displaying the result using the text() function.

The values from the buildinfo.h collected at build time are used in a similar way and will be shown to the user at runtime.

Alongside tui.cpp, there's a header file:

ch15/01-full-project/src/calc_console/include/tui.h

```
#include <ftxui/component/component.hpp>
ftxui::Component getTui();
```

This header is used by the bootstrap file in the calc_console target:

ch15/01-full-project/src/calc_console/bootstrap.cpp

```
#include <ftxui/component/screen_interactive.hpp>

#include "tui.h"

int main(int argc, char** argv) {
  ftxui::ScreenInteractive::FitComponent().Loop(getTui());
}
```

This brief code initializes an interactive console screen with FTXUI, displaying the Component object from getTui() and handling keyboard inputs in a loop. With all files in the src directory addressed, we can now progress to testing and analyzing the program.

Testing and program analysis

Program analysis and testing are essential components that work together to ensure the quality of our solutions. For instance, using Valgrind is more effective when running test code (because of its consistency and coverage). Therefore, we will configure testing and program analysis in the same place. *Figure 15.5* illustrates the execution flow and files needed to set them up:

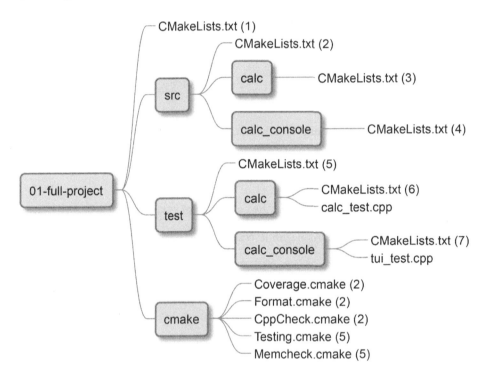

Figure 15.5: Files used to enable testing and program analysis

The numbers in parentheses represent the sequence in which listfiles are processed. Start from the top-level listfile and add the src and test directories:

- In src, include Coverage, Format, and CppCheck modules, and add the src/calc and src/calc_console directories.
- In src/calc, define targets and configure them with included modules.
- In src/calc_console, define targets and configure them with included modules.
- In test, include Testing (which includes Memcheck) and add the test/calc and test/calc_console directories.

- In test/calc, define test targets and configure them with included modules.
- In test/calc_console, define test targets and configure them with included modules.

Let's examine the listfile for the test directory:

ch15/01-full-project/test/CMakeLists.txt

```
include(Testing)
add_subdirectory(calc)
add_subdirectory(calc_console)
```

At this level, the Testing utility module is included to provide functionality for both target groups (from the calc and calc_console directories):

ch15/01-full-project/cmake/Testing.cmake (fragment)

```
include(FetchContent)
FetchContent_Declare(
  googletest
  GIT_REPOSITORY https://github.com/google/googletest.git
  GIT_TAG v1.14.0
)
# For Windows: Prevent overriding the parent project's
# compiler/linker settings
set(gtest_force_shared_crt ON CACHE BOOL "" FORCE)
option(INSTALL_GMOCK "Install GMock" OFF)
option(INSTALL_GTEST "Install GTest" OFF)
FetchContent_MakeAvailable(googletest)

# ...
```

We enabled testing and included the FetchContent module to obtain GTest and GMock. Although GMock isn't used in this project, it's included with GTest in the same repository, so we configure it as well. The key configuration step is preventing the installation of these frameworks from affecting our project's installation by using the option() command.

In the same file, we define an AddTests() function to facilitate comprehensive testing of business targets:

ch15/01-full-project/cmake/Testing.cmake (continued)

```
# ...
include(GoogleTest)
include(Coverage)
include(Memcheck)
macro(AddTests target)
  message("Adding tests to ${target}")
  target_link_libraries(${target} PRIVATE gtest_main gmock)
  gtest_discover_tests(${target})
  AddCoverage(${target})
  AddMemcheck(${target})
endmacro()
```

First, we include the necessary modules: GoogleTest is bundled with CMake, and Coverage and Memcheck are custom utility modules included in the project. The AddTests macro is then provided to prepare a target for testing, applying coverage instrumentation, and memory checking. The AddCoverage() and AddMemcheck() functions are defined in their respective utility modules. Now, we can proceed to implement them.

Preparing the Coverage module

Adding coverage across various targets involves several steps. The Coverage module provides a function that defines the coverage target for a specified target:

ch15/01-full-project/cmake/Coverage.cmake (fragment)

```
function(AddCoverage target)
  find_program(LCOV_PATH lcov REQUIRED)
  find_program(GENHTML_PATH genhtml REQUIRED)
  add_custom_target(coverage-${target}
    COMMAND ${LCOV_PATH} -d . --zerocounters
    COMMAND $<TARGET_FILE:${target}>
    COMMAND ${LCOV_PATH} -d . --capture -o coverage.info
    COMMAND ${LCOV_PATH} -r coverage.info '/usr/include/*'
      -o filtered.info
    COMMAND ${GENHTML_PATH} -o coverage-${target}
```

```
        filtered.info --legend
     COMMAND rm -rf coverage.info filtered.info
     WORKING_DIRECTORY ${CMAKE_BINARY_DIR}
   )
endfunction()

# ...
```

This implementation differs slightly from the one introduced in *Chapter 11, Testing Frameworks*, as it now includes the target name in the output path to prevent name conflicts. Next, we need a function to clear previous coverage results:

ch15/01-full-project/cmake/Coverage.cmake (continued)

```
# ...

function(CleanCoverage target)
  add_custom_command(TARGET ${target} PRE_BUILD COMMAND
    find ${CMAKE_BINARY_DIR} -type f
    -name '*.gcda' -exec rm {} +)
endfunction()

# ...
```

Additionally, we have a function to prepare a target for coverage analysis:

ch15/01-full-project/cmake/Coverage.cmake (fragment)

```
# ...

function(InstrumentForCoverage target)
  if (CMAKE_BUILD_TYPE STREQUAL Debug)
target_compile_options(${target}
                       PRIVATE --coverage -fno-inline)
    target_link_options(${target} PUBLIC --coverage)
  endif()
endfunction()
```

The InstrumentForCoverage() function is applied to src/calc and src/calc_console, enabling the generation of the coverage data files when targets calc_obj and calc_console_static are executed.

To generate reports for both test targets, execute the following cmake commands after configuring the project with the Debug build type:

```
cmake --build <build-tree> -t coverage-calc_test
cmake --build <build-tree> -t coverage-calc_console_test
```

Next, we want to perform dynamic program analysis on multiple targets we defined, so to apply the Memcheck module, introduced in *Chapter 12, Program Analysis Tools*, we need to tweak it slightly to scan more than one target.

Preparing the Memcheck module

The generation of Valgrind memory management reports is initiated by AddTests(). We begin the Memcheck module with its initial setup:

ch15/01-full-project/cmake/Memcheck.cmake (fragment)

```
include(FetchContent)
FetchContent_Declare(
  memcheck-cover
  GIT_REPOSITORY https://github.com/Farigh/memcheck-cover.git
  GIT_TAG        release-1.2
)
FetchContent_MakeAvailable(memcheck-cover)
```

This code is already familiar to us. Now, let's examine the function that creates the necessary targets for generating reports:

ch15/01-full-project/cmake/Memcheck.cmake (continued)

```
function(AddMemcheck target)
  set(MEMCHECK_PATH ${memcheck-cover_SOURCE_DIR}/bin)
  set(REPORT_PATH "${CMAKE_BINARY_DIR}/valgrind-${target}")

  add_custom_target(memcheck-${target}
    COMMAND ${MEMCHECK_PATH}/memcheck_runner.sh -o
      "${REPORT_PATH}/report"
      -- $<TARGET_FILE:${target}>
    COMMAND ${MEMCHECK_PATH}/generate_html_report.sh
      -i ${REPORT_PATH}
      -o ${REPORT_PATH}
```

```
        WORKING_DIRECTORY ${CMAKE_BINARY_DIR}
    )
endfunction()
```

We slightly improved the AddMemcheck() function from *Chapter 12* to handle multiple targets. We made the REPORT_PATH variable target-specific.

To generate Memcheck reports, use the following commands (note that generating reports is more effective when using the Debug build type for configuration):

```
cmake --build <build-tree> -t memcheck-calc_test
cmake --build <build-tree> -t memcheck-calc_console_test
```

Okay, we defined our Coverage and Memcheck modules (they are used in the Testing module), so let's see how the actual test targets are configured.

Applying testing scenarios

To implement testing, we'll follow this scenario:

1. Write unit tests.
2. Define and configure executable targets for tests with AddTests().
3. Instrument the **Software Under Test (SUT)** to enable coverage collection.
4. Ensure that coverage data is cleared between the builds to prevent segmentation faults.

Let's start with the unit tests we have to write. To keep things brief, we'll provide the simplest (and perhaps a bit incomplete) unit tests possible. First, test the library:

ch15/01-full-project/test/calc/basic_test.cpp

```cpp
#include "calc/basic.h"
#include <gtest/gtest.h>

TEST(CalcTest, SumAddsTwoInts) {
  EXPECT_EQ(4, Calc::Add(2, 2));
}

TEST(CalcTest, SubtractsTwoInts) {
  EXPECT_EQ(6, Calc::Subtract(8, 2));
}
```

Follow with the tests for the console – for this purpose, we'll use the FXTUI library. Again, understanding the source code completely isn't necessary; these tests are for illustrative purposes:

ch15/01-full-project/test/calc_console/tui_test.cpp

```cpp
#include "tui.h"

#include <gmock/gmock.h>
#include <gtest/gtest.h>

#include <ftxui/screen/screen.hpp>

using namespace ::ftxui;

TEST(ConsoleCalcTest, RunWorksWithDefaultValues) {
  auto component = getTui();
  auto document = component->Render();
  auto screen = Screen::Create(Dimension::Fit(document));
  Render(screen, document);
  auto output = screen.ToString();
  ASSERT_THAT(output, testing::HasSubstr("Sum: 102"));
}
```

This test renders the UI to a static `Screen` object and checks if the string output contains the expected sum. Not really a great test, but at least it's a short one.

Now, let's configure our tests with two nested listfiles. First, for the library:

ch15/01-full-project/test/calc/CMakeLists.txt

```cmake
add_executable(calc_test basic_test.cpp)
target_link_libraries(calc_test PRIVATE calc_static)
AddTests(calc_test)
```

And then for the executable:

ch15/01-full-project/test/calc_console/CMakeLists.txt

```cmake
add_executable(calc_console_test tui_test.cpp)
target_link_libraries(calc_console_test
                      PRIVATE calc_console_static)
AddTests(calc_console_test)
```

These configurations enable CTest to execute the tests. We also need to prepare the business logic targets for coverage analysis and ensure that the coverage data is refreshed between builds.

Let's add the necessary instructions to the calc library target:

ch15/01-full-project/src/calc/CMakeLists.txt (continued)

```
# ... calc_obj target definition

InstrumentForCoverage(calc_obj)

# ... calc_shared target definition
# ... calc_static target definition

CleanCoverage(calc_static)
```

Instrumentation is added to the calc_obj with the extra --coverage flag, but CleanCoverage() is called for the calc_static target. Normally, you'd apply it on the calc_obj for consistency, but we're using the PRE_BUILD keyword in CleanCoverage(), and CMake doesn't allow PRE_BUILD, PRE_LINK, or POST_BUILD hooks to the object libraries.

Finally, we'll instrument and clean the console target as well:

ch15/01-full-project/src/calc_console/CMakeLists.txt (continued)

```
# ... calc_console_test target definition
# ... BuildInfo

InstrumentForCoverage(calc_console_static)
CleanCoverage(calc_console_static)
```

With these steps, CTest is now set up to run our tests and collect coverage. Next, we'll add instructions for enabling static analysis, as we want our project to be of high quality during the first build and all of the subsequent builds.

Adding static analysis tools

We're nearing the completion of configuring quality assurance for our targets. The final step involves enabling automatic formatting and integrating CppCheck:

ch15/01-full-project/src/calc/CMakeLists.txt (continued)

```
# ... calc_static target definition
```

```
# ... Coverage instrumentation and cleaning

Format(calc_static .)

AddCppCheck(calc_obj)
```

We face a minor issue here: `calc_obj` cannot have a `PRE_BUILD` hook, so we apply formatting to `calc_static` instead. We also make sure that the `calc_console_static` target is formatted and checked:

ch15/01-full-project/src/calc_console/CMakeLists.cmake (continued)

```
# ... calc_console_test target definition
# ... BuildInfo
# ... Coverage instrumentation and cleaning

Format(calc_console_static .)

AddCppCheck(calc_console_static)
```

We still need to define the `Format` and `CppCheck` functions. Starting with `Format()`, we're borrowing the code described in *Chapter 12, Program Analysis Tools*:

ch15/01-full-project/cmake/Format.cmake

```
function(Format target directory)
  find_program(CLANG-FORMAT_PATH clang-format REQUIRED)
  set(EXPRESSION h hpp hh c cc cxx cpp)
  list(TRANSFORM EXPRESSION PREPEND "${directory}/*.")
  file(GLOB_RECURSE SOURCE_FILES FOLLOW_SYMLINKS
    LIST_DIRECTORIES false ${EXPRESSION}
  )
  add_custom_command(TARGET ${target} PRE_BUILD COMMAND
    ${CLANG-FORMAT_PATH} -i --style=file ${SOURCE_FILES}
  )
endfunction()
```

To integrate `CppCheck` with our sources, we use:

ch15/01-full-project/cmake/CppCheck.cmake

```
function(AddCppCheck target)
```

```
  find_program(CPPCHECK_PATH cppcheck REQUIRED)
  set_target_properties(${target}
    PROPERTIES CXX_CPPCHECK
    "${CPPCHECK_PATH};--enable=warning;--error-exitcode=10"
  )
endfunction()
```

This is simple and convenient. You may see some resemblance to the Clang-Tidy module (from *Chapter 12, Program Analysis Tools*) showcasing CMake's consistency in functionality.

The arguments for cppcheck are as follows:

- --enable=warning: Activates warning messages. To enable additional checks, refer to the Cppcheck manual (see the *Further reading* section).
- --error-exitcode=1: Sets the error code returned when cppcheck detects an issue. This can be any number from 1 to 255 (as 0 indicates success), although some numbers can be reserved by the system.

With all files in the src and test directories created, our solution is now buildable and fully tested. We can proceed to the installation and packaging steps.

Installing and packaging

Figure 15.6 shows where we'll configure our project for installation and packaging:

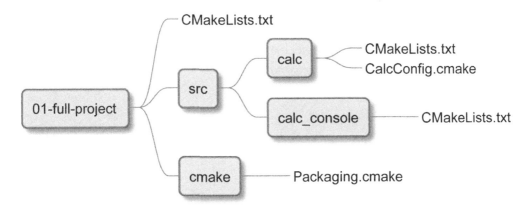

Figure 15.6: File configuring installation and packaging

The top-level listfile includes the `Packaging` utility module:

ch15/01-full-project/CMakeLists.txt (fragment)

```
# ... configure project
# ... enable testing
# ... include src and test subdirectories


include(Packaging)
```

The `Packaging` module details the package configuration for the project, which we will explore in the *Packaging with CPack* section. Our focus now is on installing three main components:

- The Calc library artifacts: static and shared libraries, header files, and target export files
- The package definition config file for the Calc library
- The Calc console executable

Everything is planned, so it's time to configure the installation of the library.

Installation of the library

To install the library, we start by defining logical targets and their artifact destinations, utilizing the `GNUInstallDirs` module's default values to avoid manual path specification. Artifacts will be grouped into components. The default installation will install all files, but you may choose to only install the `runtime` component and skip the development artifacts:

ch15/01-full-project/src/calc/CMakeLists.txt (continued)

```
# ... calc library targets definition
# ... configuration, testing, program analysis


# Installation
include(GNUInstallDirs)
install(TARGETS calc_obj calc_shared calc_static
  EXPORT CalcLibrary
  ARCHIVE COMPONENT development
  LIBRARY COMPONENT runtime
  FILE_SET HEADERS COMPONENT runtime
)
```

For UNIX systems, we also configure post-installation registration of the shared library with ldconfig:

ch15/01-full-project/src/calc/CMakeLists.txt (continued)

```
if (UNIX)
  install(CODE "execute_process(COMMAND ldconfig)"
    COMPONENT runtime
  )
endif()
```

To enable reusability in other CMake projects, we'll package the library by generating and installing a target export file and a config file that references it:

ch15/01-full-project/src/calc/CMakeLists.txt (continued)

```
install(EXPORT CalcLibrary
  DESTINATION ${CMAKE_INSTALL_LIBDIR}/calc/cmake
  NAMESPACE Calc::
  COMPONENT runtime
)

install(FILES "CalcConfig.cmake"
  DESTINATION ${CMAKE_INSTALL_LIBDIR}/calc/cmake
)
```

For simplicity, the CalcConfig.cmake file is kept minimal:

ch15/01-full-project/src/calc/CalcConfig.cmake

```
include("${CMAKE_CURRENT_LIST_DIR}/CalcLibrary.cmake")
```

This file is located in src/calc since it only includes the library targets. If there were target definitions from other directories, like calc_console, you would typically place CalcConfig.cmake in the top-level or src directory.

Now, the library is prepared to be installed with the cmake --install command after building the project. However, we still need to configure the installation of the executable.

Installation of the executable

We, of course, want our users to be able to enjoy the executable in their system, so we will install it with CMake. Preparing the installation of the binary executable is straightforward; to achieve it, we only need to include GNUInstallDirs and use a single install() command:

ch15/01-full-project/src/calc_console/CMakeLists.txt (continued)

```
# ... calc_console_static definition
# ... configuration, testing, program analysis
# ... calc_console bootstrap executable definition

# Installation
include(GNUInstallDirs)
install(TARGETS calc_console
  RUNTIME COMPONENT runtime
)
```

With that, the executable is set to be installed. Now, let's proceed to packaging.

Packaging with CPack

We could go wild and configure a vast multitude of supported package types; for this project, however, a basic configuration will be enough:

ch15/01-full-project/cmake/Packaging.cmake

```
# CPack configuration
set(CPACK_PACKAGE_VENDOR "Rafal Swidzinski")
set(CPACK_PACKAGE_CONTACT "email@example.com")
set(CPACK_PACKAGE_DESCRIPTION "Simple Calculator")
include(CPack)
```

Such a minimal setup works well for standard archives, such as ZIP files. To test the installation and packaging processes after building the project, use the following command within the build tree:

```
# cpack -G TGZ -B packages
CPack: Create package using TGZ
CPack: Install projects
CPack: - Run preinstall target for: Calc
CPack: - Install project: Calc []
CPack: Create package
```

```
CPack: - package: .../packages/Calc-1.0.0-Linux.tar.gz generated.
```

This concludes the installation and packaging; the next order of business is documentation.

Providing the documentation

The final touch to a professional project is the documentation. Undocumented projects are very difficult to navigate and understand when working in teams and when shared with external audiences. I would even go as far as saying that programmers often read their own documentation after stepping away from a specific file to understand what is happening inside.

Documentation is also important for legal and compliance reasons and to inform the users how to act with the software. If time permits, we should invest in setting up documentation for our project.

Documentation usually falls into two categories:

- Technical documentation (covering interfaces, designs, classes, and files)
- General documentation (encompassing all other non-technical documents)

As we saw in *Chapter 13, Generating Documentation*, much of the technical documentation can be automatically generated with CMake using Doxygen.

Generating the technical documentation

While some projects generate documentation during the build phase and include it in the package, we've chosen not to do so for this project. However, there could be valid reasons to opt otherwise, like if the documentation needs to be hosted online.

Figure 15.7 provides an overview of the documentation generation process:

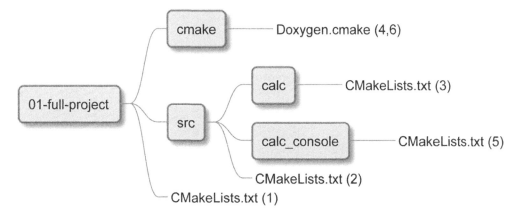

Figure 15.7: Files used to generate documentation

To generate documentation, we'll create another CMake utility module, Doxygen. Start by using the Doxygen find-module and download the doxygen-awesome-css project for themes:

ch15/01-full-project/cmake/Doxygen.cmake (fragment)

```
find_package(Doxygen REQUIRED)

include(FetchContent)
FetchContent_Declare(doxygen-awesome-css
  GIT_REPOSITORY
    https://github.com/jothepro/doxygen-awesome-css.git
  GIT_TAG
    v2.3.1
)
FetchContent_MakeAvailable(doxygen-awesome-css)
```

Then, we'll need a function to create targets that generate documentation. We'll adapt the code introduced in *Chapter 13, Generating Documentation*, to support multiple targets:

ch15/01-full-project/cmake/Doxygen.cmake (continued)

```
function(Doxygen target input)
  set(NAME "doxygen-${target}")
  set(DOXYGEN_GENERATE_HTML YES)
  set(DOXYGEN_HTML_OUTPUT    ${PROJECT_BINARY_DIR}/${output})

  UseDoxygenAwesomeCss()
  UseDoxygenAwesomeExtensions()

  doxygen_add_docs("doxygen-${target}"
      ${PROJECT_SOURCE_DIR}/${input}
      COMMENT "Generate HTML documentation"
  )
endfunction()

# ... copied from Ch13:
#     UseDoxygenAwesomeCss
#     UseDoxygenAwesomeExtensions
```

Use this function by calling it for the library target:

ch15/01-full-project/src/calc/CMakeLists.txt (fragment)

```
# ... calc_static target definition
# ... testing and program analysis modules


Doxygen(calc src/calc)


# ... file continues
```

And for the console executable:

ch15/01-full-project/src/calc_console/CMakeLists.txt (fragment)

```
# ... calc_static target definition
# ... testing and program analysis modules
Doxygen(calc_console src/calc_console)


# ... file continues
```

This setup adds two targets to the project: doxygen-calc and doxygen-calc_console, allowing for the on-demand generation of technical documentation. Now, let's consider what other documents should be included.

Writing non-technical documents for a professional project

Professional projects should include a set of non-technical documents stored in the top-level directory, essential for comprehensive understanding and legal clarity:

- README: Provides a general description of the project
- LICENSE: Details the legal parameters regarding the project's use and distribution

Additional documents you might consider include:

- INSTALL: Offers step-by-step installation instructions
- CHANGELOG: Presents significant changes across versions
- AUTHORS: Lists contributors and their contact information if the project has multiple contributors
- BUGS: Advises on known issues and details on reporting new ones

CMake doesn't directly interact with these files, as they don't involve automated processing or scripting. Yet, their presence is vital for a well-documented C++ project. Here's a minimal example of each document:

ch15/01-full-project/README.md

```
# Calc Console

Calc Console is a calculator that adds two numbers in a
terminal. It does all the math by using a **Calc** library.
This library is also available in this package.

This application is written in C++ and built with CMake.

## More information

- Installation instructions are in the INSTALL file
- License is in the LICENSE file
```

This is short and maybe a little silly. Note the `.md` extension – it stands for *Markdown*, which is a text-based formatting language that is easily readable. Websites such as GitHub and many text editors will render these files with rich formatting.

Our INSTALL file will look like this:

ch15/01-full-project/INSTALL

```
To install this software you'll need to provide the following:

- C++ compiler supporting C++17
- CMake >= 3.26
- GIT
- Doxygen + Graphviz
- CPPCheck
- Valgrind

This project also depends on GTest, GMock and FXTUI. This
software is automatically pulled from external repositories
during the installation.
```

```
To configure the project type:

cmake -B <temporary-directory>

Then you can build the project:

cmake --build <temporary-directory>

And finally install it:

cmake --install <temporary-directory>

To generate the documentation run:

cmake --build <temporary-directory> -t doxygen-calc
cmake --build <temporary-directory> -t doxygen-calc_console
```

The LICENSE file is a bit tricky, as it requires some expertise in copyright law (and otherwise). Instead of writing all the clauses by ourselves, we can do what many other projects do and use a readily available software license. For this project, we'll go with the MIT License, which is extremely permissive. Check the *Further reading* section for some useful references:

ch15/01-full-project/LICENSE

```
Copyright 2022 Rafal Swidzinski

Permission is hereby granted, free of charge, to any person obtaining a
copy of this software and associated documentation files (the "Software"),
to deal in the Software without restriction, including without limitation
the rights to use, copy, modify, merge, publish, distribute, sublicense,
and/or sell copies of the Software, and to permit persons to whom the
Software is furnished to do so, subject to the following conditions:

The above copyright notice and this permission notice shall be included in
all copies or substantial portions of the Software.

THE SOFTWARE IS PROVIDED "AS IS", WITHOUT WARRANTY OF ANY KIND, EXPRESS OR
IMPLIED, INCLUDING BUT NOT LIMITED TO THE WARRANTIES OF MERCHANTABILITY,
FITNESS FOR A PARTICULAR PURPOSE AND NONINFRINGEMENT. IN NO EVENT SHALL
THE AUTHORS OR COPYRIGHT HOLDERS BE LIABLE FOR ANY CLAIM, DAMAGES OR OTHER
```

```
LIABILITY, WHETHER IN AN ACTION OF CONTRACT, TORT OR OTHERWISE, ARISING
FROM, OUT OF OR IN CONNECTION WITH THE SOFTWARE OR THE USE OR OTHER
DEALINGS IN THE SOFTWARE.
```

Lastly, we have the CHANGELOG. As suggested earlier, it's good to keep track of changes in a file so that developers using your project can easily find out which version supports the features they need. For example, it might be useful to say that a multiplication feature was added to the library in version 0.8.2. Something as simple as the following is already helpful:

ch15/01-full-project/CHANGELOG

```
1.1.0 Updated for CMake 3.26 in 2nd edition of the book
1.0.0 Public version with installer
0.8.2 Multiplication added to the Calc Library
0.5.1 Introducing the Calc Console application
0.2.0 Basic Calc library with Sum function
```

With these documents, the project not only gains an operational structure but also communicates its usage, changes, and legal considerations effectively, ensuring users and contributors have all the necessary information at their disposal.

Summary

In this chapter, we put together a professional project based on everything we've learned so far. Let's do a quick recap.

We started by laying out the project and discussing what files will live in which directory. Based on previous experience and the desire to practice more advanced scenarios, we delineated a main application for the users and a library that another developer might use. This shaped the structure of directories and relations between the CMake targets we want to build. We then followed with the configuration of individual targets for the build: we provided the source code for the library, defined its targets, and set it up for consumption with position-independent code parameters. The user-facing application also had its executable target defined, provided with source code, and configured its dependency: the FTXUI library.

Armed with artifacts to build, we continued to enhance our project with tests and quality assurance. We added the coverage module to produce coverage reports, Memcheck to verify the solution with Valgrind during the runtime, and CppCheck to execute static analysis as well.

Such a project was now ready to be installed, so we created appropriate installation entries for the library and the executable using the techniques learned so far, and we prepared a package configuration for CPack. The final task was to ensure that the project was correctly documented, so we set up automatic documentation generation with Doxygen and wrote a few basic documents that take care of less technical aspects of the software distribution.

This led us to the completion of the project configuration and we can now easily build it and install it with just a few precisely used CMake commands. But what if we could just use one simple command to complete the entire process? Let's discover how in the final chapter: *Chapter 16, Writing CMake Presets.*

Further reading

For more information, you can refer to the following links:

- Building both a static library and a shared library:
  `https://stackoverflow.com/q/2152077`

- A FXTUI library project:
  `https://github.com/ArthurSonzogni/FTXUI`

- The documentation of the option() command:
  `https://cmake.org/cmake/help/latest/command/option.html`

- Preparing for release (of open source software) by Google:
  `https://opensource.google/docs/releasing/preparing/`

- Why we can't use Clang-Tidy for GCC-precompiled headers:
  `https://gitlab.kitware.com/cmake/cmake/-/issues/22081#note_943104`

- Cppcheck manual:
  `https://cppcheck.sourceforge.io/manual.pdf`

- How to write a README:
  `https://www.freecodecamp.org/news/how-to-write-a-good-readme-file/`

- Creative Commons licenses for GitHub projects:
  `https://github.com/santisoler/cc-licenses`

- Commonly used project licenses recognized by GitHub:
  `https://docs.github.com/en/repositories/managing-your-repositorys-`
  `settings-and-features/customizing-your-repository/licensing-a-repository`

Leave a review!

Enjoyed this book? Help readers like you by leaving an Amazon review. Scan the QR code below to get a free eBook of your choice.

16

Writing CMake Presets

Presets were added to CMake in version 3.19 to make it easier to manage project settings. Before presets, users had to memorize lengthy command-line configurations or set overrides directly in the project files, which could become complicated and prone to mistakes. Presets let users handle settings such as the generator used for configuring the project, the number of concurrent build tasks, and the project components to build or test in a more straightforward manner. With presets, CMake becomes simpler to use. Users can set up presets once and use them whenever needed, making each CMake execution more consistent and easier to understand. They also help standardize settings across different users and computers, simplifying collaborative project work.

Presets are compatible with four primary modes of CMake: configuring the buildsystem, building, running tests, and packaging. They allow users to link these parts together in workflows, making the whole process more automatic and organized. Additionally, presets offer features like conditions and macro expressions (or simply macros), granting users greater control.

In this chapter, we're going to cover the following main topics:

- Using presets defined in a project
- Writing a preset file
- Defining stage-specific presets
- Defining workflow presets
- Adding conditions and macros

Technical requirements

You can find the code files that are present in this chapter on GitHub at `https://github.com/PacktPublishing/Modern-CMake-for-Cpp-2E/tree/main/examples/ch16`.

The commands needed to execute the examples in this chapter will be provided in each section.

Using presets defined in a project

The configuration of projects can become a complex task when we need to be specific about elements such as cache variables, chosen generators, and more—especially when there are multiple ways to build our project. This is where presets come in handy. Instead of memorizing command-line arguments or writing shell scripts to execute `cmake` with different arguments, we can create a preset file and store the required configuration in the project itself.

CMake utilizes two optional files to store project presets:

- `CMakePresets.json`: Official presets delivered by project authors.
- `CMakeUserPresets.json`: Dedicated to users who wish to add custom presets to the project. Projects should add this file to the VCS ignore list to ensure that custom settings don't inadvertently get shared in the repository.

Preset files must be placed in the top directory of the project for CMake to recognize them. Each preset file can define multiple presets for each stage: configure, build, test, package, and workflow presets that encompass multiple stages. Users can then select a preset to execute through the IDE, GUI, or command line.

Presets can be listed by adding the `--list-presets` argument to the command line, specific to the stage we're listing for. For example, build presets can be listed with:

```
cmake --build --list-presets
```

Test presets can be listed with:

```
ctest --list-presets
```

To use a preset, we need to follow the same pattern, and provide the preset name after the `--preset` argument.

Additionally, you can't list package presets with the `cmake` command; you need to use `cpack`. Here's a command line for the package preset:

```
cpack --preset <preset-name>
```

After picking the preset, you can, of course, add stage-specific command-line arguments, for example, to specify your build tree or installation path. Added arguments override whatever is set in the preset.

There's a special case for workflow presets, which can be listed and applied if the additional --workflow argument is present when running the cmake command:

```
$ cmake --workflow --list-presets
Available workflow presets:
  "myWorkflow"
$ cmake --workflow --preset myWorkflow
Executing workflow step 1 of 4: configure preset "myConfigure"
...
```

That's how you can apply and review available presets in a project. Now, let's explore how the preset file is structured.

Writing a preset file

CMake searches for CMakePresets.json and CMakeUserPresets.json in the top-level directory. Both files use the same JSON structure to define presets, hence there isn't much difference between them to discuss. The format is a JSON object with the following keys:

- version: This is a required integer that specifies the version of the preset JSON schema
- cmakeMinimumRequired: This is an object that specifies the required CMake version
- include: This is an array of strings that includes external presets from file paths provided in the array (since schema version 4)
- configurePresets: This is an array of objects that defines the configuration stage presets
- buildPresets: This is an array of objects that defines the build stage presets
- testPresets: This is an array of objects that are specific to the test stage presets
- packagePresets: This is an array of objects that are specific to the package stage presets
- workflowPresets: This is an array of objects that are specific to the workflow mode presets
- vendor: This is an object that contains custom settings defined by IDEs and other vendors; CMake does not process this field

When writing a preset, CMake requires the version entry to be present; other values are optional. Here's an example preset file (actual presets will be added in subsequent sections):

ch16/01-presets/CMakePresets.json

```
{
  "version": 6,
  "cmakeMinimumRequired": {
    "major": 3,
    "minor": 26,
    "patch": 0
  },
  "include": [],
  "configurePresets": [],
  "buildPresets": [],
  "testPresets": [],
  "packagePresets": [],
  "workflowPresets": [],
  "vendor": {
    "data": "IDE-specific information"
  }
}
```

There's no requirement to add empty arrays like in the preceding example; entries other than version are optional. Speaking of which, the appropriate schema version for CMake 3.26 is 6.

Now that we understand the structure of the preset file, let's actually learn how to define the presets themselves.

Defining stage-specific presets

Stage-specific presets are simply presets that configure individual CMake stages: configure, build, test, package, and install. They allow for a granular and structured approach to defining build configurations. Here's an overview of the common features shared across all preset stages, followed by an introduction to defining presets for individual stages.

Common features across presets

There are three features that are used to configure presets regardless of the CMake stage. Namely, these are unique name fields, optional fields, and associations with configuration presets. The following sections will cover each, respectively.

Unique name fields

Every preset must have a unique name field within its stage. Given that CMakeUserPresets.json (if it exists) implicitly includes CMakePresets.json (if it exists), both files share the namespace, preventing duplicate names across them. For example, you can't have two package-stage presets with the name myPreset in both files.

A minimal preset file might look like this:

```
{
  "version": 6,
  "configurePresets": [
    {
      "name": "myPreset"
    },
    {
      "name": "myPreset2"
    }
  ]
}
```

Optional fields

Every stage-specific preset can use the same optional fields:

- displayName: This is a string that provides a user-friendly name for the preset
- description: This is a string that offers an explanation of what the preset does
- inherits: This is a string, or an array of strings, that effectively copies the configuration of presets named in this field as a base, to be further extended or modified
- hidden: This is a Boolean that hides the preset from the listings; such hidden presets can only be used through inheritance
- environment: This is an object that overrides ENV variables for this stage; each key identifies an individual variable, and values can be strings or null; it supports macros
- condition: This is an object that enables or disables this preset (more on this later)
- vendor: This is a custom object that contains vendor-specific values and follows the same convention as a root-level vendor field

Presets can form a graph-like inheritance structure, provided there are no cyclic dependencies. CMakeUserPresets.json can inherit from project-level presets but not the other way around.

Association with configuration-stage presets

All stage-specific presets must be associated with a configuration preset, as they must know the location of the build tree. While the `configure` preset is inherently associated with itself, build, test, and package presets need to explicitly define this association via the `configurePreset` field.

Contrary to what you might think, this association doesn't mean CMake will automatically execute the configuration preset when you decide to run any of the subsequent presets. You still need to execute each preset manually, or use a workflow preset (we'll get to that in a bit).

With these foundational concepts in place, we can continue into the specifics of presets for individual stages, starting with the configuration stage. As we progress, we'll explore how these presets interact and how they can be used to streamline the project configuration and building process in CMake.

Defining configuration-stage presets

As previously indicated, configuration presets reside within the `configurePresets` array. They can be listed by adding the `--list-presets` argument to the command line, specific to the configuration stage:

```
cmake --list-presets
```

To configure a project with a chosen preset, specify its name after the `--preset` argument, like so:

```
cmake --preset myConfigurationPreset
```

The configuration preset has some general fields like `name` and `description`, but it also has its own unique set of optional fields. Here are the simplified descriptions of the most important ones:

- `generator`: A string that specifies a generator to use for the preset; required for schema version < 3
- `architecture` and `toolset`: A string that configures generators supporting these options
- `binaryDir`: A string that provides a relative or absolute path to the build tree; required for schema version < 3; supports macros
- `installDir`: A string that provides a relative or absolute path to the installation directory; it is required for schema version < 3 and it supports macros
- `cacheVariables`: A map that defines cache variables; values support macros

When defining the cacheVariables map, remember the order in which variables are resolved in the project. As you can see in *Figure 16.1*, any cache variables defined through the command line will override preset variables. Any cache or environment preset variables will override those coming from the cache file or the host environment.

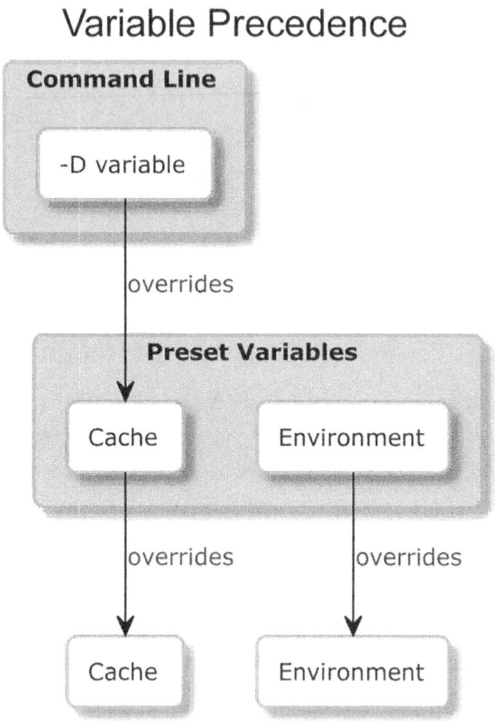

Figure 16.1: How presets override CMakeCache.txt and the system environment variables

Let's declare a simple myConfigure configuration preset that specifies the generator, build tree, and installation path:

ch16/01-presets/CMakePresets.json (continued)

```
...

  "configurePresets": [
    {
      "name": "myConfigure",
      "displayName": "Configure Preset",
```

```
       "description": "Ninja generator",
       "generator": "Ninja",
       "binaryDir": "${sourceDir}/build",
       "installDir": "${sourceDir}/build/install"
     }
  ],
  ...
```

Our introduction to `configure` presets is complete, which brings us to build-stage presets.

Defining build-stage presets

You won't be surprised to learn that build presets reside within the `buildPresets` array. They can be listed by adding the `--list-presets` argument to the command line, specific to the build stage:

```
cmake --build --list-presets
```

To build a project with a chosen preset, specify its name after the `--preset` argument, like so:

```
cmake --build --preset myBuildingPreset
```

The build preset also has some general fields like `name` and `description`, and it has its unique set of optional fields. The simplified descriptions of the most important ones are:

- `jobs`: An integer that sets the number of parallel jobs used to build the project
- `targets`: A string or string array that sets targets to build and supports macros
- `configuration`: A string that determines the build type for multi-configuration generators (Debug, Release, etc.)
- `cleanFirst`: A Boolean that ensures that the project is always cleaned before the build

That's it. Now, we can write a build preset like so:

ch16/01-presets/CMakePresets.json (continued)

```
  ...

  "buildPresets": [
    {
      "name": "myBuild",
      "displayName": "Build Preset",
      "description": "Four jobs",
      "configurePreset": "myConfigure",
```

```
      "jobs": 4
    }
  ],

...
```

You'll notice that the required `configurePreset` field is set to point to the `myConfigure` preset we defined in the previous section. Now, we're able to move on to the test presets.

Defining test-stage presets

Test presets live within the `testPresets` array. They can be displayed by adding the `--list-presets` argument to the command line, specific to the test stage:

```
ctest --list-presets
```

To test a project using a preset, specify its name after the `--preset` argument, like so:

```
ctest --preset myTestPreset
```

The test preset also has its own unique set of optional fields. The simplified descriptions of the most important ones are:

- `configuration`: A string that determines the build type for multi-configuration generators (Debug, Release, etc.)
- `output`: An object that configures the output
- `filter`: An object that specifies which tests to run
- `execution`: An object that configures the execution of tests

Each object maps the appropriate command-line options to configuration values. We'll highlight a few essential options, but this isn't an exhaustive list. Refer to the *Further reading* section for a full reference.

Optional entries for the output object include:

- `shortProgress`: Boolean; progress will be reported within a single line
- `verbosity`: A string that sets the output verbosity to one of the following levels: default, verbose, or extra
- `outputOnFailure`: A Boolean that prints the program output upon test failure
- `quiet`: Boolean; suppress all output

For exclude, some of the accepted entries are:

- `name`: A string that excludes tests with names matching a regex pattern and supports macros

- `label`: A string that excludes tests with labels matching a regex pattern and supports macros

- `fixtures`: An object that determines which fixtures to exclude from the test (see official documentation for more details)

Finally, the execution object accepts the following optional entry:

- `outputLogFile`: A string that specifies the output logfile path and supports macros

The `filter` object accepts `include` and `exclude` keys to configure the filtering of test cases; here's a partially filled structure to illustrate this:

```
"testPresets": [
  {
    "name": "myTest",
    "configurePreset": "myConfigure",
    "filter": {
      "include": {
                    ... name, label, index, useUnion ...
                 },

      "exclude": {
                    ... name, label, fixtures ...
                 }
    }
  }
],

...
```

Each key defines its own object of options:

For `include`, entries include:

- `name`: A string that includes tests with names matching a regex pattern and supports macros
- `label`: A string that includes tests with labels matching a regex pattern and supports macros

- index: An object that selects tests to run with accepting start, end, and stride integers, and a specificTests array of integers; it supports macros

- useUnion: A Boolean that enables the usage of a union of tests determined by index and name, rather than the intersection

For exclude, entries include:

- name: A string that excludes tests with names matching a regex pattern and supports macros

- label: A string that excludes tests with labels matching a regex pattern and supports macros

- fixtures: An object that determines which fixtures to exclude from the test (see official documentation for more details)

Finally, the execution object can be added right here:

```
"testPresets": [
  {
    "name": "myTest",
    "configurePreset": "myConfigure",
    "execution": {
                ... stopOnFailure, enableFailover, ...
                ... jobs, repeat, scheduleRandom, ...
                ... timeout, noTestsAction ...
                }
  }
],

...
```

It accepts the following optional entries:

- stopOnFailure: A Boolean that enables halting the tests if any fail

- enableFailover: A Boolean that resumes previously interrupted tests

- jobs: An integer that runs a number of multiple tests in parallel

- repeat: An object that determines how to repeat tests; the object must have the following fields:

    - mode – A string with one of the following values: until-fail, until-pass, after-timeout

- count – An integer that determines the number of repeats
- scheduleRandom: A Boolean that enables a random order of test execution
- timeout: An integer that sets a limit (in seconds) on the total execution time for all tests
- noTestsAction: A string that defines the action if no tests are found, with options like default, error, and ignore

While there are many configuration options, simple presets are also viable:

ch16/01-presets/CMakePresets.json (continued)

```
...

  "testPresets": [
    {
      "name": "myTest",
      "displayName": "Test Preset",
      "description": "Output short progress",
      "configurePreset": "myConfigure",
      "output": {
        "shortProgress": true
      }
    }
  ],

...
```

As with the build preset, we also set the required configurePreset field for the new test preset to neatly tie things together. Let's take a look at the last stage-specific preset type, the package preset.

Defining package-stage presets

Package presets were introduced in schema version 6, meaning you'll need at least CMake 3.25 to utilize them. These presets should be included in the packagePresets array. They can also be displayed by appending the --list-presets argument to the command line, specific to the test stage:

```
cpack --list-presets
```

To create a project package using a preset, specify its name after the --preset argument, like so:

```
cpack --preset myTestPreset
```

A package preset leverages the same shared fields as other presets while introducing some optional fields specific to itself:

- generators: An array of strings that sets the package generators to use (ZIP, 7Z, DEB, etc.)
- configuration: An array of strings that determines the list of build types for CPack to package (Debug, Release, etc.)
- filter: An object that specifies which tests to run
- packageName, packageVersion, packageDirectory, and vendorName: Strings that specify the metadata for the created package

Let's extend our preset file with a concise package preset as well:

ch16/01-presets/CMakePresets.json (continued)

```
...

  "packagePresets": [
    {
      "name": "myPackage",
      "displayName": "Package Preset",
      "description": "ZIP generator",
      "configurePreset": "myConfigure",
      "generators": [
        "ZIP"
      ]
    }
  ],

...
```

Such a configuration will allow us to streamline the creation of project packages, but we're still missing one key ingredient: project installation. Let's find out how we can make it work.

Adding the installation preset

You might've noticed that the CMakePresets.json object doesn't support defining "installPresets". There's no explicit way to install your project through a preset, which seems odd since the configure preset provides an installDir field! So, do we have to resort to manual installation commands?

Fortunately, no. There's a workaround that enables us to use the build preset to achieve our goal. Take a look:

ch16/01-presets/CMakePresets.json (continued)

```
  ...

  "buildPresets": [
    {
      "name": "myBuild",

      ...

    },
    {
      "name": "myInstall",
      "displayName": "Installation",
      "targets" : "install",
      "configurePreset": "myConfigure"
    }
  ],

...
```

We can create a build preset with a targets field set to install. The install target is implicitly defined by the project when we configure the installation correctly. Building with this preset will execute the necessary steps to install the project to installDir specified in the associated configure preset (if the installDir field is empty, the default location will be used):

```
$ cmake --build --preset myInstall
[0/1] Install the project...
-- Install configuration: ""
-- Installing: .../install/include/calc/basic.h
-- Installing: .../install/lib/libcalc_shared.so
-- Installing: .../install/lib/libcalc_static.a
-- Installing: .../install/lib/calc/cmake/CalcLibrary.cmake
-- Installing: .../install/lib/calc/cmake/CalcLibrary-noconfig.cmake
-- Installing: .../install/lib/calc/cmake/CalcConfig.cmake
-- Installing: .../install/bin/calc_console
```

```
-- Set non-toolchain portion of runtime path of ".../install/bin/calc_
console" to ""
```

This neat trick can help us save a few cycles. It would be even better if we could provide a single command for our end users that takes care of everything, from configuration to installation. Well, we can, with workflow presets. Let's take a look.

Defining workflow presets

Workflow presets are the ultimate automation solution for our project. They allow us to automatically execute multiple stage-specific presets in the predetermined order. That way, we can practically perform an end-to-end build in a single step.

To discover available workflows for a project, we can execute the following command:

```
cmake --workflow --list-presets
```

To select and apply a preset, use the following command:

```
cmake –workflow --preset <preset-name>
```

Additionally, with the --fresh flag, we can wipe the build tree and clear the cache.

Defining workflow presets is quite simple; we need to define a name and we can optionally provide displayName and description, just like for stage-specific presets. After that, we must enumerate all the stage-specific presets the workflow should execute. This is done by providing a steps array containing objects with type and name properties, as illustrated here:

ch16/01-presets/CMakePresets.json (continued)

```
...

  "workflowPresets": [
    {
      "name": "myWorkflow",
      "steps": [
        {
          "type": "configure",
          "name": "myConfigure"
        },
        {
          "type": "build",
```

```
        "name": "myBuild"
      },
      {
        "type": "test",
        "name": "myTest"
      },
      {
        "type": "package",
        "name": "myPackage"
      },
      {
        "type": "build",
        "name": "myInstall"
      }
    ]
...
```

Each object in the steps array references a preset we defined earlier in this chapter, indicating its type (configure, build, test, or package) and a name. These presets collectively execute all necessary steps to fully build and install a project from scratch with a single command:

```
cmake --workflow --preset myWorkflow
```

Workflow presets are the ultimate solution for automating C++ building, testing, packaging, and installing. Next, let's explore how to manage some edge cases with conditions and macros.

Adding conditions and macros

When we discussed the general fields for each stage-specific preset, we mentioned the condition field. It's time to return to that subject. The **condition** field enables or disables a preset, revealing its true potential when integrated with workflows. Essentially, it allows us to bypass presets that aren't suitable under certain conditions and create alternative presets that are.

Conditions require preset schema version 3 or above (introduced in CMake 3.22) and are JSON objects that codify a few simple logical operations that can determine whether circumstances, like used OS, environment variables, or even chosen generators, fit the scenario of a preset. CMake provides this data through macros, which are essentially a limited set of read-only variables usable in the preset file.

The structure of a condition object varies based on the check type. Each condition must include a type field and additional fields as defined by the type. Recognized basic types include:

- const: This checks whether the value provided in the value field is Boolean true

- equals, notEquals: This compares the lhs field value to the value in the rhs field

- inList and notInList: These check for the presence of the value provided in the string field within the array in the list field

- matches and notMatches: These evaluate whether the string field's value aligns with the pattern defined in the regex field

An example condition looks like this:

```
"condition": {
               "type": "equals",
               "lhs": "${hostSystemName}",
               "rhs": "Windows"
            }
```

The const condition's practical use is primarily for disabling a preset without removing it from the JSON file. Apart from const, all basic conditions permit the use of macros in the fields they introduce: lhs, rhs, string, list, and regex.

Advanced condition types, which function like "not", "and", and "or" operations, utilize other conditions as arguments:

- not: A Boolean inversion of the condition provided in the condition field

- anyOf and allOf: These check whether any or all conditions in the conditions array are true

For instance:

```
"condition": {
               "type": "anyOf",
               "conditions": [
                                {
                                   "type": "equals",
                                   "lhs": "${hostSystemName}",
                                   "rhs": "Windows"
                                },{
                                   "type": "equals",
```

```
                              "lhs": "${hostSystemName}",
                              "rhs": "Linux"
                          }
                     ]
              }
          }
```

This condition evaluates as true if the system is either Linux or Windows.

Through these examples, we've introduced our first macro: ${hostSystemName}. Macros follow a simple syntax and are limited to specific instances, like:

- ${sourceDir}: This is the path of the source tree
- ${sourceParentDir}: This is the path of the source tree's parent directory
- ${sourceDirName}: This is the project's directory name
- ${presetName}: This is the name of the preset
- ${generator}: This is the generator used to create the buildsystem
- ${hostSystemName}: This is the system name: Linux, Windows, or Darwin on macOS
- ${fileDir}: This is the name of the file containing the current preset (applicable when an include array is used to import external presets)
- ${dollar}: This is the escaped dollar sign ($)
- ${pathListSep}: This is the environment-specific path separator
- $env{<variable-name>}: This returns the environment variable if specified by the preset (case-sensitive), or the parent environment value
- $penv{<variable-name>}: This returns the environment variable from the parent environment
- $vendor{<macro-name>}: This allows IDE vendors to introduce their own macros

These macros provide sufficient flexibility for use in presets and their conditions, enabling the effective toggling of workflow steps as needed.

Summary

We have just completed a comprehensive overview of CMake presets, introduced in CMake 3.19, to streamline project management. Presets allow product authors to provide a neatly prepared experience for their users by configuring all the stages of the project build and delivery. Presets not only simplify the usage of CMake but also enhance consistency and allow environment-aware setups.

We explained the structure and usage of the CMakePresets.json and CMakeUserPresets.json files, providing insights into defining various types of presets, such as configure presets, build presets, test presets, package presets, and workflow presets. Each type is described in detail: we learned about common fields, how to structure presets internally, establish inheritance between them, and the specific configuration options available for the end user.

For the *configure preset*, we covered important topics like selecting the generator, build, and installation directory, and linking presets together with the configurePreset field. We now know how to handle *build presets* and set the build job count, targets, and cleaning options. Then, we learned how the *test preset* assists with test selection through extensive filtering and ordering options, output formatting, and execution parameters such as timeouts and fault tolerance. We understand how to manage *package presets* by specifying package generators, filtering, and package metadata. We even introduced a workaround to execute the installation stage through a specialized build preset application.

Next, we discovered how workflow presets allow the grouping of multiple stage-specific presets. Finally, we discussed conditions and macro expressions, providing project authors with greater control over the behavior of individual presets and their integration into a workflow.

Our CMake journey is complete! Congratulations – you now possess all the tools necessary to develop, test, and package high-quality C++ software. The best way forward is to apply what you've learned and create excellent software for your users. Good luck!

Further reading

For more information, you can refer to the following resource:

- Official documentation for presets:
  https://cmake.org/cmake/help/latest/manual/cmake-presets.7.html

Join our community on Discord

Join our community's Discord space for discussions with the author and other readers:

`https://discord.com/invite/vXN53A7ZcA`

Appendix

Miscellaneous commands

Every language includes utility commands useful for various tasks, and CMake is no exception. It offers tools for arithmetic, bitwise operations, string manipulations, and list and file operations. Although the need for these commands has diminished due to enhancements and the development of numerous modules, they can still be essential in highly automated projects. Nowadays, you might find them more useful in CMake scripts invoked with `cmake -P <filename>`.

Hence, this appendix, which is a summary of miscellaneous CMake commands and their various modes, acts as a convenient offline reference or a simplified version of the official documentation. For more detailed information, you should consult the provided links.

This reference is valid for CMake 3.26.6.

In this *Appendix*, we're going to cover the following main topics:

- The `string()` command
- The `list()` command
- The `file()` command
- The `math()` command

The string() command

The `string()` command is used to manipulate strings. It comes with a variety of modes that perform different actions on the string: search and replace, manipulation, comparison, hashing, generation, and JSON operations (the last one available since CMake 3.19).

Full details can be found in the online documentation: `https://cmake.org/cmake/help/latest/command/string.html`.

 Note that `string()` modes that accept the `<input>` argument will accept multiple `<input>` values and concatenate them before the execution of the command, so:

```
string(PREPEND myVariable "a" "b" "c")
```

is the equivalent of the following:

```
string(PREPEND myVariable "abc")
```

Available `string()` modes are search and replace, manipulation, comparison, hashing, generation, and JSON.

Search and replace

The following modes are available:

- `string(FIND <haystack> <pattern> <out> [REVERSE])` searches for `<pattern>` in the `<haystack>` string and writes the position found as an integer to the `<out>` variable. If the REVERSE flag was used, it searches from the end of the string to the beginning. This works only for ASCII strings (multibyte support isn't provided).

- `string(REPLACE <pattern> <replace> <out> <input>)` replaces all occurrences of `<pattern>` in `<input>` with `<replace>` and stores them in the `<out>` variable.

- `string(REGEX MATCH <pattern> <out> <input>)` regex-matches the first occurrence of `<pattern>` in `<input>` with `<replace>` and stores it in the `<out>` variable.

- `string(REGEX MATCHALL <pattern> <out> <input>)` regex-matches all occurrences of `<pattern>` in `<input>` with `<replace>` and stores them in the `<out>` variable as a comma-separated list.

- `string(REGEX REPLACE <pattern> <replace> <out> <input>)` regex-replaces all occurrences of `<pattern>` in `<input>` with the `<replace>` expression and stores them in the `<out>` variable.

Regular expression operations follow C++ syntax, as defined in the standard library in the `<regex>` header. You can use capturing groups to add matches to the `<replace>` expression with numeric placeholders: \\1, \\2... (double backslashes are required so arguments are parsed correctly).

Manipulation

The following modes are available:

- `string(APPEND <out> <input>)` mutates strings stored in `<out>` by appending the `<input>` string.

- `string(PREPEND <out> <input>)` mutates strings stored in `<out>` by prepending the `<input>` string.

- `string(CONCAT <out> <input>)` concatenates all provided `<input>` strings and stores them in the `<out>` variable.

- `string(JOIN <glue> <out> <input>)` interleaves all provided `<input>` strings with a `<glue>` value and stores them as a concatenated string in the `<out>` variable (don't use this mode for list variables).

- `string(TOLOWER <string> <out>)` converts `<string>` to lowercase and stores it in the `<out>` variable.

- `string(TOUPPER <string> <out>)` converts `<string>` to uppercase and stores it in the `<out>` variable.

- `string(LENGTH <string> <out>)` counts the bytes of `<string>` and stores the result in the `<out>` variable.

- `string(SUBSTRING <string> <begin> <length> <out>)` extracts a substring of `<string>` of `<length>` bytes starting at the `<begin>` byte, and stores it in the `<out>` variable. Providing -1 as the length is understood as "till the end of the string."

- `string(STRIP <string> <out>)` removes trailing and leading whitespace from `<string>` and stores the result in the `<out>` variable.

- `string(GENEX_STRIP <string> <out>)` removes all generator expressions used in `<string>` and stores the result in the `<out>` variable.

- `string(REPEAT <string> <count> <out>)` generates a string containing `<count>` repetitions of `<string>` and stores it in the `<out>` variable.

Comparison

A comparison of strings takes the following form:

```
string(COMPARE <operation> <stringA> <stringB> <out>)
```

The <operation> argument is one of the following:

- LESS
- GREATER
- EQUAL
- NOTEQUAL
- LESS_EQUAL
- GREATER_EQUAL

It will be used to compare <stringA> with <stringB> and the result (true or false) will be stored in the <out> variable.

Hashing

The hashing mode has the following signature:

```
string(<hashing-algorithm> <out> <string>)
```

It hashes <string> with <hashing-algorithm> and stores the result in the <out> variable. The following algorithms are supported:

- MD5: Message-Digest Algorithm 5, RFC 1321
- SHA1: US Secure Hash Algorithm 1, RFC 3174
- SHA224: US Secure Hash Algorithms, RFC 4634
- SHA256: US Secure Hash Algorithms, RFC 4634
- SHA384: US Secure Hash Algorithms, RFC 4634
- SHA512: US Secure Hash Algorithms, RFC 4634
- SHA3_224: Keccak SHA-3
- SHA3_256: Keccak SHA-3
- SHA3_384: Keccak SHA-3
- SHA3_512: Keccak SHA-3

Generation

The following modes are available:

- string(ASCII <number>... <out>) stores ASCII characters of given <number> in the <out> variable.

- `string(HEX <string> <out>)` converts `<string>` to its hexadecimal representation and stores it in the `<out>` variable (since CMake 3.18).

- `string(CONFIGURE <string> <out> [@ONLY] [ESCAPE_QUOTES])` works exactly like `configure_file()` but for strings. The result is stored in the `<out>` variable. As a reminder, using the @ONLY keyword restricts replacements to variables in the form of @VARIABLE@.

- `string(MAKE_C_IDENTIFIER <string> <out>)` converts non-alphanumeric characters in `<string>` to underscores and stores the result in the `<out>` variable.

- `string(RANDOM [LENGTH <len>] [ALPHABET <alphabet>] [RANDOM_SEED <seed>] <out>)` generates a random string of `<len>` characters (default 5) using the optional `<alphabet>` from the random seed, `<seed>`, and stores the result in the `<out>` variable.

- `string(TIMESTAMP <out> [<format>] [UTC])` generates a string representing the current date and time and stores it in the `<out>` variable.

- `string(UUID <out> NAMESPACE <ns> NAME <name> TYPE <type>)` generates a universally unique identifier. Application of this mode is a bit complex to use; you need to provide a namespace (which has to be a UUID), a name (for example, a domain name), and a type (either MD5 or SHA1).

JSON

Operations on JSON-formatted strings use the following signature:

```
string(JSON <out> [ERROR_VARIABLE <error>] <operation + args>)
```

Several operations are available. They all store their results in the `<out>` variable, and errors in the `<error>` variable. Operations and their arguments are as follows:

- `GET <json> <member|index>...` returns the value of one or more elements from a `<json>` string using the `<member>` path or `<index>`.

- `TYPE <json> <member|index>...` returns the type of one or more elements from a `<json>` string using the `<member>` path or `<index>`.

- `MEMBER <json> <member|index>... <array-index>` returns the member name of one or more array-typed elements on the `<array-index>` position from the `<json>` string using the `<member>` path or `<index>`.

- `LENGTH <json> <member|index>...` returns the element count of one or more array-typed elements from the `<json>` string using the `<member>` path or `<index>`.

- `REMOVE <json> <member|index>...` returns the result of removal of one or more elements from the `<json>` string using the `<member>` path or `<index>`.

- SET `<json>` `<member|index>`... `<value>` returns the result of upsertion of `<value>` to one or more elements from a `<json>` string using the `<member>` path or `<index>`.

- EQUAL `<jsonA>` `<jsonB>` evaluates whether `<jsonA>` and `<jsonB>` are equal.

The list() command

This command provides basic operations on lists: reading, searching, modification, and ordering. Some modes will change list (mutate the original value). Be sure to copy the original value if you'll need it later.

Full details can be found in the online documentation:

`https://cmake.org/cmake/help/latest/command/list.html`

The categories for the available list() modes are reading, searching, modification, and ordering.

Reading

The following modes are available:

- `list(LENGTH <list> <out>)` counts the elements in the `<list>` variable and stores the result in the `<out>` variable.

- `list(GET <list> <index>... <out>)` copies the `<list>` elements specified with the list of `<index>` indexes to the `<out>` variable.

- `list(JOIN <list> <glue> <out>)` interleaves `<list>` elements with the `<glue>` delimiter and stores the resulting string in the `<out>` variable.

- `list(SUBLIST <list> <begin> <length> <out>)` works like the GET mode but operates on range instead of explicit indexes. If `<length>` is `-1`, elements from the `<begin>` index to the end of the list provided in the `<list>` variable will be returned.

Searching

This mode simply finds the index of the `<needle>` element in the `<list>` variable and stores the result in the `<out>` variable (or `-1` if the element wasn't found):

```
list(FIND <list> <needle> <out>)
```

Modification

The following modes are available:

- `list(APPEND <list> <element>...)` adds one or more `<element>` values to the end of the `<list>` variable.

- `list(PREPEND <list> [<element>...])` works like `APPEND` but adds elements to the beginning of the `<list>` variable.

- `list(FILTER <list> {INCLUDE | EXCLUDE} REGEX <pattern>)` filters the `<list>` variable to `INCLUDE` or `EXCLUDE` the elements matching the `<pattern>` value.

- `list(INSERT <list> <index> [<element>...])` adds one or more `<element>` values to the `<list>` variable at the given `<index>`.

- `list(POP_BACK <list> [<out>...])` removes an element from the end of the `<list>` variable and stores it in the optional `<out>` variable. If multiple `<out>` variables were provided, more elements would be removed to fill them.

- `list(POP_FRONT <list> [<out>...])` works like `POP_BACK` but removes an element from the beginning of the `<list>` variable.

- `list(REMOVE_ITEM <list> <value>...)` is shorthand for `FILTER EXCLUDE` but without the support of regular expressions.

- `list(REMOVE_AT <list> <index>...)` removes elements from `<list>` at a specific `<index>`.

- `list(REMOVE_DUPLICATES <list>)` removes duplicates from `<list>`.

- `list(TRANSFORM <list> <action> [<selector>] [OUTPUT_VARIABLE <out>])` applies a specific transformation to the `<list>` elements. By default, the action is applied to all elements, but we may limit the effect by adding a `<selector>`. The provided list will be mutated (changed in place) unless the `OUTPUT_VARIABLE` keyword is provided, in which case, the result is stored in the `<out>` variable.

The following selectors are available: `AT <index>`, `FOR <start> <stop> [<step>]`, and `REGEX <pattern>`.

Actions include `APPEND <string>`, `PREPEND <string>`, `TOLOWER`, `TOUPPER`, `STRIP`, `GENEX_STRIP`, and `REPLACE <pattern> <expression>`. They work exactly like the `string()` modes with the same name.

Ordering

The following modes are available:

- `list(REVERSE <list>)` simply reverses the order of `<list>`.
- `list(SORT <list>)` sorts the list alphabetically.

Refer to the online manual for more advanced options.

The file() command

This command provides all kinds of operations related to files: reading, transferring, locking, and archiving. It also provides modes to inspect the filesystem and operations on strings representing paths.

Full details can be found in the online documentation:

https://cmake.org/cmake/help/latest/command/file.html

The categories for available file() modes are reading, writing, filesystem, path conversion, transfer, locking, and archiving.

Reading

The following modes are available:

- file(READ <filename> <out> [OFFSET <o>] [LIMIT <max>] [HEX]) reads the file from <filename> to the <out> variable. The read optionally starts at offset <o> and follows the optional limit of <max> bytes. The HEX flag specifies that output should be converted to hexadecimal representation.
- file(STRINGS <filename> <out>) reads strings from the file at <filename> to the <out> variable.
- file(<hashing-algorithm> <filename> <out>) computes the <hashing-algorithm> hash from the file at <filename> and stores the result in the <out> variable. Available algorithms are the same as for the string() hashing function.
- file(TIMESTAMP <filename> <out> [<format>]) generates a string representation of a timestamp of the file at <filename> and stores it in the <out> variable. It optionally accepts a <format> string.
- file(GET_RUNTIME_DEPENDENCIES [...]) gets runtime dependencies for specified files. This is an advanced command to be used only in install(CODE) or install(SCRIPT) scenarios. Available since CMake 3.21.

Writing

The following modes are available:

- file({WRITE | APPEND} <filename> <content>...) writes or appends all <content> arguments to the file at <filename>. If the provided system path doesn't exist, it will be recursively created.

- `file({TOUCH | TOUCH_NOCREATE} [<filename>...])` updates the timestamp of the `<filename>`. If the file doesn't exist, it will only be created in the TOUCH mode.

- `file(GENERATE OUTPUT <output-file> [...])` is an advanced mode that generates an output file for each build configuration of the current CMake generator.

- `file(CONFIGURE OUTPUT <output-file> CONTENT <content> [...])` works like `GENERATE_OUTPUT` but also configures the generated files by substituting variable place-holders with values.

Filesystem

The following modes are available:

- `file({GLOB | GLOB_RECURSE} <out> [...] [<globbing-expression>...])` generates a list of files matching `<globbing-expression>` and stores it in the `<out>` variable. `GLOB_RECURSE` mode will also scan nested directories.

- `file(RENAME <oldname> <newname>)` moves a file from `<oldname>` to `<newname>`.

- `file({REMOVE | REMOVE_RECURSE } [<files>...])` deletes `<files>`. `REMOVE_RECURSE` will also remove directories.

- `file(MAKE_DIRECTORY [<dir>...])` creates a directory.

- `file(COPY <file>... DESTINATION <dir> [...])` copies files to the `<dir>` destination. It offers options for filtering, setting permissions, symlink chain following, and more.

- `file(COPY_FILE <file> <destination> [...])` copies a single file to the `<destination>` path. Available since CMake 3.21.

- `file(SIZE <filename> <out>)` reads the size of `<filename>` in bytes and stores it in the `<out>` variable.

- `file(READ_SYMLINK <linkname> <out>)` reads the destination path of the `<linkname>` symlink and stores it in the `<out>` variable.

- `file(CREATE_LINK <original> <linkname> [...])` creates a symlink to `<original>` at `<linkname>`.

- `file({CHMOD|CHMOD_RECURSE} <files>... <directories>... PERMISSIONS <permissions>... [...])` sets permissions on files and directories.

- `file(GET_RUNTIME_DEPENDENCIES [...])` collects the runtime dependencies for various types of files: executables, libraries, and modules. Use with `install(RUNTIME_DEPENDENCY_SET)`.

Path conversion

The following modes are available:

- `file(REAL_PATH <path> <out> [BASE_DIRECTORY <dir>])` computes the absolute path from the relative path and stores it in the `<out>` variable. It optionally accepts the `<dir>` base directory. Available since CMake 3.19.

- `file(RELATIVE_PATH <out> <directory> <file>)` computes the `<file>` path relative to `<directory>` and stores it in the `<out>` variable.

- `file({TO_CMAKE_PATH | TO_NATIVE_PATH} <path> <out>)` converts `<path>` to a CMake path (directories separated with a forward slash) to the native path of the platform and back. The result is stored in the `<out>` variable.

Transfer

The following modes are available:

- `file(DOWNLOAD <url> [<path>] [...])` downloads a file from `<url>` and stores it in `<path>`.

- `file(UPLOAD <file> <url> [...])` uploads `<file>` to a URL.

Locking

Locking mode places an advisory lock on the `<path>` resource:

```
file(LOCK <path> [DIRECTORY] [RELEASE]
    [GUARD <FUNCTION|FILE|PROCESS>]
    [RESULT_VARIABLE <out>] [TIMEOUT <seconds>]
)
```

This lock can be optionally scoped to `FUNCTION`, `FILE`, or `PROCESS` and limited with a timeout of `<seconds>`. To release the lock, provide the `RELEASE` keyword. The result will be stored in the `<out>` variable.

Archiving

The creation of archives is provided with the following signature:

```
file(ARCHIVE_CREATE OUTPUT <destination> PATHS <source>...
  [FORMAT <format>]
  [COMPRESSION <type> [COMPRESSION_LEVEL <level>]]
  [MTIME <mtime>] [VERBOSE]
)
```

It creates an archive at the `<destination>` path comprising `<source>` files in one of the supported formats: 7zip, gnutar, pax, paxr, raw, or zip (paxr is the default). If the chosen format supports the compression level, it can be provided as a single-digit integer 0-9, with 0 being the default.

The extraction mode has the following signature:

```
file(ARCHIVE_EXTRACT INPUT <archive> [DESTINATION <dir>]
  [PATTERNS <patterns>...] [LIST_ONLY] [VERBOSE]
)
```

It extracts files matching optional `<patterns>` values from `<archive>` to the destination `<dir>`. If the LIST_ONLY keyword is provided, files won't be extracted but will only be listed instead.

The math() command

CMake also supports some simple arithmetical operations. See the online documentation for full details:

`https://cmake.org/cmake/help/latest/command/math.html`

To evaluate a mathematical expression and store it in the `<out>` variable as the string in an optional `<format>` (HEXADECIMAL or DECIMAL), use the following signature:

```
math(EXPR <out> "<expression>" [OUTPUT_FORMAT <format>])
```

The `<expression>` value is a string that supports operators present in C code (they have the same meaning here):

- Arithmetical: +, -, *, /, and % modulo division
- Bitwise: | or, & and, ^ xor, ~ not, << shift left, and >> shift right
- Parenthesis (...)

Constant values can be provided in decimal or hexadecimal format.

packt.com

Subscribe to our online digital library for full access to over 7,000 books and videos, as well as industry leading tools to help you plan your personal development and advance your career. For more information, please visit our website.

Why subscribe?

- Spend less time learning and more time coding with practical eBooks and Videos from over 4,000 industry professionals
- Improve your learning with Skill Plans built especially for you
- Get a free eBook or video every month
- Fully searchable for easy access to vital information
- Copy and paste, print, and bookmark content

At www.packt.com, you can also read a collection of free technical articles, sign up for a range of free newsletters, and receive exclusive discounts and offers on Packt books and eBooks.

Other Books You May Enjoy

If you enjoyed this book, you may be interested in these other books by Packt:

CMake Best Practices

Dominik Berner

Mustafa Kemal Gilor

ISBN: 978-1-80323-972-9

- Get to grips with architecting a well-structured CMake project
- Modularize and reuse CMake code across projects
- Integrate various tools for static analysis, linting, formatting, and documentation into a CMake project
- Get hands-on with performing cross-platform builds
- Discover how you can easily use different toolchains with CMake
- Get started with crafting a well-defined and portable build environment for your project

Modern C++ Programming Cookbook - Third Edition

Marius Bancila

ISBN: 978-1-83508-054-2

- Explore the new C++23 language and library features
- Become skilled at using the built-in support for threading and concurrency for daily tasks
- Leverage the standard library and work with containers, algorithms, and iterators
- Solve text searching and replacement problems using regular expressions
- Work with different types of strings and learn the various aspects of compilation
- Take advantage of the file system library to work with files and directories
- Implement various useful patterns and idioms
- Explore the widely used testing frameworks for C++

Packt is searching for authors like you

If you're interested in becoming an author for Packt, please visit authors.packtpub.com and apply today. We have worked with thousands of developers and tech professionals, just like you, to help them share their insight with the global tech community. You can make a general application, apply for a specific hot topic that we are recruiting an author for, or submit your own idea.

Share your thoughts

Now you've finished *Modern CMake for C++, Second Edition*, we'd love to hear your thoughts! Scan the QR code below to go straight to the Amazon review page for this book and share your feedback or leave a review on the site that you purchased it from.

https://packt.link/r/1805121804

Your review is important to us and the tech community and will help us make sure we're delivering excellent quality content.

Index